Ranganathan Series in Library Science, 2

CLASSIFIED CATALOGUE CODE

Ranganathan Series in Library Science

1 *Library movement in India* by P N Kaula
2 *Classified catalogue code* by S R Ranganathan
3 *Library administration* by S R Ranganathan
4 *Colon classification* by S R Ranganathan
5 *Social science research and libraries* by S R Ranganathan and Girja Kumar
6 *Library manual* by S R Ranganathan
7 *Education for leisure* by S R Ranganathan
8 *Elements of library classification* by S R Ranganathan
9 *Reference service* by S R Ranganathan
10 *Documentation and its facets*, ed by S R Ranganathan
11 *Decimal classification and colon classification in perspective* by R S Parkhi
12 *The five laws of library science* by S R Ranganathan
13 *Pustakalaya vigyan ki bhumika* by Umesh Datta Sharma
14 *Library science today*: Ranganathan Festschrift Volume I—*Essays and felicitations offered to S R Ranganathan on his seventy-first birthday*, ed by P N Kaula (*In Press*)
15 *An essay in personal bibliography*: Ranganathan Festschrift Volume II—*Bibliography of the writings on and by Dr S R Ranganathan*, compiled by A K Das Gupta (*In Press*)
16 *Library book selection* by S R Ranganathan
17 *Library manual* (Translation into Hindi by P N Kaula)

Some other books by the author

Anuvarga-suchi-kalpa
Classification and communication
Depth classification
Grantha-adhyayanartha-hai
Granthalaya-prakriya
Heading and canons
Library development plan
Library legislation
Literature for neoliterates
Organization of libraries
Philosophy of library classification
Public library provision and documentation problems
Rural adult education
Social bibliography
Social education literature
Union catalogue of learned periodical publications in South Asia

Classified Catalogue Code
with additional rules for Dictionary Catalogue Code

By

S.R. Ranganathan

National Research Professor in Library Science
(1965-72)

Assisted By

A. Neelameghan

Documentation, Research and Training Centre
Bangalore

Published by
Ess Ess Publications
4837/24, Ansari Road
Darya Ganj
New Delhi-110 002

for

Sarada Ranganathan Endowment For Library Science
Bangalore

Shiyali Ramanrita Ranganathan (1892-1972)
Arshanapalai Neelameghan (1927)

Edition 5 Reprinted 1988
Reprinted **2006**
Reprinted **2022**

2 : 55N3
qN64;N88

ISBN: 81-7000-493-4

Rs. 1700/-

Published by:
Ess Ess Publications
4837/24, Ansari Road, Darya Ganj, New Delhi-110 002
Tel: 011-23260807, 41563444 Fax: 011-41563334
E-mail: info@essessreference.com
url: www.essessreference.com

for

Sarada Ranganathan Endowment for Library Science
702, 'Upstairs', 42nd Cross, III Block, Rajajinagar,
Bangalore-560 010
Ph.no.23305109 E-mail: sreis@vsnl.com

Printed in India at:
Printline, New Delhi

To the memory of

R KRISHNASWAMY RAO

my first colleague in Cataloguing

The Five Laws of Library Science

1 Books are for use

2 Every Reader his book

3 Every book its reader

4 Save the time of the reader

5 A library is a growing organism

CONTENTS

PART A

Introduction

PART B

Canons of Cataloguing

PART C

General Normative Principles

Part D

Evolution of the Catalogue

Part E

Recording

PART F

Terminology

PART G

Conflict of Authorship

PART H

Name of Person

PART J

Rendering of Names

PART K

Class Index Entry

Part L

Cross Reference Index Entry

Part M

Single-Volumed Simple Book

Part N

Composite Book and Multi-Volumed Book

PART P

Periodical Publication

PART Q

Union Catalogue of Books

PART R

Union Catalogue of Periodical Publications

PART U

Abstracting Periodical

PART V

Incunabula and Non-Book Materials

PART W

End Matter

PART A

INTRODUCTION

CHAPTER AA

GENESIS

1 Sense of Revolt

The Classified Catalogue Code owes itself to the sense of revolt induced in the mind while learning cataloguing in 1924-25, in the School of Librarianship of the University College in London. The first cause of revolt was the method of teaching used. Each rule of the Anglo-American Code was taken by itself, to be put into rote-memory as it were. No attempt at answering the what, the why, or the how of it. No attempt to present the rules as a system. No attempt at studying an alternative code and comparing their relative merits. But this is necessary to sense the theory behind the practice. The second cause was the nature of the Code taught. It was the Anglo-American Code [A3] of 1908. Its skeleton nature, its mixing up the author entry and the subject entry, lack of unity in many of its rules—a serious drawback in the drafting of a Code—all these added to the result. There was also a third cause. The volumes of the Classified Catalogue of the Carnegie Library of Pittsburgh and of the Mitchel Library of Glasgow were fascinating. Copies of these were available in the library of the School of Librarianship. But not a word was said in the class either about Classified Catalogue or about the essential difference between it and Dictionary Catalogue. A fourth cause came out of the discrepancy between the rules taught in the theory class and those prescribed for adoption in the practical class. Here again, nothing was said or done to satisfy the curiosity of students about this difference. Fifthly, the bibliographical details about format, collation and imprint were over-emphasised in the practical class. The revolt made one say within onself, "When I go back home,. . . ."

2 Facility for Designing

On going back to Madras, facility of every kind was found to re-think the cataloguing work.

21 Freedom

In the first place, there was full freedom to do one's best in re-organisation—open access, classification, cataloguing, reference service, simplified practice in administration, staff selection, public relation, in fact in every detail in the running of the library and in building it up.

22 Need for Fresh Catalogue

Secondly, the annual accession soon rose from 500 to 6,000. Within a year, this choked the paste-down catalogue in book-form. The necessity to build the catalogue afresh provided the opportunity to change over to card catalogue. This in its turn brought in the opportunity to give up the old method of cataloguing, based on the British Museum Code, modified arbitrarily here and there. The working out of a new Code was taken on hand.

23 Unconventionalised Mind of Readers

Thirdly, much time was spent each day on floor-duty, observing the classificatory and cataloguing approach of readers to books. Their approach had not been coloured at all by any tradition, as most of them tasted library facility—and open access in particular—for the first time in their lives. This gave as good an approximation as possible to unconventionalised, free, natural mental behaviour on the part of readers.

24 One Mind in Three Bodies

Fourthly, I was fortunate in the first two colleagues selected by me—C Sundaram and K M Sivaraman. Both were young graduates fresh from university. Both were free from any kind of library tradition in any library technique whatever. Both had a participating attitude. Both were devoted to their work. Both were industrious. All the three of us were loyal to one another. In fact, we three worked together in library field, as if it were a case of one mind in three bodies. A quantum of intuition was bringing out the Colon Classification and the Classified Catalogue Code. Intellect was brought into play once a week collectively in all the three—to discuss, check up, and polish the product of intuition, in the light of the experience gained by each of the three during the hours of floor-duty.

25 Teaching of Cataloguing

Fifthly, a School of Library Science was established in 1929. Since then, the author had been teaching cataloguing every year.

26 Practice of Cataloguing

Sixthly, about 70,000 volumes were classified, catalogued, and served during the seven years from 1926 to 1932. During the last two of these years the Colon Classification occupied the conscious level. The Classified Catalogue Code was, however, shaping itself unexpressed, below the conscious level, except while teaching cataloguing, till 1933 the year of publication of the *Colon classification*.

3 First Formulation

After the *Colon classification* [C10] came out, the catalogue-valve between the conscious and the sub-conscious opened out. The simmering of the Classified Catalogue Code began within the mind. I had to go to Calcutta. It was a railway journey of 38 hours. I said to Sivaraman, "Put into my bag plenty of 5×3 slips and a few sharpened pencils." During the 20 hours of daylight in the forward journey and an equal extent of time in the return journey, the rocking of the train, the utter absence of distraction by any printed stuff, and the solitude in the railway compartment, helped concentration. Un-interrupted recording of the flow of the rules of the Classified Catalogue Code was the result. Some of the rules brought their commentaries in their train. On return to Madras, these were intellectually reviewed by all the three of us. These were checked up and polished. Examples were provided. The press-copy was typed. This was the development of the First Formulation of this Classified Catalogue Code.

CHAPTER AB

SCIENTIFIC METHOD

1 Endless Spiral

The next stage in the development of the Classified Catalogue Code was conditioned by the advent of scientific method.

In scientific method, there is a never-ending spiral:

1 From individual experiences, through generalisation, to empirical laws derived from them, with the aid of induction and normal equations;

2 Through their reduction to a few normative principles, with the aid of imagination and/or intuition;

3 Through deductive laws or canons derived from the normative principles with the aid of methods of inference and semantics;

4 Through fresh individual experiences not conforming to them;

5 Back again through another cycle; and

6 So on, without end.

2 Establishment of Cycle

Such a cycle of development has now been established in cataloguing. Therefore, both the teaching of cataloguing and the framing of Catalogue Code can have the benefit of normative principles. New types of reading materials, apparently transcending the capacity of the existing rules of a Catalogue Code, may be catalogued by a proper interpretation of its rules. If this is not adequate, the rules can be amended or extended with the aid, and as a necessary implication, of the normative principles. When the cumulated unconscious shift in the social purpose of the library calls for an altogether different kind of library service, organisation, and technique, and the current ones stand abandoned by sheer folk-force, new normative principles should replace the old ones. And the cycle should be started again [RF9].

3 Critical Study of Codes

A critical examination of a Catalogue Code can be made with the aid of the normative principles. So also can be made a comparative study of several Catalogue Codes. Lastly, any Catalogue Code can be rectified in their light.

4 Verbal Apparatus

The success of critical or comparative study will depend on the verbal apparatus used to express thought and communicate it. The verbal apparatus should not create "noise" in the process of communication. It should not do so even in self-communication. Grossly disturbing noise is usually caused by the presence of homonyms and synonyms in the verbal apparatus. Even more dangerous and virus-like is the subtle difference in the shade of meaning of a word or phrase, due to slight shift in undertones and overtones. To minimise this, we should begin any discipline with the establishment of a special, agreed, dry-as-dust terminology without even the slightest touch of fuzziness. But such a special terminology will have to begin with some undefined terms. These should be clearly stated. Again the meta-language with which we handle the special terminology both at the stage of definition and at the later stages of development of thought, should be closely watched, if it is also drawn from the same natural language as the terminology itself. This is so in the discipline of cataloguing to-day. The special terminology should become spontaneous and instantaneous. Its use should be as much the result of reflex action as that of mother-tongue. This is an essential factor in scientific method.

5 First Approximation

The first application of such a scientific method to Cataloguing and to Catalogue Code was made in 1937. Between 1934 and 1937 some of the rules of the Classified Catalogue Code came up for critical examination from time to time, both in class-room discussion, and in staff-meetings to consider problem-books in cataloguing. On the anvil of such critical discussions and as a necessary aid to them, certain normative principles of cataloguing took shape. These were different from the Five Laws of Library Science. Indeed, they were all implications of these Laws. They were also different from the normative principles common to all spheres of human action and thought. The special normative principles were called Canons of Cataloguing. These were the product of impersonal intellectual grind during the prolonged earlier stages, and of imagination with a touch of intuition at the difficult final stage. I had the unusual privilege of continuously subjecting my Classified Catalogue Code and the other codes to a severe semantic analysis and check-up in the pure intellectual plane—in the class-room and in staff-meetings. This helped the formulation of the Canons; and it also led eventually to the setting up of the scientific method in the Discipline of Cataloguing. The experience of this first attempt was recorded in *Theory of library catalogue* [RT1] in 1937.

CHAPTER AC

AID TO DEVELOPMENT

1 Comparative Study 1

It was late in 1937. The press-copy of the *Theory* was lying on the table. To write or not to write to the Vice-Chancellor for formal permission to print it—that was the question. A sullen mood for total withdrawal from intellectual work and retirement from office was undermining enthusiasm and zest. Natesa Ananda, a spiritual friend, took me for an all-night vigil. He counselled persistence in the work on hand. A new spiritual guide appeared suddenly. He was Purohit Swami. He had considerable experience both before and after enlightenment. He had just then returned from Ireland after spending some years with W B Yeats. He administered a genial warning. He said, "Salvation can come only by dogged pursuit of the allotted work in society, with neither emotional attachment nor revulsion." This corrective was working in the mental plane for about twenty-four hours. Then came suddenly a physical aid in the form of a postal packet. It contained a mimeographed copy of the draft of the Rules for the preliminary second edition of the Anglo-American Code. Along with it came also a letter from Rudolph Gjelsness, chairman and editor-in-chief of the Catalogue Revision Committee of the American Library Association. He asked for comments on the Draft Rules. A few hours were turned on them during night. Many inconsistencies were seen. Some faults were detected. But there was no agreed Terminology or Canons of Cataloguing, in terms of which the comments could be put across to a far-off correspondent precisely and briefly through a letter. The new Canons came in handy to make a comparative study of the draft of the second edition of the Anglo-American Code and the Classified Catalogue Code. These events, the close sequence of them, and the advice from spiritual friends at the nick of time led to a decision to publish the *Theory of library catalogue*.

2 Comparative Study 2

The *Heading and canons* [RH1] was a second approximation to the application of Scientific Method to cataloguing. The Spiral of Scientific Method having been formed in this field, this second approximation began with a chapter on Terminology and another on Normative Principles. Then the several topics in the Choice and Rendering of Headings were taken up successively. The corresponding rules in the five chosen codes—the Anglo-American Code, the Classified Catalogue Code, the Cutter Code [C1], the Prussian Instructions [O1], and the Vatican Code [S2]—were examined critically and comparatively. This demonstrated the convenience, if not the need, of having an International Standard for the Title-Page and its Overflow, with special emphasis on Supplement to Author-Statement. Finally came a peep into the problems of an International Catalogue Code.

3 Corrective of the Class-Room

The Classified Catalogue Code has been used by me to teach the subject even from the time it was in the first draft stage. It is still being used both in teaching theory and in practical cataloguing. This is an unusual privilege I have had—to be an author and at the same time to teach one's own book to growing minds. This gave me a great chance to discover the flaws in the book. Here is a picture of a situation in the class-room. The class as a whole critically examines the catalogue cards written in the practical hours. The "accuser" as well as the "accused" student should cite the appropriate rule from the Classified Catalogue Code in support of every statement of his. The class-room looks like a Court of Law. This method of teaching puts the Classified Catalogue itself "on trial" in this Court. This has happened for nearly twenty-five years. A few trivial flaws thus come to be spotted out from time to time. These are removed in the subsequent edition. This is a continuing process.

4 Resilience of Sutra Style

The Rules in the very first edition made some approximation to the Sutra (aphorism) style of exposition. This style is the one used for basic codes and texts in Sanskrit tradition. This style is extremely sensitive to the principle of "atomic unit-thought" in the construction of a rule. However, drafting in English does not allow thorough atomisation. But so far as it goes, it proves useful in applying the rules to refractory title-pages with the aid of the Rules of Interpretation. The ruthlessly analytical mesh, holding the rules of the Classified Catalogue Code, invests the code as a whole with a resilience of another kind. Books appear off and on with cataloguing features beyond the capacity of the existing rules, even with the prop provided by the Rules of Interpretation. A few books with one or the other of such new features have come out in recent years. This will continue for ever. Hitherto, it has been easy to interpolate the necessary new Rules consistent with the old ones in the right place in the Code. Three such new Rules have been absorbed by the Classified Catalogue Code since the first edition came out without any disturbance to the existing rules. These concern Pseudo-Series, Related Book, and Merger Book.

CHAPTER AD

SUCCESSIVE EDITIONS

1 Edition 1

Edition 1 was published in 1934 as volume 4 of the Publication Series of the Madras Library Association [RC2]. This edition furnished the members of the staff of the Madras University Library with a firm Code to do their day-to-day cataloguing work and to make full use of all the entries in the card catalogue in giving reference service to readers. Perhaps, it happened to be the first available complete Classified Catalogue Code in printed form. It was pronounced by Sayers to be "by far the largest contribution to the subject" [S1].

2 Edition 2

In 1938, the Canons of Cataloguing were first enunciated. These were applied to a critical examination of this Code. The symbiosis between Classification and Cataloguing was discovered at the same time. It was brought out by the Chain Procedure invented at that time to derive Class Index Entry from Class Number. These ideas were incorporated in the next edition [RC3] which came out in 1945. The *Theory of library catalogue* [RT12] contained also a Theory of Alphabetisation. This theory separated the "Legislative phase" and the "Executive phase" in alphabetisation. This led to the formulation of the Rules for the Style of Writing and those for Alphabetisation, in close correlation to one another. This, in its turn, led to the formulation of the Gestalt Theory of Alphabetisation. Edition 2 incorporated these new ideas also [RC4].

3 Edition 3

Edition 3 came out in 1951. It included Rules for a Union Catalogue of Periodical Publications [RC7] and Rules for an Abstracting Periodical [RC8]. This edition provided also an

English-Sanskrit Glossary of Cataloguing Terms [RC9] to form the basis for cognate terminology in the several Indian languages. This was made possible by the Hindi version of the Code [RZN], with Rules in Sanskrit Sutras, which was also printed about the same time.

4 Edition 4

Edition 4 was largely the result of the second round of the critical study of cataloguing problems embodied in the *Heading and canons* (1955). It sought to implement the lay-out for a catalogue code arrived at in that book. It added the supplementary rules needed in the building of a National Bibliography. It separated the problems of the determination of the authorship of a document, the choice of heading, and its rendering, and prescribed the rules for them in independent chapters. It made some changes in the Style of Writing headings and the corresponding changes in the Rules for Alphabetisation. The corrections suggested in the *Heading and canons* were incorporated. This edition further eliminated the need for a separate Dictionary Catalogue Code. The necessary alternative rules for a Dictionary Catalogue Code were given in appropriate places in the Classified Catalogue Code itself. They were only a few.

5 Edition 5

Ed 5 is different from Ed 4 in certain respects. The difference concerns the inclusion of the following new chapters and Part:

Chap CD Law of Symmetry;
Chap DD Physical Form;
Chap DE Centralised Cataloguing;
Chap KK Homonym in class Index Headings; and
Chap KL Feature Heading;
Part V Non-Conventional Documents.

In Ed 5, some of the typographical and other trivial mistakes have been corrected. These concern particularly the internal reference backwards and forwards, the bibliography, the examples, and the index. Several sections have been re-worded to secure uniformity, or clarity, or simplicity as the case may be. Additional commentaries have been added in several places. A major change in Ed 5 is the reorganisation of the Parts and Chapters. The 9 Parts of Ed 4 have been replaced by 19 Parts in Ed 5. Some of the longer chapters have been split into shorter chapters. All this was done to make a closer approximation to the Principle of Unity in Parts as well as in Chapters.

In this edition, Sri A Neelameghan, my colleague and Reader in the Documentation Research and Training Centre, has shared with me the work of revision. His assistance has been of immense help to me.

The work of revising the text of Ed 4 and preparing the press copy of Ed 5 has taken about 320 man-hours. This does not include the time taken by clerical work.

CHAPTER AE

CONSPECTUS

The 9 parts—A B C D E F G H and J—constitute the approach, so to speak. The 10 parts—K L M N P Q R S T and U—give the substantive rules for cataloguing.

The 5 chapters of Part A describe the evolution of the Code.

The 9 chapters of Part B expound the Canons of Cataloguing in the light of which a Catalogue Code should be written as well as interpreted while applying.

The 7 chapters of Part C deal with the Laws of Library Science, four general Laws applicable to any situation, two Principles which throw light on the need for Local Catalogue Codes, and the Principle of Osmosis by which a library can be reorganized and recatalogued at minimum cost.

The 5 chapters of Part D deal with the evolution of the library catalogue in its internal form as well as external form and with Centralised Cataloguing.

The 8 chapters of Part E deal with the mechanics of cataloguing—such as writing and arranging entries.

The 17 chapters of Part F concern themselves with the establishment of a standard terminology for use in the discipline of cataloguing.

The 5 chapters of Part G give some help in the determination of the author of a document, particularly with reference to the conflict usually arising between the claimants—a Person, a Corporate Body, a Government, and an Institution.

The 7 chapters of Part H go into the structure of Name-of-Person in different cultural groups. They lay bare the difficulties in the way of the cataloguers of any one cultural group understanding the correct method of rendering the Name-of-Person in any other cultural group.

The 8 chapters of Part J prescribe the rules for rendering different kinds of names—personal, geographical, corporate — and also names of books and series.

The 12 chapters of Part K develop the technique of Chain

Procedure devised in 1938. During the last 25 years the advantages of Chain Procedure are being appreciated all over the world. Ed 5 gives the latest version of that procedure.

The 6 chapters of Part L deal with the Cross Reference Index Entries to be given in the alphabetical part of the catalogue by way of linking up alternative headings likely to be sought.

The 11 chapters of Part M form the core of the book. They lay down strict rules for the writing of the diverse kinds of Specific Entries for a Single-Volumed Simple Book.

The 3 chapters of Part N give the supplementary rules necessary in making entries for a Composite Book and a Multi-Volumed Book.

The 11 chapters of Part P analyse the complexities normally met in Periodical Publications and provide the additional rules necessary to write entries for Periodicals with several kinds of complexities.

The 44 chapters of Parts Q to V give the additional rules necessary in building a Union Catalogue of Books, a Union Catalogue of Periodical Publications, a National Bibliography, an Abstracting or Indexing Periodical, and a Catalogue of Non-conventional Documents.

The last chapters of some of the Parts—particularly those giving rules for making entries—are devoted to the alternative rules for a Dictionary Catalogue Code.

PART B

CANONS OF CATALOGUING

CHAPTER BA

DEFINITION

0 **Canons of Cataloguing.**—The specific normative principles applicable to cataloguing—that is, to the

1 Drafting of a Catalogue Code including the formulation of each rule;

2 Interpretation of the rules to meet new situations brought up by a particular document or by changes in the practice of book production; and

3 Provision of suitable guidance for cataloguing work.

There are nine Canons of Cataloguing formulated so far. Some of them were formulated for the first time in the *Theory of library catalogue* [RT9]. They were further added to and elaborated in the *Heading and canons: Comparative study of five catalogue codes* [RH2]. The Canons are stated below with brief comments.

A word of explanation about the choice of the term 'Canons' to denote 'Normative Principles'. The following is the convention adopted about the term to be used to denote normative principles in different contexts:

Law.—In the context of a major discipline, such as Library Science.

Canon.—In the context of divisions of the first order of the major discipline, such as Book Selection, Classification, and Cataloguing.

Principle.—In the context of divisions of the second or later order of the major discipline, such as Facet Sequence in Classification, and Alphabetisation in Cataloguing.

CHAPTER BB

CANON OF ASCERTAINABILITY

0 **Canon of Ascertainability.**—The Principle prescribing that the information found in the title-page of the document catalogued and its over-flow pages should determine the choice and rendering of

1 Each Section of the Main Entry other than the Extract Note, the Extraction Note, and the Related Book Note;

2 Each Section of a Cross Reference Entry (in a Classified Catalogue) and Subject Analytical (in a Dictionary Catalogue) other than the Leading Section and the Directing Section;

3 The Heading of each Book Index Entry other than any derived from the Extract Note, Extraction Note, and Related Book Note;

4 All Sections other than the Heading and the Directing Section of each Book Index Entry;

5 All Sections other than the Heading and Directing Section of a Class Index Entry (in a Classified Catalogue), and Specific Subject Entry, and *See also* Entry (in a Dictionary Catalogue);

6 Each Section other than the Directing Section in each Cross Reference Index Entry other than Name Entry; and

7 Similar sections in any other kind of entry.

1 Internal Inconsistency

Some of the internal inconsistencies of existing catalogue codes are traceable to their being obliged to step out of the title-page and its over-flow and go into the market place so to speak, in search of data for the choice and rendering of headings of even specific entries.

2 Failure of Title-Page

Unfortunately, the title-page and its over-flow have not yet begun to give all the data needed for making the main entry in the catalogue. Nor has the Cataloguing Profession exerted itself till now in persuading the book-trade and the authors to do the needful in the matter.

3 Steady Change in Title-Page

It must however be conceded that the design of the title-page and its over-flow has been in flux all along. During the last one or two centuries sheer folk-force has led the title-page and its over-flow to evolve towards being a complete repository of the cataloguing elements of a document. Its evolution has been described in detail in the *Social bibliography: Physical bibliography for librarians* [RS2]. The title-page is a gift of the early printers. It has been exploited in succession by patrons, publishers, and authors. It is open to cataloguers too to exploit it. Exploitation here means not only using the information given in the title-page, but also endeavouring to make the title-page and its over-flow carry all such information as the cataloguer needs but is not at present given in them.

4 Reciprocity

In other words, the influence between the title-page and the Cataloguing Profession should be reciprocal. Each should enrich and help the other. To make this possible, the title-leaf and its over-flow leaves in the material plane and the Canon of Ascertainability in the idea plane—that is, the plane of normative principles—should be made the sheet-anchor of any Catalogue Code. The purpose of the commentaries in Sections FL71 to FL78 is just to plead for the establishment of such a reciprocity between the Cataloguing Profession and the book-trade, leading to the adoption of an International Standard for the title-page and its over-flow.

5 Main Entry

Even before the desired International Standard for the title-page and its over-flow is established, the Main Entry can conform to the Canon of Ascertainability to a large measure. Most of the Book Index Entries also can do so.

CHAPTER BC

CANON OF PREPOTENCE

0 Canon of Prepotence.—The principle that

1 The Potency to decide the position of an entry among the various entries in a catalogue should, if possible, be concentrated totally in the Leading Section; and even there

2 It should be concentrated, as much as possible, in the entry element; and further

3 If total concentration in the Leading Section is not possible, the minimum possible potency should be allowed to overflow beyond it to later sections; and

4 Even this spill-over should be distributed in the later sections in a decreasing sequence of intensity.

1 Distribution of Potency

The essence of a Library Catalogue is arrangement of entries. The entries get sorted letter by letter or digit by digit, beginning with the very first of these found in an entry. The potency goes on decreasing rightwards and downwards, from the first letter or digit, in most of the scripts. Any mistake in the first letter or the digit will therefore be fatal. The entry will be virtually lost in some far-off region of the catalogue. The range within which the entry may get lost goes on decreasing, as we move further on from the first letter or digit. The range is reduced to a reasonably small one, only by the time we reach beyond the end of the entry word, or of the entry element, or of the class number, as the case may be.

2 Light for Framers of Catalogue Code

The Canon of Prepotence yields an important deduced principle applicable to the choice of entry element in a multi-worded heading—that is, in the rendering of a multi-worded term chosen for use as heading. That principle is a statistical one.

"The entry element should be chosen from among that group of the words, occurring in the multi-worded term chosen for use as heading, that is more numerous than the groups of the other words occurring in it."

For, the probability for the same word to be used as entry element in several headings is inversely proportional to the numerousness of the group from which the word is chosen; and the smaller this probability, the greater will be concentration of potency in the entry element. This statistical principle is responsible—unconscious though it might have been—for the choice of the family name as the entry element in rendering western name-of-person in a heading. It is the overlooking of this statistical principle that has vitiated the Anglo-American Code's prescription of place-name as the entry element for Institution-Heading, in spite of its having accepted the place-name as the entry element in the name of a Government as improvised by cataloguing convention [A4]. This statistical principle plays some part, though again unconsciously, in the choice of entry element in the real title for title heading, as prescribed in the Prussian Instructions [O2]. This statistical principle should be exploited fully in the framing of a Catalogue Code. Its use will be demonstrated in Part J, which is on the Rendering of Names.

21 Illustration From Name of Series

Here is an example of the application of this principle to Series-Heading. Many universities and governments have established their own series. They are generally given common names, such as Publication series, Library science series, English series, Hindi series, Historical series, Economic series, Pamphlet series, and so on. These names do not have sufficient potency. They often become homonyms. To resolve the homonym and to increase the potency, the name of the university or the government or even a department of either may have to be added. If the purpose be merely individualisation, the name can be added at the end. But if the purpose is increasing the potency of the heading, the name should be added at the front. While drafting the Classified Catalogue Code in 1933, I had not consciously seized the Canons of Cataloguing. I was therefore unable to decide the issue on proper grounds. Much of indeterminancy or inconsistency was the result. It is sixteen years after the Canons of Cataloguing were enunciated, that I was able to see this difficult issue lighted up by the Canon of Prepotence.

3 Moral for the Cataloguer

The Cataloguer should prevent any casual error creeping into the Leading Section and particularly into the first word or the class number—and even more so the very first letter or digit—to be written at the very beginning of the Leading Section. He must be aware that any error in writing the Entry Element or the Class Number carries a high penalty.

4 Call Number Entry

The Canon of Prepotence has its fullest sway in the Call Number Entry of the Classified Catalogue. Even here, it is able to have its full sway, only if the Scheme of Classification in use has an individualising Call Number for every document. Today, the only scheme that does so is the Colon Classification [RC11]. If the Call Number is constructed according to that scheme, the Leading Section of the Main Entry is truly prepotent. All the potency of the entry, in respect of arrangement of entries, is concentrated in the Leading Section. Every other section in that entry is rendered impotent. In finding the position for a Call Number Entry in the catalogue cabinet, the

Filing Cataloguer need never look beyond the Call Number in the Leading Section.

5 Dictionary Catalogue

In respect of the Canon of Prepotence, the Classified Catalogue has an advantage over the Dictionary Catalogue. For, the Main Entry of the latter is an Author Entry. However much the name of an author may be individualised, it may not individualise the document described in the entry. For, the author might have written two or more documents. Even if he has written only two, the entry is not individualised by the name of the author alone. In other words, the potency is not concentrated in the Leading Section. A part of it necessarily overflows into the title-section. In finding the position for the Main Entry in the Catalogue Cabinet of a Dictionary Catalogue, the Filing Cataloguer will have often to look into the second and the later sections.

6 Specific Word Entry

A similar remark is applicable also to any specific word entry, be it of the Dictionary Catalogue or of the Alphabetical Part of the Classified Catalogue. In every such entry, every endeavour is made by a Catalogue Code for the potency to be at its possible maximum in the Leading Section. For example, the name of a person, occupying the Leading Section, is individualised by the addition of the necessary Individualising Elements to the name. Similarly, a geographical name in the Leading Section—be it as the name of a subject or as the name of a Government—is helped to carry the maximum possible potency, by the addition of the necessary Individualising Elements to the name.

7 Cross Reference Entry

In a Cross Reference Entry of a Classified Catalogue, the Leading Section has only a little potency. For, it is merely a class number. A good deal of potency necessarily flows into the Third Section, which gives the Locus. The Filing Cataloguer will have to reach that Section in the Entry.

8 Class Index Entry

The Canon of Prepotence has its full sway in a Class Index Entry of the Classified Catalogue. For, there cannot be two Class Index Entries with the same Heading. This is a result of the requirement that the artificial ordinal language of class numbers is expected to be so designed that it has no synonyms or homonyms [RP2]. In other words, the Heading of a Class Index Entry individualises the entry. All the potency, in respect of arrangement of entries, of a Class Index Entry is totally concentrated in its Leading Section. Its second section containing the directing words and its third section containing the class number are totally impotent. In finding the position for a Class Index Entry in the Catalogue Cabinet, the Filing Cataloguer need not at all look beyond the Leading Section.

91 Cross Reference Index Entry

The Canon of Prepotence is least respected by the Cross Reference Index Entry—be it in the Classified Catalogue or in the Dictionary Catalogue. For, the Filing Cataloguer must look down to the last word in the last section of such an entry to find the correct position of it in the catalogue cabinet. In other words, the potency, in respect of arrangement of entries, is distributed both in the first and the last sections of a Cross Reference Index Entry. The Filing Cataloguer will have to reach the Third Section of the Entry.

CHAPTER BD

CANON OF INDIVIDUALISATION

0 **Canon of Individualisation.**—The principle that the name of any entity—be it of a person, a geographical entity, a corporate body, a series, a document, a subject, or a language—used as the Heading of a catalogue entry should be made to denote one and only one entity, by adding to it the necessary and sufficient number of Individualising Elements.

1 Fatal Result of Homonym

Homonym may prove fatal. Tragic results have come out of homonyms. In the epic *Mahābhārata* the turning point in the Great War centres round the homonym "Aswatthama". It was the name of a General as well as of an elephant on the side of one of the belligerents. When the elephant was killed, the words "Aswatthama killed" were broadcast by the opposite belligerents. The other side took the name "Aswatthama" to denote their General. This led to the demoralisation of that side and the ultimate victory of the other.

2 Homonym Deflects an Author

Homonym may lead to serious results in a scholar's work. A traditional story, apocryphal though it might be, illustrates it. Sankara, the great philosopher of mediaeval India, wished to write a commentary on the *Sahasranama* (book of thousand names) of Lalita (the Goddess-Principle). He asked his librarian to bring a copy of the *Sahasranama*. But he brought the *Sahasranama* of Vishnu (the God-Principle). According to the tradition, Sankara ultimately saw the vision of Lalita telling him, "It is I that took advantage of the homonymous nature of the title mentioned by you, and led your librarian to bring the other *Sahasranama*. Write a commentary on it."

3 Homonym Spoils Book Selection

Homonym may lead to ridiculous mistakes. Some years ago, the Board of Studies in English Literature recommended to the Madras University Library the purchase of a book entitled *Life of Johnson*. It had taken it to to be a biography of Samuel Johnson, the well-known man of letters. But when the book arrived, it turned out to be the life of a dog !

4 Homonym in Indology

By S Kuppuswamy Sastri

The following account of the way in which homonym dissipates research-potential into trivial work had been furnished by the late Mahamahopadhyaya Vidya-Vacaspati Professor S Kuppuswamy Sastri, Professor of Sanskrit and Comparative Philology in the Presidency College and Curator of the Government Oriental Manuscripts Library in Madras. It is extracted from a note of his entitled *Authorial polyonymy and homonymy in Sanskrit literature*. This note will be found in full in the first three editions of this book [RC5.]

41 Authorial Homonym in Sanskrit Literature

In Sanskrit Literature, there are several instances of Authorial Homonym (the same name coming to be given to different authors).

This phenomenon presents many an interesting problem to the makers and students of Library Science, in their attempt to formulate the rules of library classification and cataloguing, not to speak of the various difficulties which they cause to the modern historians of Sanskrit literature. Homonym comprises all the cases where, mainly as a result of the ancient custom of naming persons after their ancestors, gods, goddesses, prophets, saints, distinguished authors, patrons and sometimes rulers, different persons have come to bear the same name. In many of the cases of homonym, it is impossible to discover exactly all the underlying causes. Homonymous parallels are bound to cause even greater trouble and confusion in the sphere of library classification and cataloguing than in the investigation of crimes and settlement of legal claims. Long-standing usage established by reliable evidence is certainly useful to a considerable extent in helping one out of difficulties. It would be certainly worthwhile for any institution intended for the promotion of culture to undertake the preparation of a concordance to Authorial Homonyms in Indian literature; and this would afford ample scope for intelligent, interesting, and useful research for a number of scholars for a number of years.

The following illustrations indicate the nature and complexity of the problems connected with Authorial Homonym. All the names given below are such as are expected to find a place in the classification of Indian literature.

42 Vyasa

Vyasa is one of the most famous names in Sanskrit literature. He is the reputed author of the *Mahabharata*. Several Puranas are attributed to one with the same name. The famous *Bhashya* on the *Yoga-sutras*, called *Vyasa-bhashya*, is also believed to have been written by Vyasa. Some later writers called Vyasaraya and Vyasatirtha bore the name Vyasa.

43 Valmiki

Valmiki is the author of the *Ramayana*. In later literature, a Tamil poet and a Prakrita grammarian came to be called Valmiki. In recent times, Subba

Rao, retired Telugu Pandit of the Presidency College came to be called Andhra-Valmiki for his *Telugu Ramayana.*

44 Gautama

Gautama is the author of the *Nyaya-sutras*. The founder of Buddhism, whose hagiological name is Siddhartha, is also known by his gotra-name, Gautama. Cataloguers have also to take into account the name Gautama, borne by the author of an ancient Sutra work of the Dharmasastra literature (*Gautama-dharmasutrani*).

45 Bad Errors

In library classification and cataloguing, the various problems connected with authorial Homonym should be carefully and successfully tackled. Otherwise, bad errors are likely to vitiate the work of higher research. The following illustration, in this connection, may not be out of place. Aufrecht, on page 46 of his famous catalogue, confounds Anandatirtha (=Madhavacarya=Purnaprajna) with Anandagiri (=Anandajnana). The former is the well-known Acarya of the Dvaita School and the latter is the well-known scholiast of the Advaita School. This is an instance in which a homonymous part of two distinct names of two distinct authors has caused trouble.

46 Inadequacy of Mere Names

This illustration will indicate the nature of the snares and pitfalls in the way of librarians who are engaged in library classification and cataloguing. The difficulties arising in this way from Authorial Homonymy in Sanskrit literature have to be surmounted necessarily with the co-operation of scholars in Sanskrit, until a reliable concordance as indicated at the end of Sec BD41 becomes available, for ready reference. One golden rule, however, which a librarian, who is concerned with the classification and cataloguing of any considerable collection of Sanskrit books, can easily remember and follow is—"*Refuse to be guided by mere names.*"

5 Dissipation of Research Potential

The unresolved homonyms of the past are dissipating much of the research potential among the Indologists of the world today. Surely the time and energy of such eminent scholars could be put to better use, if the bibliographies and catalogues of the past had respected the Canon of Individualisation. Research Potential is also dissipated by the failure of the past to have resolved homonyms in the titles of books, as and when they appeared.

6 Safeguard the Future

The directive of the Canon of Individualisation is in the words, "Sufficient is the harm done by neglecting me in the past. Provide safeguards against its recurrence at least in respect of the headings in the entries of the future documents. The safeguard is to resolve homonyms in headings by the addition of extra terms to the names proper. Call them Individualising Elements." One of the main purposes of the plan contained in Sec FL71 to FL78 for an International Standard for the Entry Statement for Author on the back of the title-page of a book is to carry out this directive of the Canon of Individualisation. Many of the Rules in the chapters of Part J are turned on the prescription of Individualising Elements in the rendering of names in headings of catalogue entries.

CHAPTER BE

CANON OF SOUGHT-HEADING

0 **Canon of Sought-Heading.**—The principle that the decision whether an entry

1 With a particular type of heading, or

2 With a particular choice for that heading, or

3 With a particular rendering of that choice, or

4 A particular added entry arising out of it,

should be based on the answer to the question: "Is reader or library staff likely to look for a book under the particular type or choice or rendering of heading or in the particuar added entry."

1 Flair and Freedom

The answer to this question is a matter of flair. The flair should be based on experience in Reference Service—that is, in eliciting from readers their requirements and finding the appropriate documents for them. Induction should be applied to the words usually brought up by readers in looking into the catalogue to choose their documents. The flair should also be based on experience in Book Selection. Induction should be applied to the types of heading found necessary to help either in filling up gaps in the library collection or in avoiding unintended duplication. It has to be based further on the obligation of the Reference Section to give a reader alternatives to a document, when the one actually sought is not in at the moment. The alternative may be essentially the same as the one sought. For, the same book might have appeared with a different title and the latter may be in the library. Or, it might have been merged into another book in the library. Or it might be an extract from some other book, which is on the shelf. Reference Section will also have the obligation to produce to a reader all the documents associated with another document mentioned by him. The apparent freedom given by the Canon of Sought-Heading should be used with great circumspection, care, and judgement.

2 Effect on Catalogue Code

The design of the Catalogue Code is itself largely guided by the Canon of Sought-Heading. Several of the Rules are determinded by it. There are several elements on the title-page and its over-flow. The Canon of Ascertainability is indifferent as to which element can be allowed the claim to become a heading. All that it is concerned with is that no element outside the title-page and its over-flow should be allowed to become the heading of a main entry or any other entry coming under its sway as prescribed in Sec BB0. It is the business of the Canon of Sought-Heading to admit or reject the claim of any element in the title-page and its over-flow to become a heading. A trivial case of rejection is the claim of the year or the place of publication or of the name of the publisher. Author-heading and subject-heading are the most popular among sought-headings. Collaborator-heading comes next in popularity. Series heading also is sought.

3 Pseudo-Series and its Discovery

The concept of Pseudo-Series owes its origin practically to the Canon of Sought-Heading. The question "What are the plays of Shakespeare with Variorum Edition ?" was asked by a scholar. The catalogue based on the 1934 edition of the *Classified catalogue code* or any other code current in that period, could not give an immediate answer to this question. Similar experiences accumulated through years while doing Reference Service. It was this that led to the concept of Pseudo-Series.

4 Extract and its Demand

A reader may ask for a document. It may have gone out on loan. But an Extract from it may be on the shelf, as a separate document. There is some probability for this Extract to satisfy his want. But he will not be able to look for it under its own heading. Because he may not know of its existence. Therefore, when he looks for the original book under its own heading which he knows, he will be helped if there is a note in its entry with the information "*A portion printed as*" followed by the heading etc of each of the extracts from it, owned by the library. Vice versa, the reader may know only of the Extract. A note in its entry saying "*Extract from . . .*" will help him to think of the original. It may be of use to him. He might not at all have thought of the original. But this note will make him seek it. This service should be done by the catalogue according to the Canon of Sought-Heading.

5 Merger Book and its Demand

Again, it was only in 1953 that the phenomenon of two or more books appearing merged into one book at a later time, came to our notice. Here again the Canon of Sought-Heading prompted the framing of a Rule to meet the cataloguing problems of such Merger Books.

6 Cross Reference Index Entry

The institution of the majority of cross reference index entries had its origin in the Canon of Sought-Heading. A reader might remember an author or a collaborator by only one of the names used by him as alternative names or variant forms of one and the same name, in different documents. Some of these may be real and some pseudonymous. This makes no difference in the problem being considered. Whatever be the name sought by the reader, the catalogue should inform him of all the documents written by him under other names too. The Canon of Sought-Heading recognised this fact. All such names are proper names. Only a few persons indulge in such alternative names. The claim of each name to be used as heading may therefore be admitted without undue disregard of the Law of Parsimony. Such is the verdict of the Canon of Sought-Heading.

7 Subject-Heading and Chain Procedure

When the Rules of Chain Procedure were formulated for the first time in 1938 in *Theory* [RT10], the rules were crude. For, practically every significant digit in the class number was given the right to claim a Class Index Entry of its own. For example, in the class number L183, the digit 3 gave the class index heading "Ear, Medicine." The digit 8 also gave the class index heading "Head, Medicine." Again, the digit 1 too gave the class index heading "Regional Organ, Medicine". This was a ruthlessly mechanical way of deriving class index entries from the digits in class number. It led to a plethora of class index entries. Some of these were irritating the mind vaguely. The Law of Parsimony protested. But there was no way of removing the irritation, till the Canon of Sought-Heading took shape. It ruled out as unsought the two headings "Head, Medicine," and "Regional Organ, Medicine". Similar weeding out of unsought headings was indicated in many classes. The Rules of Chain Procedure were themselves re-enunciated. However, it is the crudeness of the Chain Procedure, invented in 1938, that was responsible for the formulation of the Canon of Sought-Heading in 1952.

7ZD Application to Dictionary Catalogue

During my visit to London in June 1954 for consultation with colleagues in the profession, A J Wells, the Editor of the *British national bibliography*, brought an important experience to notice. While the subject-heading got by the Rules of Chain Procedure did its work well in the Classified Catalogue, it did not produce the desired result in the Dictionary Catalogue. The discussion of this subject took a fruitful turn as soon as the Canon of Sought-Heading was consciously taken as guide.

CHAPTER BF

CANON OF CONTEXT

0 **Canon of Context.**—The principle

1 That the Rules of a Catalogue Code should be formulated in the context of:

11 The nature of the cataloguing features of the book, prevalent in the mode of book production;

12 The nature of the organisation of libraries prevalent in regard to the mode and quality of library service: and

13 The coming into existence of published bibliographies and particularly bibliographical periodicals; and

2 That the rules should be amended from time to time to keep step with changes in the Context.

1 Weightage to Physical Attributes

When manuscripts were loosely assembled sheets, not firmly bound, a detailed description of size, collation, and even peculiarities of individual leaves was necessary in catalogue entry. To add to this, each copy of a book was virtually unique. It was often a rarity. It was property. Each entry in a catalogue was therefore over-weighted with details of physical bibliography. This was true as much with Manuscript as with Incunabula. They are of immense help in historical bibliography. For a long time, after the invention of printing—even long after the Incunabula Period—these practices prevailed in some measure. This mental set of the cataloguers of documents of pre-printing days and of Incunabula days continued even for ages after the context had changed. Cutter [C2] saw the continuance of this mental set even down to the last quarter of the nineteenth century. He called it "full" cataloguing. He recommended "short" cataloguing for Service-Libraries. This recommendation was opportune; and it was readily accepted by the progressive members of the profession. Because the great increase in the annual output of printed books and even in the annual accession in many a library made "full" too costly for practice. The Canon of Context gave weight to this change in context. It supported the Law of Parsimony. And Cataloguing Code was modified. The jurisdiction of the old Code was confined to the relatively few kinds of catalogues and lists obliged to give bibliographical description.

2 Back-Log of Incunabula Age

However, the back-log of the old mental set let go the retention of collation, name of publisher, name of the place of publication, and price in library catalogue. So long as library organisation put a physical barrier between reader and library collection, collation served a useful purpose. For, a reader naturally wanted to know the size of a book before applying for it. Canon of Context voted for its retention in the then prevailing Context. Publisher's name too was somewhat helpful in evaluating a book without seeing it. But the place of publication and price were hardly relevant to the needs of either the reader or of the staff. Publisher's catalogue gave this information. The staff had an additional source in the accession register. These details are necessary in catalogues of publishers and book-sellers, the accession register, and certain other forms of bibliography such as a National Bibliography. But they are not necessary in the library catalogue of a Service-Library. In the long run, they may even amount to wrong information. In spite of this, the back-log of an earlier context is still persisting in practice, unmindful of the Canon of Context. This back-log of the Incunabula Age should not be allowed today to enter the catalogue of any Service-Library. The Catalogue of a National Central Library, serving also as the National Bibliography, is the only library catalogue where such details should be continued.

3 Context of Open Access

A further change has now occurred in the Context. This change lies in the domain of the organisation of a library. It is the introduction of Open Access System. Now the barrier between the reader and the book collection has been removed except in the case of pamphlets, weakly-built books, and rare or costly books. These form only a fraction of the collection of a Service-Library. A book within direct access to reader does not need the mention of its format, collation etc, in its catalogue entry. The Canon of Context recommends a device such as that the catalogue should indicate a pamphlet by a simple device like underlining the book number; similarly it may indicate an over-size book by over-lining the book number, and so on; for, books of these kinds are not given open access. The implication of the Canon of Context is that, in the entries of any book, other than those to which open access cannot be given, all items, other than name(s) of author(s), title with puff omitted, note giving series or certain other peculiarities prescribed by the Canon of Sought-Heading, call number, and accession number, should be omitted from the main entry of the catalogue of a Service-Library. The Classified Catalogue Code was one of the first codes to cut out items other than the above, quite ruthlessly in a library catalogue. It may however be added that if centrally-printed catalogue card is used, the Unit Card System may come into force. It will be printed by the National Central Library. It will be a reprint from the Main Entry of the National Bibliography. Therefore, it will have to be allowed to have all the bibliographical details needed in the National Bibliography. For, it is cheaper to use the same card both for the National Central Library and for a Service-Library.

The Context of Open Access will also reduce annotation to catalogue entries to a minimum, and perhaps even eliminate it.

4 Expectation of Life of a Book

To-day the demand for simplification is reinforced by another factor in the Context. Books are plentiful and cheap. Only a small percentage have permanent value. Thus, the preciousness of books as permanent possession has diminished considerably. Further, democracy circulates the library copy of a book through many hands. Therefore, books perish rapidly by legitimate use. We have begun to realise that a book is a mortal, though the work embodied in it may be immortal. Except in a comparatively small percentage of works which form the classics of permanent value, even the thought-content of a work is soon out-moded. And in the case of some works, the thought-content becomes even quite wrong in course of time. A copy of a book embodying such out-moded and wrong thought-content may be necessary in a few libraries, in order to serve the interest of historical and antiquarian research. Perhaps, it should be sufficient to have copies of such out-moded works in one dormitary library in each country or in each constituent State, or in a few regions of each country. In a Service-Library, such books are not only a burden, but they may even be a social danger. Because, the lower intellectual strata in a democracy may not be able to sense the erroneousness of the information or the knowledge given in such books. I usually high-light this new element in the Context by the provocative statement: "The expectation of life of a modern book is only ten years. A Service-Library hoarding books, over ten years old, is punishable for one or other of two reasons. Either it has neglected to circulate the book properly as is evident from its being not worn out sufficiently and reduced to pulp by legitimate use to make its being weeded out a necessity; or it is retaining a book embodying out-of-date knowledge and exposing it to use by the public. Either of these is a social danger. If the work as well as the book embodying it are of fleeting value, there is no harm in weeding the book out in ten years. If the work is immortal and its body perishes by actual use, one will have to withdraw it in ten years and replace it by a fresh copy; moreover, its very lasting value will enable it to come again in a new embodiment. In that case, it is wiser to replace it by a later edition." We can generally grant that the span of life of a book of to-day is limited, even though the work embodied in it may have unlimited span of life. This context makes one scrutinise severely the cost of cataloguing. It calls for simplification of catalogue entry. A revision of Catalogue Code becomes necessary.

5 New Demand in Literature-Search

Intensification and extension of research activity in the community creates new demands on the catalogue. Over-all economy in the man-power of a nation calls for a new division of labour. There should be no dissipation of research-potential. For this, a new division of labour is necessary among the intellectuals. In this new division of labour, the Library Profession should relieve the other professions of the task of literature-search. The librarian should become a partner in every research enterprise. Moreover, the tremendous turbulance in the universe of knowledge of today throws a heavy burden on the Library Profession engaged in literature-search. The search, moreover, has to be expeditious. To discharge this new function, the Library Profession has to throw a new burden on the library catalogue. Subject-analyticals have to be multiplied, in order to bring to the notice of the reader even micro thought embodied in articles in periodicals and in portions of books, in the measure of his interest in them. Many libraries have begun to practise this—particularly research, industrial, commercial, and governmental libraries, and even public libraries.

6 Effect of International Bibliography

Another change has come in the Context. It has been brought about by the pressure of the economics of cataloguing service. There is much unfavourable disproportion between the cost of subject-analyticals and the extent of their use. However, the social value of even limited use is immense. A reconciliation of these two conflicting findings should be found. It has been found. It is the publication of subject bibliographies as an international project. This change in the Context does make the Catalogue Code add a directive that subject-analyticals should not be attempted wholesale by a Library Catalogue in the fields of knowledge provided with international bibliographies.

7 Effect of National Documentation

But there is an unavoidable time-lag between the appearance of a document and its mention in international bibliography. This is unavoidable on account of the problems created by the space to be covered and by the needs of processing. During the interval of this time-lag, a Service-Library cannot fail or fumble about in its literature-search. The failure here is particularly anti-social. Because, it is nascent micro thought that counts in research. Here again, the pressure of the economics of cataloguing comes into play. This pressure too has been removed by a new development coming into vogue just at this time. A temporary "documentation list" is being published by a nation. For this purpose, nation after nation has begun to establish a National Documentation Centre. It scans all the periodicals produced in the country or taken into the country. It classifies the articles. It publishes a classified list of them week by week. The Context changes with its establishment. The Canon of Context is sensitive to this change. It tells individual Service-Libraries "Don't attempt subject-analyticals in duplication of entries in national documentation lists." It also tells the National Documentation Centre, "Remember that your documentation list is only for temporary use. It will soon be replaced by the fully comprehensive international bibliographies in the diverse subjects. Don't waste your resources in making your documentation list exhaustive. Know what work is in progress in your country.

Include, in your documentation list, only the title justified by this Context."

8 Other Changes in Context

The world of books is not static. Context is ever-changing. Nature of book changes. Make up of title-page changes. Nature of readers changes. Out-look of library service changes. Extent of national and international co-operation changes. The Canon of Context demands that cataloguing practice should also change. For this purpose, it demands that Catalogue Code too should change in consonance with the change in the other factors. When the standard for Entry Statement for Author, recommended in Sec FL71 to FL78 comes into vogue, many of the Rules in the current Catalogue Codes, in regard to the rendering of names of authors, will have to be omitted. Probably about 60 pages of this code will be replaced by a Rule of a few lines. (See Rule C1). Several others will have to be changed. New ones will have to be added.

The refrain of the Canon of Context in its application to Library Catalogue and to Library Catalogue Code is:

Ever becoming, ever new.

नवो नवो भवति जयमानः ।

CHAPTER BG

CANON OF PERMANENCE

0 **Canon of Permanence.**—**The principle that no element in an entry, the heading in particular, should be subjected to change by the Rules of a Catalogue Code, except when the Rules themselves are changed in response to the Canon of Context.**

The Canon of Permanence and the Canon of Ascertainability work in unison. Alternative names are left to the care of Cross Reference Index Entries. Change of name of a person or of a corporate body is not allowed to ask for a change in the Heading of any entry of any book published under the old name. The Classified Catalogue Code has framed its Rules on the cataloguing of periodical publications, for the first time, in such a way that the Canon of Permanence in cataloguing and the Canon for Filiatory Sequence [RC6] in classification are both respected simultaneously.

CHAPTER BH

CANON OF CURRENCY

0 **Cannon of Currency.**—The principle that the term used to denote a subject in a Class Index Entry of a Classified Catalogue and in a Subject Entry of a Dictionary Catalogue should be the one in current usage.

1 Conflict of Canons

Name of subject keeps changing with time. Unless the current name is used in the heading, readers cannot benefit by it. To satisfy this Canon, the headings of Class Index Entries and of Subject Entries should be changed as and when a new name stabilises itself. This leads inevitably to a violation of the Canon of Permanence. This conflict between the two Canons is resolved by a partition of the field of sway. The Canon of Currency has sway only over Class Index Heading in Classified Catalogue and over Subject-Heading in Dictionary Catalogue. The Canon of Permanence has sway only over Name-Heading other than Subject-Heading. It has sway only in a heading made of name of person, geographical entity, or corporate body.

2 Dilemma

The Canon of Currency has to face a dilemma. The question is, "Current among whom ?" For, two different terms may be current at the same time among specialists and non-specialists to denote one and the same subject. The first belongs to the special terminology built up by the specialists themselves. The second belongs to the natural language spoken by the common man. The general tendency is to prefer the term in natural language. This preference often leads to a multi-worded term in natural language in preference to a single-worded term in specialist language, *e g*, "Child, Medicine" in preference to "Pediatrics". In spite of the increase in the number of words to be used, natural language is preferred. This is due to the pressure of the Second Law of Library Science [RF3]. According to it, a specialist reader knows the common name as well as the technical name of a subject. The non-specialist reader knows only the common name; he does not know the technical name. Moreover, the specialist has a highly organised personality; he has greater intellectual awareness and agility. If he does not find a technical name in the headings, he will look up its popular equivalent. It is not so with the common reader. Therefore, to serve every reader without exception, common name should be preferred to special terminology, in Subject Heading. This is the joint finding of the Canon of Currency and the Second Law of Library Science as a helpful way of getting out of the dilemma.

CHAPTER BJ

CANON OF CONSISTENCE

0 **Canon of Consistence.**—The principle that

1 The rules of a Catalogue Code should provide for all the added entries of a document to be consistent with its Main Entry; and

2 The entries of all documents should be consistent with one another in certain essentials such as choice, rendering, and style of writing the heading and the other sections.

The Canon of Consistence does insist that the Main Entry of all documents should be of the same species. For example, in a Dictionary Catalogue the main entry should be an Author Entry in all cases. It should not be a Subject Entry.

We should not make one species of entry take the place of another. Again a catalogue code should not prescribe for the heading of one and the same entry, Main Heading and Sub-Heading of different species, such as Author Heading and Subject Sub-Heading. But this canon is violated by some of the Rules of the Anglo-American Code, as shown in the *Heading and canons* [RH3].

PART C

GENERAL NORMATIVE PRINCIPLES

CHAPTER CA

LAWS OF LIBRARY SCIENCE

0 **Laws of Library Science.**—The specific normative principles applicable to any problem arising in library science, library service, and library practice.

1 **First Law:**—Books are for Use.

2 **Second Law:**—Every Reader His Book.

3 **Third Law:**—Every Book Its Reader.

4 **Fourth Law:**—Save the Time of the Reader.

41 **Corrollary to the Fourth Law:**—Save the Time of the Staff.

5 **Fifth Law:**—Library is a Growing Organism.

1 Fundamental Laws

There are Five Laws of Library Science formulated so far. They were first formulated in Madras in 1928. In 1931, they were first published in a book [RF1] along with an exposition of their implications.

These Laws are the Fundamental Laws of Library Science. These form the Normative Principles containing in a latent form all the library practices current at any time and to be evolved at a later time. A new chapter in its second edition [RF8] published in 1957 shows how some of its implications not current in library practice a quarter of a century ago, have now become current to suit the boundary conditions of Library Service set up by the pressure of the social concepts of to-day. In particular, the term "Book" should be generalised in the present-day context to mean a "Document" as defined and elaborated in the Rules of Chap FE.

2 Final Court of Appeal

The Canons of Cataloguing given in Part B are all implications of the Five Laws, specific to the sphere of cataloguing. If any conflict arises between the Canons, it is resolved by an appeal to the Five Laws. If a cataloguing problem exceeds the capacity of the Canons, an appeal is made to the Five Laws to suggest a solution. But we do not invoke the Five Laws on the occasions in which the Canons can manage the situation. The Five Laws are like the Head of a State, in whose name and on whose authority, every government action is done by the ministers and the secretaries, without his explicit and immediate intervention. The Five Laws are like Lord Narayana, resting in his flowery float on the Ocean of Milk,—ever-watchful and ever-alert, but abstaining from visible intervention except when the laws of the universe are over-powered by the happenings in the universe not anticipated by them.

3 Agency for Compromise

It occasionally happens that the Canons of Cataloguing come into conflict with certain general Normative Principles, such as those given in the later Chapters of this Part. On such occasions, a compromise is effected in the light, and with the aid, of the Five Laws of Library Science.

CHAPTER CB

LAWS OF INTERPRETATION

0 **Laws of Interpretation.**—The well-known principles of interpretation, such as the 1,008 principles of interpretation listed in the *Nyaya-kosa* [J1].

1 Application to Catalogue Code

These principles have been evolved to a remarkable extent by the philosophers of the Purva-Mimamsa and the Nyaya Schools of Indian philosophy. In law too, such principles are applied necessarily. A Catalogue Code is like a legal document. Any Rule in it should be interpreted like a legal text. For example, there may be conflict between one Rule and another. In actual application, the conflict should be resolved with the aid of the Laws of Interpretation. A new cataloguing problem created by a document may have to be met by a proper interpretation of the Rules in the Catalogue Code. Periodically, the Rules should be amended in the light of experience, so as to remove conflicts or at least to reduce them to a minimum, if they could not be totally removed. It is the application of the Laws of Interpretation that led to a revision of the definition of Composite Book and to the concept of Pseudo-Series. One of the Laws of Interpretation is called "Lost-horse, Burnt-chariot" Principle. Its application in the field of classification occurs in the article *Classification of allusion books* [RZS].

2 Resolution of Conflict

There is often conflict between the Law of Parsimony, the Laws of Library Science, and the Canons of Cataloguing. The conflict has to be removed quite often with the aid of the Laws of Interpretation. One of the Laws of Interpretation, for example is this: The claim of the normative principles special to the business on hand—cataloguing, in this case—should be given greater weightage than a normative principle of general application—say, a Law of Library Science. Conflict may arise between one Law of Library Science and another in framing a particular Rule in Catalogue Code. The Fifth Law—Library is a Growing Organism—often sides the Law of Parsimony and gets into conflict with the other Laws of Library Science. If possible, a compromise has to be arrived at in every such case of conflict. If a compromise is not at all possible the principle of "the later the law, the greater its weightage" is applied.

3 Subject for Thesis

It has been an unfulfilled ambition to scrutinise the entire Classified Catalogue Code from the angle of the Laws of Interpretation. My friend Mahamahopadhyaya Professor S Kuppuswamy Sastry was an eminent specialist in the subject. He and myself had intended to take up such a scrutiny of the Classified Catalogue Code, after both of us would retire from the salary-earning stage of life. But, alas, he died before I could retire. I then sought to do the work in collaboration with a student of his. But it did not mature. The application of the Laws of Interpretation to the Classified Catalogue Code will be an eminent subject for investigation by an aspirant to a Doctorate in Library Science.

CHAPTER CC

LAW OF IMPARTIALITY

0 **Law of Impartiality.**—The principle that between two or more claimants—say, for use as heading—the preference of any one should be made only on sufficient grounds, and not arbitrarily.

1 Joint Authorship

For example, in the case of joint authorship, the Law of Impartiality would recommend equal right to the names of all the authors for choice as heading.

2 Multiple Series

Again, a book may belong to more than one publisher's series. The Law of Impartiality would recommend equal right to each of the series to have a note devoted to itself. Further, as a consequence of this, this Law would recommend equal right to the names of each of the series for choice as heading for a book index entry of its own. (*See* Examples 1 to 5 in Sec MK232).

3 Locus Statement

Here is another example. The locus of a micro document has to be given both in the case of a Cross Reference Entry and of an entry in indexing or abstracting periodical. The locus consists of the name of a host document and often also of the exact part, chapter, section or page of occurence in the host document. The punctuation marks to be used in the locus section should be along similar lines in the case of either class of entry according to the Law of Impartiality.

CHAPTER CD

LAW OF SYMMETRY

0 **Law of Symmetry.**—The principle that of two entities or situations which admit of being regarded as symmetrical counterparts of each other, if one of the entities or the situations is given weight in any particular context, the other entity or situation should also be given a corresponding weight.

1 Joint Authorship

For Example: Let us consider a book of two joint authors. In the heading of the main entry, we are obliged to write the names of the two authors in the sequence in which they occur on the title page. As a result of this, there will be a book index entry using as heading the names of the two authors in the same sequence. But considerations of symmetry would make us write another book index entry using the names of the two authors in the reverse sequence. (*See* examples 7 and 8 in Sec MK 211).

2 Concurrent Prescription

In this type of cases, the prescription of the Law of Symmetry is concurrent with the prescription of the Canon of Sought-Heading formulated in Chap BE. The difference between the Law of Impartiality and the Law of Symmetry is somewhat subtle. A little thought will however show that they are not identical.

3 Conflict with Law of Parsimony

Conflict may arise often between the Law of Impartiality and the Law of Symmetry on the one side and the Law of Parsimony on the other. It will require a considerable judgement to resolve the conflict in actual cataloguing work.

CHAPTER CE

LAW OF PARSIMONY

0 **Law of Parsimony.**—The principle that between two or more possible alternative rules bearing on a particular phenomenon, the one, leading to overall economy of man-power, material, money, and time considered together with proper weightage, is to be preferred.

1 Sobering the Chain Procedure

The sobering effect of the Law of Parsimony of the Chain Procedure has been described in Sec BE7.

2 Pruning According to Context

The Alternative-Name Entries, the special notes in the Main Entry and their Associated Added Entries, the Cross Reference Entries in a Classified Catalogue, the Subject-Analyticals in a Dictionary Catalogue, the Class Index Entries in a Classified Catalogue and the *See also* Subject Entries in a Dictionary Catalogue promoted by the Canon of Sought-Heading, may swell to disproportionate dimensions, unless the answer to the question, "Is it truly a Sought-Entry ?" is considered with great care. The Law of Parsimony would ask for considerable pruning. This pruning can be done to an appreciable extent with the aid of the Canon of Context explained in Chap BF and its commentaries.

3 Printed vs Written Card

The Law of Parsimony would make a fundamental difference in the Rules about Specific Added Entries, according as the catalogue card is printed or machine duplicated, or typed (or hand-written). In the former case, it would recommend the Unit-Card-System. In this, a copy of the Main Entry Card itself would be used as any Specific Added Entry Card, by merely inserting in the Leading Section the heading of the Added Entry. For this purpose, the first line of the printed card should be left vacant. On the other hand, if the catalogue card is typed or hand-written, the Law of Parsimony would recommend a Multiple-Card-System. In this, each Added Entry would have only the minimum information necessary to satisfy the Canon of Context. To achieve this, the Law of Parsimony would allow a number of additional Rules in the Catalogue Code to take care of the different kinds of Added Entries. Such additional Rules for Specific Added Entries would prescribe omission of Series Note and Accession Number, shortening of Title, and shortening of every other category not acting as a link between a Specific

Added Entry and its Main Entry. For example, in the Classified Catalogue, Rules would provide for the omission, in the Second Section of a Specific Added Entry, of the Individualising Elements added to the Author's Name in the Heading of the Main Entry.

CHAPTER CF

PRINCIPLE OF LOCAL VARIATION

0 **Principle of Local Variation.**—The principle that

1 The International Catalogue Code should mark out the factors to be left to the care of each National Catalogue Code;

2 A National Catalogue Code should mark out the factors to be left to the care of each Linguistic Catalogue Code in a multilingual country such as India;

3 A National Catalogue Code or a Linguistic Catalogue Code, as the case may be, should mark out the factors, to be left to the care of the Local Catalogue Code of each individual library;

4 The Catalogue Codes in each hierarchical line should be consistent with one another without any mutual contradiction; and

5 Each lower link in each hierarchical line should be a Supplement to all the upper links taken together.

1 Intimacy Inherent in Service

Catalogue is a tool for a reader to find out his requirement in the library. It is an important tool in library service. Intimacy characterises service. Intimacy underlines the individuating particularities in the reader-library setting. The catalogue is a medium of communication in this intimate setting. Thus, local colour should be inherent in library catalogue. A library catalogue does have to conform to a pattern conceivable in abstract. The pattern should also be prescribed in abstract. But to invest it with the intimacy inherent in service, it should be impressed with the essential local colour. This is the message of the Principle of Local Variation. This local colour is to be assumed by the library catalogue in successive stages. Three or four stages are unmistakable—International, National, Linguistic, and Local. Corresponding to each stage there should be a different catalogue code, consistent with the code corresponding to each of the earlier stages. The International Catalogue Code gives only a general blue print, as it were.

2 Languages and Their Reconciliation

Difference in language will be the first point of deviation from the International Code. It has been shown in *Library catalogue: Fundamentals and procedure* that the Language of the Heading in a Catalogue Entry is an artificial language [RL5]. Its syntax is different from that of any Natural Language. It generally admits of nouns only,—with the exception that, when a language has no single word to denote an isolate idea, the Heading may have to admit a noun qualified by an adjective—as for example, "Digestive System" to denote the functional organ concerned. Again the nouns in the Heading should be in the nominative case. But the title-page in some of the languages such as Sanskrit and Russian give the names of authors and collaborators in the instrumental case. Therefore the Linguistic Catalogue Code in such a language should give an appropriate note under Sec JA7. The punctuation system of the artificial language of Headings is also artificial. Linguistic Variation should be allowed in respect of punctuation.

3 Style of Writing and Printing

The style of writing or printing the elements in a catalogue entry depends on the script and the type-faces available. For example, Roman character admits of upper case, lower case, and italics. It admits also of antique face and small capitals. Even when written by hand, it is possible to have corresponding varieties. But many of the Indian characters do not admit of all of them. As it is to-day, we have to have recourse only to white and black, and variation of *matra* (size). The International Catalogue Code should therefore deal with style, only in general terms—of dominance, subordination, and the like. The actual method of implementing these prescriptions will have to be stated only in a National Catalogue Code or a Linguistic Catalogue Code as the case may be. The importance and inevitability of a Linguistic Code providing its own specification for the style of writing was realised in a compelling way while compiling a Tamil Bibliography [RZM]. In this sense, either of these has to fill up some details in the blue print sketched by the International Catalogue Code. Thus the Principle of Local Variation has sway over this problem.

4 Arrangement of Entries

The arrangement of word-entries is intimately bound up with the style of writing and printing. At any rate, it is desirable that they should be so bound up. As the Rules on the Style of Writing and Printing have to be left to the care of a National Catalogue Code or Linguistic Catalogue Code, the Rules on the Arrangement of Word-Entries should also be left to its care. Thus, the Principle of Local Variation has sway over this problem.

5 Rendering of Personal Names

At present, certain National Catalogue Codes claiming international status presume competence to prescribe rules for the rendering, in heading, of a Name-of-Person of any culture whatever. This is attempting the impossible. Considerable research awaits to be done to delimit the boundary of the International Catalogue Code in this respect. The first step in this direction was taken by Unesco through its International Advisory Committee on Bibliography in 1952. In 1951, the Indian Library Association and the Indian National Commission for Unesco accepted a resolution of mine to request Unesco to make the rendering of Asian names the subject of one of its bibliographical projects. This was done. The task was in the end entrusted to me. This gave me an opportunity to face the problem squarely. The details of this Unesco Project are given in Sec FL 75 and FL 76. Meetings with several cultural groups slowly allowed some awareness to dawn on the problem. Some streak of light has fallen on the problem.

51 Entry Element

It was the Canon of Prepotence that let the light in. A modern Name-of-Person has many words. The potency from the angle of arrangement is not equally incident on all the words. In many names, it is greatest on one word. Generally speaking, a prepotent word in the name can be found. But in an appreciable number of cases, potency is concentrated most, not on one word, but on a doublet—that is on two words. Sometimes it is spread over even three words. Whether a single word is prepotent or a double or a treble word is prepotent, it is obvious only to a native of the country to which the name belongs. An alien cataloguer cannot ordinarily acquire sufficient competence in this matter. Even if a persevering cataloguer is enterprising enough to master alien names, it is doubtful if he can do it for all the foreign cultural groups. If he attempts to do it, he will become a specialist in cultural sociology at the cost of his loyalty and duty to the Library Profession in general and the Cataloguing Profession in particular. Our experience with such cultural-cum-linguistic specialists, functioning as cataloguers, confirms this fear. For, by the sheer impossibility of doing two things at one time, they are found to be naturally un-informed about current progress in the discipline of cataloguing and about the great changes coming over library service in our own days. They even show a tendency towards bigotry which denies even the very existence of Library Science and the Discipline of Cataloguing. A step in the right direction appears to be to entrust the problem of "single-worded or multi-worded entry element" to the care of the respective National or Linguistic Catalogue Codes. It is the duty of each National or Linguistic Catalogue Code to devise a method by which the singleness or multipleness of the entry element could be mechanically found out by a cataloguer of an alien culture. The most obvious method will be to append to the National Catalogue Code schedules of multi-worded entry elements, assuming that these are fewer in the cultural group concerned than the single-worded entry elements. There may be less cumbersome methods available in certain cultural groups. For example, while discussing this problem with Sinhalese scholars in Ceylon, the concept of "Starter Word" emerged. By a "Starter Word" is meant a word which is the first of a multi-worded entry element. The other words are found to be consecutive to the Starter Word, exactly as they occur in the full name as it is uttered or printed on title-page. Perhaps a reprint of such national schedules may be separately issued for use by other national groups.

6 Script and Transliteration

Headings in many catalogue entries are proper names. They are names of persons, geographical entities, or corporate bodies. They do not admit of translation. For they are terms of extension. They are not expressive terms. Whatever be the script used in a catalogue entry, the heading should represent the proper name phonetically. This indicates transliteration. All the letters of one script do not have phonetic equivalents in another script. Therefore, transliteration is not a simple affair. Till now, the Roman script has been largely playing the part of the host-script. This has been due to historical circumstances. For, the renaissance phase of the present cultural cycle appeared in areas of Roman script a few centuries earlier than in areas of any other script. Therefore, during the last few centuries, transliteration had virtually meant transliteration into Roman script. This has become such a rigid part of the mental set of the cataloguers of the West that the reverse movement of transliteration seems to have very little chance to be recognised, even at international level. This is again due to a historical factor. For, international bodies have been all along effectively confined to the membership of the West. Therefore, the idea produced by reflex action, on hearing the term transliteration, is that of the Roman script as the host-script. Therefore, the so-called International Catalogue Codes provide only for one-way transliteration. This is a violence to the Principle of Local Variation. The newly awakening countries have much to do to remove this violence. In my recent experience with the Unesco Project on the Rendering of Asian Names, I had found this mental set in the Librarians of the West too rigid to be broken. They cannot dissociate transliteration from rendering. Nor do they see the reciprocal feature of transliteration. For them, Rendering of Asian Names is mostly transliteration in Roman script. This is a vexatious barrier I had met with in many international meetings. The West should become a little more aware of the "whole problem". Perhaps it is due to the viscosity of the mental set created in the years of Western dominance that the Indian National Bibliography contemplated the adoption of Roman script. May better sense dawn upon those responsible for this !

7 Analytical Entry

The extent of the putting in of subject analyticals and author analyticals is subject to Local Variation of a narrower variety. This is bound to vary from library to library. Therefore a National or an International Catalogue Code should make the rules on such entries permissive, and not compulsory. The Supplementary Catalogue Code of a library should have rules defining their permissible extent in more rigid terms. For example, a library in India need not give analytical entries for essays in English, as there is the *Essay index* of Wilson and Co. But it should give analytical entries for essays in Indian languages, until an *Essay index* comes to be published for them.

8 Fleeting Material

In a governmental library and in the library of a business body or an academic institution, a large and even exhaustive collection may have to be made from time to time, in connection with a particular problem engaging attention at the moment. After the problem is disposed of, the collection may not have use in the library. A few years ago, the Library of the United Nations had to amass considerable material on the Palestine Problem. After the settlement of the problem, that library could not afford to continue to keep on its shelves the entire load. Such materials have only a limited period of use. We shall therefore denote them by the term "Fleeting Material". The duration of the accession as well as of the use of fleeting material may be too small to complete their cataloguing except by putting an enormous strength of temporary staff on it. And yet, it will all amount to a waste after a short while. The Canon of Local Variation would allow such Fleeting Materials to be merely shelf-listed; perhaps even this would be too much in some cases. It will be sufficient merely to arrange them on the shelves and deem them to stand "self-catalogued" so to speak. This was, for example, enunciated as follows by the United Nations International Committee of Library Experts which went into "the kinds of library service required by the United Nations and the methods by which such service can be most effectively provided," during its meeting from 2 to 9 August 1948. I was a member of that Committee. And I had to stress hard this point of Local Variation and Fleeting Materials. This was because I had seen mad proposals of librarians in India that every scrap of printed paper coming into the library had an absolute claim to a share of the cataloguing time of the library. Lay-managements are often misguided into this absurd insistence. The document *Library services of the United Nations* (U1) gives the recommendation of the International Committee in the following terms:

"No attempt should be made to build up the collections for purposes of general historical research beyond the needs of the United Nations. . . . The library should be free to provide more summary treatment for much of its material and in some categories may omit cataloguing altogether."

91 Selective Cataloguing

Even in other kinds of libraries, the Principle of Local Variation will prescribe Selective Cataloguing. Materials used only occasionally may have to stand on the shelves or in vertical files, "self-catalogued". For example, my advice to the Central Secretariat Library in New Delhi was that such a treatment might be given to the large mass of annual reports and similar documents of various governments including those of the United Nations, accumulated for years in that library. Ignorance of this has led to the wastage of the meagre library fund in certain places and to other kinds of havoc in other places. At the same time, they should be properly classified and catalogued in a research library, such as that of the Gokhale Institute, where they form the very basis of much of the work in the Institute.

92 Differential Rules

Another application of the Principle of Local Variation is the freedom given to an individual library or to a Local Catalogue Code to cut down details rigorously for entries of certain kinds of materials. The *Prussian instructions* (O3) gives the following list of categories of documents where the application of selective cataloguing may be allowed in public reference libraries:

1 Manuals for schools or self-education;
2 Guides for elementary knowledge including books on sports;
3 Materials on domestic economy lacking scientific interest;
4 Popular informative books, especially in science, medicine and law;
5 Instructions for non-commissioned officers and privates;
6 Books of superstitious and occult content (!);
7 Light reading materials and songs for social purposes;
8 Juvenile and picture books;
9 Prayer and devotional books;
10 Minor works of local interest such as reports on festivities, exnibition catalogues etc.

For these books, added entries are almost omitted, various editions are combined on the same card and various other simplifications are made.

Again, cataloguing may have to be done to different degrees of fullness for different categories of materials. Mere shelf-listing may be sufficient for some. At the other extreme, for Incunabula, for instance, detailed bibliographical cataloguing is necessary. A Local Catalogue Code must have freedom to adopt Differential Rules for different groups of materials. The Principle of Local Variation will call for all degrees of play of Selective Cataloguing.

93 Areas for Variation

There is need for a hierarchy of catalogue codes, from the International Code, through Regional and National Code, through Linguistic Code, to Local Code. There are limitations in the competence of the above successive codes. Where a code is not competent to lay down specific rules, it should lay down broad principles to guide the codes lower down in the hierarchical lines. The problems in cataloguing have all been analysed and found to fall in ten levels. It is also possible to allocate the different levels to the different members of the hierarchy [RI2].

CHAPTER CG

PRINCIPLE OF OSMOSIS

0 **Principle of Osmosis.**—The principle that, when a change in the Catalogue Code or in the Scheme of Classification becomes necessary in deference to the Canon of Context, on and after a chosen date

1 All the new accessions be catalogued and classified according to the new Catalogue Code and the new Scheme of Classification;

2 Just those of the old collection as are known to be in much use be recatalogued and reclassified, with an additional temporary staff, if necessary, during the first few months;

3 The new accessions and the recatalogued and reclassified books be kept in a New Collection and similarly their catalogue cards too kept in a New Collection;

4 The rest of the old collection be kept as Old Collection and similarly their catalogue cards too be kept as Old Collection;

5 Readers' attention be invited by the Reference Librarian to the existence of the Two Collections;

6 If any book is taken out by a reader from the Old Collection, on its return by him it be recatalogued and reclassified and absorbed in the New Collection and similarly with its catalogue cards.

1 Capitulation to the Dead Past

The Canon of Context will bring about now and again changes in the Rules of Catalogue Code and in the Scheme of Classification. At present this change is met in one of two ways in cataloguing practice.

According to one, the entire collection of a library is recatalogued and reclassified. The cost of this is enormous. Often, to find the necessary money, active service is starved; reference service is cut out; book-fund is depleted. All this amounts nearly to a criminal waste of library fund. Law of Parsimony is therefore chagrined.

In the second way of practice, eyes are closed in the ostrich way to the change in the Catalogue Code and in the Scheme of Classification. The obsolete Code and Scheme are perpetuated in defiance of the Canon of Context and of the Laws of Library Science, and to the neglect of readers' unexpressed needs. This way amounts to tying the future up to the dead past. This capitulation to the dead past is fatal to any social institution; and library is a life-giving social institution.

2 Living the Present

The right way shown by the Canon of Context is to live the present. We should neither waste the resources nor do disservice to readers. The Principle of Osmosis helps us to chalk out the right way. According to it, the documents of a library fall into three groups:

1 New documents;

2 Documents—usually or mostly of recent past—continuing to be in active use; and

3 Old documents rarely, or only occasionally, in use.

When the Catalogue Code or the Scheme of Classification has to be changed, the three groups should be treated differently [G3].

3 New Documents

From the date of change over, all the new documents should be catalogued by the New Code and classified by the New Scheme of Classification. These should be kept as "New Collection". Their catalogue cards also should be kept as a "New Collection", according to the Principle of Parallel Movement enunciated in the *Library administration* [RL3], and the *Library manual* [RL6]. This does not mean any extra cost.

4 Recent Documents in Active Use

Within a short period after the date of change over to the New Catalogue Code and to the New Scheme of Classification or even in anticipation of it, the active documents of the recent past should be rapidly re-catalogued. In some cases, no serious change will be necessary. The only work to be done will be to pick out their cards from the old collection, and insert them in the new collection. The documents themselves should be similarly transferred from the old to the new collection, as and when the cards are transferred, according to the Principle of Parallel Movement. A suitable mark should be put above the class number on the tag in the back and in the back of title page to indicate the absorption of the document in the New Collection. In some cases, slight changes in the existing cards may prove sufficient. Only in a few cases, total re-cataloguing may become necessary. In all cases the routine of absorption should be completed for each quantum of documents recatalogued at one time as if it were a single indivisible job; otherwise, chaos will result. The quantity of man-hour needed for this routine of absorption will depend upon the number of documents to be so absorbed within the short time. In a Service-Library, eighty percent of use is estimated to be confined to the accessions of the last five years. Even this eighty percent is likely to be distributed as follows:—50 percent of the current year, 25 percent of the last year, 12 percent of the second last year, and so on in diminishing sequence. One method of systematically picking out the documents in active use is to register for the Catalogue Revision Section all the documents of the "Old Collection" going out on loan. When they are returned by readers, the documents will automatically go to the Catalogue Revision Section. Their catalogue cards should be checked up and the routine of their absorption into the New Collection should be completed. The pressure of this work will be high only for about three months in most libraries. Thereafter, it will decrease progressively. This way of absorption of old documents in current use will require additional staff only for a short period. The number of volumes to be so treated may not exceed 10,000 in a Service-Library. The extent of extra work to be done on this kind of absorption in a National Central Library can be worked out from experience. Even there, the proportion of the special staff needed to the permanent staff, and the duration for which the special staff will be needed will not be very different from that of a Service-Library.

5 Osmotic Pressure of Use

After the first few months of high-pressure absorption, the daily quota of absorption will become small. It will go on thinning almost to a vanishing point in about five years. By that time, all the "Live Books" would have been transferred by the "Osmotic Pressure of Use" from the Old Collection to the New Collection. The "dead books" will for ever remain in the Old Collection, without any harm to any reader. This is the **Principle of Osmosis.** This is a contribution of the Principle of Local Variation applied in one of its extreme spheres of jurisdiction. This Principle of Osmosis suggested itself to me, while visiting many aged libraries during my tour of Europe and America in 1948. The pathetic look of the younger members of the cataloguing sections of big libraries caught my eye. They were internally revolting against having to use the Catalogue Codes of earlier centuries. But their chiefs, who had given up active cataloguing and active reference service and had become mere administrators and committee men, did not have the time or the willingness to understand the urge of the juniors to change over, in order to make library service real. Or, cataloguing was, in some places done by the old guards in whom mental fibrosis had set in and who did cataloguing without any awareness of the latest thought on library service or sensitiveness to the social changes since the time their Catalogue Codes were framed. When their thought was disturbed, they immediately struck the disturber, crying, "Theory, theory, all theory !" This made me think out the deeper reason for such wide-spread resistance to any change in cataloguing and classification. It was found to be the cost of re-cataloguing of the whole of a large collection. This simmered in the mind for some time. The Principle of Osmosis came forth and gave a possible solution of the problem.

PART D

EVOLUTION OF THE CATALOGUE

CHAPTER DA

FUNCTIONS OF THE CATALOGUE

1 Introduction

A Library Catalogue is essentially a tool. Hence, its parts and details are to be designed so as to make it an efficient tool. This means that in designing the Catalogue we must take its chief functions into consideration. The functions to be performed by a Library Catalogue have been discussed in detail in the light of the Laws of Library Science elsewhere [RF5]. That discussion may be summarised by the statement that a Library Catalogue should be so designed as to

1 Disclose to every reader his or her document;
2 Secure for every document its reader;
3 Save the time of the reader; and for this purpose
4 Save the time of the staff.

To pursue Cutter's line of approach and restate the purpose in a more specific way, the functions of a library catalogue are to [C3]:

1 Enable a person to find a book of which either the
   A Author, or
   B Title, or
   C Subject is known;
2 Show what the library has
   D by a given author,
   E on a given subject, and
   F in a given kind of literature; and
3 Assist in the choice of a book as to its
   G Edition, and
   H Character.

2 Museum Tradition

Historically, however, the nature of the Library Catalogue has been for long influenced by a powerful tradition. In this tradition, undue emphasis was placed on the library as a museum, where books are housed for preservation. Under its influence, the primary purpose of the catalogue was naturally taken to be that of serving as an inventory of the contents of the library. To make this inventory catalogue as simple as possible, it was made of the title-a-line type, listing the books in the accession sequence, with the books themselves arranged on the shelves in the same accession sequence. The task of building up a catalogue of this primitive type is not difficult and calls for no very elaborate code.

3 Spirit of Salesmanship

The force that has been trying to oust this museum tradition may be described as the force of 'Salesmanship'. This force emanated from a new view of the library. According to this view, a library is an institution charged with the duty of converting every person in its area into its regular customer and serving the customers so well, so promptly, and with such exact reference to their specific needs, that they would gladly keep on as customers. A library is not a museum but a workshop, full of life and activity. It is not the book which gets rapidly worn out by constant use that should worry a library according to this view, but it is the book which would seldom leave the shelf that needs anxious attention and effective treatment. This view is now revolutionising everything connected with the library—book selection, shelf arrangement, architecture, furniture, location, hours, finance, staff, attitude towards readers, and last but not least the Library Catalogue. It is also among other things trying to relegate the spirit of inventory to its legitimate far off place in the back-ground so as not to smother the nascent spirit of service—service at any cost, service at any risk—which is slowly but rightly enlivening the libraries of to-day.

4 Struggle of the Catalogue

41 First Victory

The first struggle over the Library Catalogue between the inventory tradition and the service spirit resulted in a compromise. The title-a-line entry was preserved but the entries were to be, not in the accession sequence, but in the alphabetical sequence of the names of authors. This replacement of the vagaries of accession by the vagaries of the alphabet was, to some extent, due to the service spirit not knowing its own mind, not having had enough experience to know what interested readers most—the author or the subject-matter.

42 Second Victory

But it did not take long to see the importance of subject-matter. The first result of seeing it was to get one more concession, *viz*, replacing the single alphabetical sequence by a number of such sequences—at the rate of one sequence to each of a few—say fifteen or twenty—broad classes into which knowledge was divided. The catalogues of a few of our libraries are still at one or other of these stages.

43 Emancipation

The real emancipation of the Library Catalogue from the hold of the inventory tradition dates from the invention of the shelf-register, which, as the name implies, lists the books on the basis of a title-a-line entry, in a sequence which is exactly parallel to the sequence of the books on the shelves. The inventory spirit being thus cut off with a special register of its own, the catalogue began to develop along lines natural to itself and conducive to the fulfilment of the new service-spirit of the Libraries.

CHAPTER DB

PARTS OF LIBRARY CATALOGUE

1 Unipartite Dictionary Catalogue

The first line of development led to what is known as the Dictionary Catalogue. It consists of a single part, with the components differentiated to suit the different functions to be performed by the catalogue. The perfection of this form has engaged many an inventive brain from the middle of the last century. It has developed some new techniques—the fixing of subject headings being an example of colossal magnitude.

11 New Bigotry

The revolutionaries—the tradition-breakers—of one generation themselves become the conservatives of the next, fondly clinging to the new tradtion, which they themselves founded in the place of those broken down by them. So it is in library cataloguing. The fascination of grappling with the difficulties with which the dictionary catalogue bristles seems to have so narrowed the vision that the immediate and next stage of evolution in the catalogue is either not perceived or resisted with bigotry.

2 Bipartite Classified Catalogue

The next stage in the evolution of the library catalogue consists in splitting it into two parts, on the basis of the differences of function—one part holding all the components giving information about what the library has on various subjects and the other holding all the other components. The arrangement in the former is by Call Numbers and Class Numbers; and this is filiatory. The arrangement in the latter is alphabetical as in a dictionary. That this bipartite form of catalogue is a more evolved form than the unipartite dictionary catalogue will be conceded by those that believe that evolution means differentiation in structure to meet differentiation in function. Those who, however, hold the view that the ultimate stages of evolution lead to unification and not to differentiation, must learn by experience the enormous difficulties of a dictionary catalogue and the comparatively easy elimination or handling of such difficulties in the classified from of catalogue emphasised in this code.

21 A Cause for Delay

The delay in the emergence of the bipartite form as the dominant form has been due, not merely to the resistance of the practitioners of the unipartite Dictionary Catalogue, but also to the then absence of a scheme of book-classification which

1 Individualises specific subjects of any degree of intension whatever;

2 Arranges specific subjects at all levels in an acceptable filiatory sequence; and

3 Individualises the different books in a specific subject.

22 A Fallacy

A subtle fallacy also leads to the retention of the Dictionary Catalogue in preference to the Classified. The ordinary reader, it is argued, is familiar only with alphabetical arrangement and that the catalogue, being primarily for his use, should be *purely* alphabetical. The premises of this argument are correct but a fallacy lurks in the introduction of the epithet 'purely'. All that the premises warrant is that there should be an alphabetical part through which the ordinary reader can enter the catalogue. The second part of the bipartite Classified Catalogue is alphabetical just for this purpose.

CHAPTER DC

RIGHT APPROACH

1 A Deeper Function

If the reader's interest is for a particular book or a book by a particular author, the alphabetical part is sufficient by itself to satisfy his want. But if it is interest in a subject which takes him to the library, his wants will be better served if the catalogue can spread before him a full, connected, panorama of all the materials on his specific subject, all its subdivisions, and all broader subjects of which it is itself a subdivision. Moreover, few readers are able to name their specific subjects exactly. It is a broader or a narrower subject that is usually thought of. But whatever is brought up and however wide of mark it may be, the alphabetical part tells him, as it were, "For all books on the subject you mention and on all connected subjects, look up the region of the Classified Part covered by number so and so." There he finds displayed the full field of his interest. When he enters it, he finds all that he was vaguely conscious of having wanted; and indeed it is only then that he is able to know the exact subject he wanted.

11 Unexpressed Wants

The function of the number is exhausted as soon as the reader enters the region indicated by it. Thereafter the numbers do not occupy this thought or distract him. His mind is fully occupied with the helpful filiatory way in which the names of his books follow one after another. He is delighted. This delight is at bottom due to the satisfaction of unexpressed wants and to the getting of something which he did not know how to ask for. This represents a deeper function to be performed by the library catalogue.

2 Duty of the Library

It is the duty of the library to meet such unexpressed wants, particularly because an ordinary reader does not know how to give shape to them and state them. The Dictionary Catalogue, with its inevitable alphabetical scattering of subjects instead of collocation, cannot satisfy this want. Its maze of '*See also*' directions will virtually tire out the ordinary reader by sending him from pillar to post.

3 Holism in the Catalogue

It is unchivalrous to say to the reader, as it were, "You say you can enter the catalogue only with the alphabetical key. Ergo, then you shall have it! But you will have to use the alphabet not only at the beginning but throughout and to the very end." This is too great a penalty to be imposed upon the reader. It is pushing the 'alphabet' beyond its legitimate function. Real efficiency and gracefulness consist in confining the use of each tool to the purpose for which it is best suited or designed. To display the resources of a library in a filiatory sequence the correct means is the classified arrangement and not the alphabetical one. As the library catalogue has to do this and as the reader can enter it only with the alphabetical key, a bipartite catalogue with a classified and an alphabetical part is the only suitable one. Such a holism should prevail in the catalogue. It can be seen that the Classified Part is designed to suit the functions marked by Cutter as (C), (E), (F), (G) and (H); while the Alphabetical Part corresponds to the functions (A), (B), (D) and to some extent (H) also. It can also be seen that the Alphabetical Part is virtually the Dictionary Catalogue *minus* the Specific Subject Entries.

4 Future of the Catalogue

If the bipartite form of catalogue comes into general use, it will doubtless lead to more evolved and more efficient forms in the future. For the time being, however, the bipartite Classified Catalogue should be popularised and this code is, therefore, devoted mainly to the rules relating to its compilation. And yet to help those lagging behind in the times of the Dictionary Catalogue, supplementary Rules to suit this form of catalogue are given wherever warranted.

CHAPTER DD

PHYSICAL FORM OF THE LIBRARY CATALOGUE

1 Book Form

The book form of the Library Catalogue, whether printed or manuscript, has been made an anachronism by the Fifth Law. Nearly a century ago, Jewett wrote the epitaph of the printed catalogue in his address to a conference of librarians held in New York City:

> "While the catalogue of a large library is passing through the press, new books are received, the titles of which it is impossible in the ordinary manner of printing, to incorporate with the body of the work. Recourse must then be had to a supplement. In no other way can the acquisitions of the library be made known to the public. If the number of supplements be multiplied as they have been in the Library of Congress, the student may be obliged to grope his weary way through ten catalogues, instead of one, in order to ascertain whether the book which he seeks be in the library. He cannot be certain, even then, that the book is not in the collection, for it may have been received since the last appendix was printed. Supplements soon become intolerable. The whole catalogue must then be rearranged and reprinted. The expense of this process may be borne so long as the library is small, but it soon becomes burdensome, and, ere long, insupportable, even to national establishments.
>
> "There is but one course left—not to print at all. To this no scholar consents, except from necessity. But to this alternative, grievous as it is, nearly all the large libraries of Europe have been reluctantly driven."

2 Move Forward

India has been reputed to be the dumping ground for practices discarded elsewhere. Long experience of this seems to have developed even a special fascination for the antediluvian. It is often welcomed and fondled, instead of allowing it to die a peaceful death. The printed library catalogue evidently belongs to this category. There may not be enough money to buy books, to maintain an adequate staff, to get the books better circulated and used, to extend the hours of the library or to light or furnish it attractively; but money is found, or rather whatever money there may be is diverted, to print or reprint the catalogue. Let us hope that this will not continue for ever even in India. India should move forward.

3 Evolution to Card Form

The *Five laws* traces the evolution of the physical form of the Library Catalogue from the closely written bound book, through the interspaced and interleaved one, through paste-down form, through the sheaf form, to the present card form.

4 Card Form, Not the Last Word

The pressure of the Fifth Law is not yet felt anywhere in India to the same extent as in Europe and America. Most libraries still maintain their catalogues in the primitive book form. Some of these even conspire to pull down the more forward ones from the card stage they have reached back to the old book stage. Further, even in the libraries that have adopted the modern card form, the rate of growth is by no means of the order that has become common in the West. The card catalogue is thus believed to be the last word in the physical form of the catalogue. But it is not wise to proceed with that belief. The inexorable Fifth Law of Library Science may have something in store for the next stage in the evolution of the physical form of the catalogue.

5 Service Library

In a local Service Library, the Fifth Law itself would put a ceiling to the number of volumes to be stored in it. In its case the Fifth Law would make the growth in the stock of the library take the form of replacement of the different out-moded and worn-out books by new books comparable in number. Therefore, it is likely that the card form of catalogue does not create much difficulty in the case of a local Service Library. A card form may continue for a long time as the most helpful form.

6 National Central Library

The position, however, is different in the case of a National Central Library and even of a Regional or State Central Library. In their case, the Fifth Law would allow growth by continuous addition of volumes without withdrawal of old ones. The size of the catalogue will therefore grow continuously. It will soon reach a size, obstructing its efficient use. In fact, such a size has already been reached by the card catalogue of libraries, such as, the Library of Congress (USA), the New York Public Library, and the Lenin Library in Moscow. The very catalogue room of such a library is bigger than the entire building of many a service library. Apart from the cost of the maintenence of such a huge catalogue, the readers too may find using of such a leviathan catalogue irksome and time-consuming. What is the solution ?

7 Micro Film Form

One possible solution may be to have the catalogue in micro form, such as micro film or micro card. But there will be a practical difficulty in using that form. The Fifth Law itself will cause that difficulty. In a huge library, about a hundred books may be added almost every day. This rate of growth in the stock carries with it the implication that about six hundred entries will have to be interpolated at different conceivable points among the already existing entries. What will technology say to this ? Can the micro film technologists handle this problem successfully and at a reasonable cost ?

8 A Compromise

If they cannot, one can think of a compromise. The compromise is suggested by the Principle of Osmosis already described in Chap CG. Entries of reading materials, other than those in current use, may be micro-filmed. The entries of the volumes in current use may be maintained in the conventional card form. Then the catalogue will be in two forms and sequences—one in micro-film form for the older books, and the other in card form for current books. This may be a solution for the present. In due course, however, a separation of the entries in the card form will have to be made again into those to be reduced to the micro-film form and those to be retained in card form. To pursue this matter will almost amount to a speculation at this stage. Moreover, the number of libraries in the world that will have to face this situation will be relatively small.

CHAPTER DE

CENTRALISED CATALOGUING

1 Beginnings

The first stage in the national centralisation of cataloguing was brought into vogue in the United States in 1901. From then, the Library of Congress prints the catalogue card of each book. Copies of this card are available for sale. I saw such a system in vogue in Denmark also during my tour in 1948. The Bibliographical Institute was in charge of the work. Since 1950, the *British national bibliography* is unobtrusively and obliquely influencing the British libraries to accept centralised classification and cataloguing. It has begun to supply catalogue cards within 48 hours of order. Often, the catalogue cards arrive even before the books arrive [W1]. Centralised Service of printing catalogue cards is also practised by the Deutsches Bucherei, the Central Bibliographical Institute in Leipzig. It seeks to cover all German books in whatever country published. It can be no wonder if the Fifth Law of Library Science dances with joy, on observing this development in the organisation of cataloguing work.

2 National Saving

If Centralised Cataloguing is done, national saving will be as much as 79 per cent [RH3] in respect of all the publications in the country.

3 International Saving

If each country establishes Centralised Cataloguing and all countries cooperate with one another in the exchange of the results of central cataloguing, there will be a saving of 79 per cent [RH7] in respect of the books published in all the cooperating countries. This will of course require, as condition-precedent, prevalence of peaceful intercourse between nations.

4 Position in India

There is a great shortage of well-trained cataloguing man-power in the country. But the libraries are growing in number as a result of the current renaissance. The economical method of meeting the situation will be to adopt Centralised Cataloguing. This cannot be done for the country as a whole. There should be a diversified organisation for it. In each of the Constituent States, there should be a State Central Cataloguing Body for the books in the language of the State. There should be a Union Central Cataloguing Body to take charge of the books in English, Sanskrit, and in any other Indian languages in which books are published in different parts of the country [RI1].

5 Pre-Natal Cataloguing

The next step in the evolution of the organisation for cataloguing will be for the National Central Body and the State Central Body for Cataloguing to get the proof copies of books even before they are published and provide the call number and the catalogue entries for each book. Then the class number can be printed in the back of the title page. The catalogue cards can be printed even before the book is released. This is called Pre-Natal Cataloguing [RP1].

Λ

PART E

RECORDING

CHAPTER EA

LANGUAGE OF ENTRIES

1 Favoured Language

The language in which the majority of the documents of the library occur.

Normally the language of the country or region or State is likely to be the Favoured Language. But in a specialist library, the Favoured Language may be different from the language of the country or region or State. Due to historical causes, English is now the Favoured Language in many of the generalist libraries in India.

2 Scale of Languages

A list of languages, to be kept by a library, in which the Favoured Language is given the first place and the other languages are entered in the descending scale of popularity.

It is not easy to give a definite and unique sequence of popularity for arranging the languages. But each library may be able to decide from experience some working scale. All that is wanted is that this should be a fixed one. For example, in the University Library at Madras, English was used as the Favoured Language. The scale of languages was as follows: English, Tamil, Malayalam, Telugu, Kanarese, Sanskrit, Hindi, Urdu, French, German, etc.

3 Most Popular Language

Among a given set of languages, the language occurring earliest in the scale of languages.

4 Preference of Favoured Language

Generally speaking, an entry in a library catalogue is to be in the Favoured Language of the Library. The Rules in Sec 5 of this Chap deal with the elements in an Entry to be written in a different language.

5 Use of Non-favoured Language

51 Proper Noun

Proper Nouns in any Entry are to be written in the language in which it occurs on the title-page and its over-flow of the document, except that the special rules of Chap JB are to be followed in the case of the name of a Geographical Entity.

This is obvious. It is wrong to translate a Proper Noun on the basis of the dictionary meanings of the word(s) constituting it. For example, it is wrong to enter my name in an entry in the translated form 'Lord of the Stage'. It is equally wrong to enter the name of my collaborator, in this edition, in an entry in the translated form 'Blue Cloud.'

52 Title of a Document

The title of a document is to be written in the language in which it occurs on the title-page.

521 POLYGLOT TITLE

If the title of a document is given on the title page in two or more languages, it is to be written in the Most Popular Language of the library.

522 ADDITION OF TRANSLATION

If the title of the document is not in the Favoured Language and it is not a proper noun but is descriptive, its translation in the Favoured Language may be added within square brackets as a separate sentence in the title section, either in the Main Entry alone or also in specific Added Entries according to a subsidiary rule to be framed by each library in conformity to the Principle of Local Variation.

CHAPTER EB

SCRIPT OF THE ENTRIES

1 Favoured Script

The script of the Favoured Language of the library; and in exceptional cases any other script chosen by the library as the Favoured Script.

For example, the Favoured Language of a Library of Books in Sanskrit in USA will be Sanskrit. But, it may choose as its Favoured Script, not the Nagari—i e, the Sanskrit—Script, but the Roman Script.

2 Preference of Favoured Script

Generally speaking, the script of an entry in a library catalogue is to be in its Favoured Script.

An alternative is considered in Sec SA5

3 Transliteration

If the title-page is not in the Favoured Script of the library, the words taken from the title page are to be transliterated in that Script in accordance with an accepted table of transliteration.

The script of this book being Roman all the examples in it are in Roman script. It is equivalent to saying that the examples are printed as for a library whose favoured script is Roman.

31 Transliteration Table

The table given in the *Journal* of the Royal Asiatic Society of Great Britain and Ireland or any other standard table, put up as an international or national standard, as the case may be, is to be used for the scripts covered by them.

The table mentioned first in the above Rule is based on the agreement arrived at in an International Congress of Orientalists.

4 In Edition 1

The first edition of this book reproduced a slightly modified form of that table. But in actual practice, we found it unhelpful because it did not indicate the shapes of consonant-vowel combinations. Twenty more pages would be required to indicate them. It was felt that the frequency of use of the tables would not justify sparing so many pages for them. Further, the bodies of the types of the different languages are so different that they cannot be composed in the same line. This necessitated the making of blocks for all the pages of the tables. This would increase the cost beyond economic limits. The tables have, therefore, been omitted in this edition.

5 Transliteration into Indian Scripts

At present, tables exist only for transliteration into Roman Script. Tables for transliteration into most other scripts—particularly the Indian scripts—are yet to be standardised.

We cannot expect any other country to take up this task. The Indian Standards Institution should seize this task and complete it in collaboration with the linguists of the different regions of the country. Its EC2—Documentation Committee—should co-opt linguistic scholars and establish a standard for transliteration from western scripts into Indian scripts. There is another task even more urgent than this. It is the establishment of standards for transliteration from one Indian script to another. For, apart from the Tamil script and the Urdu script differing considerably in the phonetic make up from the other Indian scripts, even among the other Indian scripts there are substantial differences in respect of the phonetic values of a few letters of the alphabet. Thus there is scope for considerable work to be done in internal transliteration by the Documentation Committee of the Indian Standards Institution. The present drive for emotional integration through literature service calls immediate attention to this problem of internal transliteration.

CHAPTER EC

ARTICLES AND CONTRACTIONS

1 Articles

Some Rules prescribe omission of initial articles. The following list of articles is given to facilitate recognition:

Arabic: ad, al, ar, as, at, ez.
Dutch: de, het, 't, een, eene.
English: a, an, the
French: le, la, les, un, une
German: das, der, die, ein, eine
Hebrew: Ha, he
Hungarian: a, az, egy
Italian: gli, gl, i, il, l', la, le, lo, un, una, uno
Portuguese: a, as, o, um, uma
Scandinavian: de, den, det, en, et, ett
Spanish: el, la, lo, los, un, una
Yiddish: der, di, dos

The numeral adjective meaning "one" should be distinguished from an article of the same form and should not be omitted.

2 Contractions

The following are the contractions to be used, in writing entries:

Abkürzung	..	Abkurz
Abridged	..	Abr
Abteilung(en)	..	Abt
Annotated	..	Annot
Annotation	..	Annot
Annotator(s)—	..	Annot
Assistant	..	Assis
Auflage(-n)	..	Aufl
Ausgabe(n)	..	Ausg
Ausgewahlt	..	Ausgew
Author(s)	..	Auth
Band	..	B
Bearbeiter	..	Bearb
Bearbeitet	..	Bearb
Before Christ	..	BC
Century	..	Cent
Commentary	..	Comm
Commentator(s)	..	Comm
Compiled	..	Comp
Compiler(s)	..	Comp
Dedicated	..	Ded
Dedicatee(s)	..	Ded
Dedication	..	Ded
Director	..	Dir
Edited	..	Ed
Edito	..	Ed
Editor(s)	..	Ed
Edition	..	Ed
Edizione	..	Ed
Epitome	..	Epit
Epitomised	..	Epit
Epitomiser(s)	..	Epit
Erklärung(en)	..	Erkl
Fascicule	..	Fasc
Gekürzt	..	Gek
Gesammelt	..	Ges
Heft	..	H
Herausgeber	..	Her
Herausgegeben	..	Her
Illustration	..	Ill
Illustrator(s)	..	Ill
Illustrazione	..	Ill
Introduction	..	Introd
Introduction writer(s)	..	Introd
Introductory	..	Introd

Word		Contraction
Introduzione	..	Introd
Joint	..	J
Nouveau	..	Nouv
Nouvelle	..	Nouv
Number(s)	..	N
Omarbeide(t)	..	Omarb
Oversat	..	Overs
Page(s)	..	P
Popular	..	Pop
Preface	..	Pref
Prologo	..	Prol
Pseudonym	..	Pseud
R digirt	..	Red
Report	..	Rep
Reported	..	Rep
Reporter	..	Rep
Revidierte	..	Rev
Revised	..	Rev
Revision	..	Rev
Revisor(s)	..	Rev
Samlede vaerker	..	Sam
Sammlung	..	Sam
Special	..	Sp
Teil(e)	..	Te
Tome	..	T
Tradotto	..	Tr
Traduction	..	Tr
Traduit	..	Tr
Traduzione	..	Tr
Translated	..	Tr
Translation(s)	..	Tr
Translator(s)	..	Tr
Udgave(r)	..	Udg
Udgiver(e)	..	Udg
Übersetzt	..	Übers
Übersetzung	..	Übers
Uitgaaf	..	Uitg
Vertaler	..	Vert
Volume(s)	..	V

3 Cognate Words

As far as possible, cognate words are provided the same contraction.

4 Homonymous Contractions

Some of the contractions prescribed are homonymous. For example, the contraction 'Tr' denotes 'Translated,' 'Translation,' and 'Translator(s)'. The context of its occurrence will resolve the homonym.

CHAPTER ED

STYLE OF WRITING

1 Introduction

The style of making the entries is, to some extent, to depend on the physical form of the catalogue. From this point of view, three physical forms may be recognised—the bound-book form; the loose-leaf form; and the card form. The choice of form has to be made in the light of the Fifth Law of Library Science. The main concern of the Fifth Law is to give full weight to the need for casual repairs and frequent addition of entries even while the catalogue continues to be in use. It has been discussed in detail in the *Five laws of library science* [RF9].

11 Physical Form of the Catalogue

The days of time-honoured bound-book form are gone for ever—never to return—at least in the case of a growing Service-Library. The loose-leaf form and the card form are so much alike, that they admit of nearly the same style of making the entries. As the card form marks a later stage of evolution, as it is rightly more popular, and as it is desirable to make the rules definite, this chapter deals only with the style of making entries for a card catalogue.

12 Card Catalogue

In order that the right sequence of all entries—old as well as new taken together—may always be easily maintained, each card is to get only one entry, except where rules provide for the consolidation of several consecutive entries into a single 'Consolidated Entry.'

Experience has singled out cards, 124×75×0.25 mm, as of the most convenient size. They are referred to as 'standard cards' for cataloguing purposes. If the catalogue, as a tool, is to have the longest lease of life possible, it is desirable that cards of the best texture should be used. To secure elegance, it is better to have ruled cards.

13 Printed Card

Next to the choice of the material on which the entry is to be made, we have to examine the mode of making the entry. Is the entry to be printed, type-written, or written by hand ? Printing will be ideal, if economically possible. As the cost of printing goes to-day, it is not economical for individual libraries. It may be possible in countries where co-operative cataloguing is practised. The number of such countries is, however, now small [RT6].

14 Typed Card

As for typing, the chief problem is the availability of the right sort of ribbon which will leave behind it an indelible impression. The handling of single cards need not be considered however a serious handicap, as it may be possible to produce the cards in reels of suitable length. Typing may be too expensive for some libraries.

15 Written Card

Thus writing by hand may be the only mode practicable in many individual libraries—at least for some time in the newly developing countries.

16 Unit Card System

No library can get on with a single copy of the catalogue. Further, the tendency now is to have groups of small libraries knit together. This organisation involves having a number of copies of the catalogue. The number is usually too small, however, to make printing economical. Hence the library world is now engaged in carrying on various experiments in the matter. Many near-printing processes have now come into use. Libraries which use these processes or printing itself will find it economical to use the 'Unit Card' system. This system uses copies of the Main Entry Card for Added Entries also by adding the Headings of the latter at the top or underlining those words in the title-portion which should be regarded as Headings. Detailed rules for these are easily framed by individual libraries.

The rules of this chapter bear upon the style of *writing* the entries in cards in individual libraries. This brings us to two other issues, *viz*, the writing fluid to be used and the hand in which the entries are to be written.

2 Writing

21 Writing Fluid

The indelibility of the ink used should be such as to make the entry last as long as the card lasts.

The catalogue is a permanent record and the cost of renewing it wholesale would be prohibitive. Hence this rule.

22 Use of Pencil

Call Numbers and Class Numbers should, however, be in pencil.

These are liable to revision and change. Hence this rule.

23 Library Hand

All words and numbers in an Entry are to be in a bold upright hand, their letters and digits being detached from one another.

As regards the hand, we are between two opposing factors. On the one side, the hand in which a person writes is singularly personal. The science of graphology is based on this fact. On the other hand, the catalogue of a growing library accretes to itself several entries from week to week, over in indefinitely large number of generations. Hence, if all the calligraphic idiosyncrasies of all the successive cataloguers be given full play, the catalogue would certainly become an unattractive hotchpotch. The library world would rather sacrifice the individuality in the handwriting of cataloguers than make the heterogeneous style of the catalogue offend or repel the readers. Accordingly, it has, in recent years, developed an impersonal hand and dubbed it the 'Library Hand.' It is claimed that even a person with a bad hand can practise it with success and, what is more, can write it fairly fast. Here is Library Hand for the Roman Script and the Indo-Arabic Numerals.

A similar standard should be established for the favoured script of a library and implemented.

24 Rules on Style of Writing

Before we proceed to state the rules of this chapter, an apology is due to the reader. An actual demonstration of writing the various kinds of cards would be more effective than a chapter of rules. But, as the author of a book is denied the privilege of personal demonstration, he is driven to the circumlocutory mode of describing them by rules. Hence, I would request the reader to bear with me in this matter and follow the rules by actually writing out sample cards.

25 Lines in an Entry

1 **Leading Line.**—The top-most horizontal line of a card.

2 **First Vertical.**—The left-most vertical line of a card.

3 **Second Vertical.**—The vertical line which is to the right of the First Vertical of a card.

In what follows, some of the definitions given in Chap B7 are assumed.

3 Leading Section

The Leading Section—that is, the section beginning on the Leading Line—and all its continuation lines are to be commenced at the First Vertical.

4 Other Sections

41 General

All the other Sections except an Index Number Section, an Accession Number Section, and the Second Section in a Series Index Entry are to be commenced at the Second Vertical.

42 Continuation Lines

The continuation lines of all sections are to be commenced at the First Vertical.

43 Index Number Section

The Index Section is to be as far to the right as possible in the Section preceding it or in the first line after the said last line.

44 Serial Number

The Serial Number in the Second Section of a Series Index Entry is to be commenced at the First Vertical, while the word which follows the Serial Number is to be commenced at the Second Vertical or as far further to its right as may be necessary if the Serial Number is so long as to go beyond the Second Vertical.

45 Accession Number Section

The Accession Number Section is to begin at the First Vertical of the bottom-most line.

451 TWO OR MORE ACCESSION NUMBERS

If two or more Accession Numbers are to be written in the same Main Entry, they are to be in a sequence parallel to that of the Book Numbers to which they correspond.

5 Typography

51 Entry Element

The words, other than auxiliary ones, in an Entry Element in a Block in a Heading are to be in Block Letters.

52 Directing Element

A Directing Element is to be underlined. In print, it is to be in italics.

53 Descriptive Element

A Descriptive Element is to be underlined. In print, it is to be in italics. The first letter of each word in it other than an auxiliary word is to be in capital.

54 Other Words

All the words in an Entry, other than those covered by Sections ED51, ED52, and ED53 are to be written in ordinary hand as in prose.

The word "and" connecting two Descriptive Elements also should be in ordinary hand according to this Section.

55 Numerals

All numbers, other than those forming part of the name of a monarch or a pope or any other person or of a corporate body and usually written in Roman Numerals, and other than Call Numbers and Class Numbers are to be in Indo-Arabic Numerals.

6 Sequence of Words

The words in a section are to be in their normal sequence, except where a different sequence is specifically laid down by a Rule.

7 Use of Capitals

The use of capitals is to be regulated by the rules of grammar of the favoured language of the library, subject to Sec 51 and 53 of this Chap.

8 Punctuation Marks

Punctua on marks are to be given as in ordinary prose, subject to Rules 81 to 84 of this Chap.

It cannot be said that the rules of grammar regarding the use of capitals and punctuation marks are very rigid or definite. They are, I believe, made purposely elastic so that some freedom may be given to individual tastes. But the result of giving freedom to the varying tastes of the individual cataloguers of a library will make the Library Catalogue unseemly. Hence, it is recommended that the freedom, given by the rules of grammar, should not be extended by a library to its individual cataloguers but that each library should draw up its own rules and enforce them rigidly. On the other hand, it is felt that it is not desirable that the freedom of the libraries also should be cut out and a uniform set of rigid rules enforced on all libraries. But to make cooperative cataloguing among countries possible, the International Catalogue Code itself should fix the rules of punctuation marks for all the national centres of cataloguing.

81 A Comma is to separate two consecutive Blocks in a Heading.

82 A Comma is to separate a Descriptive Element in a Block in a Heading, from what it describes.

83 Circular brackets are to enclose each Individualising and Secondary Element.

84 The conjunction between Blocks in a Heading may be replaced by a comma. If this is done, semicolon should precede a Descriptive Element instead of a comma.

This rule will be of use in a language calling for an inflection of the words connected and instead of the use of an auxiliary word equivalent to 'and'—for example, Tamil. By this means, the words can be in the nominative case form.

91 Varieties of Notation

910 Inclusive Notation

A set of consecutive numbers represented by the symbol consisting of

1 The first number of the set;
2 A dash; and
3 The last number of the set.

Example : 3—18.

911 Years

Notwithstanding Rule 910 of this Chap, if the numbers denote years, the second member of the inclusive notation is to consist of:

1 The last digit alone when the earlier digits are common to both the members;

2 The last two digits alone when the earlier digits are common to both the members; and

3 So on.

Example : 1962-3, 1952-63, 1852-963, 1963-2112.

912 Open Notation

An indefinite continuation of consecutive numbers beginning from a specific number and represented by the symbol consisting of

1 The specific number forming the beginning; and
2 A dash.

Example : 3—

913 Non-consecutive

The members of a sequence of non-consecutive numbers and non-consecutive sets of consecutive numbers in inclusive notation, are to be separated by commas.

Example : 3—18, 41—57, 85—

CHAPTER EE

SIZE OF BOOK

1 Each library is to maintain a specification for deciding whether a volume is to be regarded as

1 Undersized; or,

2 Oversized; or,

3 Abnormal for the reason of having too many plates or maps or for any other peculiarity in its build or for any other reason such as rarity.

It is found from experience that it is convenient to have the pamphlets, the giant folios and the other abnormal volumes, arranged in separate collections of their own. On the other hand, it is not desirable to have the entries corresponding to them taken out of their natural place in the catalogue. Hence, there must be some simple method of showing, in their entries, the collections in which they will be found in the stack-room.

One does not wish to be dogmatic in fixing the size for a 'pamphlet,' 'giant folio' and so on. That is why this rule leaves the specification in the hands of individual libraries. It is expected that each library should, in the light of experience, write out a specification as a supplement to this rule.

An illustrative specification is given here.

A volume is deemed to be undersize if its

11 Breadth is less than 300 mm; and

121 Thickness is not greater than 5 mm;

or

122 Thickness is not greater than 30 mm and its height is less than 150 mm.

or

123 Thickness is not greater than 50 mm and its height is less than 120 mm.

or

124 Thickness is not greater than 150 mm and its height is less than 50 mm.

2 A volume is deemed to be oversized if its breadth is not less than 300 mm.

3 A volume is deemed to be abnormal if

31 It contains not less than 50 plates or maps or both plates and maps taken together;

or

32 The paper is very poor, such as unpressed paper or paper loaded with clay;

or

33 The Reference Section recommends its inclusion in the abnormal sequence because of the peculiar nature of the contents or the scarcity value of the volume.

2 The Book Number of an undersized volume is to be underlined.

3 The Book Number of an oversized volume is to be overlined.

4 The Book Number of an abnormal volume is to be both underlined and overlined.

5 In all the entries of a volume put in any other collection, an appropriate collection symbol is to be put consistently above the Class Number or below the Book Number.

In a public library, the sequence symbol may indicate the branch in which the volume is housed; in a university or college library, the department in which it is housed [RL4], and in a school library, the standard to which it is assigned [RS1].

The symbol indicating collection should be inserted in all the Entries of the volume concerned.

It must be remembered that the primary collection has no symbol.

CHAPTER EF

CONTINUED CARDS

1 If an Entry is too long for one card, it is to be continued in another card; the connecting phrase '*continued in the next card*' is to be at the right end of the bottom-most line of the earlier card and the connecting word '*continued*' is to be at the right end of the top of the latter card. Further the Leading Section is to be repeated in all continued cards. The sequence of such cards may be referred to as a set of 'Continued Cards.'

2 A sequence of Main Entries of periodical publications, having the same class number in their respective Leading Sections, written in different cards because of break in the set, or change of name or any other of the causes covered by Rule PA2 is also to be treated as a set of 'Continued Cards.'

3 If a set of 'Continued Cards' consists of three or more cards, the first card is to have the connecting phrase at the bottom only; the last card is to have the connecting word at the top only and the intermediate cards are to have the connecting words at the top as well as at the bottom.

4 The 'Continued Cards' are to be numbered serially, the serial number being written after the connecting word '*continued*' near the top of the card.

CHAPTER EG

ARRANGEMENT OF ENTRIES IN CLASSIFIED PART

1 By Class Numbers

1 The entries in the Classified Part are to be arranged by the Class Numbers in their respective Leading Sections.

The ordinal arrangement of Class Numbers would depend on the Scheme of Classification used. If the Colon Classification is used, the ordinal arrangement is governed by Rules 024, 025 and 0251 of the *Colon classification*.

11 Main and Cross Reference Entries

2 The entries having the same Class Number in their respective Leading Sections are to be arranged among themselves in accordance with the succeeding Rules.

Such entries will be either Main Entries of works dealing chiefly with the specific subject represented by the Class Number in question or Cross Reference Entries of works dealing with it in a subsidiary way.

2 Main Entries

21 Among the entries with the same Class Number in their respective Leading Sections, those with one or more Book Numbers are to have precedence over those without them.

The result of this Rule is to separate the Main Entries and Cross Reference Entries, relating to a given specific subject and to give precedence to the former group.

22 Entries with Book Numbers in their respective Leading Sections are to be arranged among themselves by the Book Numbers.

The ordinal arrangement of Book Numbers would depend on the System of Book Numbers used. If the Colon Classification is used, the ordinal arrangement is governed by Rules 03015 and 03016 of the *Colon classification*.

23 The position of a consolidated Main Entry is to be determined by the last Book Number in it.

24 Entries with the same Class Numbers as well as Book Numbers in their respective Leading Sections will be a sequence of "continued" entries and they are to be arranged among themselves in their numerical sequence.

3 Cross Reference Entries

31 Entries with the same Class Number and without Book Numbers in their respective Leading Sections are to be arranged among themselves by the Book Numbers, if any, in their respective Third Sections.

The result of this rule is that the Cross Reference Entries for a given specific subject will get grouped by the languages of the works cross-referred and those in each language group will get arranged chronologically by the year of publication of the book to which reference is made.

32 Such of the entries coming under rule 31 of this Chap as have the same Book Numbers in their respective Third Sections, are to be arranged among themselves by the Class Numbers occurring in their respective Third Sections.

This is simply one convenient way of making the arrangement definite.

4 Periodical Publications

Entries with no Book Numbers in their Leading Sections and no Class Numbers in their respective Third Sections, but with the same Class Number in their respective Leading Sections will be a sequence of "continued" entries of a Periodical Publication; and they are to be arranged among themselves in their numerical sequence.

The result of this rule is that the entries for a given periodical publication will get arranged in their natural sequence.

CHAPTER EH

ARRANGEMENT OF ENTRIES IN ALPHABETICAL PART

1 By Alphabet

1 The entries in the Alphabetical Part are to be arranged strictly by the alphabet, as in a dictionary and in conformity with the succeeding rules of this chapter.

The possibility and advantages of ruthless all-through alphabetisation are examined in the paper on *Alphabetical arrangement* [RA1].

2 Initial Articles

2 In the alphabetical arrangement no attention is to be paid to initial articles.

3 Umlaut

31 German words spelt with the vowels ä, ö, and ü are to be arranged as if they were spelt, a, o, and u respectively.

The help of Cross Reference Index Entry is to be sought to link up umlauted vowel with its representation with an 'e', by the application of Sec LA3.

4 Scottish Names

Scottish names with the prefix Mac and its abbreviated forms such as Mc and M' are to be arranged according to their apparent alphabetical make-up.

The help of Cross Reference Index Entry is to be sought to link up the prefixes Mac, Mc, and M' by the application of the Sec LA3.

5 'Saint' and its Variants

Names beginning with St and Ste are to be treated on the analogy of Rule 4 of this Chap.

6 Superior Comma

The superior comma in a Scottish or Irish name or in a possessive case is to be ignored.

7 Gestalt Alphabetisation

70 The following ascending scale of ordinal values is to be borne in mind in arranging the entries in the Alphabetical Part:

1 Section space;
2 Full stop;
3 Comma;
4 Numerals in their natural sequence;
5 Bracket;
6 Words in Roman;
7 Words in italics, or underlined words;
8 The word "and", or its substitute semicolon; and
91 Etc.

71 Certain Terms

The priority of Section Space over Full Stop may be called the Rule of "Section before Full Stop." Similarly we can speak of the "Rule of Full Stop before Comma"; the Rule of "Comma before Bracket," the Rule of "Bracket before Words in Roman," and Rule of "Words in Roman before Words in Italics or underlined."

72 Abandonment of the Rule of "Nothing before Something"

The above prescription omits the Rule of "Nothing before Something," followed in other methods of arrangement. It has to be omitted on account of the uncertainty and the inconsistency with which authors and other persons write a word in their names either as a single word or as two or more words with empty space between them, or with hyphens between them. This phenomenon is described fully in Sec HC5 and its Subdivisions. For example, one and the same name may occur in the same list in any of the following three forms:

1 Sivasankaranarayana.
2 Siva-Sankara-Narayana.
3 Siva Sankara Narayana.

The "Nothing before Something" rule will scatter these three entries. At the same time, a person who looks up the Alphabetical list cannot be sure in which of these three forms his reference is likely to be found. It is for these reasons that the Rule of "Nothing before Something" has been abandoned in this edition.

73 Traditional Method of Alphabetisation

It has been usual to direct that homonymous words and phrases should be arranged among themselves according to their meaning, say, in the sequence:

1 Names of places;
2 Names of subjects;
3 Names of books;
4 Names of things; and
5 Names of persons.

But such a direction implies deliberation of a delicate nature during alphabetisation, which ought to be a purely mechanical affair [RT8]. In this Code, absolute mechanisation of arrangement is sought to be secured by specifying the Rules of Writing and the Rules of Alphabetisation in a fully integrated manner. This is indeed an attempt to apply the Gestalt Theory of Alphabetisation enunciated in the *Theory of library catalogue.*

74 Oscillation between Extremes

In the first three editions of this Code, the Gestalt Principle was implemented to a severe degree. Between 1951, the year of edition 3 and now, some re-thinking has been done. As a kind of extreme swing away from the severe Gestalt Alphabetisation, the All-through Alphabetisation was practised. The Documentation Section of the Indian Standards Institution established a Standard on the basis of the latter. In this standard, arrangement is to be guided only by what is visible. For example "Mac" and "Mc" are not to be equated at all. It also refused to give different ordinal values to the different styles of writing. In the Indian Standards Convention held at Madras in December 1957, these two extreme positions were reviewed. It was decided that what could be truly helpful to the users of an alphabetical list, should be found somewhere midway between these two extremes.

75 Midway Position

The present edition of this Code has made an attempt to find this midway position. The Rules on the Style of Writing given in Chap ED, and the Rules on Alphabetical Arrangement given in this Chap are so co-ordinated as to implement that midway position.

76 Example

The combined effect of these two co-ordinated sets of Rules is illustrated by the sequence in which the following entries get arranged. The Headings alone are given in most cases. The word "Cambrije" has been improvised just for purpose of illustration.

1 Cambridge.
Three hundred years' progress.

2 CAMBRIDGE.
See also
CAMBRIJE.
3 CAMBRIDGE, BIBLIOGRAPHY.
4 CAMBRIDGE, EDUCATION COMMITTEE.
5 CAMBRIDGE, GEOGRAPHY.
6 CAMBRIDGE, LIBRARY COMMITTEE.
7 CAMBRIDGE, TAXATION COMMITTEE.
8 CAMBRIDGE, *Pseud.*
9 CAMBRIDGE (City).
10 CAMBRIDGE (City), LIBRARY COMMITTEE.
11 CAMBRIDGE (Duke of) 1.
12 CAMBRIDGE (Duke of) 2.
13 CAMBRIDGE (John).
Aesthetics.
14 CAMBRIDGE (John).
Metaphysics.
15 CAMBRIDGE (John), DRAMA.
16 CAMBRIDGE (John), PHILOSOPHY.
17 CAMBRIDGE (John), *Ed.*
18 CAMBRIDGE (John), *Tr.*
19 CAMBRIDGE (John) and ROSS (E B).
20 CAMBRIDGE (John) and ROSS (E B), *Ed.*
21 CAMBRIDGE (John) and SMITH (John).
22 CAMBRIDGE (Massachusetts).
23 CAMBRIDGE ARCHAEOLOGICAL SOCIETY.
24 CAMBRIDGE GOWN.
25 CAMBRIDGE PHILOSOPHICAL SOCIETY.
26 CAMBRIDGESHIRE.
27 CAMBRIDGE TROPHY.
28 CAMBRIJE.
29 NEWALL (J T).
30 NEWARK.
31 NEW SHAKESPEARE SOCIETY.
32 NEW SOUTH WALES.
33 NEW YORK.
34 NEW ZEALAND.
35 SHIVASANKARANARAYANA AYYAR (Ramanathan).
36 SHIVA-SANKARA-NARAYANA AYYAR (Subramaniyam).
37 SHIVA SANKARA NARAYANA AYYAR (Tiruvellore).
38 SHIVASANKARANARAYANA PILLAI.

In alphabetical works of reference such as *Who's who* and *Telephone directory*, punctuation marks and italics are not likely to occur. Therefore, the compromise between strict All-through and Gestalt arrangements is not likely to cause any serious difficulty to the users of such reference works.

8 Guide Card

In the Alphabetical Part, one guide card for about every three inches may prove sufficient. The Classified Part must be guided more profusely. The fact that the guide cards should be separated sufficiently so as to stand out distinctly is the only limiting factor. Subject to this, every possible Class should be guided. Even this limiting factor may be evaded to some extent by putting an inclusive class on the tab and featuring its subclasses in two or three columns on the body of the card to which the tab is affixed.

PART F

TERMINOLOGY

CHAPTER FA

WORK

1 **Knowledge-Unit.**—An assumed term.

It may extend in print to several volumes at one extreme or to only a single sentence or even a single word at the other extreme. For example, the Knowledge-Units, contained in and denoted by the following, stand arranged in the decreasing sequence of size:

1 Encyclopaedia of general knowledge;

2 Encyclopaedia of library science;

3 This book itself—*Classified catalogue code with additional rules for dictionary catalogue code;*

4 Part F of this book—Terminology (of cataloguing);

5 Chap FA of this book—Terms connected with "Work"; and

6 The definition given in the Sec in the first line of this Chap.

2 **Thought.**—Knowledge-unit.

This term is introduced for brevity. We often speak of the Thought-Content of a book or of the work that it embodies.

21 **Macro Thought** and **Micro Thought.**—These are relative terms, with meanings loosely fixed by convention. Examples 1, 2, and 3 given under Sec FA1 may be taken to denote Macro Thought. And examples 4, 5, and 6 may be taken to denote Micro Thought. Ordinarily, a book greater in size than a pamphlet may be said to embody Macro Thought. So also, a pamphlet, an article in a periodical, a section of a book, a picture, or a map, may be said to embody Micro Thought.

3 **Expressed Thought.**—Thought expressed in language, or symbols, or in any other mode, and thereby made communicable.

The above definition itself is Expressed Thought. It is expressed in the English language. A picture is also Expressed Thought. A mathematical or a chemical formula is again Expressed Thought. A gesture is equally an Expressed Thought.

4 **Work.**—Expressed thought.

This term is introduced for brevity and elegance.

41 **Abridgement.**—Reduced form of a work got by condensation and/or omission of details, but retaining the whole general sense and the unity of the original work.

For example, Chap 1 of my *Library manual* gives an Abridgement of my work entitled *Five laws of library science*.

42 **Adaptation.**—A version of a work, re-written for a particular purpose, but not so changed as to be deemed an independent work on the basis of the quality of its thought and expression. The Adaptation may be either in the language of the original work or in any other language.

For example, the chapter on Cataloguing in my *Library manual* is an Adaptation of the work contained in this book, for use in small libraries. So also, the chapter on Classification in my *Library manual* is an Adaptation of the work contained in my *Colon classification* and of the work contained in the *Decimal classification*. The *Ramayana* of Kamban may appear to be an Adaptation of the *Ramayana* of Valmiki. But it is an independent work on account of its own individualistic quality of thought and expression. So also, the Bengali and the English versions of the *Gitanjali* of Tagore should be taken as independent works and not as Adaptations of each other.

5 **Sacred Work.**—Basic work of a religion, generally accepted as such among its followers.

Vedas, Upanishads, Tantras, Tripitakas, Talmud, Bible, New Testament, and *Koran* are examples. A Sacred Work is often treated as if it were a class or subject. To distinguish such a class or subject from a normal class or subject, it is called a quasi-class or quasi-subject. Each part of a Sacred Work is also treated as a quasi-class which is a subclass of it. Chains of such subclasses of it are usually enumerated in an articulated sequence.

6 **Work of Literature.**—Work in the form of a poem, drama, fiction, prose, *champu*, or any other literary form, of which the outstanding qualities are taken to be beauty of form, emotional or intuitional appeal, and endless layers of suggestions in regard

to meaning, and/or which is of intuitive or trans-intellectual origin.

For example, *Ramayana*, *Iliad*, *Sakuntala*, *Canterbury tales*, *Hamlet*, *Hound of heaven*, *Post office*, and *Apple cart* are Works of Literature. A work of Literature is treated as if it were a class or a subject. That is, it is regarded as a quasi-class or quasi-subject.

7 **Classic.**—Work usually having embodiments in several versions, adaptations, and translations, attracting other works on itself, and getting copied out and/or brought out in print even long after its origin.

For example, Aristotle's *Poetics*, Newton's *Principia* and Marx's *Capital* are Classics. A Classic too is often treated as if it were a class or a subject. That is, it is regarded as a quasi-class or quasi-subject.

8 **Quasi-Class.**—Work which is treated as a class in a classification scheme, or whose title is used as a subject-heading in cataloguing practice.

As we have seen in Sec FA5, FA6 and FA7, a Quasi-Class is usually a Sacred Work, or a Work of Literature, or a Classic. Such works are usually governed by special rules in a Cataloguing Code.

91 **Pedestrian Work.**—Work not eligible to be made into a Quasi-Class or a Quasi-Subject.

Most of the works published today are Pedestrian Works. They are not Sacred Works of religion. Nor are they Classics. All works passing for poems, dramas, or any other form of work of literature may not, in reality, deserve to be treated as Quasi-Classes or Quasi-Subjects. Some may be only Pedestrian Works. And yet, it is the practice in cataloguing to treat them as if they are Quasi-Classes or Quasi-Subjects. This is because the line of demarcation between a true Work of Literature and a Pedestrian Work in verse, drama or any other literary form is not sharp enough. To distinguish them and treat them as Pedestrian Works would amount to a violation of the Canon of Reticence on the part of the classifiers or the cataloguers as the case may be. However, a poem whose value is the exposition of Positive Knowledge, need not be taken as poetry. So also with other forms of exposition.

CHAPTER FB

TITLE

1 **Title.**—Name of work.

For example, *Classified catalogue code with additional rules for dictionary catalogue code* is the Title of the work contained in this book.

2 **Subtitle.**—A secondary or subordinate title usually explanatory, and forming part of the title.

For example, in the full title of my book *Heading and canons: Comparative study of five catalogue codes*, the part *Comparative study of five catalogue codes* is Subtitle.

3 **Alternative Title.**—A subtitle introduced by "or" or its equivalent, and forming part of the title.

For example, in the full title of my work, contained in the book *Social bibliography or physical bibliography for librarians, authors, and publishers*, the part *Physical bibliography for librarians, authors, and publishers* is Alternative Title.

4 **Short Title or Abbreviated Title.**—The name of a work, more brief than its full title, without prejudice to intelligibility and help in identifying the work.

For example, *Library development plan* is the Abbreviated Title of my work contained in the book with the title *Library development plan, with draft library bills for the Union Government and the Constituent States*.

Generally speaking, initial words other than an article,—such as, Elements, Handbook, Introduction, Primer and Treatise—may have to be preserved.

5 **Half-Title.**—Title, usually short, given on the page of a printed book, usually found before the page containing the full title of the work contained in the book.

For example, "Classified Catalogue Code" is printed as the Half-Title of the work contained in this book. It is so printed in the half-title-page which is on the recto of the leaf preceding the title-leaf.

6 **Running Title.**—Short title usually found printed in the top line of each verso page or all the pages of a book.

For example, "Classified Catalogue Code" is printed as Running Title in the top of each verso page of this book.

7 **Binder's Title.**—Short title usually found tooled on the spine of a book.

For example, "Classified Catalogue Code" is tooled on the spine of this book as the Binder's Title.

8 **Tell-Tale Title.**—Title that discloses the subject of the work.

For example, the title of this book is a Tell-Tale Title.

91 **Uniformised Title.**—Title uniformised by popular or cataloguing usage in lieu of listless, and often unintended, variants of the title of one and the same work in different editions or the titles of different volumes of one and the same work.

For example, the work which had for its original title *Code civil des Français* was later given the title *Code Napoleon*. It is helpful to use one uniform title for it in the place of its variants. Generally, a Sacred Book of a religion is given slightly varying titles from time to time, without any significance. There is therefore a need for adopting a Uniformised Title for it. *Bible*, *Vedas*, and *Talmud* are examples of such Uniformised Titles. The same thing happens also in the case of Classics and Works of Literature. Many Governmental and other Annual Reports change their titles listlessly. For example, it may be *Administration report on agriculture* in one year, *Annual report on agriculture* in another year, and *Review of agriculture* in a still another year. This is also a case where a Uniformised Title is called for. Uniformisation of the title may also be necessary in respect of a Periodical Conference. This is a case in which the Canon of Ascertainability is not followed rigidly.

92 **Fanciful Title.**—Title that does not disclose the subject of the work.

93 **Proper Name Title.**—Either a Fanciful Title or a Title beginning with a Proper Noun and for this or other reason having the status of a Proper Name.

For example, the title *Library cheque-book of five leaves*, which is the name of a work of mine given as an address to the German Library Conference in Berlin in 1956 and published as an article in the *Granthalaya*, the organ of the Hyderabad Library Association, in the same year, is a Fanciful Title or a Proper Name Title. For, its thought-content is my Five Laws of Library Science. This subject of the work is not disclosed by its title. In fact, most of the people in the conference felt intrigued by the title announced for my address, until they listened to the address. A title like *Oxford book of English prose*, which contains a proper noun, may also be taken to be a Proper Name Title.

94 **Title Proper of a Periodical Publication.**—Includes the name of the sponsor if it occurs at the beginning and excludes it if it occurs at the end.

Examples:

1 Aslib proceedings.
2 Library Association record.
3 Unesco bulletin for libraries.
4 Annals only in the case of the Annals of the Indian Library Association.
5 Journal only in the case of the Journal of the Indian Mathematical Society.
6 *Transactions* only in the case of the Transactions of the Royal Society.

CHAPTER FC

AUTHOR

1 **Person.**—An assumed term.

2 **Corporate Body.**—

Sense 1 A number of persons taken collectively—usually as united, or organised, or coming together informally, in a common cause or for common action such as governmental business, or commercial or industrial or service or political or any other business, or for deliberation, or for collective expression of opinion or statement.

Sense 2 A number of corporate bodies, in sense 1, taken collectively—usually as united, or organised, or coming together informally, in a common cause or for common action such as governmental business, or commercial or industrial or service or political or any other business, or for deliberation, or for collective expression of opinion or statement.

For example, Government of India, Madras Chamber of Commerce, Union of Textile Mill Owners of Coimbatore, Ramakrishna Mission, Indian National Congress, Indian National Trade Union Congress, Constituent Assembly of India, Villagers' Gathering at Ubhiavedantapuram, District Board of Tanjavur, Corporation of Madras, Panchayat Board of Sirkali, Madras Library Association, Indian Mathematical Society, and Old Boys' Association of the Hindu High School (Sirkali) are corporate Bodies in sense 1.

United Nations, Afro-Asian Conference, International Federation of Library Associations, Federation of Indian Chambers of Commerce, Inter-University Board of India, and Commonwealth Universities' Conference are Corporate Bodies in sense 2.

21 **Organ of a Corporate Body.**—Non-autonomous part of a corporate body formed by

1 The constitution of the parent body; or

2 A legislative, executive, or administrative measure, for administrative or deliberative work for an indefinite period, within the field of function of the parent body; or

3 A legislative, or executive, or administrative measure for

a specific piece of work for a specified duration, within the field of function of the parent body.

211 **Constitutional Organ.**—Organ of the category 1 mentioned in Sec FC 21.

212 **Administrative Organ.**—Organ of the category 2 mentioned in Sec FC 21.

213 **Permanent Organ.**—Organ of the categories 1 or 2 mentioned in Sec FC 21.

214 **Temporary Organ.**—Organ of the category 3 mentioned in Sec FC 21.

215 **Organ of the First Remove.**—Organ intrinsic to the constitution of the parent body.

216 **Organ of the Second Remove.**—Organ of any organ of the first remove.

217 **Organ of the Third Remove.**—Organ of any organ of the second remove.

218 Organ is itself a corporate body.

For example, 1 The President of India, the Parliament of India, the Supreme Court of India, the Governor of Madras, the Madras Legislative Assembly, the High Court of Madras, the Madras Council of Ministers, the Senate, the Academic Council, the Syndicate, and the Faculties of the Vikram University, the Council of the Madras Library Association are all Constitutional Organs of their respective parent bodies.

2 The Ministry of Education of the Government of India, the Library Committee of the Vikram University, the Publication Committee of the Madras Library Association, the Reception Committee of the Indian Mathematical Conference of 1957, and the Professors' Council of the Vivekananda College are Administrative Organs of their respective parent bodies.

4 The Indian Taxation Enquiry Commission of 1956 was a Temporary Organ of the Government of India.

6 The Privileges Committee of the Lok Sabha is an Organ of the Second Remove of the Government of India.

7 The Subcommittee of the Privileges Committee, and the Advisory Committee for Secondary Education of the Ministry of Education are Organs of the Third Remove of the Government of India.

22 **Government.**—

Sense 1 Corporate body with full or limited sovereign power over a territory. It has generally functions of execution, legislation, justice, and administration. Other functions, such as defence, taxation, regulation of commerce, public transport, communication etc, will vary with the degree of limitation in the sovereign power.

Sense 2 Local Authority in charge of the regulation, promotion, and/or provision of specified local public services in an area, under power delegated by the government within the territory of which its own area lies, and with a defined extent of autonomy.

Sense 3 Organ of Government in sense 1 or 2 defined above.

For example, 1 the Government of India, the Government of Madras, and the Government of the United Kingdom are Governments in sense 1.

2 The District Board of Tanjavur, the Corporation Madras, and the Panchayat Board of Sirkali are Governments in sense 2.

3 The President of India, the Parliament of India, the Supreme Court of India, the Council of Ministers of Madras, and the Council of the Corporation of Madras are Governments in sense 3.

23 **Institution.**—

Sense 1 Independent or autonomous corporate body other than a government. It may be created by a government, or constituted under a statute, or formed voluntarily—either formally or informally. It has or it is intended to have continued existence and functions beyond that of merely convening a conference.

Sense 2 Organ of an Institution in sense 1 defined above.

For example, the Madras Library Association is an Institution in sense 1. And the Council of the Madras Library Association is an Institution in sense 2. Instances of autonomous bodies are discussed in Part G.

24 **Conference.**—Sense 1 *Ad hoc* assembly for deliberation or formulation and expression of opinion or sentiments

1 Not convened by

11 A Government and made up solely of its own personnel or as a Constituent Assembly to form a Sovereign State, or

12 An Institution and made up solely of its members or as a Foundation Assembly to form an Institution, or

13 More than one Government jointly and confined solely to their own personnel, or

14 More than one Institution jointly and confined solely to their members;

2 Convened and conducted by

21 A number of persons and/or corporate bodies, spontaneously, to consider matters of common interest, or

22 A body with no function or existence beyond the conference convened and held by it, or

23 A body with only the convening and holding of conferences at intervals, as its primary function.

For example, the Indian Mathematical Conference of 1957 is a Conference in sense 1. The Reception Committee of the Indian Mathematical Conference of 1957 is a Conference is sense 2.

241 **Organ Conference.**—Any category of Assembly excluded from the definition of a Conference in Sec FC4. It is an Organ of the Corporate body (ies) convening it.

3 **Author of a Work.**—

Sense 1 Person creating the work, that is, the thought and the expression constituting it.

Sense 2 Corporate body owning responsibility for a work that is, for the thought and the expression constituting it.

31 **Personal Author.**—Person as author, the responsibility for the thought and the expression constituting the work resting solely on his private capacity and not on the capacity of any office being held by him within a corporate body, nor on the capacity of that body.

For example, S R Ranganathan is the Personal Author of ed 4 of the work contained in this book, although he holds the office of President of the Madras Library Association which sponsored that edition. For, the responsibility for the thought and the expression constituting the work rests solely on him in his private capacity, and not at all on the Madras Library Association or on him in his official capacity as its President.

32 **Corporate Author.**—Corporate body as author, the responsibility for the thought and expression constituting the

work resting solely on it or any organ of it, and not on the private capacity of any person or persons forming part of or holding office in or in any other way connected with that body.

For example, 1 the Library Committee of the University of Rangoon is the Corporate Author of the *Catalogue of periodicals in the University and other libraries of Rangoon*, 1937, though it might have been actually compiled by the librarian of that University.

2 The work contained in the book entitled *Rulings of S Satyamurti, the Mayor of Madras*, 1940, does not have Satyamurti as its personal author. But it is of Corporate Authorship. The Author is the Mayor of Madras. As the Mayor of Madras is elected only for a period of one year, it had been necessary to add the name of Satyamurti also, not as name of the personal author, but as a means of individualising the particular Mayor who gave the Rulings. The Rulings were given not in his private capacity, but only in the capacity of Mayoral Office..

3 The work contained in the book *Despatch including a report as to irrigation projects on the Upper Nile*, 1901, by the Agent and Consul-General of Great Britain in Cairo is of Corporate Authorship and not of personal authorship. For the *Despatch* was written by the gentleman working as the Agent of the Government of Great Britain in Cairo not in his private capacity but in his corporate capacity as an organ of the Government of Great Britain.

4 **Compiler.**—Author, personal or corporate, making up a work by collecting information from various sources and arranging them in a particular way.

For example, the so called compiler of the *Concordance to the Bible*, or of the *Concordance to Keats*, or of a Directory, or of a Who's Who, or of any other kind of serial is in reality its Author.

5 **Joint Authors.**— Two or more authors, personal or corporate, sharing responsibility for the thought and expression constituting the work, the portion for which each is separately responsible not being either specified or separable.

For example, the responsibility for the thought and expression constituting the work contained in the book *Library manual*, 1951, by S R Ranganathan and K M Sivaraman is shared by the two authors. The portion for which each is separately responsible is neither specified in the work nor is it separable. Therefore this work is of Joint Authorship.

6 **Pseudonymous Author.**—An author assuming a false or fictitious name or any other specification different from the real

name. A pseudonym may also be given by others to an author or it may even get started in a casual way, either in his own time or in later times.

The motive for the suppression of the real name may be various—diffidence; sense of shame; fear of consequences; freakishness; joking, mystifying, or hoaxing instinct; and so on. I myself used the pseudonym 'Arithmeticus' in an article to the *Educational review* of Madras in 1922, and the pseudonym 'Libra', made up of the first five letters of the word 'Librarian', in articles contributed in 1931 to the *Hindu*, a daily of Madras, as it was found expedient not to disclose my identity. While the psychology of such motives may be of interest for its own sake, it is not directly relevant to cataloguing. But the various degrees, to which the element of fiction and concealment is introduced in the pseudonym assumed or given, are not without interest.

1 At one extreme, there is the adoption or the gift of what appears like a regular name, though different from the real name. George Eliot is an example. The author's real name might have been forgotten and he may be remembered by some other name.

2 Secondly, the words constituting the real name may be permuted. For example, Arthur Travers Crawford used the pseudonym T C Arthur.

3 Thirdly, the letters in the essential word in the real name or in all or some of its words may be permuted. For example, Anne Lake wrote under the pseudonym Ekalenna. While such anagrams occur at all times, there appear to be some periods in the history of each community when the anagrammatic mood is in an epidemic phase.

4 Fourthly, the anagram may involve the omission of some of the letters.

5 Fifthly, the real name may be disfigured by the interpolation of letters or words among the legitimate letters and words.

6 Sixthly, the real name may be replaced by the initial letter of its words, or their end-letters, or by any combination of these, with or without intervening punctuation marks. When the initial letters are strung together, they are said to form Initionym. For example, Edward Hamilton Aitken adopted the initionym Eha. Pronounceable initionyms are nowadays frequently used to denote corporate bodies. Here are a few examples:

Uno=United Nations Organisation.
Unesco=United Nations Educational Scientific and Cultural Organisation.
Ifla=International Federation of Library Associations.
Afla=Asian Federation of Library Associations.
Insdoc=Indian National Scientific Documentation Centre.
Scapa=Society for Checking the Abuses of Public Advertising.
Socony=Standard Oil Company of New York.

7 Seventhly, a single pseudonym may be used to represent two or more joint authors; and conversely, a double pseudonym may be used to represent

a single author, producing the illusion of joint authorship. For example, the two joint authors I Zangwill and L Cowen used the pseudonym 'J Freeman Bell'.

8 Eighthly, the same pseudonym may be used by different authors; and conversely, the same author may assume different pseudonyms for different works of his. Voltaire is reported to have used 137 pseudonyms, and Franklin 57 pseudonyms.

9 Ninthly, the real name may be replaced by the name of place of birth, place of residence, nationality, or profession; academic or titular distinctions; real or assumed relationship; horoscopic peculiarities; personal peculiarities; political leanings; authorship of previous publications; pictures or diagrams; and in every other conceivable way.

61 Unmasking of Pseudonyms

The unmasking of fictitious names and anonymity is a recognised field for bibliographical and cultural scholarship.

Germany appears to have been one of the first countries to devote attention to this problem. Two results are:

1 Placcii (Vincentii). Theatrum anonymorum et pseudonymorum. 1708.

2 Mylius (Johenn Christoph). Bibliotheca anonymorum et pseudonymorum detectorum. 2 V. 1740.

France soon followed with

1 Barbier (Antoine Alexandre). Dictionnaire des ouvrages anonymes et pseudonymes. 4 V. 1806

2 Querard (Joseph Marie) Les supercheries litteraires devoilees. 7 V.

Italy was later provided with

1 Melzi (Gaetano). Dizionario di opere anonime e pseudonime di scrittori italiani. 3 V. 1848

The **Scandinavian** countries own jointly

1 Collin (E). Anonymer og pseudonymer. 1869.

The **Netherlands** has been supplied by

1 Doorninck (Jan Izaac van). Vermonde en naamlooze schrijvers opgespoord op het gebiet. 2 V. 1883

The **Anglo-Saxon** countries are armed with the following publications:

1 Halkett (Samuel) and Laing (John). Dictionary of anonymous and pseudonymous English literature. 7 V. 1926-32.

2 Stonehill (Charles A) etc. Anonyma and pseudonyma. 4 V. 1926.

3 Taylor (Archer) and Mosher (Frederic J). Bibliographical history of anonyma and pseudonyma. 1951.

The **Indian languages** are yet to be provided with such bibliographical tools.

7 Anonymous Work.—Work of unknown authorship either personal or corporate.

Many of the sacred books are anonymous. Some of the classics of old are also anonymous. A few pedestrian books also occasionally come out anonymously. In the German library practice, a work of corporate authorship also is treated as an anonymous work.

CHAPTER FD

COLLABORATOR AND SPONSOR

1 **Collaborator.**—Person or corporate body associated with a work and/or its author or authors in a secondary capacity not amounting to authorship—for example, director, guide, assistant, commentator, illustrator, engraver, translator, reviser, editor, reporter, writer of introduction or foreword, epitomiser, adapter, libratist, writer of the words in a musical composition, writer of the words in a pictorial book.

For example, in the work contained in the book *Manual of chemical technology* (1904) by Rudolf Von Wagner, it is stated that the work was revised by Ferdinand Fischer, that it was translated from the German edition 13 by William Crookes, and that it was also edited by the same Crookes. We therefore say that Fischer and Crookes are collaborators associated with the work contained in the book in secondary capacities not amounting to authorship.

2 **Sponsor.**—Person or corporate body with whose good will, authority, or finance or under whose auspices a work is published, though the responsibility for the thought and the expression constituting the work does not at all rest with the said person or corporate body, but rests solely on the author of the work as a whole or on the respective authors of the different contributions in the work.

A sponsor is not author. But a periodical publication is often traced by a reader through the name of its sponsor. This tradition is more than a century old. Cataloguing practice has to strive hard to get away from the tradition of treating the sponsor as if he were the author.

CHAPTER FE

DOCUMENT

1 **Embodied Thought.**—Record of work on paper or other material, fit for physical handling, transport across space, and preservation through time.

This book itself is Embodied Thought. It is recorded on paper by the process of printing. The record is bound in stiff board in order to make it fit for physical handling. Because it is so embodied, it is possible to send it to any part of the world. If it be not embodied as a record, it will soon be forgotten; and the work embodied in it cannot be preserved through time accurately, or preserved at all. The work known as the *Vedas* was not recorded in a document, for a long, long time. It could therefore be communicated to others in those far off days only by word of mouth. It could not therefore be known all through the world in those days, as it is today after being embodied in a document. Again it has to be handed down from generation to generation only through word of mouth. This had necessarily led to hundreds of versions of the same work. So it was with the ancient epic poems the *Ramayana* and the *Iliad*.

Such ancient works were first recorded on materials such as leaves, silk cloth, and stones. Later they came to be recorded on other materials and finally on paper. But even then, enough copies could not be produced economically for being sent out to many distant places. The invention of printing from movable metallic types and the continuous improvement of it have led to the overcoming of all such difficulties.

2 **Document.**—Embodied thought.

This term is introduced for brevity. It was brought into use a few decades ago to emphasise embodied micro thought. It is now extended in use to include any embodied thought, micro or macro.

3 **Macro Document.**—Usually a work expressing macro thought is embodied into a document all by itself. Such a document may be called Macro Document.

4 **Micro Document.**—Usually a work expressing micro thought is not embodied into a document all by itself. Several micro documents are embodied in one and the same document.

Then we say that the several Micro Documents are clubbed together in a single macro document.

5 **Host Document.**—A macro document is called the Host Document for each of the micro documents embodied in it.

For example, a periodical is a macro document. Each article in it is a micro document. The periodical is the Host Document for each of the articles contained in it. So also, a book is the Host Document for each of its chapters and sections, which may be looked upon as micro documents.

6 **Locus.**—The Host Document in which a Micro Document occurs and its exact position within it.

For example, the Locus of the micro document *Indian national bibliography* by me is the *Annals of library science*. 4; 1957; 65-72—that is pages 65 to 72 of volume 4, of the said periodical, which was published in 1957.

7 **Volume.**—Several leaves of paper or other material used for recording, either the whole or a part of a work, fastened together so as to be opened at any desired place.

A volume is an independent physical unit.

8 **Thought-Content.**—Expressed thought embodied within a document or a volume of it.

CHAPTER FF

KINDS OF DOCUMENTS

1 **Conventional Document of Kind 1.**—Document with paper as basic material and with the work recorded on it in the phonetic symbols forming the script of an articulate natural or artificial language, with or without illustrations used as a help in the communication of the thought-content. The recording is done by printing, or by some near-printing process; or the record is a reproduction of the above or of the original manuscript of it by photographic, chemical, or any other so-called mechanical process, to a size more or less the same as that of the original.

For brevity, this may be denoted by the term **Printed Book**, using it in a general sense.

The conventional book, the periodical publication, and a fascimile reproduction of either are common examples. This book is a Conventional Document of Kind 1. The quarterly *Annals of library science* is also so. A facsmile copy of this book made by photographic process will also be a Conventional Document of Kind 1.

11 **Periodical Publication.**—Conventional Document of Kind 1 with the following attributes:

1 A volume, or a small group of volumes of it, is intended to be published or completed normally once in a year (or at other regular intervals), though irregularity in interval is not ruled out;

2 Each successive volume, or periodical group of volumes, is usually distinguished by the year of publication and/or by a number belonging to a system of simple or complex ordinal number. Such a number is usually called a **Volume Number.**

3 The intention had been to continue the publication of the volumes for ever, though not actually carried out; and

4 The intention had been to continue the same title in all the volumes, though not actually carried out.

The term **Periodical Publication** is also used to denote any single volume of a Periodical Publication as defined above.

111 **Periodical.**—Periodical publication of which each volume is made up of distinct and independent contributions, not forming a continuous exposition, normally by two or more personal authors and normally the specific subjects and the authors of the contributions in successive volumes also being, in general, different, but all the subjects falling within one and the same region of knowledge, contemplated to be brought within its purview. It is not usually released complete as a volume but only in fascicules or numbers, as they are called. It essentially expounds knowledge and not repeat the same kind of information, usually in the same pattern, in each of its volumes just bringing the information up-to-date from volume to volume.

The term **Periodical** is also used to denote any single volume of a periodical as defined above.

Examples:

1 Annals of library science.
2 Proceedings, Royal Society of London.
3 Zeitschrift, Deutschen Morgenlandischen Gesellschaft.

112 **Serial.**—Periodical publication of which each volume or each periodical group of volumes embodies more or less the same kind of information, usually in the same pattern, mainly relating to its year (or other period) of coverage. It is usually released complete as a volume. It is not made of diverse contributions each forming a continuous exposition of knowledge.

The term **Serial** is also used to denote any single volume of a serial as defined above.

Examples:

1 Annual report of the Director of Agriculture, Madras.
2 Madras telephone directory.
3 Statesman's year-book.
4 Who's who in America.
5 Year-book of the Carnegie Institution of Washington.

21 **Indexing Periodical.**—A periodical giving a bare catalogue of articles bearing on a stated subject and appearing in the current fascicules of periodicals. It may also include bare entries of books currently published.

Examples:

1 Agricultural index.
2 Technical index.
3 Law index.

22 **Abstracting Periodical.**—A periodical giving a catalogue of articles bearing on a stated subject and appearing in the current fascicules of periodicals, each entry being provided with an abstract of the article described by it. It may also include annotated entries of books currently published.

Examples:

1 Biological abstracts.
2 Library science abstracts.
3 Science abstracts: Electrical engineering.

23 **Reviewing Periodical.**—A periodical giving in narrative form an account of the contributions bearing on a stated subject and appearing in the fascicules and the books published during its period of coverage.

Examples:

1 Year's work in librarianship.
2 Reports on progress in physics.
3 Annual review of biochemistry.

3 **Book.**—Conventional Document of Kind 1, other than periodical publication—that is, it has been completed or has been intended to be completed in a finite number of volumes. It is generally in one volume. Some are in many volumes.

The above definition really connotes what is commonly understood by the term Book. This book, for example, is a "Book" according to the above definition.

31 **Multi-Volumed Book.**—Book in two or more volumes giving a continuous exposition, and, for this or for any other reason in the distribution of thought among the volumes, compelling the treatment of all the volumes as an inseparable set, *i e* as if they together formed a single volume.

Examples:

1 The book *Principles of economics* of Frank William Taus published in two volumes in 1920.

2 The book *Letters* of Sir Walter Scott, edited by H J C Grierson and published from 1932 onwards in several volumes.

3 The book *Dictionary of the inorganic compounds* edited by M K Hoffmann and published in 1921 in four volumes. This book is said to be in three volumes. But the first volume consists of two parts published as independent volumes.

4 **Composite Book.**—Book with two or more contributions, each with its own title, not forming a continuous exposition and often, though not necessarily, by different authors.

41 **Ordinary Composite Book.**—Composite book provided with a single, generic title to denote all the contributions collectively.

Anthology of several authors, christomathy, hymn-book, prayer-book, song-book, symposium, Festschrift and similar compilations come under this category.

Examples:

1 The book *Happy baby*, published in 1926. It has contributions from L Emmett Holt, Ralph Lobenstine, Harvey J Burkhart, and Henry L K Shaw.

2 The book *University of Saint Andrews. Five-hundredth anniversary: Memorial volume of scientific papers*, published in 1911. This contains contributions by several authors.

3 *Science and religion, a symposium*, published in 1931.

42 **Artificial Composite Book.**—Composite book without a generic title to denote all the contributions collectively.

An Artificial Composite Book may be created by the publisher by issuing two or more different books within one and the same cover but without a common title-page. It may also be created by a library by binding several books together into a single volume.

5 **Contribution.**—Work forming a part of a composite book, or a periodical, or a serial.

51 **Article.**—Contribution in a periodical.

52 **Contributor.**—Author of a contribution.

6 **Simple Book.**—Book which is not composite, that is which embodies work by a single author or by joint authors. It may also be anonymous.

This book is a Simple Book.

7 **Incunabula.**—A book printed within a few decades of the invention of modern printing—say in the fifteenth century.

8 **Restricted field of this Code.**—This code confines itself to the cataloguing of convenitional books and periodical publications mentioned in Sec FF1 to FF 6 only. This restricts its field to modern books and periodicals without any special features of physical bibliography needing description. In particular, it does not provide Rules for Descriptive Cataloguing or for the Cataloguing of Incunabula. These are of interest only to historical bibliographers and not to ordinary readers. A Supplementary Code is necessary for each of these excluded categories.

91 **Conventional Document of Kind 2.**—Document similar to Conventional Document of Kind 1 but the recording being in a non-conventional script, such as braille, stenograph, music in notatoin, and cipher.

92 **Conventional Document of Kind 3.**—Document similar to Conventional Document of Kind 1, except that the graphic medium is not phonetic symbols but essentially drawings, pictures, maps, and similar ones.

93 **Conventional Document of Kind 4.**—Document similar to Conventional Document of Kind 1, but the recording being done by handwriting. This is usually called Manuscript.

931 **Non-Conventional Manuscript.**—Manuscript using material other than paper.

94 **Non-Conventional Document of Kind 1.**—Photograph i e, chemical, or any other so called mechanical reproduction of any Kind of Conventional Document on an extremely reduced scale needing the use of special reading apparatus.

Micro card, micro film, micro filmstrip and kindred materials are examples. One micro card of size 125×75 mm may contain the reproduction of a hundred pages of a normal book.

95 **Reprograph.**—Non-conventional document of kind 1 or a photographic, chemical, or any other so-called mechanical reproductions of any kind of conventional document to a size more or less the same as that of the original.

96 **Non-Conventional Document of Kind 2.**—Document made of sound-record, whether of articulate sound or of music. This is called Audio Document.

961 **Speaking Book.**—Printed book with a companion-attachment of the sound-record of the words in it.

97 **Non-Conventional Document of Kind 3.**—Document made of cinema reels. This is called **Visual Document.**

98 **Non-Conventional Document of Kind 4.**—Document made of talkie reels. This is called **Audio-Visual Document.**

991 **Non-Conventional Document of Kind 5.**—Document made of record of natural or social phenomena made directly by an instrument, without being passed through human mind and without being woven into thought created and expressed by human mind. This may be called **Instrument-Record of Phenomena.**

An account of all these kinds of documents, and particularly of the new kind called Instrument-Record of Phenomena will be found in a paper entitled *Document: Conventional and non-conventional* [RD 2].

Supplementary Catalogue Codes are necessary for cataloguing each of the varieties described in Sec FF7 and Sec FF91 to FF991 respectively. The Rules in this Code form only the basic Rules for such documents.

CHAPTER FG

PRELIMINARY PAGES

1 **Title-Page.**—Page, of a document or a volume of it, containing its Title-Statement. Usually, it also contains the Author-Statement, the Collaborator-Statement, and the Imprint. It also indicates the Edition in many cases.

Page 3 of this book is its Title-Page.

2 **Over-Flow of Title-Page.**—Page (s) immediately succeeding or preceding the title-page of a document or a volume of it and containing part of the information usually given on the title-page and/or some of the statements mentioned in Sec FL4, FL7 and FL81, and information about other additional factors such as the Series to which the document may belong.

Pages 1, 2 and 4 form the Over-Flow of the Title-page of this book.

21 In the case of a Composite Book, Over-Flow of Title-Page is deemed to include every page in which the names (s) of the author (s) and collaborators and the title of any of the contributions or constituent works, as the case may be, are found.

3 **Title-Leaf.**—The leaf of which the recto is the Title-Page. In this book the verso of the title-leaf contains the Entry Statement for Author, the Edition-Statement, and the Call Number which is virtually the Subject-Statement.

4 **Half-Title Page.**—The recto of the leaf usually preceding the title-leaf and containing the half-title of the document.

Page 1 of this book is its Half-Title Page.

5 **Half-Title Leaf.**—The leaf of which the recto is the Half-Title Page.

CHAPTER FH

SERIES

1 **Series.**—A set of books, not constituting a multi-volumed book, and with the following attributes:

1 The books are issued, normally successively by one publisher or by one sponsoring body or person, usually in a uniform style, and having some similarity of subject or standard or purpose;

2 Each book has normally a distinct and independent title and/or other features of its own;

3 Each book has normally a different author;

4 There is a collective name to denote the set, called the **Name of the Series** and given in all or at least in one of the books of the set; and

5 Each book is or can be assigned a distinct number, called the **Serial Number.** It may belong to a system of simple or complex ordinal numbers such as 1, 2, 3, etc; 3.1, 3.2, 3.3, etc; or 1957. 1, 1957.2, 1957.3, etc.

For example, this book belongs to the Ranganathan Series in Library Science. Its serial number is 2. Other examples of Series are:

1 Broadway oriental library.
2 Cambridge tracts in mathematics and physics.
3 Library of philosophy.
4 Modern world series.
5 University of Delhi, library science series.

There is a list of such publishers' series, current in Great Britain, in the earlier pages of the *English catalogue* of any year.

2 **Pseudo-Series of Kind 1.**—A set of books not constituting a multi-volumed book and with the following attributes:

1 All the books are of common authorship;

2 All the books belong to the same edition in sense 2;

3 The title of each book has a distinctive part in addition to the name of the edition in sense 2;

4 Each book is or can be assigned a **Serial Number** belonging to a system of simple or complex ordinal numbers; and

5 The name of the author taken along with the name of the edition in sense 2 is suitable to be used as if it were the Name of a Series.

Example:

Consider the book, whose spine has the following words: Works of Leo Tolstoy / Childhood, Boyhood and Youth / Centenary Edition / 3 / 1928.

It belongs to the Pseudo-series of Kind 1. It may be named Tolstoy (Leo). Centenary ed.

3 **Pseudo-Series of Kind 2.**—A set of books, not constituting a multi-volumed book and with the following attributes:

1 All the books are of common authorship;

2 The titles of the various books have a common part capable of being used as their common generic title;

3 The title of each book has a distinctive part of its own in addition to the generic part;

4 Each book is or can be assigned a **Serial Number** belonging to a system of simple or complex ordinal numbers; and

5 The name of the author taken along with the generic title is suitable to be used as if it were the Name of a Series.

Example:

Consider the book whose title-page reads as follows: E Grimsehl / Text-book of physics / Edited by R Tomaschek / Volume 4 Optics.../ Translated ... by L A Woodward / 1933. It belongs to the Pseudo-series of Kind 2.

It may be named "Grimsehl (E): Text-book of physics ed by R Tomaschek".

4 **Pseudo-Series of Kind 3.**—A set of books not constituting a multi-volumed book and with the following attributes:

1 All the books are not of a common authorship;

2 The titles of the various books have a common part capable of being used as a common generic title;

3 The title of each book has a distinctive part of its own in addition to the generic part;

4 Each book is or can be assigned a Serial Number belonging to a system of simple or complex ordinal numbers; and

5 The generic title is suitable to be used as if it were the Name of a Series.

Example:

The volumes edited by Charles Oman under the generic title "History of England".

CHAPTER FJ

RELATED DOCUMENTS

1 **Related Books.**—A set of books whose Main Entries will not always file consecutively, but which all the same call for their being linked up by the catalogue on account of their being related to one another for some important reasons.

Five kinds of Related Books have so far been isolated. These are described in succeeding Rules. In a sense, the books belonging to a series may also be considered as forming a kind of Related Books. But these usually contain in themselves all the necessary information about the Series unlike the other kinds given in this chapter. Therefore, "Series" has been treated in a separate chapter—Chap FH.

2 **Extract.**—A document which embodies a portion of another document.

Examples:

1 The book *Library science and scientific method* is an Extract from the book *Five laws of library science*, ed 2, 1957.

2 The book *Libraries in the District of Columbia* (1921) by W I Swanton is an extract from *Special libraries*. 12; 1921.

3 **Separate.**—A portion of a document—usually, but not necessarily, a periodical publication—issued in the same format as the original, whether printed from the types or plates of the original, or reset.

4 The word **Reprint** is loosely used to denote either

1 A separate; or

2 A reproduction of an edition of a work without alteration.

5 **Merger Book.**—A book formed by the merging of two or more books.

Examples:

1 The book "Theory of economic dynamics, an essay on cyclical and long-range changes in capitalistic economy" (1953) by M Kalaeck contains the note "Published in lieu of the second editions of:

'Essays in the theory of economic fluctuations'; and
'Studies in economic dynamics.'"

2 The book "Economics and economic policy of dual societies as exemplified by Indonesia" (1953) by J H Boek contains the note "Revised and enlarged version of the author's two earlier studies published separately under the titles:
'Structure of the Netherlands Indian economy' (1942); and
'Solutions of the Netherlands Indies economy' (1946)".

6 Other Kinds of Related Books.—

Examples:

1 The books "Short history of the British Empire" (1934) by Anderson and Marsdon; and "Teacher's hand-book to Anderson and Marsdon's Short history of the British Empire" (1955).

2 The books "Elementary practical physics" (1938) by N H Black Davis; and "Laboratory experiment in elementary physics: To accompany Black and Davis's "Elementary practical physics" (1938) by N H Black.

CHAPTER FK

EDITION

1 **Edition in Sense 1.**—One of the different printings or reproductions of a document with or without slight change in thought-content, each being distinguished form the others, either numerically or by some other equivalent term such as "New", "Revised", and "Enlarged".

2 **Edition in Sense 2.**—One of the different forms in which one and the same work is published, each form having a distinctive name almost amounting to a proper noun—such as "Arden Edition", "Variorum Edition", "Memorial Edition", and "Loeb Classics".

An edition in sense 2 forms Pseudo-Series of Kind 1. (*See* Sec FH2).

3 Each book in a series or a pseudo-series may be brought out in seccessive Editions of Kind 1, independently of one another.

Examples:

1 This book in the Ranganathan Series in Library Science is in edition 5, whereas the book *Colon classification* in the same series is now in edition 6.

2 The Variorum Editions of the different plays of Shakespeare are now in different editions of kind 1. Some are in edition 1; some are in edition 2; and so on.

3 The same usually happens also in respect of pseudo-series of all kinds.

Sections FK1 and FK2 show that the term edition is used in two senses. When it is used in sense 2, the application of sense 1 also becomes possible. It will be a convenience if this homonym is resolved and different terms are used to denote the two different senses.

Even in respect of sense 1, the term edition is not used alike by all the publishers. Some call a mere reprint also a new edition and give it a new number. At the other extreme some give the new number to the edition only if there is considerable change introduced. Between these two extremes there are all kinds of usages depending upon the degree of change introduced. It is the continuity of the degree of changes between the editions that makes it difficult to arrive at a definite standard for the denotation of the term Edition.

CHAPTER FL

CATALOGUER'S NEEDS

1 **Format.**—A statement of the size of the leaf of a document.

2 **Collation.**—A statement of the number of volumes, pages, plates, maps, and other illustrations, of a conventional document, and an equivalent statement in the case of a non-conventional document.

A statement of Format and Collation is essential in a catalogue of incunabula and of documents of all kinds other than the conventional documents of kinds 1 to 3. It is necessary also in a National Bibliography, State Bibliography, and other bibliographies even of modern conventional books and periodicals. But it is not necessary in a library catalogue of modern conventional books and periodicals in a Service-Library of the normal kind.

3 **Imprint.**—Record, in a document or a volume of it, of the name(s) of its publisher (s), of the name (s) of the place (s) of its publication, and of the year of its publication.

4 **Edition-Statement.**—Record, in a document or a volume of it, of the number of each of the successive editions of it or of a distinctive edition of it with a proper name, along with the year of publication of each.

'Edition' and 'Distinctive edition' are defined in Chap FK. Page 4 of this book gives the Edition-Statement.

5 **Title-Statement.**—Record, in a document or a volume of it, of the title of the work embodied in it.

6 **Author-Statement.**—Record, in a document or a volume of it, of the name(s) of the author(s) of the work embodied in it.

Page 3 of this book contains the Title-Statement as well as the Author-Statement of the work embodied in it.

7 **Entry Statement for Author.**—Record, in a document or a volume of it, of the year of birth (and also the year of death in the case of a deceased person), and of the alternative name(s),

if any, of each author of the work embodied in it, and in addition an indication of the Entry Element and the Secondary Element in each name.

'Entry element' and 'Secondary element' are defined in Sec FN.

It has not yet become a common practice to give the Entry Statement for Author in documents.

71 Homonym

But cataloguers find that the years of an author are the sharp elements to *resolve* homonyms in the names of authors. On account of universal literacy and cheap methods of printing, several authors with the same name are now producing works which are embodied into documents. It becomes difficult to distinguish the different authors with the same name. For some years, certain libraries have been endeavouring to ascertain the years of birth of the authors, in order to use them for resolving homonyms. The Library of Congress of U S A has been doing this work for all authors in the world, whose works it gets. But the response is not always satisfactory. In 1946 I attempted to get the years of birth of several authors whose names were not found in *Who is who*. Appeal through newspapers brought little information. Addresses of many authors could not be found out. Even when found out, requests did not elicit replies.

72 Alternative Name

Again, cataloguers need help from Entry Statement for Author to link up the different alternative names including pseudonyms, which an author might have used in different works of his. If this help is not given by each of the documents embodying the several works in respect of each of the earlier documents, the cataloguer has to make inquiries to find them out. This would involve waste of cataloguing time. This waste will occur in all the hundreds of libraries acquiring documents, by the same author. Thus the total wastage involved will be huge in any community. The magnitude of this wastage is not easily realised. For, it is scattered into many libraries and is thus hidden. Such a wastage is easily avoided by each document giving the Entry Statement for Author.

73 Choice of Entry Element

Thirdly, a new phenomenon is gaining in its dimensions in our own days. Firstly, authors are appearing in many more countries than in the past. Secondly, books of any one country are acquired in many other countries far more than in the past. These factors result from practically every country coming out of its cultural exhaustion and throwing forth many creative citizens on the one side, and the great increase in international exchange of thought and documents on the other. When the books of other countries come into a country, they bring with them new problems in cataloguing.

These new problems are greatest in determining the Entry Element and the Secondary Element in the name of an author. A modern name-of-person is, in most cases, muiti-worded. Three words may be taken as the average in a name-of-person. All the words do not have equal potency in individualising the name. The cataloguer has therefore to find out the most potent word or word-group and use the same as the Entry Element in the heading of the entry. But different cultural groups often put the most potent elements in a name, as it is in public usage, in different positions in the name. For example, the Chinese put it at the beginning of a name. The British put it at the end. In some cultural groups, the potent Element consists of two words, or three words of which one is a conjunction. In the names in some cultural groups, the potent word carries with it the preceding conjunction or preposition, and the Entry Element has to include it. In some cultural groups, a name-of-person has honorific and other removable words. Even within a single culture such as that of India, each linguistic subgroup of a cultural group follows different practices in this matter. It is not easy for a cataloguer born in one cultural group to spot out such removable words in the name of person of every other cultural group. The situation is best met by the author of a document and its publisher indicating the Entry Element and the Secondary Element in the name of the author, in the Entry Statement for Author to be recorded in the document itself in a standard place.

74 Enunciation of the Problem

The third of the above problems formed the subject of an appeal in my *Theory of library catalogue* [RT11]. The appeal read as follows:

"Library Associations throughout the world should put their heads together and arrive at an agreed set of rules for the treatment of names-of-persons. Such an international code is very necessary now-a-days when the libraries of almost every country have books by authors belonging to almost every one of the others."

It is now realised that the production of such an international code is not practicable and simple as each book giving the necessary information on the back of its own title page.

75 Problem Taken to Unesco

The following calendar of events shows how the problem was taken by me to the level of Unesco.

1938 Appeal made in my *Theory of library catalogue.*

Nov 1949 Unesco's Conference in Paris on the Improvement of Bibliographical Services.

14 Mar 1951 The following resolution was tabled by me for the Second Conference in Delhi of the Indian National Commission for Unesco:

"That the following items be recommended for inclusion in the agenda for the proposed Conference

	of National Commissions to be held at Bangkok in 1951: "That an Asian Committee be set up to produce an authoritative set of rules for the rendering of Asian Names in bibliographical entries."
25 Mar 1951	Approval of the above resolution by the Delhi Conference, on being supported by Torres-Bodet, the Director General of Unesco, who was present at the Conference.
13-14 May 1951	Approval of the above resolutions by: 1 the First Conference of Asian Librarians held at Indore; and 2 the Ninth All India Library Conference held at Indore.
14 Sept 1951	The document Unesco/Reg Conf II/16 contained the remark that the proposed Project would be in keeping with the Unesco's programme.
25 Nov 1951	Meeting of the Head of the Libraries Division of Unesco with a group of Indian librarians in Delhi and formulation of the contents and the stages of the Project.
26 Nov to 10 Dec 1951	Passing of the following resolution by the Second Regional Conference of Unesco National Commissions in South Asia and South Pacific, held at Bangkok; "(4) That consideration should be given to the proposals from the Indian Library Association to undertake the tasks outlined in document, Unesco/Reg Conf II/16 as follows: (*a*) Establishment of a committee for framing standard rules for the rendering of Asian names in bibliographical and catalogue entries."
6 Jan 1952	Circulation of my draft Working Paper on the Project to all the probable participating countries, soliciting opinion.
Mar 1952	Receipt of general approval from several countries and communication of the same to Unesco.
21-25 Apr 1952	Approval of the Project by Unesco's Provisional International Committee on Bibliography and Documentation held in Paris, and its assignment to India.
12 May 1952	Assignment of the Project to me by the Indian Library Association.
May-July 1952	Field-work and Group-Meetings in the regions of the following Languages: Marathi, Kannada, Tamil, Malayalam, and Telugu.
31 July 1952	Finalising the Contract on the Project.

August 1952	Circulation of the provisional findings of the Group-Conferences of May to July to other linguistic regions in India and the other participating countries.
Sep 1952	Field-work and Group-Meeting in Gujarathi linguistic region and the testing and the enlargement of the findings.
Dec 1952	Field-work and Group-Meeting in Bengali linguistic region.
Dec 1952	Discussion in Calcutta with some nationals of Pakistan, Indonesia, Malaya, and Siam, about the structure etc, of the names in the respective languages.
Jan 1953	Field-work and Group-Meetings in Hindi and Punjabi areas.
Mar 1953	Circulation to participating countries of a pamphlet embodying the findings arrived at up to March 1953.
20-23 Apr 1953	Presentation of interim report to the First Session of Unesco's International Advisory Committee on Bibliography, held in Paris.
21 May 1953	Circular letter to all National and Regional Rapporteurs and to other helpers in all participating countries, furnishing a copy of the latest findings and asking for the final report to be sent within three months—that is by the end of August 1953.
1-4 June 1953	Meetings with Muslim scholars in Hyderabad.
July 1953	Receipt of hints from Siam, Indo-China, and Indonesia.
29 August 1953	Reminders sent to all participating countries and regions.
1-14 Sept 1953	Meetings with Muslim authors and scholars in Delhi.
22-29 Sept 1953	Field-work and Group-Meetings in Sinhalese region in Ceylon.
8 Oct 1953	Receipt of report from Viet Nam.
11 Oct 1953	Discussion of the draft rules for Indian names at a meeting of the Expert Committee for Documentation (=EC 2) of the Indian Standards Institution.
12-18 Oct 1953	Correspondence with Pakistan on the draft rules for Muslim names.
31 Oct 1953	Despatch of the final report to Unesco, Paris.

76 General Findings in the Unesco Project

Though there is demand for the above Report of mine to Unesco on the *Rendering of South Asian names*, Unesco has not yet published that report. One year was spent in getting opinions from France, Great Britain, and the United States of America. The French report gave general approval. The British report had no relevant substance in it. The American report was a long one. It largely dealt with style and terminology. It also contained a few useful suggestions. My remarks on the three reports were sent to Unesco promptly from Zurich in October 1954. But nothing more has been heard of the further action intended to be taken by Unesco on this matter of great importance to the library profession.

It is worth mentioning here that the report mentioned the following general findings in the sections 72 and 81 of its annexure:

"72 It is impossible to make all the cultural groups of the world to conform to a single efficient standard in Name-Formation. But it is possible to agree upon a single efficient standard for printing the name on the title-page. This will easily guide readers in changing over from Title-Page-Name to Entry-Name and vice-versa.

"81 Laying down of a standard for Title-Page-Name by all concerned including Unesco, Iso, Ifla, Fid and the corresponding bodies in the several countries, (along lines suggested below or in alternative ways).

1 The Entry Word or Entry Word-Group, as the case may be, should be printed in Black Face.
2 The Honorific Words, to be omitted in the Entry Name, should not be printed on the Title-page. If printed, they should be in Roman Cap and lower case, preferably in different lines and in a font of smaller size.
3 Any titular word, which should be included among the Additional Words following the Entry Word (or Entry Word Group) should be printed in italics.
4 Pseudonym should be separated from real name and printed in a distinctive style in a separate block.
5 Compound Family Names and Compound Individual Names should be hyphenated if the practice of the language does not admit of their being written as one word or if the author habitually separates them."

77 Indian Standard

By the end of 1954, it was possible to guess that there was some reluctance in some quarters in Unesco either to give wide publicity to my Report or to take any further positive action on it. This might have been partly due to the racial discrimination which is slow to die out. I felt, however, that the hard work put into it for two years should not be totally wasted. Therefore I took action at the national level in India, as the Chairman of the Expert Committee for Documentation (=EC 2) of the Indian Standards Institution. I requested that Committee to take action on the General Findings in my Unesco Report, quoted in the preceding Section. It really went up to the Committee as a general proposal to establish Standards for the Preliminary Pages of a book. The most difficult of these Standards was the one relating to the Entry Statement for Author. The Committee co-opted representatives of the publishing and printing trades for this purpose. It struggled long and experimented with various styles of printing the Entry Statement for Author and with various places in the preliminary pages where it could be printed. The final standard arrived at is elegance itself. According to it, the Entry Statement for Author is to be printed near the top of the back of the title-page in small type. Words in the name, which are removable while rendering the name in the heading of a catalogue entry, should be omitted. The Entry Element alone in the name should be in antique face. The other irremovable words in the name should be printed in Roman. It costs nothing extra to print it. This Indian Standard does not interfere with the creative freedom of the artist in designing the title-page. The Entry Statement for Author printed on page 4 of ed 4 of this book is in accordance with the Indian Standard. It would have given additional lines for the alternative names of the author, if he had any, and for joint authors and collaborators if there were any.

78 International Standard

In the Indian Standard, all the information necessary for a cataloguer in rendering the name of an author in catalogue entry will be readily found in the preliminary pages of the book itself. In other words the Canon of Ascertainability (Sec BB0) can have full sway in the matter. To make this possible, the Indian Standard in question throws a definite responsibility on the authors and the publishers. The information needed for the Entry Statement for Author is best known to the author himself. The publisher can get it from him without any difficulty when he gets the press-copy and can print it in the book as prescribed in the Indain Standard. A stitch in time saves nine, as the saying goes. If the publishers implement the Standard, it will save the cataloguing time, the cataloguing man-power, and the cost of cataloguing now involved in the search for the necessary information by several libraries. It often happens that the source of information—the author himself—is no longer available. In view of this, the Indian Standards Institution entrusted me with the task of proposing the Indian Standard for consideration and adoption by ISO/TC46—the Documentation Committee of the International Standards Organisation. I did so at the Stutgart meeting of ISO/TC46 in June 1956. All the cataloguers of the world should make common cause to get this Standard accepted at the international level, and to get it implemented universally by all the publishers in their respective countries.

8 **Collaborator-Statement.**—Record, in a document or a volume of it, of the name (s) of collaborator (s) in respect of the work embodied in it, along with an indication of the role of each.

Whenever warranted, a modern document gives the Collaborator-Statement in the page giving the Title-Statement and the Author-Statement.

81 **Entry Statement for Collaborator.**—Record, in a document or a volume of it, of the year of birth (and also of the year of death

in the case of a deceased person), and of the alternative name(s), if any, of each collaborator in respect of the work embodied in it, and, in addition, an indication of the Entry Element and the Secondary Element in each name.

Commentary on this Rule is similar to that on Sec FL 7.

91 Anonymous Document.—A document without Author-Statement.

CHAPTER FM

CATALOGUE

1 **Library Catalogue.**—List of the documents in a librarry or in a collection forming a portion of it.

For brevity we shall use in this book the term **Catalogue** in the sense of "Library Catalogue." Whenever any other kind of catalogue is meant, a suitable epithet will be added. A catalogue may be printed; or it may be in manuscript. It may be in cards, or in loose leaves. It may be in the form of a continuous book, or in the paste-down form with gaps for the interpolation of new entries in between existing entries.

2 **Union Catalogue.**—List of all the documents in two or more libraries giving the names of all the libraries where copies of each document can be found.

A Union Catalogue may cover all kinds of documents or any restricted kind of them.

Examples:

1 *Union catalogue of learned periodical publications in the libraries of South Asia*, brought out in 1953 by S R Ranganathan.

2 *Union list of serials in libraries of the United States and Canada*, ed 2, brought out in 1943 by Winiefred Gregory.

3 *List of scientific periodicals in the Bombay Presidency*, sponsored in 1931, by the Royal Institute of Science, Bombay.

3 **Documentation List.**—List of documents listed together for some purpose.

The purpose is usually to bring to the notice of reader an exhaustive or select list of documents relevant to the pursuit of his enquiry or study.

This term is used to emphasise the inclusion of micro documents. The fortnightly *Insdoc list*, published by the Indian National Scientific Documentation Centre, is an example. It is usual for a library to prepare special Documentation Lists on particular topics in anticipation or on demand by individual readers or by groups of readers.

4 **Bibliography.** The older name for Documentation List.

Originally it was mostly a list of macro documents. Now it may include also micro documents. It is differently named according to the group of persons to be served by them, or according to the agency which prepares them. These are enumerated and discussed in *Reference service and bibliography* [RZSU].

41 **Micro Bibliography.**—Bibliography exclusively or mostly of Micro documents.

42 **Macro Bibliography.**—Bibliography exclusively of Macro documents.

5 **National Bibliography in Sense 1.**—List of the books and periodicals published in a country.

It is now becoming the practice for each nation to publish its National Bibliography on a periodical basis. For example, the *British national bibliography* is being published as a weekly, with monthly, quarterly, annual, and five-yearly cumulations or versions. The *Indian national bibliography* began in 1958. In my article on the subject [R11] in the *Annals of library science*, I have outlined a scheme for producing the *Indian national bibliography* on economic and helpful lines. An account of the *British national bibliography* by A J Wells is also given in the same issue [W4].

51 **National Bibliography in Sense 2.**—List of books published in a country, and books published on the country and on the citizens of the country, and books written by any citizen of the country, in whatever country they may be published.

6 **State Bibliography.**—List of the books and periodicals published in a Constituent State of a country.

Remarks similar to those on National Bibliography are applicable to State Bibliography.

7 **Linguistic Bibliography.**—List of the books and periodicals published in a language.

Examples:

1 *Deutches Bucherii*, of the Leipzig Bibliographical Institute, is planned to cover all the books published in the German language in any country whatever.

2 The *Cumulative book index: World list of books in the English language* of H W Wilson and Co of New York.

8 The Abstracting Periodical defined in Sec FE22 and the Indexing Periodical defined in Sec FE24 are also catalogues. They do not list documents in a particular library or libraries. Like the national, state, or linguistic bibliography, they list documents which have been published.

9 This Code gives the Basic Rules needed for all kinds of catalogues and bibliographies of modern conventional books and periodicals.

They are by themselves sufficient to construct the Catalogue of a Service-Library.

This Code gives also the Supplementary Rules necessary for Union Catalogues, National Bibliographies, Abstracting Periodicals, and Indexing Periodicals.

CHAPTER FN

ENTRY

1 Entry.—Ultimate unit-record in a catalogue or a documentation list.

The examples given in the succeeding Rules are taken mostly from the examples in the later parts of this book.

11 **Specific Entry.**—Entry mentioning a specific document.

Examples:

1 2: 55N3 N58
RANGANATHAN (Shiyali Ramamrita) (1892).
Classified catalogue code with additional rules for dictionary catalogue code. Ed 4.
(Madras Library Association, publication series. 24).
(*For extract see* 2: 55 *y* (PIII) N58)
122519

2 RANGANATHAN (Shiyali Ramamrita) (1892).
Classified catalogue code. Ed 4. 2: 55N3 N58

3 MADRAS LIBRARY ASSOCIATION, PUBLICATION SERIES.
24 Ranganathan: Classified catalogue code. Ed 4. 2:55N3 N58

The above three examples of specific entry pertain to a book. It can be seen that each of these entries mention a specific book.

12 **General Entry.**—Entry not mentioning any specific document.

Examples.

1 CLASSIFIED CATALOGUE CODE.
For books in this Class and its Subdivisions see the Classified Part of the catalogue under the Class Number 2:55N3

2 CLASSIFIED CATALOGUE.
For books in this Class and its Subdivisions see the Classified Part of the catalogue under the Class Number 2:55A5

3 CATALOGUE, LIBRARY SCIENCE.
For books in this Class and its Subdivisions see the Classified Part of the catalogue under the Class Number 2:55

4 LIBRARY SCIENCE.
For books in this Class and its Subdivisions see the Classified Part of the catalogue under the Class Number 2

5 BHARAT.
See
INDIA.

2 **Consolidated Entry.**—Two or more entries consolidated into a single entry.

21 **Consolidated Specific Entry.**—Entry mentioning two or more specific documents.

Example:

1 2:55N3 N34, N45, N51
RANGANATHAN (Shiyali Ramamrita) (1892).
Classified catalogue code. Ed 1, 2, 3.
(Madras Library Association, publication series. 4, 13, 17).
63421, 87453, 111601

22 **Consolidated General Entry.**—General entry replacing two or more general entries.

Examples:

1 LIBRARY SCIENCE.
See also
BOOK SELECTION.
CATALOGUE, LIBRARY SCIENCE.
CLASSIFICATION, LIBRARY SCIENCE.

2 RANGANATHAN.
Variant Forms of the above word to be looked up.—
RANGANADAN.
RENGANATHAN.
RUNGANATHAN.

31 **Number Entry.**—Entry beginning with a Call Number or a Class Number.

Examples:

The Entries given as Example 1 under Sec FN11 and as Example 1 under FN21.

32 **Word Entry.**—Entry beginning with a Word, or in rare cases, with a symbol given in the author-statement of a document as a substitute for name of author.

Examples:

The Entries given as Examples 2-3 under Sec FN11, Examples 1-5 under Sec FN12, and Examples 1-2 under Sec FN22.

4 Varieties of Entry

41 **Main Entry.**—Specific entry giving maximum information about the whole of a document. All the other entries—specific or general—relating to the document, are normally derived from the Main Entry.

Examples:

The Entries given as Example 1 under Sec FN11 and as Example 1 under Sec FN21, and the following entry:

1 RANGANATHAN (Shiyali Ramamrita) (1892).
Classified catalogue code with additional rules for dictionary catalogue code. Ed 4.
(Madras Library Association, publication series. 24).
122519 2:55N3 N58

42 **Added Entry.**—Entry other than main entry.

43 **Specific Added Entry.**—Added entry mentioning a specific document.

In the book-form and the multiple-card-system of catalogue, it is briefer than the main entry.

In the unit-card-system of catalogue, it differs from the main entry only in its top-most line, which is filled up by hand or by typing.

It does not usually draw any information from outside the main entry or its back.

Examples:

The Entries given as Examples 2 and 3 under Sec FN11.

44 **General Added Entry.**—Added entry not mentioning any specific document.

Examples:

Entries given as Example 1-5 under Sec FN12, and as Examples 1-2 under Sec FN22.

45 **Cross Reference Index Entry.**—General added entry

referring from one word or set of words to another synonymous word or set of words.

451 **Referred-To Heading.**—The word or the word-group with which a Cross Reference Index entry, or a *See also* Subject Entry in a Dictionary Catalogue ends.

The Referred-to Heading in a cross Reference Index Entry is usually the name of a person, a geographical entity, a series, or a document, which is preferred for use in the Main Entry.

The Referred-to Heading in a *See also* Subject Entry in a Dictionary Catalogue is usually the name of a Specific Subject of a document.

452 **Referred-From Heading.**—The word or the word-group with which a Cross Reference Index Entry or a *See also* Subject Entry in a Dictionary Catalogue begins.

It is usually an alternative name of the person, the geographical entity, the series, or the document respectively, named in the Referred-to Heading. It is likely to be brought up by some readers while looking up the catalogue.

Examples:

Entry given as Example 2 under Sec FN22 and the following entry:

1 SALISBURY.

See

HOWARD (Henry)

In this example, "Howard (Henry)" is the Referred-To Heading. And "Salisbury" is the Referred-From Heading. This means that documents are entered under the name "Howard (Henry)". But the author is also known as "Salisbury". This is an alternative name for him. Some reader may look up for his books under "Salisbury". To him, the catalogue gives the direction that "Howard (Henry)" should be looked up.

The Referred-From Heading in a *See also* Subject Entry of a Dictionary Catalogue is usually the name of a subject forming an upper link in the chain having the Main Heading of the Referred-To Heading as the last link. It is likely to be brought up by some readers while looking up the Catalogue (*See* end of Chap KZD).

Example:

Entry given as Example 1 under Sec FN22.

A Cross-Reference Index Entry may draw information from outside the main entry and even from outside the document.

46 **Author Analytical.**—Specific Added Entry referring from the name of the Author and the Title of a Contribution occur-

ring in a host document, to its Locus, that is, the host document and the place of occurrence in it.

Example:

1 WEBB (Sydney) (1859).
Diseases of organised society.
Forming part of
Adams: Modern state. W N35

47 Title Analytical.—Specific Added Entry referring from the Title of a Contribution occurring in a host document, to its Locus, that is, the host document and the place of occurrence in it.

Example:

1 DISEASES OF organised society.
By Webb.
Forming part of
Adams: Modern state. W N35

5 Subject Entry

51 Subject Entry.—Entry giving information about a subject.

52 Specific Subject Entry.—Subject entry which mentions a document in which the subject is treated.

Examples:

The Entries given as Example 1 under Sec FN11, and as Example 1 under Sec FN21, and the following:

1 CLASSIFIED CATALOGUE CODE.
Ranganathan (Shiyali Ramamrita) (1892): Classified catalogue code. Ed 4. 2: 55N3 N58

53 Cross Reference Entry.—Specific subject entry which mentions a portion of a document, in which the subject is treated. It may also be called a **Subject Analytical.**

Examples:

1 BwM87
See also
BxM87 N27
Ramanujah.
Collected papers, P xi-xix

2 BIOGRAPHY, RAMANUJAN (S) (1887-1919).
Ramanujan (S): Collected works, P xi-xix. BxM87 N27

54 **Class Index Entry.**—Subject entry which refers from the name of a class to its class number.

Examples:
The Entries given as Examples 1-5 under Sec FN12, and Example 1 under Sec FN22.

55 **Chain Procedure.**—Procedure for deriving Class Index Entry from a class number, in a more or less mechanical way.

Chain Procedure is used to derive Class Index Entries in Classified Catalogue, and Specific Subject Entries, Subject Analyticals, and *See also* Subject Entries in Dictionary Catalogue.
The Rules of Chain Procedure are given in Part K.

6 Names of Entries

61 A Specific Entry is usually named after the occupant of its first section, which is called its Leading Section.

SERIAL NUMBER	NAME OF ENTRY	EXAMPLE: ENTRY GIVEN AS
1	Call Number Entry	Example 1 under Sec FN11 and Example 1 under Sec FN21
11	Specific Subject Entry	Example 1 under Sec FN11 and Example 1 under Sec FN52
2	Class Number Entry	Example 1 under Sec FN53
3	Author Entry	Example 2 under Sec FN11 and Example 1 under Sec FN41
31	Joint Author Entry	Example 2 under Sec MK211
4	Collaborator Entry	Example 5 under Sec MK211
41	Joint Collaborator Entry	Example 7 under Sec MK211
42	Commentator Entry	
43	Editor Entry	Example 5 under Sec MK211
44	Illustrator Entry	
45	Reviser Entry	Example 1 under Sec MK221
46	Translator Entry	Example 6 under Sec MK221
5	Title Entry	Example 1 under Sec FN47
6	Series Entry	Example 1 under Sec MK231
61	Pseudo Series Entry	
7	Related Book Entry	Example 1 under Sec MK6
71	Extract Entry	Example 1 under Sec MK4

62 A General Entry is usually called after its function.

Examples:

Serial Number	Name of Entry	Example: Entry given as
1	Class Index Entry	Examples 1-5 under Sec FN12
2	Cross Reference Index Entry	Example 2 under Sec FN22 and Example 1 under Sec FN45
3	*See also* Subject Entry	Example 1 under Sec FN22

63 An entry may also be called as shown below according to the kind of name occupying its Leading Section:

Serial Number	Name of Entry	Example: Entry given as
1	Personal Name Entry	Example 2 under Sec FN11
2	Corporate Name Entry	
3	Subject Name Entry	Example 1-4 under Sec FN12 and 1 under Sec FN22

7 Number of Entries

Every book or periodical publication will get at least one entry—*viz* Main Entry. But it may also get one or more Added Entries.

While each entry is made in relation to a particular document, once it is written out, its assignment to the appropriate part of the catalogue and its relative position among the entries in its part are determined entirely by the numbers and the words written in it. In other words, the document to which it relates may be eliminated from view, while arranging the entries so as to form a catalogue.

To put it in a different way, each entry forms one of the fundamental units out of which the catalogue is made—one of the ultimate bricks which are built into the structure. Just as the bricks needed for a structure are made in several patterns, so also the entries in a catalogue are of several species and varieties and carry different names.

The number of each species or variety of entry will vary with the document catalogued. The relation between a document and the number of its entries may be described as 1 to *n*, where *n* is at least 1 and may be any integer whatever.

71 Main Entry

There is one and only one Main Entry for each document. It enters it under its chief Specific Subject. It is, as its name implies, the basic entry for the document. All the other entries are derived from it. It gives us more information about the document than any other entry. Further, as can be seen from Chap MH and its subdivisions, it acts as a key which lets us know what Added Entries the document has received in the catalogue. Chap MA and MB and Chap MZD are on its construction.

72 Cross Reference Entry

The number of Cross Reference Entries to be given for a document is variable. It may be zero or one or two or three, etc.,—even quite a large number. The why of this variability will be appreciated if the purpose of the Cross Reference Entry is understood. This question has been fully discussed, in the light of the Laws of Library Science, in the *Five laws of library science* [RF4]. A Cross Reference Entry enters a document under one or other of the classes other than its dominant focus or class. And a document is to get as many Cross Reference Entries as there are different subsidiary classes so dealt with by it.

This variety of entry is necessitated by the inevitable composite nature of most of the documents. Few are of the monograph type. Very often a document, whose chief interest is in a certain class, may devote a chapter or a few pages to some other topic. It may also happen that throughout a work, primarily devoted to a particular class, information about some others is diffusely scattered. If a catalogue lists a work only under its dominant class and makes no attempt whatever to give analytical cross references, it will offend the Laws of Library Science. At the same time, practical consideration, such as staff, finance, and the policy of the library, may not permit of the cross-referencing work to be done as profusely and as thoroughly as the Laws would demand [RT5].

Thus, the nature of the document and the limitations of the library would make the number of Cross Reference Entries of a document vary widely. Chap MJ is devoted to the construction of this variety of entries.

73 Class Index Entry

Each document has also associated with it Index Entries which index names of classes. These direct the reader to the region of the Classified Part where he can find his materials enumerated and featured in a filiatory way. Normally, every document will have at least one Class Index Entry relating to it. Part K is devoted to the construction of this variety of entries.

74 Cross Reference Index Entry

A Cross Reference Index Entry occurs only occasionally. It is only a very small percentage of documents that gives rise to this variety of entries. It is devised to economise in the number of Index Entries. It usually directs the reader's attention from one heading to another synonymous one in the

Alphabetical Part. Part L is devoted to the construction of this variety of entries.

75 Book Index Entry

The number of Book Index Entries for a document is also variable. Governmental and similar annual and other periodical reports, of an administrative nature, do not get any Book Index Entry. Normally every other document will get at least one such entry. It may get more, but seldom more than half a dozen.

These entries enable a reader to get his document, provided he has some information or other about it. For, the Book Index Entries enter a document under the names of authors, editors, translators, etc, under the name of series and, in certain cases, under the title. Chap MK and other Sec in Part N onwards are devoted to the construction of this variety of Entries.

CHAPTER FP

CLASSIFIED CATALOGUE

1 **Classified Catalogue.**—Catalogue in which some entires are Number Entries and some are Word Entries.

Consequently a Classified Catalogue consist of two parts—the Classified Part and the Alphabetical Part.

2 **Classified Part.**—The part of a Classified Catalogue containing all its Number Entries.

21 Its entries are arranged by their Call Numbers and Class Numbers, as the case may be.

22 It serves as a Classified or Systematic Subject Catalogue.

23 It helps a reader to get a panoramic view of the entries of all the documents in the specific field of his interest, arranged by their specific subjects in a helpful sequence.

3 **Alphabetical Part.**—The part of a Classified Catalogue containing all its Word Entries.

31 The entries are arranged alphabetically as in a dictionary.

32 It serves as an Alphabetical Catalogue.

33 It serves also as an Alphabetical Index to Classes of Knowledge.

34 It thus forms an over-all Alphabetical Index to the Classified Part.

35 It helps a reader to get a document of which he knows the author, or any collaborator, or the series it may belong to, or its title, or the title of any part of it.

36 It also helps the reader to find out the Class Number of the class of knowledge in which he is seeking a document. This Class Number will enable him to alight on the particular spot in the Classified Part, where the documents on his subject are listed. He will also find just earlier than them the documents on subjects of which his subject is a subclass. Further, he will also find after those in his own subject, the documents on subjects which are subclasses of his subject.

4 Main Entry in a Classified Catalogue begins with Call Number in the case of a book and with Class Number in the case of a periodical publication.

41 It is thus a Number Entry.

42 Therefore it belongs to the Classified Part.

Examples:

The Entries given as Example 1 under Sec FN11 and as Example 1 under Sec FN21.

5 Cross Reference Entry.—Specific Added Class Number Entry in a Classified Catalogue.

51 It refers from the Class Number of a subject to its Locus in a Host Document.

52 It is a Number Entry.

53 Therefore, it belongs to the Classified Part of the Catalogue.

54 It corresponds to the Subject Analytical in a Dictionary Catalogue.

Example:

Entry given as Example 1 under Sec FN53.

6 Class Index Entry.—General Added Word-Entry in a Classified Catalogue, referring from the name of a Class to its Class Number.

61 It is derived, by Chain Procedure, from the class number of the Main Entry or of a Cross Reference Entry of a document.

62 It enables a reader to know the class number of the subject on which he seeks documents.

Examples:

Entries given as Examples 1-4 under Sec FN12.

7 Cross Reference Index Entry.—Same as Sec FN45.

It enables a reader to find out the call number of the document, for which he looks up the catalogue under the name of its author, collaborator, title, series, or any related book.

Examples:

Entries given as Examples 2 and 3 under Sec FN11, and Example 1 under Sec FN46 and Sec FN47 respectively.

8 Book Index Entry.—Specific Added Word Entry in a Classified Catalogue.

91 In a Classified Catalogue, Main Entry, Cross Reference Entry, and Class Index Entry are Subject Entries.

92 In a Classified Catalogue, Main Entry is a Specific Subject Entry.

93 In a Classified Catalogue, Cross Reference Entry is a Subject-Analytical.

94 In a Classified Catalogue, Class Index Entry is a General Subject Entry.

CHAPTER FQ

SECTIONS OF ENTRY

0 **Section of an Entry.**—That which is prescribed to be a separate paragraph in an entry in a Card Catalogue.

01 When an entry occurs in a catalogue in book-form, all its sections may occur as separate sentences of a single paragraph.

1 **Leading Section.**—Section 1 of an Entry.

2 **Heading Section.**—

1 Leading Section of a Word Entry.

2 Section 2 of a Call Number Entry of a book or of a Class Number Entry of a periodical publication, *i e* of a Main Entry in a Classified Catalogue

3 Section 3 of a *See also* Subject Entry.

4 Section 3 of a Cross Reference Index Entry.

3 **Title Section.**—Section of a Main Entry, giving the title of the document catalogued, along with the names of Collaborators and of Edition if any.

31 **Bibliographical Section.**—Section giving format, collation, and imprint, in the Main Entry of a Macro Document.

32 **Locus Section.**—

1 Section in the Main Entry giving the locus of a Micro Document, in its host document.

2 Section in a Cross Reference Entry of a Classified Catalogue, giving the locus.

3 Section in a Subject Analytical in a Dictionary Catalogue, giving the locus.

4 **Note Section.**—Section of a Main Entry giving the name of series and/or the name(s) of related book(s) and certain other information in the case of a Periodical Publication.

41 **Annotation Section.**—Section in a Main Entry giving an Annotation, or a Synopsis, or an Abstract of the document catalogued.

5 **Accession Number Section.**—Last section in the front of a Main Entry Card, giving the Accession Number of the Document.

6 **Tracing Section.**—Back of a Main Entry Card, indicating all the Added Entries of the document.

61 Tracing Section is not normally given in a catalogue in book-form.

91 **Directing Section.**—Section in an Added Entry directing attention to a Document, or a Class Number, or Name of a Class, or an Alternative name.

This section occurs in a Cross Reference Entry, a Class Index Entry, a *See also* Subject Entry, and a Cross Reference Index Entry.

92 **Second Section.**—Section in a Book Index Entry giving the specification of the concerned document(s).

93 **Index Number Section.**—

1 Section in a Book Index Entry, giving the Call Number of the document.

2 Section in a Class Index Entry, giving the Class Number of the class.

3 Section in a Specific Subject Entry, giving the Call Number of the document.

4 Section in a Subject Analytical, giving the Call Number of the document.

5 Section in the Main Entry of a Dictionary Catalogue giving the Call Number in general and Class Number in the case of the Periodical Publication.

CHAPTER FR

HEADING

0 **Heading.**—The occupant of a Heading Section (*See* Sec FQ2).

01 A Heading may be the name of
1 A person;
2 A geographical entity;
3 A corporate body;
4 A series;
5 A document;
6 A subject; or
7 A language.

02 A person or corporate body whose name is used as Heading may be
1 An author;
2 A joint author;
3 A collaborator;
4 A joint collaborator; or
5 The subject of a document.

03 The name of a geographical entity, used as Heading, may represent the name of
1 A Government;
2 A Document; or
3 A Subject.

1 **Homonym in Sense 1.**—One and the same name denoting two or more entities of any one of the categories, such as

1 Person;
2 Geographical Entity;
3 Corporate Body;
4 Document;
5 Series;
6 Subject;
7 Language.

11 **Homonymous Heading in Sense 1.**—A heading which is a Homonym in Sense 1.

12 **Individualising Element in Sense 1.**—Term(s) added to a name in a Heading to resolve Homonym in Sense 1—that is, so as to individualise the entitv intended to be denoted.

Examples:

1 HALL (James) (1755).
HALL (James) (1761).

These are both names-of-persons. The elements in brackets are Individualising Elements in Sense 1.

2 TANJORE.
TANJORE (City).
TANJORE (Taluk).

These three are geographical names. The words in brackets are Individualising Elements in Sense 1. The first of the above headings is the name of the geographical area of the largest extent denoted by the homonym being considered. It is a district of which the taluk is only a part.

3 GODAVARI.
GODAVARI (City).
GODAVARI (River).
GODAVARI (Taluk).

These four are geographical names. The words in brackets are Individualising Elements in Sense 1.

4 RAMAYANA (Kamban).
RAMAYANA (Tulasidas).
RAMAYANA (Valmiki).

These three are names of books. The words in brackets are Individualising Elements in Sense 1.

5 CAMBRIDGE.
CAMBRIDGE (Borough).
CAMBRIDGE (Maryland).
CAMBRIDGE (Massachusetts).
CAMBRIDGE (Ohio).

2 **Homonym in Sense 2.**—One and the same name denoting entities of any two or more of the categories mentioned in Sec FR1.

21 **Homonymous Heading in Sense 2.**—A Heading which is a Homonym in Sense 2.

22 **Individualising Element in Sense 2.**—Term(s) added to a name in a Heading to resolve a Homonym in Sense 2—that is, so as to individualise the entity intended to be denoted.

Examples:

1 SALISBURY.
SALISBURY (Book).
SALISBURY (City).
SALISBURY (Subject).

The words in brackets are Individualising Elements in Sense 2. The first of the above headings is the name of a person.

3 **Homonym in Sense 3.**—A Homonym simultaneously in Senses 1 and 2.

31 **Homonymous Heading in Sense 3.**—A Heading which is a Homonym in Sense 3.

32 **Individualising Element in Sense 3.**—A succession of Individualising Elements in Senses 1 and 2 added to a name in a Heading to resolve Homonym in Sense 3—that is, so as to individualise the entity intended to be denoted.

Example:
CAMBRIDGE (Massachusetts) (Book).
Here, "Massachusetts" is Individualising Element in Sense 1 and "Book" is Individualising Element in Sense 2. Both taken together form Individualising Element in Sense 3.

4 **Individualised Heading.**—Heading including Individualising Element(s) added to resolve homonym.

41 **Word-Group in a Heading.**—One or more words, constituting the name forming the heading, which are inseparable and should be taken together, to make the specification of the entity intelligible.

Examples:
1 "HALL" in Example 1 under Sec FR12 is a Word-Group of one word only.
2 DE QUINCY, LE SAGE, NI NI, QUILLER-COUCH, RAJENDRA PRASAD, SIVASWAMI AYYAR, YUSUF ALI;
CHIN HILLS, COSTA RICA, LA PLATA, MADHYA PRADESH, NEW DELHI, NEW YORK, NOVA SCOTCIA, PORTO RICO, WEST LOTHIAN;
BOOK SELECTION, ELEMENTARY EDUCATION, INTEGRAL CALCULUS, RESPIRATORY SYSTEM;
are Word-Groups of two words.
3 BASU RAY CHAUDHURI, LEON Y ROMAN, MARTIN DU GARD, MUHAMMAD IBN ALY, SANKARA NARAYANA PILLAI;
CLACTON-ON-SEA, DERA GHAZI KHAN, PRINCE EDWARD ISLANDS, NEW SOUTH WALES, RIO DE JANEIRO;
are Word-Groups of three words.

42 **Individualised Word-Group in a Heading.**—A Word-

Group in a heading taken along with the Individualising Elements if any.

Example:

"HALL (James) (1755)" in Example 1 and "TANJORE (City)" in Example 2 under Sec FR12 are examples of Individualised Word-Groups in a Heading.

43 **Block in a Heading.**—Individualised Word-Group in a Heading.

This term is introduced for brevity.

5 Heading of an entry may be Simple or Multiple.

51 **Simple Heading.**—Heading consisting of a single Block.

Examples:

1 HALL (James) (1755).
2 TANJORE (City).
3 CAMBRIDGE (Massachusetts) (Book).

52 **Multiple Heading.**—Heading consisting of two or more Blocks, usually separated by a punctuation mark such as a comma.

Examples:

See under Sec FR56 and FR57.

53 **First Heading or Main Heading.**—The First Block in a Multiple Heading.

Examples:

The following remarks pertain to the successive examples given in Sec FR56:

1 "INDIA" is First Heading or Main Heading in Example 1.
2 "LAW" is First Heading or Main Heading in Example 2.
3 "DIAGNOSIS" is First Heading or Main Heading in Example 3.

The following remarks pertain to the successive examples given in Sec FR57:

1 "MADRAS" is First Heading or Main Heading in Example 1.
2 "MADRAS (City)" is First Heading or Main Heading in Example 2.
3 "MADRAS" is First Heading or Main Heading in Example 3.
4 "WESTERN RAILWAY (India)" is First Heading or Main Heading in Example 4.

5 "UNIVERSITY COLLEGE (London)" is First Heading or Main Heading in Example 5.

54 Second Heading or First Subheading.—The Second Block in a Multiple Heading.

Examples:

The following remarks pertain to the successive examples given in Sec FR56:

1 "LAW" is Second Heading or First Subheading in Example 1.

2 "CONSTITUTION" is Second Heading or First Subheading in Example 2.

3 "TUBERCULOSIS" is Second Heading or First Subheading in Example 3.

The following remarks pertain to the successive examples given in Sec FR57:

1 "COUNCIL OF MINISTERS" is Second Heading or First Subheading in Example 1.

2 "COUNCIL" is Second Heading or First Subheading in Example 2.

3 "DISTRICT COURT (Coimbatore)" is Second Heading or First Subheading in Example 3.

4 "AUDIT (Department of—)" is Second Heading or First Subheading in Example 4.

5 "BIOMETRIC (Laboratory)" is Second Heading or First Subheading in Example 5.

56 Multiple Subject Heading.—Subject Heading having, in its successive blocks, the names of successive classes.

These are normally of increasing extension.

Examples:

1 INDIA, LAW, LIBRARY.

2 LAW, CONSTITUTION, GREAT BRITAIN.

3 DIAGNOSIS, TUBERCULOSIS, LUNGS.

561 It can be seen that normally any class mentioned in a subheading in a Multiple Subject Heading will have the earlier classes mentioned in the heading as its subclasses.

562 The Main Heading and the Subheadings of a Multiple Subject Heading are derived from a Class Number by the Chain Procedure described in Part K.

57 Multiple Corporate Heading.—Corporate Heading having, in its successive blocks, the name of a Corporate body and the names of its successive organs of increasing remove.

Examples:

1 MADRAS, COUNCIL OF MINISTERS.
2 MADRAS, (City), COUNCIL, WORKS (Standing Committee for—).
3 MADRAS, DISTRICT COURT (Coimbatore).
4 WESTERN RAILWAY (India), AUDIT (Department of—).
5 UNIVERSITY COLLEGE (London), BIOMETRIC (—LABORATORY).

6 **Descriptive Element.**—Term(s) added after the name of a person or a corporate body including its individualising element(s), if any, to denote the role of the person or the corporate body, if it is other than that of author—such as, *J Auth; Ed; J Ed; Tr; J Tr; Assis; Dir; Ded; etc.*

7 **Connecting Element.**—Word like "and", "of", etc occurring within a Block in a Heading or between the names of J Authors, or J Collaborators.

Examples:

1 "y" in "LEON Y ROMAN."
2 "on" in "CLACTON-ON-SEA."
3 "de" in "RIO DE JANEIRO."
4 "and" in "RANGANATHAN (Shiyali Ramamritha) (1892) and SIVARAMAN (Kesarimangalam Manikam Aiyar) (1903)."
5 "and" in "LIBRARY ASSOCIATION (Great Britain) and AMERICAN LIBRARY ASSOCIATION."

8 **Entry Element.**—The Word or Word-Group occurring First in a Block in a Heading, that is before any Individualising or Descriptive or any other Element belonging to the Block.

81 **Entry Word.**—The First Word in an Entry Element.

CHAPTER FZD

DICTIONARY CATALOGUE

1 **Dictionary Catalogue.**—Catalogue in which all the entries are Word Entries.

11 Consequently, a Dictionary Catalogue consists of one part only.

2 The entries in a Dictionary Catalogue are arranged alphabetically as in a dictionary.

3 In a Dictionary Catalogue, the Main Entry begins with the Name of the Author or a substitute for it.

Example:
Entry given as Example 1 under Sec FN11.

4 **Subject Index Entry** in a Dictionary Catalogue;
1 Specific Subject Entry;
2 Subject Analytical;
3 *See also* Subject Entry.

41 **Specific Subject Entry.**—Specific Added Word Entry in a Dictionary Catalogue, entering a document under the name of the class treated in, if it is unifocal, or under that one of its classes, which is most dominant, if it is multifocal.

Example:
Entry given as Example 1 under Sec FN52.

42 **Subject Analytical.**—Specific Word Entry in a Dictionary Catalogue entering a document under the name of a class treated in it in a subsidiary way, that is occurring as a secondary focus in the document.

Example:
Entry given as Example 2 under Sec FN53.

43 *See also* **Subject Entry.**—General Added Word Entry in a Dictionary Catalogue referring from the name of one Subject to that of another.

44 All the Subject Index Entries are derived from the Class Number of the document or of any portion of it for which a Specific Subject Entry has been made.

Example:
Entry given as Example 1 under Sec FN22.

7 Cross Reference Index Entry—Same as Sec FN45.

8 Book Index Entry.—A Specific Added Word Entry in a Dictionary Catalogue.

Example:
Entry given as Example 2 under Sec FN53.

PART G

CONFLICT OF AUTHORSHIP

CHAPTER GA

INTRODUCTION

1 Difficulties

Difficulties arise in deciding the author of a Work. These difficulties may be taken to centre round the following issues:

1 Person *vs* Person
2 Person *vs* Corporate Body
3 Government *vs* Institution
4 Ecclesiastical Polity
5 Institution *vs* Institution
6 Delegation-from-Body *vs* Delegated-to-Body
7 Legal Publications
8 Author's Name Merged in Title

2 Problem for International Catalogue Code

It is desirable from the point of view of international intercourse in the Library field such as, International Library Loan and Centralized Cataloguing, that a uniform practice should be followed in respect of the problems mentioned in Sec GA1. Unesco took interest in this problem. It requested the International Federation of Library Associations to pursue the problem, promising as usual the necessary financial help. Accordingly at its meeting held in Zagreb in September 1954, the International Federation of Library Associations seized this problem. After several years of work, the problem was brought for consideration at the International Conference on Cataloguing held in Paris from 9 to 18 October 1961. The attention of the International Conference was invited to these problems in a paper circulated to the authorities of the Conference early in 1961 [R13].

3 Evasion of the Problems

However, the Conference did not consider the problems on the basis of accepted Canons and Principles of Cataloguing. In fact, the work of the Conference was not at all guided by such canons and principles. The Conference dealt in detail with certain problems that are best left to National and Linguistic Codes. But this question of Conflict of Authorship was not adequately discussed by the Conference [R14].

CHAPTER GB

PERSON *VS* PERSON

1 Spoken Word

In certain types of works, the thought expressed in the spoken word is not committed to writing by the author of the spoken word. The words are not even published always exactly in the form in which they were spoken. Usually they are edited, rearranged, and featured. The person, who creates the thought, is taken as the author; while the person who collects or notes down the words uttered by the creator of the thought and gives them the shape of a work is regarded as a collaborator. He may be called Reporter. The reporter may even prompt the author by his own questions and suggestions; and yet he is not given the status of a joint author. It must be stated that the steno-typist of an author is not even regarded as a collaborator.

Ser N	*Type of Work*	*Author*
1	Ana, table-talk	Talker
2	Dialogue, conversation, debate	Participants
3	Interview	Person(s) interviewed
4	Lecture	Lecturer
5	Narration (real and not fictitious)	Narrator
6	Mediumistic communication	Medium(s) and not the disembodied souls

Example:

Consider the book whose title page reads as follows:

Plasma Physics: A Course Given by S Chandrasekhar at the University of Chicago. Notes compiled by S K Trehan.

The Author of the book is S Chandrasekhar. Trehan is only the Reporter—that is, a Collaborator.

2 Correspondence

In the case of correspondence, the correspondent(s) should be taken as joint author(s). If, however, the document contains the correspondence of one person only with several others—then the one person alone may be taken as the author.

3 Map and Atlas

The cartographer should be taken as the author of a map or atlas.

4 Dependent Work

Dependent Work is a work got by some modification of another work or by the augmentation of it. The modification or augmentation, as the case may be, need not necessarily be by the author of the original work. It may be done by some other person or corporate body. Conflict in authorship arises in respect of the original author and the modifier or the augmenter. The decision in such cases is to be in accordance with Sec GB5 and GB6.

5 Author of the Original

The author of the **Original** should be taken as the **Author** of the following kinds of dependent works:

1 Abridgement
2 Adaptation
3 Paraphrase
4 Revision
5 Selection
6 Translation

6 Author of Dependent Work

The author of the **Dependent work** should be taken as the **Author** of the following kinds of dependent works:

1 Commentary (Of greater importance than the basic work)
2 Concordance
3 Continuation
4 Dramatisation
5 Imitation
6 Index
7 Libretto
8 Music-setting
91 Novelisation
92 Parody
93 Sequel
94 Supplement
95 Versification
96 Version in the same or another language, which has sufficient new qualities in thought and/or expression to deem it an independent work on its own right.

CHAPTER GC

PERSON *VS* CORPORATE BODY

0 Introduction

The title-page of a document may indicate corporate authorship or may contain the name of a corporate body, in addition to containing the name(s) of person(s). Such a document raises a conflict in authorship. This conflict can be resolved in most cases by observing the rules given in this chapter.

1 If the title-page mentions the name(s) of person(s) only in the author-statement and does not mention or indicate the name of any corporate body(ies) other than the one(s) belonging to the publishing trade mentioned in the imprint, the work in the document is of personal authorship.

2 If the title-page does not mention the name(s) of person(s) in the author-statement, but mentions or indicates somewhere in itself or in the overflow of title-page the name of a corporate body(ies) other than a body belonging to the publishing trade mentioned in the imprint, and if there is also internal evidence of corporate authorship, the work in the document is of corporate authorship; provided that, even in the case of the name(s) of the corporate body(ies) mentioned in the imprint being only that of a body belonging to the publishing trade, if it is a work by the corporate body itself—such as its catalogue, administration report, history—the work in the document is of corporate authorship.

3 If the title-page mentions or indicates the name(s) of a corporate body(ies) other than a body belonging to the publishing trade mentioned in the imprint, and also the name(s) of person(s) in the place usually giving the name of the author.—

31 The work in the document is of corporate authorship, if it is of a deliberative, legislative, directive, judicial, administrative or routine character limited by the purpose or function or outlook of the corporate body. The mere fact that a document is published, financed, aided, approved, sponsored, or authorised by a corporate body is not sufficient reason to deem the work in

it to be of corporate authorship, and not to be of personal authorship.

32 The work in the document is of personal authorship, if its primary function is the extension of the boundary of a field of knowledge or its intensification, and the responsibility for the thought and expression of it rests on the person and not on the office held by him in the corporate body, in spite of his being a paid or an honorary employee or a member of the corporate body. The mere mention of the personal name of an official of the corporate body in the place in which author's name is usually mentioned in a book, is not sufficient reason to deem the work in it to be of personal authorship and not to be of corporate authorship.

4 Legal Publication

Legal publications raise certain issues of their own in regard to authorship. For example, a bill is usually the work of a Ministry. Its modification may be the work of a Select Committee. The Act, before the assent of the Head of the State, is the work of the Legislature. These cases give no difficulty. But the final Act is the work of the Legislature and the Head of the State. Constitutionally, the part of each of these limbs of the government is of equal weight. Quantitatively, they are quite unequal. Further, the details have to be filled up usually by the Executive or even by a Department. For these reasons, we may have the following Rule:

41 The whole government should be taken as the author of an Act and a collection of Acts, with or without the Rules framed under them.

Another difficulty may arise in respect of legal publications. Editions of an Act may be brought out by a private author with notes, commentaries, and case laws in various degrees of proportion. Such publications are perhaps best treated according to Sec GB82.

42 An edition of an Act, brought out by a private author with introduction, notes, commentaries, case laws, and over-all observations, should be treated as provided in Sec GB6.

5 **Person vs Conference.**—A Conference is deemed author only of its agenda, minutes, resolutions, report of proceedings, and similar collectively created thought. But a collection of

learned papers or memoranda presented by person(s) or corporate body(ies) at the conference is deemed to have the respective person(s) or body(ies) as author(s).

CHAPTER GD

CORPORATE BODY *VS* CORPORATE BODY

1 GOVERNMENT *VS* INSTITUTION

Several institutions are government-owned or nearly so. Some of these are autonomous. Some are managed directly by government as if they were departments or other organs. There are all possible grades of transition from an unmistakable organ of government to an independent institution. Now and again, there is also shift of the same institution in course of time from the status of an independent institution to any status short of an unmistakable organ and vice versa. A useful test is this:

Organ of first remove is usually mentioned in a modern written constitution On the analogy of this, organ of first remove of a nation with unwritten constitution may be recognised.

Another fact has to be remembered. There is a tendency for the state to take up more and more functions, beyond the traditional and primary ones of government—*viz*, policy decision, legislation, defence, judiciary, and administration. It takes up many service functions such as:

1 Construction and maintenance of high-ways, bridges, harbours, airports and such other essentials of transport;

2 Astronomical and meteorological observations through its own observatories;

3 Transport systems such as railways, tramways, bus system, and airways;

4 Communication systems such as postal, telegraph, telephone, wireless and radio services;

5 Healing the sick and wounded through its own hospitals and its own sanatoria;

6 Teaching through its own schools, colleges, and universities; and

7 Banking service through its own banks.

Perhaps none of the above seven categories except the first is usually included among the primary functions of a government. At any rate, this may be adopted as a cataloguing convention.

But for such a convention, most institutions will come into the category of organs of government, as the state progresses towards socialisation. In a truly totalitarian state, there may not be any corporate body other than the government and its organs. To break up this octopus-type of governmental authorship, cataloguing practice has to adopt a convention to distinguish between an organ of a government and an institution. The conventions may be put in the form of Sec GD2 and GD3.

2 Government as Author

For a work bearing on the discharge of primary functions—administiation report, report of deliberation, direction, and any kindred work embodying thought created and expressed by an organ of government of first remove, second remove, etc as defined in Sec FC21 to FC217—the government or its appropriate organ(s), as the case may be, should be taken as its author.

3 Institution as Author

Any autonomous or even non-autonomous organisation, engaged in the work of research, production, commerce and supply of commodities and services to the public, may have to be taken to be the institutional author for an work for whose thought and expression it is responsible. It is so even if the institution is owned and managed by the government.

4 Elusive Cases

The above-mentioned criterion to distinguish between governmental and institutional authorship will be sufficient in most cases. But there will occasionally be refractory cases baffling this criterion. No help except the personal judgment of the cataloguer will be of avail in such cases. By a periodical review of such elusive cases, the criterion can be made progressively sharper.

5 Ecclesiastical Polity

Ecclesiastical polity has features similar to those of a government. There are organs of different removes from the central authority. There are also autonomous institutions. The criterion to resolve conflict of authorship between an ecclesiastical organ and institution is similar to that for the conflict between a governmental organ and institution, as given in Sec GD2 and GD3.

6 Institution *vs* Institution

The criterion to resolve the conflict about authorship between a parent institution or one of its organs on the one side, and an autonomous affiliated institution on the other is similar to that for the conflict between a governmental organ and institution as given in Sec GD2 and GD3.

7 Delegation—Conflict about Parent Bodies

Delegation to a conference or an international body such as the United Nations appears to be amphibious. A delegation is itself a corporate body. It implies the existence of two other corporate bodies—Delegated-from-Body and Delegated-to-Body. The kind of document, about whose authorship conflict arises, may comprise memoranda submitted, resolutions tabled, and utterances made, by the delegation at the conference, and report by the Delegation to the Delegated-from-Body. There is no doubt about the authorship belonging to the Delegation. But the Delegation is not an independent body. It is only an organ. The name of the body of which it is an organ should be mentioned along with its own name to establish its identity. The question is, "Is it an organ of the Delegated-from-Body or of the Delegated-to-Body ?" The answer to this question depends upon the answer to another question: "Which body takes the ultimate responsibility for the thought-content of the document created by the delegation? Is it the Delegated-from-Body or the Delegated-to-Body?" There can be no difference of opinion about the answers to these questions. The answers lead to the following Rule:

71 The **Delegated-from-Body** should be taken to be the parent body of a **Delegation to a Conference** or to a body such as the United Nations or a Peace Conference in respect of any work embodying any thought and expression created by the Delegation.

8 Synopsis of Cataloguing Conventions

The following is a synopsis of the cataloguing conventions more or less stabilised at present, in deciding the corporate body to be deemed the author of a work—parent body or an organ of it on the one side and a dependent of affiliated institution on the other.

Group 1

81 Each of the following **Institutions** should be taken as **Author** of its works, as if it were independent of the parent body, if any exists, be it government or institution:—

Abbey
Bank
Board of Trade
Cathedral
Cemetery
Chamber of Commerce
Church (place of worship)
College
Convent
Endowment
Exchange (Money)
Firm of Enterprise
Foundation
Guild
Masonic Body
Monastery
Mosque
Mutt
Park

Political Party	**School**	**Telephone Exchange**
Post Office	**Stock Exchange**	**Temple**
Produce Exchange		
Religious Order	**Telegraph Office**	**University**

Group 2

82 Each of the following **Institutions** should be taken as **Author** of its works as if it were independent of the parent body, if any exists, be it government or institution, **provided it has a distinctive name**:—

Botanical Garden	**Experimental Station**	**Museum**
		Observatory
	Festival	**Shop**
Chapel	**Hospital**	
	Laboratory	**Zoological Garden**
Exhibition	**Library**	

If any of the above institutions has **no distinctive name**, it should be treated as an **organ** of its parent body.

Group 3

83 Any formal or informal group of the members of a parent body formed for recreative, ameliorative or any other economical or social purposes should be treated as an **organ** of the parent body **even if it has a distinctive name.**

Group 4

84 Each **Section** or **Branch** of an institution should be taken as **Author** of its work, as if it were independent of its parent body, provided it has a **distinctive name not involving the name of the parent body.**

If a section or a branch has no **distinctive name not involving the name of the parent body,** it should be treated as an **organ** of the parent body.

Group 5

85 Each **International Institution or Conference**—isolated or continuing,—of private persons, non-governmental institutions, or national governments should be taken as **Author** of work made up of its deliberations.

91 Refractory Cases

The preceding Rules of this Chapter will prove sufficient to resolve the conflict that may arise in respect of authorship in most of the cases. The commentaries in Sec GD4 and GD7 and their subsections amount to some loud-thinking in resolving the conflict in some of the difficult cases in the light of the definition of authorship and the Sec given in this Chap. All the same, it cannot be asserted that every possible refractory case involving conflict in authorship can be solved unambiguously. New guiding principles will have to be evolved as and when new types of refractory cases arise. A few more discussions and directions are given here. These are chosen to counteract a wrong tradition brought into vogue by the Anglo-American Code.

911 Charter

The author of the charter granted by a government to a city or a rural district or any other body is the government and not the recipient of the charter. For, the charter is a document, for the thought-content and the expression of which the government is responsible.

The prescription in Rule 87 of the Anglo-American Code implies a violation of this fact, if it is to be taken as a rule for author-entry.

912 Law of Territory

The author of a law of a territory promulgated by a suzeraine power is the government of the suzeraine power and not that of the territory. For the law in question is a document, for the thought-content and expression of which the government of the suzeraine power is responsible.

The prescription in Rule 84B of the Anglo-American Code implies a violation of this fact, if it is to be taken as a rule for author-entry.

913 Constitution of Dependency

The remarks are similar to those for Law of Territory.

914 Decision of a Court of Law

A Court of Law is the author of any of its decisions or a collection of them.

915 Report of Legal Proceedings

A report of the legal proceedings in a Court of Law raises some conflict in regard to its authorship. A full report of the case will contain an account of the plaint and the defence statements of all the parties concerned. It may also contain a verbatim report of the chief-examination and the cross-examination of the parties and the witnesses. It may further contain the arguments of the advocates of all the parties. It must necessarily contain the verdict of the jury, if any, and the judgment of the court. Even if the report is brief, it will contain a summary of all these elements. The different elements have different authors. And yet, the contribution of each is not conveniently separable from those of the others. At the same time, the report cannot be regarded to be of joint-authorship, as the portion for which each author is responsible is specified. Perhaps, it resembles a document embodying correspondence between several persons. There, however, the thought-content of the document gets developed jointly by all the correspondents. Such a description cannot apply with sufficient propriety to the report of legal proceedings of a case in a court. Can we take the following view ? It is the court which co-ordinates and guides the course of the proceedings, and finally summarises the entire proceedings and gives the judgment. The real focus or the culmination of the report is the part played by the court from the beginning right up to the judgment. Therefore, the court may be taken as the author of the report of the legal proceedings of a case tried by it.

CHAPTER GE

NAME OF ORIGINAL AUTHOR MERGED IN TITLE

1 Introduction

Some works are almost immortal. They have elements of permanent value. They are saturated with the personality of the author, which itself is very powerful and highly organized. It is usually a seminal book cutting new ground, blazing new trail, stimulating new thought, and so on. It gets printed repeatedly even after centuries. It stimulates other works on itself. Such a work is called a classic (*See* Sec FA7). Since a classic outlives the author, the title page of any later edition of it has often necessarily to contain the name of a collaborator as editor or as translator or in any other capacity. The author's name may be merged in the title of the work. It may even happen that the name of the original author is totally absent from the title page. The conflict of authorship in the case of classics is dealt with elsewhere (*See* Chap GB).

11 Long-Lived Work

We are only concerned here with other fairly long-lived works. The essential value of such a long-lived work does not centre round its seminal nature or on the personality of the author or on the elements of permanent value contained in it so much as in classics. On the other hand, it embodies current knowledge or current information. For this reason it has to be revised and brought up to date from time to time. In other words, its current validity essentially requires correction or omission of old matter and addition of new matter from time to time. But the frame work of the original edition is retained in all the successive editions. Such a work often occurs in all the sciences—particularly in the taxonomic works of natural sciences, medical works, and legal works.

12 Extent of Change

At one extreme, the change in a new embodiment of a long-lived work may be slight—that is, it may affect only a small fraction of the work. At the other extreme, it may affect most of the work—at any rate, more than half the work. The change-over from the one extreme to the other may be in gradual steps from embodiment to embodiment.

13 Need for Collaborator

From certain edition onwards, a long-lived work of the nature described above will necessarily require a collaborator. It may be due either to the incapacity of the original author or to his having been dead. Surely thereafter, the original author can have no responsibility for the changes made in the later editions. The entire responsibility for bringing the work up to date falls on the collaborator alone. This factor has resulted in the title page of the later editions reflecting the change of responsibility in diverse ways.

2 Examples

Example 11:

Dewey/Decimal Classification/and Relative Index/Devised by/Melvil Dewey/16 *Edition*/Volume 1/Tables/Forest Press Inc/Lake Placid Club/Essex Country/New York.

First published anonymously in 1876 under the title: A Classification and Subject Index. Ed 2 to 14 published under the title: Decimal Classification and Relative Index.

In P 19, the Editor's Introduction says, "The editors have tried to provide enough subdivisions but not too many... In this respect the 16th edition varies distinctly from earlier editions... Edition 14 has 31,364 separate entries in the Tables... While edition 16 has 17,929.

"There are in this edition 1,603 relocations. Of these 832 are total, meaning that the entire number has been 'dropped'."

On P 27 the Editor's Introduction is signed "Benjamin A Kuster/Editor." Thus, there is no doubt that there is a considerable alteration in ed 16. About 10 per cent of the classes have been relocated. The number of classes has been nearly halved. This has certainly involved a good deal of judgment. Surely no responsibility for this can go to the original author Melvil Dewey who died two decades earlier. The responsibility can only rest with the editor Kuster. But Kuster has not allowed his name to be printed even in the Collaborator Statement in the title-page.

The only hint that somebody other than the original author has played a a large part in Ed 16 is to be found in the Author-Statement. In that statement we find "Devised by Melvil Dewey."

Another peculiarity is that there is no mention either in the Foreword or in the Editor's Introduction of the policy decision to merge the original author's name in the title, though it is found to be merged in the title-page.

Example 14:
Rider's/International/Classification/for the arrangement of books/on the shelves of general libraries/By Fremont Rider/Librarian Emeritus, Olin Memorial Library,/Wesleyan University/Preliminary Edition/Printed as manuscript for the receipt of corrections, amendations and amplifications./The Author/Middletown, Conn./1961.

This example is of a different kind. The author's name is merged in the title by the author himself, in addition to his name appearing in the 'Author-Statement' in the title-page.

Example 221:
James Duff Brown's/Manual/of/Library Economy/ Seventh Edition/ Completely rewritten/By/R Northwood Lock F L A/Grafton & Co/London/ 1961.

Unlike in example 231 the title-page indicates Lock's role as a reviser of Brown's work.

Example 222:
Thomson's Outlines/of/Zoology/Revised by/ James Ritchie, M.A., D.Sc. Ninth Edition/Geoffrey Cumberlege/Oxford University Press/London New York Toronto.

Extract:
"The present edition, the first to appear since the death of Sir J Arthur Thomson, has been carefully revised, and apart from amendations, rearrangements and additions suggested by advancing knowledge, takes more cognizance of fossil forms, without which a just survey of animal progress is impossible. The short section on tissue structure has been expanded and illustrated, and I have made close upon a hundred new figures to supplement the text and to replace diagrams less suitable, particularly in connection with animals customarily examined in first courses . . ."

Ed 8 1929; Ed 9 1944.

In this case probably the change introduced is not sufficient to justify regarding Ritchie as the author instead of Thomson.

Example 231:
James Duff Brown/Manual of/Library Economy/Sixth Edition/By/W. C. Berwick Sayers/Lecturer in Public Library Administration in/The University of London School/of Librarianship/Illustrated/London/Grafton & Co.,/1949.

In this case, it is not merely the family name "Brown" that is merged in the title, but the full name including the words forming the personal name. This may tempt one to treat Brown as the Author of the work, though his name does not occur in the Author-Statement. But this would be a violation of the Canon of Ascertainability. This view has a further support in Ed 7 as example. There what is merged is not the word group "James Duff Brown," but "James Duff Brown's."

While Lock states in the title-page of ed 7 that he has "completely re-written" the work, Sayers does not say whether he is a reviser or editor. His name just occurs in the Author Statement on the title-page. This definitely implies, according to the Canon of Ascertainability, that he should be taken as the author of the work contained in ed 6. This gains support in the following words occurring in the preface: "Hardly a page of Brown's now remains, but the book was his and his name will always be associated with it." This statement is delightedly vague in respect of the conflict of authorship. Perhaps this is sufficient ground to infer that the intention is that Brown should not be taken as the author of the work contained in ed 6.

There is, however, something in usage which may shake a cataloguer from the straight path laid down by the Canon of Ascertainability. For, in common usage the book is referred to as "Brown and Sayers."

Example 232:

Archbold's/Pleading, Evidence and Practice/in/Criminal Cases/Thirty-third Edition/By/T R Fitzwalter Butler/of the Inner Temple and Midland Circuit,/Barrister-at-Law, Recorder of Neward/and/Marston Grasia/of the Middle Temple and South Eastern Circuit,/Barrister-at-Law/London/Sweet and Maxwell Limited/2 & 3 Chancery Lane W C 2/1954.

Extract from the Preface:

"The 32nd edition had to incorporate the then very recent and far-reaching changes introduced into the administration of criminal law by the passing of the Criminal Justice Act, 1948, and the adaptation of the book so as to include these manifold new developments was at that time the chief concern of the editors . . . has necessitated alterations great in number and occasionally of importance in substance."

Information about previous editions:

Ed 1 1822 by J. F. Archbold; Ed 6 1835 by John Jervis; Ed 9 1846 by W. N. Welsby; Ed 16 Ed 16 1867 by W. Bruce; Ed 22 1900 by W. F. Craies and G. Stephenson; Ed 31 1943 by T R F Butler and M Grasia.

In this case more than a century has passed since Archbold wrote his book. It is still Archbold only in the Irish sense—of the table knife in the family being still the same which has been used continuously for five hundred years, each year one and only one part being renewed—handle in one year, blade in another and so on. The pattern of the book might have been continued but the thought-content should have become totally different. In this case it is probably more appropriate to take the word Archbold as the first word of the title, instead of promoting it to the Heading, and some other approrpiate person as the author. However, the book is likely to be sought under the word 'Archbold.' This situation is met by the book getting a title entry as a result of its being a Proper Name Title (*See* Sec FB 93).

Example 233*:*
Sear's List/of Subject Headings/Seventh Edition/By/Bertha Margaret Frick/Associate Professor, School of Library Service, Columbia University/ With Practical Suggestions for the Beginner/in Subject Heading Work,/by Minnie Earl Sears/New York/The H W Wilson Company/1950.

Extract from the Preface:
"In recognition of Miss Sear's pioneer and fundamental contributions, in the sixth edition the title was changed into 'Sear's List of Subject Headings', the name by which it is usually cited. ... New subjects for this edition have been gathered ... Many references have been added for these new subjects as well as for those already in the List, when it seemed desirable. On the other hand, some of the outmoded references have been removed ... Some subjects have been changed to agree with changes made in the Congress Library headings."

In this case Frick, responsible for the seventh edition, does not even designate herself as a reviser or editor. Her name appears in the Author-Statement and not in the Collaborator Statement in the title-page. But the content of the book does not differ from the last edition, which Sears herself brought out sufficiently to deny to Sear's name the right of becoming the heading.

Example 32*:*
Mellor's Modern/Inorganic Chemistry/*Revised and Edited by*/G. D. Parkes, M.A., D.Phil.,/Fellow of Keble College/Oxford/in *collaboration with*/J. W. Mellor, D.Sc./*With diagrams and illustrations*/Longmans, Green and co./London. New York, Toronto/(1939).

Preface:
"This new edition of Mellor's *Modern inorganic chemistry* embodies extensive changes in comparison with the previous editions. ... Mellor's *Modern inorganic chemistry* was first published in 1912 and very quickly achieved widespread popularity in many parts of the world. It had run to eight editions ... when it became clear that in preparing a further edition and time had come for a drastic revision and re-arrangement of its contents. The present volume is the consequence. By the time that this decision had been made, Dr Mellor was, unfortunately, in failing health, and this in conjunction with his numerous commitments made it necessary for the work of revision to be undertaken jointly. Although Dr Mellor passed away before it could be published, he had given a final revision to the whole of the joint work in manuscript form; so that the new edition is now issued with the confidence that it has his full authority."

In this case, G D Parkes, the editor has collaborated with Mellor, the original author of the work. The name of the editor and that of the original author are given in the Collaborator Statement.

This is an unusual case. Virtually during the very life-time of the author his name loses its place in the Author Statement and occupies only a secondary position even in the Collaborator Statement. But to signify that the book was that of Mellor, his name has been fused with the very title of the book as its very first word. Thus those who look for it under the name Mellor in the catalogue will not miss it. For, the new title is a Proper Name Title. As such it will have a Proper Name entry.

Example 33:

May's Chemistry/of synthetic Drugs/Fifth edition/*Revised and rewritten by*/G. Malcolm Dyson/M. A. (Oxon), R.Sc. (London) F.R.I.C., M.I. Chem. E.F.I.S./*in consultation with* Percy May/D.Sc. (London), F.R.I.C., C.P.A. (Longmans)./(1959).

Preface:

"The fifth edition of this work has very drastic rewriting of all sections. The enormous growth of the subject since the publication of the fourth edition in 1939 has made the sub-division into chapters according to chemical classification unworkable. The broadening of the number of organic chemical types showing specific therapeutic action has been so great that any attempt to preserve the original chemical subdivisions would involve much overlapping of chapters. We have therefore redistributed the material according to the main biological activity of the drugs, except for a part of the field of chemotherapy where the retention of special sections devoted to the consideration of general antiseptic, dyestuff, sulphonamides and organo-metallic compounds assist in clarifying the subject matter."

The fact that the preface is signed by both Dyson and May, confirm that the fifth edition is a joint product. However, the title-page mentions May as a consultant to Editor Dyson. In this case May is further removed from the author's position than Mellor in the previous example. For, Mellor was at least a co-editor whereas May is only consultant to the editor.

Example 43:

Garrison and Morton's/Medical Bibliography/An Annotated Check-list of Texts/Illustrating the History of Medicine/By/Leslie T Morton/Information Officer, British Medical Journal;/Formerly Librarian,/St. Thomas's Hospital/Medical School/Second Edition/London/Andre Deutsch/A Grafton Book/1961.

Extract from the Introduction to Ed 2·

"The publication of a second edition of this bibliography has provided opportunity to close some gaps and to bring the book into line with recent discoveries in medicine. Several sections have been considerably expanded and the whole work has been completely overhauled, although no attempt has been made to come close to the present in all subjects. About 1,400 entries have added and a few removed. The total number of items (6,808) includes some 3,800 from Garrison's original *Check List*."

Extract from the Introduction to Ed 1

"To Sir William Osler belongs the credit of first suggesting such a work as this. The late Fielding H Garrison carried his suggestion into effect, and the list compiled by him appeared in the *Index-Catalogue of the Library of the Surgeon-Generals Office*, Washington, 1912, 2nd Series, xvii, 89-178. Garrison himself wrote that he used the list "as convenient scaffolding for a book on the history of medicine . . . Later Garrison revised the list and republished it in the Bulletin of the *Institute of the History of Medicine*, Baltimore, 1933; i, 333-434, entitling it, A Revised Students' Check-List of Texts Illustrating the History of Medicine," and it is this later Check-List which forms the basis of the present work. Much has been added and a little deleted. The Check-List 1933 contained 4,186 entries, of which 3,826 have been retained, and to which 1,680 new entries have been added. . . . Many sections have been expanded, and modern representative works have been added in most sections."

In the title-page of ed 1 of the work, the name of Morton occurs in the Collaborator Statement, as a reviser. But in ed 2 his name occurs in the Author-Statement of the title-page.

Example 52:

Blakiston's/New Gould/Medical Dictionary/*A modern comprehensive dictionary of the terms* used in/all branches *of medicine and* allied sciences, including/*medical physics and chemistry, dentistry, pharmacy/nursing, veterinary medicine, zoology and botany, as well/as medico—legal terms* with *illustrations and tables*/Editors/Harold Wellington Jones, M. D./Normand L Hoerr, M. D./Arthur Osol, Ph.D/with the co-operation of an Editorial Board/and 80 contributors/252 illustrations on 45 plates, 129 in color/First Edition/The Blakiston Company/Philadelphia. Toronto/1951.

Preface:

"*Blakiston's New Gould Medical Dictionary* is a completely new reference work. Based upon *Gould's Medical Dictionary*, which through many editions since 1890 has carried on the tradition of scholarship laid down by the first editor, this new work reflects, much more accurately and thoroughly than could a mere revision, the advances of recent years in the various fields of medicine and the allied sciences. The Editors were convinced that even the most judicious modernization of older material would prove inadequate to the need. They therefore undertook the preparation of an entirely new work—a task which they approached with full realization of its difficulty and one which they now complete with an enhanced realisation of the problems and complexities of modern lexicography."

The progressive changes in the title of this work are worth recording.

What is more, with every change in title, edition numbering is restarted with one. Here is the table of information:

Title	*Year*	*Ed N*
New Medical Dictionary	**1890**	**1**
Illustrated Dictionary of Medicine, Biology, and Allied Sciences	**1894**	**1**
Dictionary of Medical Terms	**1904**	**1**
Gould's Medical Dictionary	**1926**	**1**
	1928	**2**
	1931	**3**
	1935	**4**
	1941	**5**
Blakiston's New Gould Medical Dictionary	**1949**	**1**
	1956	**2 (current)**

3 Variety of Practices

The above examples indicate the possibility of the following varieties of practices:

Original Author's Name in the title-page (1)	*Collaborator's Name given in the title-page in the place of* (2)	*See Example N given in Sec 2* (3)
1 Merged in the title and also retained in the place of the Author's name	**11 (Omitted altogether)**	**11**
	12 Collaborator's Name	**—**
	13 Author's Name	**—**
	14 (No Collaborator)	**14**
2 Merged in the title, but not retained in the place of the Author's Name	**21 (Omitted altogether)**	**—**
	22 Collaborator's Name	**221; 222**
	23 Author's Name	**231; 232; 233**
3 Merged in the title, not retained in the place of Author's Name, but mentioned in the Collaborator Statement	**31 (Omitted altogether)**	**—**
	32 Collaborator's Name	**32; 33**
	33 Author's Name	**—**
4 Merged in the title along with Collaborator's Name	**41 (Omitted altogether)**	**—**
	42 Collaborator's Name	**—**
	43 Author's Name	**43**
5 Merged in the title but occulted by the first word of the title being that of the publisher	**51 (Omitted altogether)**	**—**
	52 Collaborator's Name	**52**
	53 Author's Name	**—**

No doubt no example has been given for 12, 13, 21, 31, 33, 41, 42, 51, and 53. But examples may be forthcoming, if they do not already exist.

4 The Conflict

Whose name are we to use as the heading of the Main Entry in such cases ? That is the conflict. At a deeper level, this question implies another, namely, who is the author of the successive editions of the work ?

The person who easily has the knowledge to resolve the conflict is the one who brings out the later editions. Even the decision by him is subject to common human frailties affecting him. He may be too sentimental and either give the name of the original author as **The Author** in the title page and give his own name only as a collaborator, or he may even omit his name altogether from the title-page, even when more than half of the work embodied in the new edition is different from the work of the original edition.

At the other extreme, an egotistic editor of a new edition may omit the name of the original author and insert his own name as the author even though the change in the work embodied in the new edition is much less than half of the original work. The merging of the name of the original author in the title may be due to one of three causes:

1 It may be in recognition that the frame work designed by the original author continues to be valid though the details need change from time to time.

2 It may be out of deference to the memory of the original author.

3 It may be as a means of having the benefit of the goodwill established for the work by the original author.

5 Follow the Canon of Ascertainability

The safest course to determine the choice of the heading is to rely on the Canon of Ascertainability—that is, by what is indicated in the title-page, rather than sit in judgement over what is given in the title-page.

6 The Result

The result of so relying on the Canon of Ascertainability will be as follows:

Example N as given in Sec 2	*Heading to be chosen*
11	Dewey (Melvil)
14	Rider (Fremont)
221	Lock (R Northwood), *Rev.*
222	Ritichie (James), *Rev.*
231	Sayers (William C Berwick)
232	Butler (T R Fitzwalter)
233	Frick (Bertha Margaret)
32	Parkes (G D) and Mellor (J W), *Ed.*
33	Dyson (G Malcolm), *Ed.*
43	Morton (Leslie T)
52	Jones (Harold Wellington) etc, *Ed.*

7 A Suggestion

Even if the Canon of Ascertainability is adhered to, this class of books would baffle the Canon of Consistency. Perhaps this stage of uncertainty is neither necessary nor unavoidable. The Entry Statements for Author and the Collaborator to be given at the back of the title can be used by the person responsible for an edition to indicate clearly what the intention is. If the name of the original author should go only with the title, his name should not be mentioned on the back of the title-page. Further, the role of the person responsible for the edition should be definitely described on the back of the title-page. The Standards Organisations in different countries and the International Standards Organisation should strive to bring such a standard into vogue.

PART H

NAME OF PERSON

CHAPTER HA

INTRODUCTION

Examples will be found in Chap JA, Part 4 and in the later Sec of this Chap.

0 Places of Occurrence

A Name-of-Person occurs in most of the entries of a library catalogue. It occurs in the Headings of entries. It also occurs in their Title-Sections. In a Heading it may occur as the name of an Author, or of a Collaborator of one kind or another, or of a person forming the subject of study, or of a person whose name forms the title of a document. It may occur in a Title-Section in any of the above ways except as name of author. The variety of ways in which a Name-of-Person can occur increases the frequency of its occurrence in entries. A Catalogue Code has, therefore, to pay special attention to a Name-of-Person. Its features creating problems in cataloguing are:

1 The number of words in it;
2 Their grammatical nature;
3 Their functions;
4 Their sequence;
5 Their relative potency; and
6 The complexities in their structure.

1 Number of Words

In the far-off days, the number of persons writing books was small. Formation of homonym among names of authors was not frequent. Therefore the name of an author often consisted of one word only—such as, Valmiki, Homer, and Kalidasa. However, the increase in the number of persons writing and written upon has led to many-worded Names-of-Persons. Apart from the need to have an extra word to resolve homonym, additional words began to cumulate for one reason or other. In Names-of-Persons of Arabic origin or influence, we come across the largest number of words. Is the cataloguer to retain all these words in the Headings in full ? Can any of the words be removed ? Can any of the words be abbreviated ? Such questions arise today. An author himself reduces some of the words in his name to their initial letters. Is the cataloguer to retain them as they are ? Or, is he to expand them to their full names ?

2 Nature of the Words

The essential words in a Name-of-Person are Proper Nouns. Some

Names-of-Persons include also common nouns and auxiliary words, such as article, preposition, and adjective. When the language of a Name-of-Person is quite foreign to the cataloguer, it may be difficult for him to recognise the the nature of the Words. Modern intercourse among nations brings into a library books published in diverse languages. It will be difficult for any cataloguer to know all the languages. This causes a difficulty. Can the Catalogue Code provide any aid in this matter ?

3 Functions of the Words

Some help can be formulated as we consider the functions of the words in a Name-of-Person. The Proper Nouns are irremovable.

31 Proper Noun

Some of the Proper Nouns denote the Given Name of the person. These words are essential in the Name. One or two of the words may denote the Family Name. It occurs in some cultural groups; and it does not occur in others.

32 Common Noun

Common Nouns may or may not occur in a Name-of-Person. If they do, they may denote some attributes of the person such as academic, civic, military, ritualistic, or other distinction, or the profession of the person or some or his dominant ancestors. They may also denote denomination by caste, creed, or religion. Some may be terms of respect. Most of these are removable. Some are irremovable attachments to the proper nouns in certain cultural groups. Can the Catalogue Code help the cataloguer of a foreign culture to distinguish between the removable and the irremovable common nouns ?

33 Auxiliary Word

The auxiliary words are peculiar to certain cultural groups only. They occur between the Given Name and the Family Name. They are deemed irremovable.

4 Sequence of the Words

Every conceivable sequence is found in a Name-of-Person among the Given Name, the Family Name, and the common nouns, and the auxiliary words.

41 Position of Common Noun

The common nouns may lie at the very beginning, or at the end, or anywhere in the middle as in Buddhistic or Viet-Namese Names-of-Persons. They cannot, therefore, be spotted out in every case by their position, and removed.

42 Family Name at the end

In a Name-of-Person of European, Japanese, Marathi, Gujarathi, Sindhi, Kashmiri, Bengali, Oriya, and Assamese cultural groups, the Family Name occurs last; and the Given Name precedes it. Of the words forming the Given-Name the one specific to the individual usually comes first; and those of father, godfather, or patron may come thereafter in European, Marathi, and Gujarathi Names.

43 Family Name at the Beginning

In a Name-of-Person of Chinese, Viet-Namese, Malayalam, Kannada, and Telugu cultural groups, the Family Name comes first and the words of the Given Name come thereafter.

44 Given Name the Last Proper Noun

In a Name-of-Person of Tamil, Malayalam, Kannada, Telugu and Viet-Namese cultural groups, the last proper noun is usually the Name specific to the individual.

45 Tamil Name

In Tamil the preceding proper nouns may be the names of father and place of birth or place of ancestors.

46 Burmese and Hindi Names

In a Name-of-Person of the Burmese cultural group and in some Names-of-Persons of the Hindi cultural group, the Given Name alone occurs without any other proper nouns.

5 Potency of the Words

51 Common Noun

If there is any common noun in a Name-of-Person, which is an irremovable attachment, it has no potency as a result of its being a common noun. It has no claim to become the Entry Element.

52 Proper Noun

Among the proper nouns, either the Family Name, or the word in the Given Names specific to the individual, may have greater potency than the other.

53 Potent Family Name

In Western, Japanese, and Chinese names, the Family Name is drawn from a far more extensive and larger group of words than the Given Name. The group of the former runs to many thousands, while the group of the latter does not have more than a thousand words or so. Therefore, in a Name-of-

Person in those cultural groups, the Family Name has a greater potency than the Given Name. It has, therefore, a greater right than the Given Name to become the Entry Element.

54 Viet-Nam

On the other hand, in a Name-of-Person of the Viet-Namese culture, the Family Name has to be only one out of about two hundred words. It is, therefore, not usual to make it the Entry Element.

55 Thailand

In Thai culture, the Family Name was brought into use only after 1916. Its number is still small. It is, therefore, not usual to make it the Entry Element.

56 Bengal

In a Name-of-Person of Bengali culture, the Family Name has to be drawn from a group of less than 1000 words; while the Given Name has a very large group running to many thousands to draw from. In spite of this, the English-educated persons prefer to give the Family Name the status of Entry Element. But there is a section of opinion in Bengal which would deny it that status.

57 Potent Given Name

Generally speaking in Indian, Burmese, Ceylonese, and Islamic cultural groups, the Given Name has great potency. It is chosen as Entry Element in a Name-of-Person in Tamil, Malayalam, Kannada, Telugu, Burmese, Ceylonese and Islamic cultural groups.

58 Names for Investigation

The relative numerousness of the reservoir of Family Names and Given Names in the Marathi, Gujarathi, Hindi, Oriya, and Assamese cultures needs investigation, to see if the status of Entry Element given to the Family Name satisfies the Canon of Prepotence.

6 Complexities of Structure

61 Compound Name

Compound Family Names and Given Names form one kind of complexity in Names-of-Persons. In some cases the components are linked by a hyphen or by a conjunction or by some other auxiliary word. In some other cases there is no such visible indication that two or more words together form a compound Family Name or a compound Given Name. This happens in Names-of-Persons in Bengali, Marathi, Gujarathi, Sinhalese, and the Islamic cultural groups of India and Pakistan. Can the Catalogue Code give aid to foreign cataloguers in this matter ?

62 Name of Married Woman

A Compound Family Name among the Names of married women of some of the European cultural groups present great difficulty. It is a compound of the Family Names of the Husband and the Wife. Their sequence varies. The connecting word also is not the same. Their claim to the status of Entry Element cannot be determined by their position alone. Can the Catalogue Code give aid to foreign cataloguers in this matter ?

63 Auxiliary Word

The auxiliary word between Given Name and Family Name in European cultural groups gives difficulty. In some it is deemed to go with the Family Name and in some others with the Given Name. Here again can the Catalogue Code give aid to foreign cataloguers ?

64 Arabic Name

The Names based on Arabic culture present peculiarities of their own. These will become clear in Chap HF, dealing with the rendering of such names.

7 Cultural Impact

To add to the five important problem-cases pointed out in the preceding sections as needing special aid from the Catalogue Code, more tantalising problems are created as a result of the cultural impact between different cultural groups. It leads to imitation as well as counter-imitation. The order of King Rama VI of Thailand calling for the adoption of Surnames by all his people and arranging to confer them officially was a result of his travel in Europe. But in spite of its adoption, the surname has not been made the Entry Element. In Bengal, there is conflict between Family Names and Given Names as stated in Sec HA5, as a result of British contact. In Uttar-Pradesh and Punjab, Family Name came into vogue as a result of British impact. But the dropping of the Family Name has begun in more recent years. While the Muslims of India and Pakistan do not generally go in for Family Name, a few do so. In some places, but not in all, the Christians imitate the West. In Indonesia, the father's name is being treated as if it were Family Name, just during the present generation. This vogue may or may not be continued. In Bengal and Uttar-Pradesh, and to a smaller degree in other areas, the Given Name, which is a single word, is broken into two parts and written out as if they were two distinct words,—Ganesh Prasad instead of Ganeshprasad, Prithvi Nath instead of Prithvinath, Sankara Narayanan instead of Sankaranarayanan, and Vidya Bhushan instead of Vidyabhushan. As a result of British contact, some contract the former of these two parts into its initial letter and use the second part as it if were the true name by itself. In the name of Sir C V Raman, the real name should be C Venkataraman. Some abbreviate all the proper nouns into their respective initial letters and retain only the last attached common noun in full. A S P Ayyar is an example. It should be A S Panchapakesa Ayyar. Ayyar is a common noun attached to the proper noun.

8 Towards Aid

The terminology introduced and the procedure laid down in the succeeding sections of this chapter, taken along with the Rules on the rendering of Names-of-Persons, form a sample of one way in which a Catalogue Code can give some aid to foreign cataloguers. The best aid can come only by the implementation of the standard for Entry Statement for Author (*See* Sec HG 5).

CHAPTER HB

TERMINOLOGY : SIMPLE NAME

1 Introduction

In my report to Unesco on Asian Names [RR1], I developed a certain terminology in the process of probing into the structure of a Name-of-Person and the problem of rendering it in the Heading of an Entry. Perhaps some of these terms may be of help in the further pursuit of this problem. They are therefore given here.

2 Name-of-Person

2 **Name-of-Person.**—Word or set of words arranged in a definite sequence and used to denote a person.

21 **Name.**—Name-of-Person.

This briefer term will be used in any context where it is not likely to denote any entity other than a person.

3 Kinds of Word-Group

31 Given Name

Word or word-group usually given to a person, shortly after birth, as the individual's name, by the parents or their deputy. It consists of proper nouns. It is also denoted by the terms Christian Name, Personal Name, Forename, and First Name.

The last two terms are valid only in Western, Japanese, Marathi, Gujarathi, and Bengali Names. In Tamil, Malayalam, Kannada, Telugu, Sinhalese, Viet-Namese, and Indonesian Names, it is the last proper noun. In Hindi and Punjabi also, it may be the last proper noun in some cases. But it may be followed by a common noun (*See* Sec HB33). In Marathi, Gujarathi, Kashmiri, Punjabi, Hindi, Assamese, Bengali, and Oriya names, it is the first proper noun. But it may be preceded by a common noun or other honorifics. (*See* Sec HB34).

32 Family Name

32 **Family Name.**—Word or word-group normally inherited by a person as denoting the name of his family. It consists of proper noun(s). It is also denoted by the terms Surname and Last Name.

The last term is valid only in Western, Japanese, Marathi, Gujarathi, Bengali, and Hindi names. In Chinese, Viet-Namese, Malayalam, Kannada, and Telugu names, it is the First Name.

33 Irremovable Attachment

33 **Irremovable Attachment.**—A Word or word-group made of common nouns attached after the Given Name, deemed to be an Irremovable Attachment to the Given Name, and always taken along with it.

It is difficult for a foreign cataloguer to recognise an Irremovable Attachment. Therefore, the next Sec provides some aid in this respect.

331 The following list gives some of the oft-recurring Irremovable Attachments in names of Burmese, Ceylonese, Hindi, Kannada, Malayalam, Punjabi, Telugu, and Tamil cultural groups. Similar lists should be prepared for other cultural groups.

Note:

1 The language of the word is enclosed in brackets in most cases.

2 If a word may occur in two or more languages, all the languages are given within the brackets.

3 Variants due to transliteration are listed in many cases.

4 In Burmese, the Irremovable Attachment occurs as a Prefix and in all other languages as a Suffix.

5 In Islamic name, the Irremovable Attachment may be a Prefix or a Suffix.

Abhar (Tamil)
Achar (Kannada)
Acharaya (Telugu)
Acharayalu (Telugu)
Acharayalu (Telugu)
Achari (Kannada)
Achariar (Tamil)
Acharya (Kannada/Tamil)
Achchan (Malayalam)
Adigal (Tamil)
Agha (Islamic)
Agha (Islamic)
Aiya (Tamil/Telugu)
Aiyangar (Tamil)

Aiyar (Kannada/Malayalam/
 Tamil)
Aiyengar (Kannada)
Aiyer (Kannada)
Akka (Kannada)
Alwar (Tamil)
Amba (Kannada/Tamil)
Ambal (Kannada)
Ambalakkarar (Tamil)
Ambalavasi (Tamil)
Amma (Kannada/Malayalam/
 Tamil/Ceylon)
Ammaiyar (Tamil)
Ammal (Tamil)
Ammanni (Kannada)
Anna (Kannada/Tamil)
Annavi (Tamil)
Annaiya, Annaya (Kannada)
Anniah (Kannada)
Appa (Kannada/Tamil)
Appiah, Appaiya, Appaji, Appana,
 Appaya (Kannada)
Appu (Ceylon)
Appusamy (Ceylon)
Aradhya (Kannada)
Arasu (Kannada)
Arya (Kannada/Tamil)
Aryan (Kannada)
Asan (Malayalam/Tamil)
Asari (Tamil)
Atiyodi (Malayalam)
Atreya (Telugu)
Avadhani (Kannada/Tamil)
Avadhaniar (Tamil)
Ayya (Kannada)
Ayyangar (Kannada/Tamil)
Ayyar (Kannada/Tamil)
Babu (Tamil/Telugu)
Bagavathar (Tamil)
Bai (Kannada/Tamil)
Banda (Ceylon)
Bandara (Ceylon)
Bayi (Kannada)
Bhadra (Kannada)
Bhadran (Kannada)
Bhar (Hindi/Punjabi)
Bharati (Tamil)
Bharatiar (Tamil)
Bhat (Tamil)
Bhatta (Kannada)
Bhatta (Kannada/Tamil/
 Telugu)
Bhattachari (Tamil)
Bhattacharya (Kannada)
Bhattar (Tamil)
Bhattatiri (Malayalam)
Bhattatiripad (Malayalam)
Bhan (Hindi/Punjabi)
Bhupala (Telugu)
Bhusan, Bhushana (Kannada)
Bhushan (Hindi/Punjabi)
Bihari (Hindi/Punjabi)
Bihari Lal (Hindi/Punjabi)
Boyi (Kannada)
Chand (Hindi/Punjabi)
Chander (Hindi/Punjabi)
Char, Chari, Charya (Kannada)
Chauduri (Telugu)
Chetti (Kannada/Tamil)
Chettiyar (Tamil)
Chetty, Chettiar (Kannada)
Das (Kannada/Tamil)
Dasa (Kannada)
Dasan (Tamil)
Dasappa (Kannada)
Dass (Hindi/Punjabi)
Dasu (Tamil/Telugu)
Daw (Burmese)
Dayal (Hindi/Punjabi)
Deo (Hindi/Punjabi)
Desika (Kannada)
Desikan (Tamil/Kannada)
Desikar (Tamil/Kannada)
Dev (Hindi/Kannada/Punjabi)
Deva, Devaru (Kannada)
Devi (Tamil)
Dhar
Dikshit (Kannada)
Dikshitalu (Telugu)
Dikshitan(r) (Tamil)
Ditta (Hindi/Punjabi)
Dorai (Tamil)

Elayalu (Malayalam)
Embirandri (Malayalam)
Ezhuthatchan (Malayalam)
Giri (Kannada)
Gowd, Gowda (Kannada)
Gownd, Gownden, Gownder (Kannada/Tamil)
Gramani (Tamil)
Gupta (Kannada)
Gurukkal (Malayalam)
Haji (Islamic)
Hakim (Islamic)
Hami (Ceylon)
Hamina (Ceylon)
Hegde, Heggade (Kannada)
Iah (Kannada)
Iya (Kannada)
Iyengar (Kannada/Tamil)
Iyer (Kannada/Tamil)
Jain
Jatavallabhan(r) (Tamil)
Jetty (Kannada)
Jogi (Kannada)
Jois, Joisa, Jc ni (Kannada)
Josi (Tamil)
Josiyar (Tamil)
Josyer (Kannada)
Jotidar (Tamil)
Kaimal (Malayalam)
Kamath (Kannada)
Kander (Tamil)
Karan (Hindi/Punjabi)
Karanth(a) (Kannada)
Karayalar (Tamil)
Kartha (Malayalam)
Kavi (Telugu)
Kavinjnan (Tamil)
Kavirayan(r) (Tamil)
Khau (Islamic)
Khwaja (Islamic)
Kirth (Hindi/Punjabi)
Kirthi (Kannada)
Kishen (Hindi/Punjabi)
Kishore (Hindi/Punjabi)
Kizhar (Tamil)
Ko (Burmese)
Konan(r) (Tamil)
Kone (Tamil)
Kounder (Tamil)
Krishen (Hindi/Punjabi)
Kudumban (Tamil)
Kumar (Hindi/Kannada/Punjabi)
Kumara (Kannada)
Kumari (Hindi/Kannada/Punjabi/Tamil)
Kumarihami (Ceylon)
Kurukkal (Malayalam)
Kurup (Malayalam)
Kutti (Malayalam)
Labbai (Tamil)
Lal (Hindi/Punjabi)
Lemaltani (Ceylon)
Linga, Lingan, Lingiah (Kannada)
Mahavidwan (Tamil)
Maistri (Tamil)
Mal (Hindi/Punjabi)
Mandradiyar (Tamil)
Manigar (Tamil)
Manikkaran(r) (Tamil)
Mannadiyar (Malayalam)
Mappillai (Malayalam)
Marakkayar (Tamil)
Marar (Malayalam)
Maung (Burmese)
Melakaran (Tamil)
Menike (Ceylon)
Menon (Malayalam)
Mian (Islamic)
Mirza (Islamic)
Mohan (Hindi/Punjabi)
Molvi (Islamic)
Moopan(ar) (Tamil)
Moorthi, Moorthy, Moorty (Kannada)
Moosad (Malayalam)
Moulavi (Islamic)
Mudaliar (Tamil)
Mufti (Islamic)
Murthi (Kannada/Tamil)

Murthy (Telugu)
Murti (Kannada)
Murty (Kannada)
Nachiyar (Tamil)
Naicken (Tamil)
Naidu (Tamil/Telugu)
Naik (Kannada)
Nair (Malayalam)
Nambi (Malayalam/Tamil)
Nambisan (Malayalam)
Nambudri (Malayalam)
Nambudripad (Malayalam)
Namburi (Malayalam)
Nand (Hindi/Punjabi)
Nandan(r) (Tamil)
Narain (Hindi/Punjabi)
Nath (Hindi/Kannada/Punjabi)
Natha, Nathan (Kannada)
Nattan(r) (Tamil)
Navalan(r) (Tamil)
Nawab (Islamic)
Nawabzada (Islamic)
Nayadu (Tamil/Telugu)
Nayak (Kannada)
Nayaka (Kannada/Telugu)
Nayakadu (Telugu)
Nayakan(r) (Tamil)
Nayaki (Kannada/Tamil)
Nayanar (Tamil)
Nayar (Malayalam)
Nedungadi (Malayalam)
Odeya (Kannada)
Odeyar (Tâmil)
Othuvar (Tamil)
Padayachi (Tamil)
Pakir (Tamil)
Pal (Hindi/Punjabi)
Pandaram (Tamil)
Pandit (Tamil)
Pandithan(r) (Tamil)
Pandiyan (Tamil)
Pani (Kannada)
Panickar, Panikker (Malayalam)
Parkash (Hindi/Punjabi)
Parshad (Hindi/Punjabi)
Pathi, Pathy, Pati, Paty (Kannada)
Patrachari (Tamil)
Patrudu (Telugu)
Pattanayakan (Tamil)
Pattar (Tamil)
Pavalan(r) (Tamil)
Peer (Islamic)
Peerzada (Islamic)
Perumal (Tamil)
Pilla (Malayalam)
Pillai (Tamil)
Pishoroti (Malayalam)
Poduval (Malayalam)
Potthi (Malayalam)
Prabhu (Tamil/Telugu)
Prakash (Hindi/Kannada/Punjabi/Telugu)
Prasada (Kannada)
Pujari (Tamil)
Pulavar (Tamil)
Pusari (Tamil)
Qarzi (Islamic)
Rai (Hindi/Punjabi)
Raj (Hindi/Kannada/Punjabi)
Raja (Kannada/Malayalam/Tamil)
Rajan, Rajiah (Kannada)
Raj Kumar (Hindi/Punjabi)
Raju (Kannada/Tamil/Telugu)
Ram (Hindi/Punjabi)
Rao (Hindi/Kannada/Punjabi/Tamil/Telugu)
Rao Naidu (Telugu)
Rasu (Tamil)
Ratnam, Ratna (Kannada)
Rau (Kannada/Tamil)
Rauttar (Tamil)
Raya (Kannada)
Rayalu (Telugu)
Rayappa (Kannada)
Rayaru (Kannada)
Razu, Razulu (Telugu)
Reddi (Tamil/Telugu)
Reddy (Kannada/Tamil)

Roop (Hindi/Punjabi)
Row (Kannada/Tamil)
Rowthar (Tamil)
Sa (Tamil)
Saheb (Tamil)
Saib (Tamil)
Saila, Sailam (Kannada)
Sain (Hindi/Punjabi)
Sami (Kannada)
Saran (Hindi/Punjabi)
Saraswati (Tamil)
Sardar (Islamic)
Sarma, Sarman (Kannada/ Malayalam/Tamil/Telugu)
Sarup (Hindi/Punjabi)
Sastri, Sastrigal (Kannada/Tamil/ Telugu)
Sastrulu (Telugu)
Sastry (Kannada)
Sawmy (Kannada)
Saya (Kannada)
Sayab (Tamil)
Sayans (Kannada)
Sayed (Islamic)
Sekhar (Kannada)
Sen (Hindi/Punjabi)
Seniyan(r) (Tamil)
Servai (Tamil)
Setty, Setti (Kannada)
Setupathi (Tamil)
Shafzada (Islamic)
Shaik (Islamic)
Sharma (Kannada)
Shastri, Shastry (Kannada)
Shetti, Shetty (Kannada)
Sholiyan (Tamil)
Shyam
Siddar (Tamil)
Simha (Kannada)
Singh (Hindi/Kannada/ Punjabi/Tamil)
Singho (Ceylon)
Siva (Tamil)
Sivachariar (Tamil)
Sivan (Tamil)
Somayaji (Kannada/Tamil Telugu)
Srouthi (Kannada)
Sufi (Islamic)
Sundar (Hindi/Punjabi)
Suri (Kannada)
Swami (Kannada/Tamil)
Swamigal (Tamil)
Swamy (Kannada)
Swarup (Hindi/Punjabi)
Syed (Islamic)
Tambiran (Tamil)
Tamburan (Malayalam)
Tamburatti (Malayalam)
Tampan (Malayalam)
Tampi (Malayalam)
Tattachari (Tamil)
Thangal (Malayalam)
Thevan(r) (Tamil)
Tirumalpad (Malayalam)
Tooran (Tamil)
Turai (Tamil)
U (Burmese)
Udayar (Tamil)
Unni (Malayalam)
Unnithan (Malayalam)
Vaidhyan(r) (Malayalam)
Vaithiyan (Tamil)
Vajapeyar (Tamil)
Vallal (Tamil)
Vandayar (Tamil)
Varma (Malayalam)
Varriar (Malayalam)
Vathiyar (Tamil)
Velan(r) (Tamil)
Vellalan (Tamil)
Velu (Tamil)
Warrior (Malayalam)
Wodeyar (Kannada)
Yalaydu (Malayalam)
Yogi (Tamil)

34 Removable Attachment

34 **Removable Attachment.**—A word or word-group made of common nouns or adjectives, attached as honorific or courtesy term after or before or in the middle of a name, deemed removable, and not to be retained in the Heading of an Entry.

341 The following list gives some of the oft-recurring Removable Attachment in names of Buddhistic, Ceylonese, Indian, Indonesian, Malayan, and Viet-Namese cultural groups. Similar lists should be prepared for other cultural groups.

Note:

1 After each word in the succeeding table of Removable Attachment, the language or the culture of occurrence is mentioned within brackets.

2 It is also mentioned within the brackets whether it will occur as a prefix or as a suffix or in the middle of the name.

Adigal, Adigalar (Tamil. Suffix)
Adigar (Ceylon. Suffix)
Andavan (Tamil. Suffix)
Andavar (Tamil. Suffix)
Aratchi (Ceylon. Suffix)
Ashtavadanam (Tamil. Prefix)
Asukavi (Tamil. Prefix)
Avar (Kannada/Tamil. Suffix)
Avargal (Tamil. Suffix)
Avaru (Kannada/Tamil. Suffix)
Avarugal, Avarugalu (Kannada. Suffix)
Ayurveda Bhushanam (Tamil. Prefix)
Be (Viet-Namese. Middle)
Baba (Hindi/Punjabi. Prefix)
Bakshi (Hindi/Punjabi. Prefix)
Basnayake Nilame (Ceylon Suffix)
Bawa (Hindi/Punjabi. Prefix)
Bhagavatam (Tamil. Preffix)
Bhai (Hindi, Punjabi. Prefix)
Bibi (Punjabi. Prefix)
Brahma Sri (Tamil. Prefix)
Brahma Sri Pandit (Tamil. Prefix)
Brahmesri (Tamil. Suffix)
Brahmesrigal, Brahmesrigalavaru (Kannada. Suffix)
Chaophya (Thai. Prefix)
Che (Malayan. Prefix)
Choudhury (Hindi/Punjabi. Prefix)
Chittirakavi (Tamil. Prefix)
Dasu (Tamil. Prefix)
Dato (Malayalan. Prefix)
Dato Nuda (Malayan. Prefix)
Datoh (Malayan. Prefix)
Datoh Panglima (Malayan. Prefix)
Dekchai (Thai. Prefix)
Dekying (Thai. Prefix),
Dewan (Hindi/Punjabi. Prefix)
Dinh (Viet-Namese. Middle)
Diwan Bahadur (India. Prefix)
Diwan Sahib (India. Prefix)
Disave (Ceylon. Suffix)
Diyawadana Nilame (Ceylon. Suffix)
Duc (Viet-Namese. Middle)
Enche (Malayan. Prefix)
Gal, Galu, Galavaru (Kannada. Suffix)
Gate-Mudaliyar (Ceylon. Prefix)
Gate-Muhandiram (Ceylon. Prefix)

Giani (Hindi/Punjabi. Prefix)
Haji (Malayalan. Prefix)
Hakim (Tamil. Prefix)
Huu (Viet-Namese. Middle)
Inche (Malayalan. Prefix)
Jagatguru (Tamil. Prefix)
Jalaviddai (Tamil. Prefix)
Jathidar (Punjabi. Prefix)
Jatida Bhushanam (Tamil. Prefix)
Kanwar (Punjabi. Prefix)
Katikacarya (Ceylon. Title Prefix)
Kaviraj (India. Prefix)
Kaviraj Pandithan (Tamil. Prefix)
Kaze (Tamil. Prefix)
Khun (Thai. Prefix)
Koon (Thai. Prefix)
Koonnai (Thai. Prefix)
Koonnying (Thai. Prefix)
Korale Mahatmaya (Ceylon. Suffix)
Kumari (India. Prefix/Suffix)
Lala (Hindi/Punjabi. Prefix)
Lekam (Ceylon. Suffix)
Lung (Thai. Prefix)
Madhusri (Tamil)
Madura (Indonesian. Prefix)
Madurakavi (Tamil. Prefix)
Mahacarya (Ceylon. Title Prefix)
Maha Mudaliyar (Ceylon. Prefix)
Maharaj (India. Prefix/Suffix)
Maharshi (India. Suffix)
Mahopadyaya (Tamil. Prefix)
Makan (Tamil. Suffix)
Malik (Punjabi. Prefix and Suffix)
Maniyagar (Ceylon. Suffix)
Mas (Indonesia. Prefix)
Master (Hindi/Punjabi. Prefix)
Mian (Hindi/Punjabi. Prefix)
Moulvi (India. Prefix)
Mudaliyar (Ceylon. Prefix)
Muhandiram (Ceylon. Prefix)
Munivar (Tamil, Suffix)
Munshi (India. Suffix)
Nai (Thai. Prefix)
Nang (Thai. Prefix)
Nangsao (Thai. Prefix)
Nawab (India. Prefix)
Nawabzada (India. Prefix)
Nawabram (Tamil. Prefix)
Nilame (Ceylon. Middle)
Nu (Viet-Namese. Middle)
Padikara Mudaliyar (Ceylon. Prefix)
Padikara Muhandiram (Ceylon. Prefix)
Padukasevakan (Tamil. Prefix)
Pandit (Hindi/Punjabi/Ceylon. Prefix)
Pandita (Ceylon. Prefix)
Panditacarya (Ceylon. Prefix)
Panjangam (Tamil. Prefix)
Paramahamsa (Tamil. Prefix)
Paravastu (Tamil. Prefix)
Phra (Thai. Prefix)
Phya (Thai. Prefix)
Prathivathi bayankara (Tamil. Prefix)
Pujiya Pandita (Ceylon. Prefix)
Pulavar (Tamil. Prefix)
Quf (Viet-Namese. Middle)
Raden (Indonesia. Prefix)
Raden Aryo (Indonesia. Prefix)
Raden Mas (Indonesia. Prefix)
Raden Pandji (Indonesia. Prefix)
Rai (Punjabi. Prefix)
Rai Bahadur (India. Prefix)
Rai Sahib (Hindi/Punjabi. Prefix)
Raizada (Punjabi. Prefix)
Raja (Malayan. Prefix)
Raja Bahadur (Tamil. Prefix)
Rajah (India. Prefix)
Raja Mrutyjaya Nisanka
Raj Kumari (India. Prefix)
Rana (Hindi/Punjabi. Prefix)
Rao Bahadur (India. Prefix)
Rao Sahib (India. Prefix)

Rate Mahatmaya (Ceylon. Suffix)
Ratnakara (Tamil. Prefix)
Rishi (Punjab. Prefix)
Ru (Kannada/Tamil. Suffix)
Sadavatanam (Tamil. Prefix)
Sadguru (Tamil. Prefix)
Sahitya Siromani (India/Ceylon. Prefix)
Sahitya Visarada (India/Ceylon. Prefix)
Sami (Tamil. Suffix)
Sannadigal (Tamil. Suffix)
Sardar (India. Prefix)
Sardar Bahadur (Punjab. Prefix)
Sardar Sahib (Punjab. Prefix)
Sastri (Hindi/Punjabi. Prefix)
Sastracarya (Ceylon. Prefix)
Sastra Visarada (India/Ceylon. Prefix)
Seth (Punjab. Prefix)
Si (Viet-Namese. Middle)
Sodasavatanam (Tamil. Prefix)
Sodasavatani (Tamil. Prefix)
Soetan (Indonesia. Prefix)
Sowbhagyavati (Tamil. Suffix)
Sri (India/Ceylon. Prefix. Suffix)
Sridhasri (Tamil. Suffix)
Sri-la-Sri (Tamil. Prefix)
Sriman (Tamil. Prefix)
Srimathi (India. Prefix)
Srungarakavi (Tamil. Prefix)
Sultan (Malayan. Prefix)
Swami (India. Prefix)
Swamigal (Tamil. Suffix)
Syed (Malayan. Prefix)
Thakur (Hindi/Punjabi. Prefix)
Thi (Viet-Namese. Middle)
Tikka (Punjabi. Prefix)
Tiru (Tamil. Prefix)
Tirumathi(Tamil. Prefix)
Tiruvalar (Tamil. Prefix)
Toh (Malayan. Prefix)
Trong (Viet-Namese. Middle)
Tuan (Malayan. Prefix)
Tungku (Malayan. Prefix)
Udayar (Ceylon. Suffix)
Ungku (Malayan. Prefix)
Vaid (Hindi/Punjabi. Prefix)
Vaidraj (Hindi/Punjabi. Prefix)
Van (Viet-Namese. Middle)
Vanniyar (Ceylon. Suffix)
Varakavi (Tamil. Prefix)
Veda Aratchi (Ceylon. Prefix)
Veda Mudaliyar (Ceylon. Prefix)
Veda Muhandiram (Ceylon. Prefix)
Velvidance (Ceylon. Suffix)
Vi (Viet-Namese. Middle)
Vidan Aratchi (Ceylon. Suffix)
Vidane (Ceylon. Suffix)
Vidwan (Tamil. Prefix)
Vidya Visarada (India/Ceylon. Prefix)
Viet (Viet-Namese. Middle)
Visarada (India/Ceylon. Prefix)
Wan (Malayan. Prefix)
Yang Mutia (Malayan. Prefix)

35 Irremovable Auxiliary Word

35 **Irremovable Auxiliary Word.**—An article or a preposition, or a combination of article and preposition, or any other auxiliary word occurring between the Given Name and the Family Name. It is usually retained in the Heading of an Entry.

A list of the articles in some of the languages is given in Sec EC1. Prepositions and their combinations with articles can be easily recognised.

This list should be completed and similar lists should be prepared for other languages.

36 Abbreviated Word

36 **Abbreviated Word.**—A proper noun in a Name, not fully spelt out but abbreviated to one or more initial letters, either habitually by the person himself, or in public usage or reference, or in the title-page, or anywhere else in the preliminary pages, or elsewhere in the document.

Examples:

1	J Boswell	*for*	James Boswell
2	A W Cardinall	*for*	Allen Wolsey Cardinall
3	G W C Kaye	*for*	George William Clarison Kaye
4	B C Pal	*for*	Bepin Chandra Pal
5	S N Sen	*for*	Surendar Nath Sen
6	R P Sood	*for*	Ramraksh Pal Sood
7	A J Wells	*for*	Arthur James Wells

CHAPTER HC

TERMINOLOGY : COMPOUND NAME

1 Compound Family Name

1 **Compound Family Name.**—Family Name made up of two or more proper nouns, either

1 Connected by a hyphen; or

2 Connected by a conjunction or any other kind of auxiliary word; or

3 Written separately without any connecting symbol or auxiliary word.

Examples:

The compound Family Name is in Capitals and Small Capitals.

1 Arthur Thomas QUILLER-COUCH
2 Hermann SCHULZE-DELITZSCH
3 Theodore WATTS-DUNTON
4 Ricardo LEON Y ROMAN
5 Giorgio LEVI DELLA VIDA
6 J J MARCUET DE VASSELOT
7 Roger MARTIN DU GARD
8 Garo MERHART VON BERNEGG
9 Henri Joachim de BIJLL NACHENIUS
10 Vicente Antonio de ESPIRITO SANTO
11 Dipak DAS GUPTA
12 Krishna Row Mukund DIXIT PATWARDHAN
13 Surendar Nath BASU RAY CHAUDHURI
14 Kumara Munindra Deb RAI MAHASAI

If the component words of a Compound Family Name are connected by a hyphen or an auxiliary word as in the first eight of the above examples, the Compound Name can be easily recognised. In the absence of such an indicator, it is not possible to recognise it. To help a foreign cataloguer, there appears to be no aid other than giving a list of Compound Surnames, unless the International Standard for the Entry Statement for Author on the back of the title-page (*See* Sec FL78), prescribing the printing in dominant type-face the whole compound Family Name, is followed. In the meantime some aid is given in the three succeeding rules for Bengali, Gujarathi, Kannada, Marathi, and Sinhalese names.

2 Sinhalese Starter Word for Three-Worded Family Name

2 If the last-but-two proper noun in a Sinhalese name is any one of the following, that word and the next two words taken together form a Three-Worded Family Name.

Casie	D, Da, De	Dias

3 Bengali and Sinhalese Starter Word for Two-Worded Family Name

3 If the penultimate proper noun in a Bengali or a Sinhalese name is any one of the following, that word and the next word together form a Two-Worded Family Name.

Abaya (Sinhalese)
Acharya (Bengali)
Ayan (Bengali)
Baidya (Bengali)
Bal (Bengali)
Bandyopadhyay (Bengali)
Barr (Sinhalese)
Barua (Bengali)
Basu (Bengali)
Bej (Bengali)
Bhanja (Bengali)
Biswa (Bengali)
Brito (Sinhalese)
Casie (Sinhalese)
Chakravorty (Bengali)
Chakrabarti (Bengali)
Chel (Bengali)
Christie (Sinhalese)
Croos (Sinhalese)
Crosett (Sinhalese)
Das (Bengali)
Datta (Bengali)
De (Bengali, Sinhalese)
Deb (Bengali)
Dias (Sinhalese)
Don (Sinhalese)
Dutta (Bengali)

Flamer (Sinhalese)
Gairik (Bengali)
Gandha (Bengali)
Ghose (Bengali)
Ghosh (Bengali)
Gogerly (Sinhalese)
Guha (Bengali)
Gupta (Bengali)
Herat (Sinhalese)
Home (Bengali)
Homer (Sinhalese)
Izadeen (Sinhalese)
Jayasinha (Sinhalese)
Jayaweera (Sinhalese)
Kanja (Bengali)
Kansa (Bengali)
Kar (Bengali)
Kohoban (Sinhalese)
Kuriwita (Sinhalese)
Lata (Bengali)
Lorenz (Sinhalese)
Macan (Sinhalese)
Mallik (Bengali)
Manicka (Sinhalese)
Marika (Sinhalese)
Mendis (Sinhalese)
Mitra (Bengali)

Nag (Bengali)
Nama (Bengali)
Nandi (Bengali)
Omer (Sinhalese)
Pal (Bengali)
Pandita (Sinhalese)
Patta (Bengali)
Pinto (Sinhalese)
Pujita (Sinhalese)
Puran (Bengali)
Raj (Bengali)
Rajak (Bengali)
Ray (Bengali)
Rudra (Bengali)
Sadhu (Bengali)
Saha (Bengali)
Sama (Bengali)
Samaddar (Bengali)
Samuel (Sinhalese)
Sarkar (Bengali)
Satra (Bengali)
Sen (Bengali)
Senathi (Sinhalese)
Ṣha (Bengali)
Sharma (Bengali)
Shukla (Bengali)
Shyam (Bengali)
Silva (Sinhalese)
Singha (Bengali)
Sinha (Bengali)
Siv (Bengali)
Sri (Sinhalese)
Suriya (Sinhalese)
Syam (Bengali)
Thakur (Bengali)
Vijaya (Sinhalese)

4 Compound Family Name without Starter Word

4 The following Compound Family Names occur in Gujarathi, Kannada, Marathi, and Sinhalese names, in addition to those indicated in Sec HC2 and HC3.

Abhang Ateetakar (Marathi)
Atmaram Bhukhanvala (Gujarathi)
Baheli Homji (Gujarathi)
Bal Mahajan (Marathi)
Bapat Dikshit (Marathi)
Barwe Wad (Marathi)
Bhat Peshawe (Marathi)
Bhrugu Shastri (Gujarathi)
Biradar Patil (Kannada)
Chapte Sikhatma (Marathi)
Dehai Kulkarni (Kannada)
Deo Inamadar (Kannada)
Deo Paranjpa (Marathi)
Deodhar Dhamdhere (Marathi)
Desai Kolhatkar (Marathi)
Deva Aditya (Sinhalese)
Dikshi Sana (Marathi)
Dixit Patwardhan (Marathi)
Ehelepola Seneviratne (Sinhalese)
Flamer Caldera (Sinhalese)
Gogerly Moragoda (Sinhalese)
Gokhale Raste (Marathi)
Gokhale Tasgaokar (Marathi)
Gora Gandhi (Gujarathi)
Hans Boedkar (Marathi)
Jhaver Laxmichandvala (Gujarathi)
Joshi Ghorpade (Marathi)
Joshi Palashetakar (Marathi)
Kadam Sonaalkar (Marathi)
Kadim Diwan (Kannada)
Kamat Dalal (Marathi)
Kanawade Patil (Marathi)
Kankani Thanki (Gujarathi)
Kara Kalyanavala (Gujarathi)
Kashi Parekh (Gujarathi)
Kathiavad Divanji (Gujarathi)

Khot Bhagwat (Marathi)
Khirasagar Kulkarni (Marathi)
Kunte Mahajan (Marathi)
Lohar Khamgaokar (Marathi)
Mahajan Kunte (Marathi)
Maji Patil (Kannada)
Mamle-Desai (Kannada)
Modak Howaldar (Marathi)
Mondhe Kulkarni (Marathi)
Mulki Patil (Kannada)
Mutalik Desai (Kannada)
Mutalik Deshapande (Kannada)
Mutalik Madagouda (Kannada)
Naik Nimbalkar (Marathi)
Naik Thigale (Marathi)
Orpe Potdar (Marathi)
Pai Raikar (Kannada)
Pathak Vadiya (Marathi)
Patil Kulkarni (Kannada)
Pawar Bane (Marathi)
Pestan Jampsa (Gujarathi)
Phadtari Deshmuk (Marathi)
Phaphe Manohar (Marathi)
Prabhu Desai (Kannada)
Prabhune Pisarwakar (Marathi)
Puranic Dikshit (Kannada)
Raje Shirke (Marathi)
Salunke Rao (Marathi)
Saraf Wakde (Marathi)
Savare Bhagavat (Marathi)
Sawant Tirawadekar (Marathi)
Shamal Becharvala (Gujarathi)
Soman Narawana (Marathi)
Thorat Gadgil (Marathi)
Ulli Pradhan (Kannada)
Vachchha Gandhi (Gujarathi)
Vaidya Shastri (Gujarathi)
Varmani Thanki (Gujarathi)

5 Compound Given Name

5 **Compound Given Name.**—Given Name made up of two or more proper nouns, either

1 Connected by a hyphen, or

2 Connected by a conjunction or any other auxiliary word; or

3 Written separately without any connecting symbol or auxiliary word.

If the component words of a Compound Given Name are connected by a hyphen or by an auxiliary word, the compound name can be easily recognized.

In a Name-of-Person of a cultural group, which invariably ends or begins with a Family Name, it is not of very great importance that one should recognize a set of words in the Given Name as a Compound. Generally speaking, this is true of a Western, Japanese, Assamese, Bengali, Gujarathi, Kashmiri, Marathi, or Oriya name, each of which ends with a Family Name. This is also true of a Chinese or Viet-Namese name, each of which begins with a Family Name.

But in a Name-of-Person without a Family Name, the Given Name will have to be made the Entry Element. In a Gujarathi or a Marathi name of a period prior to early nineteenth century, Family Name was not used by many authors and the Given Name began with a name specific to the individual and ended with the name specific to his father. But neither of these was a compound name. In any other cultural group where the Given Name has to be made the Entry Element, it is often the last proper noun in the name—*i e*, it will be the last noun barring any common noun which may occur at the end as an Irremovable Attachment to the Given Name. This is what happens invariably in Viet-Namese, Kannada, Malayalam, Tamil and Telugu names. In these cases, if the words with a Compound Given Name are written separately without a hyphen connecting them, it will not be possible for the cataloguer to decide where the Entry Element should begin and which of the Proper Nouns before the last one should be taken with the Secondary Element.

In Viet-Namese, there is a tendency to insert the hyphen. But in Kannada, Malayalam, Tamil, and Telugu names, there is the opposite tendency of breaking a single fused word into its parts in violation of the Rules of Grammar and putting them down as if they were separate words.

It is not easy even for a cataloguer born within the cultural group to meet this situation successfully. It is particularly so in the case of a Tamil name. Because the word preceding the Given Name of the individual is usually the Given Name of the father. These are similar. It will be very difficult to decide where the father's Given Name ends and where the son's Given Name begins.

CHAPTER HD

SPLIT GIVEN NAME

1 South India

Here are some examples of this tendency in Kannada, Malayalam, Tamil, and Telugu Names.

The words in Capital and Small Capitals should be treated as a Single Word denoting the Split Given Name specific to the individual. The words in the Split Given Name taken together are to be used as Entry Element.

1 Pannambal VISHNU MURTHI
2 Kasargode YOGESHA ANANDA ROW
3 Candeth SIVA SANKARA MENON
4 Chettur VISVA NATHA NAIR
5 Rama Nathan ANANTHA RAMAN
6 Kalyana Raman BADARI NARAYANAN
7 Ramu Mudaliar BHIMA SANKARAN
8 Kesava Pillai DESIKA VINAYAGAM
9 Umapathi GANAPATHI SUBRAMANIAN
10 Partha Sarathy GOPALA KRISHNA
11 Panchapakesan SANKARA NARAYANAN
12 Muthu Krishna Mudaliar SANKARA SUBRAMANIA MUDALIAR
13 Sita Raman SATYA NARAYANAN
14 Kesarimangalam Manikam Ayyar SIVA RAMAN
15 Sundara Raman SIVA RAMA KRISHNAN
16 Siva Raman SIVA SANKARA NARAYANA
17 Duggiraia RAMA KRISHNA ROW
18 Durba SUBRA MANIAN

It is difficult to make an exhaustive list of such split words constituting a Given Name. For, it is not known what fused word will be split by a person in his own Given Name or that of his father.

The first two are Kannada Names. The last two are Telugu Names. The others are Tamil Names.

In 2, 3, 4, and 5, the last word is an Irremovable Attachment to the Given Name.

In 7, 8, and 12, the second word is an Irremovable Attachment to the Given Name of the Father.

In 14, the third word is an Irremovable Attachment to the Given Name of the Father.

2 Split Words Alone

In Punjabi and Hindi Names without a Family Name, there is often no proper noun other than the Given Name in a Split Form. If one can recognize it as a Punjabi or Hindi Name, it will be easy to escape making the second word the Entry Element and the First Word the Secondary Element. But it will not be possible for a foreign cataloguer to recognize the name as a Punjabi or a Hindi one. It is conjectured that the total number of words likely to occur as the second part of a split Given Name in Punjabi or Hindi name will not exceed a few hundreds. But the number of the first of the split words will be far more numerous. Therefore, if a fairly exhaustive list of the second of the split words could be provided, it will help a foreign cataloguer to recognize with its aid a Punjabi or a Hindi name and use it merely as if it were an Irremovable Attachment to the preceding word.

3 Two-Worded Given Name in the Islamic Names in India and Pakistan

An Islamic Name in India and Pakistan may have one of the following words as Family Name:

Abidi	Hasani	Naqvi	Rizvi
Alavi	Hashimi	Qadiani	Sabzwari
Alvi	Husani	Qadri	Siddiqi
Burnie	Husaini	Qidwai	Shirani
Chishtie	Hussaini	Qizilbash	Shirwani
Chughtai	Jafri	Qadsi	Tirmazi
Durrani	Kidwai	Quraishi	Usmani
Farooqi	Nadvi	Qutbi	Zaidi
Faruqi	Naqavi	Rizavi	Zubairi

This is not an exhaustive list.

If a Family Name occurs at all, it occurs as the last proper noun. But it occurs only in a comparatively few names. In most cases, there is only a Two-Worded Given Name excluding any Irremovable Attachment, if any, at the beginning or at the end. Of the two words in the Given Name, the second is usually a word denoting God or the Prophet, or meaning "Religion". The first word is a common word—such as Asad (=Lion), Nur (=Light), and Rahimat (=Grace). The result is a Two-Worded Given Name such as Asad Ullah, Nur Elahi, and Rahimat ul-Islam. It is conjectured that the total number of the words likely to occur as the second word in an Islamic Given Name in India and Pakistan will be considerably smaller than the number of the words likely to occur as the first word. Therefore if a fairly exhaustive list of the possible second words could be given, it will help a foreign cataloguer to recognize with its aid an Islamic Name without a family name and use it as if it were an Irremovable Attachment to the preceding words.

4 Gujarathi and Marathi Given Name without Family Name

In a Gujarathi or Marathi name without a Family Name, the first proper noun is the Given Name specific to the individual; and the second is the

Given Name specific to his father. The Entry Element should be the first of the two Given Names. But it will not be easy for a foreign cataloguer to recognize the name as a Gujarathi or a Marathi Name. Both the words in the name are alike and are taken from the same group of words. Therefore, the kind of help to a foreign cataloguer suggested in Sec HD2 and HD3 for Hindi, Punjabi, and Islamic names cannot be given. The only way will be to give an exhaustive list of such Two-Worded Names without a Family Name, likely to occur in Author Headings and Subject Headings. But their number is very great. Only a sample is given here. The Given Name of the Individual is in Capitals and Small Capitals.

ANANT Atmaram
ATMARAM Kesavji
KESAVJI Vishvanath
VISHVANATH Govindji
EDALJI Jamshedji
JAMSHEDJI Faramji
AMBALAL Dinarakadas
JIVANLAL Ambalal
BALLUBHAI Kahandas
CHEGANLAL Ballubhai
NARAYAN Hemachandra
SANKARANAND Narayan

5 List of Second Words

The following is a combined list of the more important words likely to occur as the second word in a Two-Worded Punjabi or Hindi Given Name or an Islamic Given Name of India or Pakistan.

Abbas (Islamic)
Afzal (Islamic)
Ahmed (Islamic)
Alam (Islamic)
Ali (Islamic)
Allah (Islamic)
Anand
Aziz (Islamic)
Anant
Askari (Islamic)
Asre
Autar
Ayyub (Islamic)
Azhar (Islamic)
Babu
Badan
Bahadur
Bai
Bala
Ballabh
Bhanu
Bhuj
Bhushan
Bandhu
Bansh
Bari (Islamic)
Bashir (Islamic)
Behari
Bhan
Chand
Chandra
Charan
Das
Dayal
Deo
Dev
Devi
Dhar
Dhawan
Din
Din (Islamic)
Dular
Dulare
Dulari
Dutt
Farooq (Islamic)
Ganesh
Gopal
Govind
Haider (Islamic)
Haleem (Islamic)
Hameed (Islamic)
Hanif (Islamic)
Haq (Islamic)
Haque (Islamic)
Hari
Hasan (Islamic)
Husain (Islamic)
Idris (Islamic)
Iqbal (Islamic)
Is-haq (Islamic)
Islam (Islamic)
Ismail (Islamic)
Jabbar (Islamic)
Jalil (Islamic)
Jit

Jiwan
Kamini
Kant
Kanta
Kanti
Karan
Kaur
Kaushal
Kishan
Kishore
Kishori
Krishna
Kumar
Kumari
Lal
Lakhan
Lata
Laxman
Majid (Islamic)
Mal
Malik (Islamic)
Mohan
Mohini
Mukhtar (Islamic)
Muni
Murari
Murti
Mushtaq (Islamic)
Mustafa (Islamic)
Nabi (Islamic)
Nand
Nandan
Nanddini
Narain
Naresh
Nath
Nazir (Islamic)
Nivas
Pal
Pati
Phool
Prabha
Prakash
Prasad
Pratap
Pyari
Qadir (Islamic)
Qayyum (Islamic)
Rafiq (Islamic)
Rahim (Islamic)
Rahman (Islamic)
Rai
Raj
Ram
Raman
Rani
Ranjan
Raoof (Islamic)
Rashid (Islamic)
Rasool (Islamic)
Ratan
Raza (Islamic)
Rezzaq (Islamic)
Roshan
Sagar
Sahai
Salam (Islamic)
Sanehi
Saran
Sarup
Sen
Sewak
Shah (Islamic)
Shamim (Islamic)
Shanker
Shekar
Shiv
Shyam
Singh
Suleman (Islamic)
Sunder
Swarup
Umar (Islamic)
Vallabh
Vanti
Vati
Vilas
Vinayak
Vir
Yagya
Yahya
Yunus (Islamic)
Yaqub (Islamic)
Yusuf (Islamic)
Zaki (Islamic)

CHAPTER HE

FORMS OF NAME-OF-PERSON

The following terms correspond to the different stages in the successive reduction of a Name-of-Person to the form in which it is finally entered in the the Heading of an Entry.

1 **Usage Name.**—Name-of-Person used in denoting a person for public purposes.

The Usage Name will contain a Given Name in one or more words. It may also contain a Family Name in one or more words, an Irremovable Attachment at the beginning or at the end, a Removable Attachment at the beginning, the middle, or the end and an Irremovable Auxiliary Word between the Given Name and the Family Name.

2 **Title-Page Name.**—Name-of-Person as it occurs on the Title-Page of the document.

The Title-Page name also may present the various kinds of Removable or Irremovable Attachment, and Irremovable Auxiliary Word, and Family Name along with the Given Name, even as the Usage Name may do. But it has usually less of Removable Attachment.

3 **Full Name.**—Usage Name or Title-Page Name as the case may be.

Full Name is the starting point in the reduction of a Name-of-Person. In an Author-Entry, Title-Page name will be the starting point, for arriving at the form in which the name is to be entered in the Heading of an Entry. In a Subject Entry which has the name of a Non-Author as the Heading the Usage Name will be the starting point.

4 **Pure Name.**—Name derived from Full Name by removing all the Removable Attachments, if any.

A Removable Attachment will be a common noun or an honorific word depending on the cultural group to which the Name-of-Person belongs. The table given in Sec HB341 will be of help in deriving the Pure Name from the Full Name in the case of Indian, Ceylonese, Indonesian, Malayan, and Viet-

Namese names. Similar tables should be constructed for other cultural groups. Words denoting academic qualifications, offices held, and civil or military decorations are removable attachments.

5 **Reduced Name.**—Name derived from Pure Name by temporarily coupling together with a hyphen the components of a Compound or multi-worded Given Name or Family Name, if any, if they are not already coupled together by a hyphen or an auxiliary word, and coupling the irremovable attachment at the end if any, with the preceding word or compound word as the case may be.

Any auxiliary word between the Family Name and the Given Name is to be temporarily linked by hyphen to one or other of them according to the practice in the cultural group.

The coupling is to be done only temporarily to facilitate further work. The tables given in Sec HC2, HC3 and HC4 will be of use in recognizing Compound Family Names. With regard to inseparable Two-Worded and artificially Split Given Names, the list given in Sec HD4 and HD5 will be of help.

51 Auxiliary Word

The following table gives some of the conventions prevailing in regard to the attachment of the Auxiliary Word occurring between the Family Name and Given Name in Western names. In column 3, the Family Name is printed in capitals and small capitals. The auxiliary word to be attached to the Family Name is in small caps; while the auxiliary word to be attached to the Given Name is in Roman smalls.

Language	Auxiliary Word to be Attached to	Example
Danish	1 Family Name, if of romance origin and the auxiliary consists of or contains and article	Jans Lessen LA COUR
	2 Given Name if the auxiliary is *av*, *af* or *von*	Carl von LINNE
Dutch	Given Name	Jan ten BRINK
English	Family Name	John DE MORGAN
French	1 Family Name if the auxiliary consists of or contains an article	Jean de LA FONTAINE
	2 Given Name if the auxiliary is a preposition	Eugene de FAYE

Language	Auxiliary Word to be Attached to	Example
German	Given Name	Peter von der MUHLL
Italian	1 Family Name if auxiliary is an article 2 Given Name if auxiliary is or contains a preposition	Antonio degli ALBERTI
Norwegian	Same as in Danish	
Swedish	1 Family Name, if of romance origin 2 Same as in Danish	Magnus Gabriel DE LA GARDIE

6 **Entry Element.**—In the case of a Name-of-Person, other than Chinese, the Entry Element, is to consist of the last word or the last coupled word-group in the Reduced Name. If Chinese, the entire Pure Name, without any change in the sequence of its words, is to be the Entry Element.

7 **Secondary Element.**—In the case of a Name-of-Person, other than Chinese, the Secondary Element is to consist of all the words of the Reduced Name, not included in the Entry Element.

8 **Entry Name.**—Entry Element followed by the Secondary element, if any, in a Name-of-Person, with all the temporary hyphens removed.

CHAPTER HF

ARABIC NAME

0 Word Groups

An Arabic name may consist of one or more groups of words representing respectively:

1 Conventional or professional title or *laqab;*

2 The personal name or *ism;*

21 The name of the father or the brother of the author preceded by the word "Ibn" or "Bin" or "B" and "Akhu" respectively;

22 A succession of the names of grandfather, great grandfather, etc, each name being preceded by "Ibn" or its variants;

3 The paternal or matronymical name or *kunyah,* usually beginning with the word "Abu";

4 The conferred title or *laqab;*

5 The nickname or *urf;*

6 The relative name or *nisbah* usually eding in *i* or *y;*

7 The literary name or *takhallus,* usually of one or two syllables only; and

71 The "familiar name" or the name by which the person is generally referred to by the public and in books, such a name being usually preceded by the words "*almaruf ba*", or "*asaheer*", if it is given on the title page.

These groups of words generally, but not in all cases, come in the sequence indicated above; but it is not to be understood that all the groups will necessarily occur in all the names.

The *Kunyah* is an indirect name. Normally it consists of the word 'Abu' meaning 'father of' followed by the name of the eldest son or daughter; but there are many exceptions. Certain *Kunyahs* go regularly with certain names owing to the first owner of the name having had that *Kunyah*. Again, *Kunyahs* are given to infants and to persons without children. Hence, we cannot infer from the *Kunyah* the existence of a child bearing the name which follows the word 'Abu'. In some cases, the *Kunyah* does not at all express paternity. It may express some other characteristic. While the normal position of the *Kunyah* is after the name of the father and the names of other ancestors, occasionally it is also placed at the beginning before the personal name. In such cases it will not be difficult to identify the *Kunyah* part of the name.

The conventional title occurring at the beginning may be invariably removed from the Heading in an Entry, for example Hakim, Qazi, Moulvi, Aga, Habib, Khaga, Mir, Sirdar and Syed. But care must be taken to see that it does not constitute the Given Name. This will not be easy for a foreign cataloguer.

2 Entry Element: Ism

The Given Name or Ism will usually consist of one or two words and in rare cases of more than two words. A rough test to spot out the Given Name is this. If the word 'Ibn' or its equivalent or 'Akhu' occurs in the Pure Name, it may be taken that the word immediately before the first 'Ibn' is the Given Name and the word after the first 'Ibn' or 'Akhu' is the father's name or the brother's name respectively. In such a case, the group of words consisting of

1 Given Name; and
2 The word 'Ibn' or its equivalent and the father's name; or
3 The word 'Akhu' and the brother's name;

form the Entry Element.

The groups 2 and 3 form an Irremovable Attachment to the Given Name. If there is no 'Ibn' or 'Akhu' in the name, the first word (or two) in the Pure Name is (are) likely to constitute the Given Name; and it forms the Entry Element.

21 Kunyah as Entry Element

In certain cases, the *Kunyah* may be the only name known, the 'Ism' or the Given Name having never been conferred or having been forgotten. In such a case, the *Kunyah* is to be the Entry Element.

3 Secondary Element: Kunyah

In the heading in a catalogue, the *Kunyah*, if it occurs as part of the name, is to be included in the Secondary Element.

4 Conferred Title: Laqab

The *Laqab* may be defined negatively as a name other than that which the holder received at birth and yet not substituted for it.

The conferred title or *Laqab* is to be omitted.

5 Nick-Name: Urf

The nickname or *Urf* is to be used, if at all, as an Alternative Name or as a Pseudonym.

6 Individualising Element: Nisbah

The *Nisbah* is an adjective which locates the person to whom it is given, as a member of a tribe, as a resident of some place, as one following some trade or in any other way. It can be identified by the fact that it usually ends in '*i*' or '*y*'. It is not unusual to find two or more *Nisbahs* as part of the same name. The *Nisbah* is to be treated as an Individualising Element.

7 Pseudonym: Takhallus

The *Takhallus* is the literary name which most men of letters assume. It is a pseudonym. An author usually puts this pseudonym at the end of his real name. But others refer to him only by his pseudonym. The *Takhallus* can be easily identified by the fact that it comes at the end of the real name and by remembering that it is usually of one or two syllables only. It has to be dealt with in accordance with Rule MD42, if it occurs along with the real name, or in accordance with Rule MD41 and its subdivisions if it occurs alone on the title-page.

71 Pseudonym: Familiar Name

The 'Familiar Name', or the name by which the person is generally referred to by the public and in books, is a source of some difficulty. In the books written by the author himself and in such of their editions as he himself is responsible for, his 'Familiar Name' will not ordinarily be found on the title-page. But in later editions brought out by others, it may happen that the title-page contains the 'Familiar name' alone. This too is a pseudonym.

8 Definite Article

The definite article '*Al*' and its variants may occur before one or more words in a name. Wherever it occurs, it is to be written, but ignored in alphabetisation. If it occurs in the *Nisbah* it is to be underlined. Can we not omit it altogether ?

91 Appeal

It is no easy matter for cataloguers without a special knowledge of Arabic culture to deal with names of such complexity. Linderfelt's *Eclectic card catalogue rules* is said to contain definite instructions on the subject. But I have not had access to a copy of that book. Generally the volumes of the British Museum catalogue dealing with books in Muslim languages and the entries in the *Encyclopaedia of Islam* will be of help in deciding the significance and the sequence of the words in Arabic Names. It must be stated that there is still room for systematisation. There is scope for research in Arabic Names. In addition to the intrinsic complexity of such names, there seem to be also some special features characterising Muslim names of different nationalities such as Spanish, Moorish, Turkish, Egyptian, Arabic, Persian, Afghan, and Indian. The whole problem is bristling with difficulties and uncertainties. The present practice in libraries can at best be described as 'drifting'. The Aligarh University will be doing a great service, if it would set some young men on the investigation and systematisation of this problem and publish an authoritative direction for the rendering of Muslim names.

CHAPTER HG

ILLUSION AND SOLUTION

1 Illusory Solution

Though the terminology and prescription in Chap HE and HF in regard to Name-of-Person, taken along with the auxiliary tables given in Chap HB, HC, and HD appear to be over-elaborate, in fact, they are over-simplified. It is doubtful whether a cataloguer, who is not intimately familiar with the social practices connected with the formation of a Name-of-Person in a cultural group, can successfully and consistently pick out the Entry Element and the Secondary Element respectively. The individual variations—one may almost say idiosyncrasies—in making up one's own name may baffle even a cataloguer born in the same cultural group. A word may be split into two unmeaning parts. A common noun which is only an attachment may be used as if it were a proper noun denoting either a given Name or a Family Name. The greater the deviation of the cultural group of the cataloguer from that of a Name-of-Person, the greater will be the uncertainty.

2 Cultural Groups in Exhaustion

Till now, cataloguing involved only the names of a few cultural groups in most of the libraries. This was the result of nearly two-thirds of the people of the world being in a state of cultural exhaustion, producing few books, and consuming even fewer books by authors belonging to other cultural groups. Therefore the problem of rendering a Name-of-Person has been dealt with in a more or less light-hearted way, and there has been only a small percentage of deviations from the correct rendering. But today practically all the cultural communities of the world are entering into the ascending phase of their current cultural cycles.

3 Creative Activity Everywhere

Creative activity has begun everywhere in the world. New thought is being created by the reviving cultural groups. They cannot be ignored by any other cultural group. The reviving cultural groups are also keen to have access to documents published in every part of the world. Modern transport conditions permit a free circulation of documents throughout the world, whatever be the cultural group of their origin. The consciousness of one world, being helped by international bodies such as the United Nations and its Specialised Agencies, is intensifying this desire on the part of every cultural group of the world to use documents produced in every other cultural group.

4 Conservation of Research Potential

Moreover, the unbalancing between population pressure and the availability of natural and near-natural commodities makes it imperative that the research-potential of the world should be conserved, without any wastage due to any unwanted repetition of one and the same piece of investigation. This requires that any document on nascent thought produced in any cultural group whatever should be served unerringly to the workers in every other cultural group. In this process, the rendering of Name-of-Person will play a very important part. The impracticability of any one cutlural group to render the Names-of-Persons of all other cultural groups will lead to inefficiency of service. Ultimately such an inefficiency of service will be traceable to the insolubility of the problem of Name-of-Person by cataloguing rules, however involved and however clever. Solution of the problem of rendering Names-of-Persons on a world-scale through a number of cataloguing rules is only an illusion.

5 The Right Solution

The one person who knows the Entry Element and the Secondary Element in a Name-of-Person is the person himself. International economy and efficiency in cataloguing requires that the author should indicate in his documents the Entry Element and the Secondary Element in his name, along the lines laid down in the Indian Standard IS : 792-1962 *Specification for title page and back of title page of a book*. This is to be printed at the back of the title-page of a book or in a suitable place in any other kind of document. If this is done, the rule on the rendering of a Name-of-Person need not be anything more than Sec JA1. With this single rule it will be more easy to secure accuracy and consistency in rendering a Name-of-Person than with the plethora of rules crowding cataloguing codes at present. This appears to be the only right solution.

PART J

RENDERING OF NAMES

CHAPTER JA

PERSONAL NAME

1 Entries of Occurrence

A Name-of-Person has to be rendered in the Headings of Main Entries, Book Index Entries, Class Index Entries, and Cross Reference Index Entries.

2 Rule To be Worked For

If the back of the Title-Page of the book conforms to the Standard for Entry Statement for Author mentioned in Sec FR77 the Entry Element is to be the Word(s) printed in a dominant type-face in the Entry Statement for Personal Author; the Secondary Element is to be the rest of the Word(s) in it; and the further Individualising Element is to be the Year(s) mentioned in it.

The task of rendering a Name-of-Person will be quite simple in all entries except in the few Class Index Entries in which the name of the person, who has not written any book, is to be the Heading. For the Entry Element and the Secondary Element in the name of a person would be clearly indicated in all future books, in the Entry Statement for Personal Author on the Back of the Title-Page, after the Standard for this Statement is implemented. It will also cover each Alternative Name of the Person. The Year(s) of the Person will also be given by it. With this Standard implemented, Part H will become unnecessary and this chapter need to have only the above two Rules. We can really have "Cataloguing without tears".

In case this help of the Entry Statement for Personal Author is not available, the Entry Element and the Secondary Element in the name of a person should be found out with the aid of the Definitions and the Rules of Part H and in particular the Sec HE and HF.

The Part H and the Sec of this Chap will be necessary for the documents not conforming to the Standard for the Entry Statement for Personal Author. They may also be of some help to publishers and authors in framing and printing the Entry Statement for Personal Author.

3 One-Worded Name

The rendering of a Title-Page Name consisting of one word only is to write it as it occurs in the Title-Page.

Examples: 1 HOMER. 2 KALIDASA. 3 VALMIKI.

4 One Fully Spelt-Out Word Only

The rendering of a Title-Page Name consisting of one and only one Fully spelt-out word, though preceded by initials, is to write the fully spelt-out word as the Entry Element and to write the expansion of the initials as the Secondary Element.

41 LOCAL RULE FOR EXPANSION OF INITIALS

Each library is to make its own Local Rule authorising the initials alone to be written as the Secondary Element, in case their expansion is beyond its means and the homonym arising, if any, can be resolved in some other convenient way.

Example: RANGANATHAN (S R).

5 Year of the Person

The year of birth of the person is to be added as a further Individualising Element, after the Secondary Element.

It may be possible to find the year from source books, such as biographical dictionaries, *Who's who*, *Who was who*, year-books, and other books. In the last resort, the year of birth can be got by writing to the person himself or his relatives, or by more involved research, or by guess work.

51 LOCAL RULE FOR YEAR OF PERSON

Each library is to make its own Local Rule prescribing the addition of years, only in case of their being needed for the resolution of homonyms actually occurring among the names-of-persons in the Headings of the Entries.

6 Multi-Worded Name

For the rendering of a Title-Page Name consisting of two or more words, it should first be reduced to the Entry Name, and the Entry Element and the Secondary Element should be separated out with the aid of the Definitions and the Sec of Part H and in particular the Chap HE and HF. The rendering is to consist successively of the

1 Entry Element;
2 Secondary Element; and
3 Year(s) of the person.

Examples:

61 One-Worded Entry Element

1 Adams (Mary) (1898).
2 Black (Newton Henry) (1874).
3 Foucher (Alfred) (1865).

62 Hyphenated Entry Element

1 Pringle-Pattison (Andrew Seth) (1856-1931).
2 Quiller-Couch (Arthur Thomas) (1863-1944).
3 Watts-Dunton (Theodore) (1832-1914).

63 Entry Element with Conjunction

1 Leon y Roman (Ricardo) (1877).
2 Levi della Vida (Georgio) (1886).
3 Martin du Gard (Roger) (1881).

64 Two-Worded Entry Element without Hyphen or Conjunction

1 Bal Mahajan (Gopala Krishna) (1875-1932).
2 Kankani Thanki (Anant Atmaram) (1852-1922).
3 Das Gupta (Sachidulal) (1912).

65 Three-Worded Entry Element

1 Basu Ray Chaudhuri (1870-1915)
2 Chen Wen Mou (1919).
3 Datta Rai Mahasai (Kumara Munindra) (1880-1942).

66 Given Name without Attachment as Entry Element

1 Radhakrishnan (Sarvapalle) (1889).
2 Ranganathan (Shiyali Ramamrita) (1892).
3 Venkatachalam (Ramamurti) (1900).

67 Single-Worded Given Name with Irremovable Attachment as Suffix, as Entry Element

1 Ramaswami Ayyar (Chetpet Pattabhirama Ayyar) (1879).
2 Ramaswami Mudaliar (Arcot) (1887).
3 Ramaswami Rao Naidu (Krishna Rao Naidu) (1874-1914).
4 Koman Nayar (Chetur) (1870-1920).
5 Maman Mappillai (Panampalli) (1890-1948).
6 Krishna Shaila (Baindur) (1885-1958).

68 Split-Worded Given Name as Entry Element

1 Anand Prakash (1832).
2 Rajendra Prasad (1884–1963).
3 Rashik Shah (1900-1954).

691 Irremovable Attachment as a Prefix

1 Lay (U) (1903).
2 Ni Ni (Da) (1875-1930).
3 Mohammad Zaki (Syed) (1884-1948).

692 Name with Auxiliary Words in Middle

1 Brink (Jan Ten) (1834-1901).
2 De la Gardie (Magnus Gabriel) (1622-1686).
3 Faille (Jacob Baat de la) (1795-1867).

693 Arabic Names

1 Kasim Ibn Ali (Abu Muhammad).
2 Muhammad Ibn Ali (Abu Abdulla).
3 Mohammad Ibrahim (Farid al-Din Abu Hamid).

7 Nominative Case

A Name-of-Person in a Heading is to be rendered in the Nominative-Case-Form.

In books in Sanskrit, Russian, and other highly inflectional languages, the Title-Page-Name may occur in the instrumental-case-form. This fact makes the above Rule necessary. It will however become unnecessary if such books conform to the Standard for Author Statement in the Title-Page and particularly the Standard for the Entry Statement for Personal Author in the Back of the Title-Page.

CHAPTER JB

GEOGRAPHICAL NAME

1 Language

11 Favoured Language

The name of a Geographical Entity is to be written in the Favoured Language of the library, if it has a name in that language.

Usually continents, countries, constituent states of a large country, large cities, other large land areas, inter-state and inter-continental mountains, oceans, and large seas, bays, gulfs, straits, and rivers may have names in the Favoured Language of the library.

Examples:

1 Germany in English; Deutchland in German.
2 South America in English; Sud Amerika in German.
3 Switzerland in English; Schweisz in German; Suisse in French.
4 Munich in English; Munchen in German.
5 Ganges in English; Ganga in Hindi; Gangai in Tamil.

12 Language of Locality

The name of a Geographical Entity is to be written in the Language of its Locality, if it does not have a name in the Favoured Language of the library.

Usually counties, districts, and smaller areas of a country, small towns and smaller localities, and small mountains, hills and other small land areas, and rivers, lakes, etc within a single linguistic area, may not have names in the Favoured Language of the library.

13 Sources for Name

The name of a Geographical Entity, to be written in the Favoured Language or in the language of the locality, is to be taken from standard gazetteers and atlases in the language concerned. Preference is to be given to official sources.

Examples:

1 *Bartholomew's survey gazetteer*.

2 *Sixth report* (1933) of the U S Geographical Board.

3 *Decision* of the U S Board on Geographical Names.

4 The publication of the Permanent Committee on Geographical Names for British Official Use.

5 The publication of Canada Geographic Board.

6 Ritter's *Geographisch-statistisches lexikon*.

7 Vivien de Saint-Martin. *Nouveau dictionaire de geographie universelle*.

2 Multi-Worded Name

21 Proper Name

The words in the Multi-Worded geographical name, which has come into current use as if it were a proper name, are to be written in full.

22 Sequence of Words

The words in a Multi-Worded geographical name are to be written in the sequence in which they occur in usage and in documents, whether the first word is a substantive, an adjective, or any other auxiliary word, or a generic word that denotes the class of geographical entities to which the entity belongs, or a specific word that individualises it.

Examples:

1 Frankfurt on Main.

2 Far East.

3 Lake Placid; and not Placid, Lake.

4 New Delhi; and not Delhi, New.

5 Bad-Eilsen; and not Eilsen, Bad.

6 Bay of Bengal; and not Bengal, Bay of.

7 Citta Sant' Angelo; and not either Angelo, Citta Sant' or Sant' Angelo, Citta.

8 Mount Everest; and not Everest, Mount.

9 Rio de Janeiro; and not Janeiro, Rio de.

23 Inseparable Initial Article

If the name of a geographical entity begins with an Article as if it were inseparable from the word following it, the Article is to be retained.

Examples:
1 THE HAGUE; and not either HAGUE, or HAGUE, THE.
2 LE MANS; and not either MANS or MANS, LE.
3 LA PLATA; and not either PLATA or PLATA, LA.

3 Homonym

Areas Outside One Another

31 DIFFERENT COUNTRIES

If two or more Geographical Entities

1 Have the same name, and
2 Lie in different countries,

the Individualising Element for resolving the Homonym is to be the name of the Country in which it lies, except that it may be omitted if it is the Country of the Library.

Examples:
1 UXBRIDGE; and
2 UXBRIDGE (United States of America);
respectively in a British Library.

32 SAME COUNTRY

If two or more Geographical Entities

1 Have the same name, and
2 Lie within the same country, but
3 Lie outside one another,

the Individualising Element for resolving the Homonym is to be the name of the Largest Geographical Area, among the Areas of the constituent states, countries, districts, taluks, etc containing the Geographical Entity and sufficient to individualise it.

Examples:
1 SATTANUR (Kumbakonam).
SATTANUR (Tanjavur).
Here Kumbakonam and Tanjavur are Taluks.
2 TIRUVALANGADU (Chingleput).
TIRUVALANGADU (Tanjavur).
Here Chingleput and Tanjavur are Districts.

3 SALEM (India).
SALEM (New Jersey).
SALEM (Ohio).
SALEM (Oregon).
SALEM (Virginia).

The second word in each of the last four is the name of a constituent state of the United States of America.

4 Homonym
Area Within Area

If two or more Geographical Entities

1 Have the same name, and

2 Lie one within another in succession,

the Individualising Element for resolving the Homonym is to be the name of the state, district, country, taluk, city, borough, town, village, etc, as the case may be, except that it is to be omitted if it is the name of the largest of the above mentioned areas among those needed for resolving the Homonym.

Examples:

1 MYSORE.
MYSORE (District).
MYSORE (Taluk).
MYSORE (City).

Here, the first denotes the Mysore state.

2 TANJAVUR.
TANJAVUR (Taluk).
TANJAVUR (Town).

Here the first denotes the Tanjavur District.

3 KUMBAKONAM.
KUMBAKONAM (Town).

Here the first denotes the Kumbakonam Taluk.

41 SECOND INDIVIDUALISING ELEMENT

If the application of two of the Sec JB1, JB2, and JB4 is necessary for resolving the Homonym, the Individualising Element prescribed in Sec JB4 is to be the second of the Individualising Elements.

Example: CAMBRIDGE (Great Britain) (City).

5 Alternative Names in Subject Headings

51 Standard Name

If a geographical entity has two or more names and if one of them has been recognised as the Standard Name in the source materials, the Standard Name is to be used in a Subject Heading.

Examples:
India has the alternative name "Bharat", according to the Constitution Act. But, "India" is now being recognised as the Standard Name in most of the publications and in the *Gazetteer*. Therefore "INDIA" should be written in any Subject Heading or any Specific Book Heading. "BHARAT" is to be used as Heading only in a Cross Reference Index Entry. It may be stated that in an Author Heading, the Canon of Ascertainability is to determine the name.

52 Local Rule for Geographical Name

If a Geographical Entity has two or more names and if all of them are equally current in the title-pages of documents, each library should have a Local Rule for the choice of one of these names as the Standard Name.

Examples:
The Madras University Library uses "GREAT BRITAIN" as the Standard Name and uses "UNITED KINGDOM" as the Heading for a Cross Reference Index Entry only.

53 Current Geographical Name

If a Geographical Entity has had different names at different times, the name current at the time of cataloguing is to be used in a Subject Heading.

It may be mentioned that the headings in the documents catalogued earlier need not be changed. This is to satisfy the Canon of Permanence. Cross Reference Index Entry is to be given for each of the other names used in the catalogue entries made earlier, in order to satisfy the Canon of Currency. It may be stated that in an Author Heading, the Canon of Ascertainability is to determine the name.

CHAPTER JC

GOVERNMENT

1 Whole Government

If the Corporate Body is a Government as a whole, its name is to be the name of its Territory.

Examples:

1 INDIA—is the rendering of "Government of India".

2 MYSORE—is the rendering of the "Government of the constituent state Mysore" in India.

3 MYSORE (District)—is the rendering of the "District Board of Mysore District".

4 MYSORE (Taluk)—is the rendering of the "Local Body or the Taluk Board of Mysore Taluk".

5 MYSORE (City)—is the rendering of the "Local Body of the city of Mysore," that is of the "Mysore Municipality".

The Name of a Government is thus established artificially by a Catalogue Code. In the document itself, it may occur in a form such as "Government of India".

2 Organ of Government

21 MULTIPLE CORPORATE HEADING

If the Corporate Body is an Organ of a Government, a Multiple Corporate Heading is to be used.

22 NAME OF GOVERNMENT AS A WHOLE

The First Heading in the rendering of the name of an Organ of a Government is to be the name of the Government as a whole as prescribed in Sec JC1.

3 Constitutional Organ

The rendering of the name of a Constitutional Organ of a Government, used as Second Heading, is to be the name of the

Organ as it is current in the language of the library, and otherwise in the language of the territory concerned.

Examples:

1 CHINA, EXECUTIVE YUAN.

2 FRANCE, MINISTRY.

3 GREAT BRITAIN, CABINET.

4 HYDERABAD, EXECUTIVE COUNCIL.

This was before 1948.

5 INDIA, CABINET.

This is from 1948.

6 INDIA, EXECUTIVE COUNCIL.

This was before 1948.

7 MADRAS, COUNCIL OF MINISTERS.

8 MYSORE, COUNCIL.

This was before 1948.

9 MYSORE, COUNCIL OF MINISTERS.

This is from 1949.

10 NORWAY, COUNCIL OF STATE.

11 UNION OF SOVIET SOCIALIST REPUBLICS, UNITED COUNCIL OF PEOPLE'S COMMISSERIES.

12 UNITED STATES OF AMERICA, CABINET.

32 LEGISLATURE

1 FRANCE, CHAMBER OF DEPUTIES.

2 FRANCE, SENATE.

3 INDIA, RAJYA SABHA.

4 INDIA, LOK SABHA.

This is from 1949.

5 INDIA, LEGISLATIVE ASSEMBLY.

This was before 1948.

6 MADRAS, LEGISLATIVE ASSEMBLY.

7 MADRAS, LEGISLATIVE COUNCIL.

8 MADRAS (City), COUNCIL.

9 NORWAY, STORTING.

10 TANJAVUR, DISTRICT BOARD.

11 TANJAVUR (Taluk), TALUK BOARD.

12 TANJAVUR (Town), MUNICIPAL COUNCIL.

13 UNITED STATES OF AMERICA, CONGRESS.

14 UNITED STATES OF AMERICA, HOUSE OF REPRESENTATIVES.

15 UNITED STATES OF AMERICA, SENATE.

33 JUDICIARY

1 GREAT BRITAIN, CENTRAL CRIMINAL COURT.

2 GREAT BRITAIN, COURT OF APPEAL.
3 INDIA, FEDERAL COURT.
This was before 1950.
4 INDIA, SUPREME COURT.
This is from 1949.
5 JAPAN, COURT OF ADMINISTRATIVE LITIGATION.
6 MADRAS, HIGH COURT.
7 UNITED STATES OF AMERICA, COURT OF CLAIMS.

Usually an Organ of the First Remove has a name of its own in the language of the country. It is almost a proper name. Therefore, that name is to be used in the Heading. This is to satisfy the Canon of Ascertainability. However an Organ of the First Remove may be denoted by a standard term in the language of the library. It is likely to be sought by a reader of the library under this standard term. To satisfy the Canon of Sought Heading, the claim of the standard term has also to be considered. This claim is to be provided for by linking them up by a Cross Reference Index Entry.

4 Head of the Government

The rendering, of the name of the Head of a Government, used as Second Heading, is to be provided with the name of the occupant of that office as an Individualising element.

As a Corporate Body, the Head of a Government is more or less immortal, therefore the number of documents claiming its name as Second Heading will be ever-increasing and will be large. Therefore, a good deal of its potency will overflow into the Title Section. But the Canon of Prepotence would like minimising such an overflow. This Rule prescribes a means of arresting this overflow.

The Canon of Sought Heading may also welcome this prescription by the Canon of Prepotence. For the Individualising Element may have to be used as the Heading for a Cross Reference Index Entry, in order to satisfy the Canon of Sought Heading.

Examples:
1 GREAT BRITAIN, CROWN (Elizabeth II).
2 GREAT BRITAIN, CROWN (George V).
3 INDIA, GOVERNOR GENERAL (C Rajagopalachari).
4 INDIA, PRESIDENT (Rajendra Prasad).
5 INDIA, VICEROY AND GOVERNOR GENERAL (Hardinge).
6 JAPAN, EMPEROR (Hirohito).
7 MADRAS (City), MAYOR (S Muthia Chetty).
8 MADRAS (City), MAYOR (S Satyamurty).
9 MADRAS, GOVERNOR (Sriprakasa).

10 MYSORE, GOVERNOR (Jayachamaraja Wodeyar).
This is after 1957.
11 MYSORE, MAHARAJA (Jayachamaraja Wodeyar).
This was before 1948.
12 MYSORE, RAJAPRAMUKH (Jayachamaraja Wodeyar).
This was between 1948-1957.
13 RUSSIA, TSAR (Alexander III).
14 UNITED STATES OF AMERICA, PRESIDENT (Woodrow Wilson).
15 UNION OF SOVIET SOCIALIST REPUBLICS, PRESIDENT (Joseph Stalin).

It must be remembered that this kind of Corporate Heading is to be used only in the case of official publications such as messages, proclamations, despatches, ordinances, and so on, emanating from the Head of the Government. This kind of Heading is not applicable to works written by a king, a president, etc in his private capacity. For example, in the case of the *War message* read by President Wilson before a joint session of the Senate and the House of Representatives on 2 April 1917, the Heading is to be

UNITED STATES OF AMERICA, PRESIDENT (Woodrow Wilson).

But, in the case of the book *George Washington* written by Woodrow Wilson, the Heading is to be simply

WILSON (Woodrow).

See Chap GC.

5 Subordinate Court of Law

If two or more Courts of Law of the same Government have similar names, the Individualising Element for resolving the Homonym is to be, in sequence of preference, a term denoting either

1 The Area of Jurisdiction; or
2 The Headquarters; or
3 Any other necessary and sufficient attribute.

Examples:

1 GREAT BRITAIN, COUNTY COURT (Yorkshire).
2 MADRAS, DISTRICT COURT (Coimbatore).
3 MADRAS, DISTRICT COURT (Salem).
4 MADRAS, DISTRICT MAGISTRATE'S COURT (Salem).
5 MADRAS, DISTRICT MUNSIF'S COURT (Salem) (Taluk).
6 MADRAS, HONORARY MAGISTRATE'S COURT (Kumbakonam) (Town).
7 MADRAS, HONORARY MAGISTRATE'S COURT (Salem) (Town).
8 UNITED STATES OF AMERICA, CIRCUIT COURT OF APPEALS, (Third Circuit).
9 UNITED STATES OF AMERICA, DISTRICT COURT (Alaska).

6 Administrative Department

The Entry Element in the name of an Administrative Department of a Government is to be the Word or the Word-Group denoting its sphere of Work.

The word or word group denoting the sphere of work of an Administrative Department is by no means easy to determine. There are many refractory cases. They cannot all be brought under specific foolproof rules. A cataloguer will have to exercise considerable judgement [K1].

61 Nominative form for Sphere of Work

It should if possible be reduced to a noun form in the nominative case.

62 Secondary Element

The other words in the name of the Administrative Department are to be deemed to form **Secondary Element.**

63 Use of Dash

If the Entry Element had occurred in any position other than the first in the name of the Administrative Department, its place should be indicated by a dash among the words of the Secondary Element.

Examples:

1 Great Britain, Education (Ministry of—).
2 Great Britain, Scottish Education (Department).
3 India, Finance (Ministry of—).
4 India, Labour and Employment (Ministry of—).
5 Madras, Instruction (Department of Public—).
6 Madras (City), Education (Department of—).
7 New York, Excise (Department of—).
8 New York (County), Excise (Department of—).
9 United States of America, Education (Bureau of—).

64 Designation of Officer

If an Administrative Department of a Government has no

special name, the Designation of its Officer is to be used as its name.

See Examples 1, 2, and 3 under Sec JC65.

65 Homonym in Administrative Department

If two or more Administrative Departments of the same Government have similar names, the Individualising Element for resolving the Homonym is to be an appropriate term denoting either

1 Its area of jurisdiction; or
2 Its function; or
3 Its headquarters; or
4 Any other necessary and sufficient attribute.

Examples:

1 Canada, Fuel (Controller).
2 Great Britain, Agent and Consul-General (Cairo).
3 Illinois, Entomologist (State—).
4 India, Archaeology (Department of—) (Northern Circle).
5 India, Archaeology (Department of—) (Southern Circle).
6 Madras, Education (District—Officer) (Salem).
7 Madras, Education (District—Officer) (Tanjavur).
8 Madras, Girls' Schools (Inspectress of—) (First Circle).
9 Madras, Girls' Schools (Inspectress of—) (Fourth Circle).
10 Madras, Instruction (Deputy Director of—) (Elementary Education).
11 Madras, Instruction (Deputy Director of—) (Finance).
12 United States of America, National Resources Planning (Board) (Region 8).

66 Interpolation of Subheadings

If the Administrative Department is an Organ of Second or Later Remove and if its name is not individualising or if a Homonym cannot be resolved without the addition of the name(s) of the Organ(s) of Earlier Remove in its hierarchy, such name(s) is (are) to be interpolated as Subheading(s) between the name of the Government as a whole and of the name of the Administrative Department in question.

The minimum number of such subheadings is to be interpolated. If the number of such Subheadings is two or more, they should be inserted in their descending hierarchical sequence.

Examples:

1 MANCHURIA, FINANCE (Department of—), GENERAL AFFAIRS (Bureau of—).

2 MANCHURIA, INDUSTRY (Department of—), GENERAL AFFAIRS (Bureau of—).

3 MADRAS, LEGISLATIVE ASSEMBLY, ACCOUNTS (Public—Committee).

4 UNITED STATES OF AMERICA, INTERSTATES COMMERCE (Commission), ACCOUNTS (Bureau of—).

5 UNITED STATES OF AMERICA, TREASURY (Department), ACCOUNTS (Bureau of—).

7 Temporary Organ

The Entry Element in the name of a Temporary Organ of a Government is to be rendered on the analogy of Sec JC6 and its sub-divisions for the Administration Department.

71 INDIVIDUALISING ELEMENT

In the case of a Temporary Organ of a Government, its Year of Formation is to be added as an Individualising Element.

72 NAME OF CHAIRMAN

In the case of an *Ad hoc* Commission, Committee etc of a Government, the name of its Chairman is to be added within circular brackets after the Individualising Element in the following style:

1 The term "*Chairman*";

2 A colon; and

3 The words in the Reduced Name of the Chairman written in their natural sequence.

Examples:

1 INDIA, FINANCE (Commission) (1951) (*Chairman*: Kshitish Chandra Neogy).

2 INDIA, FINANCE (Commission) (1956) (*Chairman*: Kasturi Santhanam).

3 INDIA, TAXATION ENQUIRY (Commission) (1953) (*Chairman*: John Mathai).

8 Common Organ of Governments

In the case of a Common Organ set up jointly by two or more Governments, its name is to be preceded by the names of the Governments setting it up; and a conjunction is to connect them.

Examples:

1 UNITED STATE and GERMANY, CLAIMS (Mixed—Commission) (19).

2 INDIA, LOK SABHA and RAJYA SABHA, NATIONAL BANK BILL (Joint Committee on—) (19).

CHAPTER JD

INSTITUTION

1 Name in Shortest Form

The name to be used in rendering the name of an Institution is to be the one in the shortest form found in the

1 Title-page; or
2 Half-title page; or
3 Any other part of the document.

11 Language of the Name

If the name of an Institution occurs in two or more languages, the name in the language occurring earliest in the scale of languages of the library is to be used for rendering.

12 Initial Article

In rendering the name of an Institution, the initial article is to be omitted.

13 Honorific Word

In rendering the name of an Institution, every honorific word, not forming an inseparable part of the name, is to be omitted, if found either at the beginning or at the end, or in any other position in the name.

Examples:

1 ACCADEMIA NAZIONALE DEI LINCEI.

"Reale" at the beginning of the name of this Institution is omitted as it is a separable honorific word.

2 ANDHRA UNIVERSITY.
3 ASIATIC SOCIETY OF BENGAL.
4 BODLEIAN LIBRARY.
5 CAMBRIDGE PHILOSOPHICAL SOCIETY.
6 CARNEGIE INSTITUTION OF WASHINGTON.
7 CHURCH OF ENGLAND.
8 INDIAN MATHEMATICAL SOCIETY.
9 INTERNATIONAL MARITIME ASSOCIATION..
10 JOHNS HOPKINS UNIVERSITY.
11 MADRAS CHRISTIAN COLLEGE.
12 MADRAS MAHAJANA SABHA.
13 MOUNT WILSON OBSERVATORY.

14 Ramanujan Memorial Committee.
15 Royal Society of London.
"Royal" is retained as it is inseparable from the name of the Institution.
16 Saraswati Mahal Library.
17 Srinivasa Sastri Entertainment Committee.
18 University of Madras.

14 Title of Honour of Person

In rendering the name of an Institution, beginning with the name of a person, carrying an Initial Term denoting a title of honour or distinction, or profession, that Initial Term is to be omitted.

Examples:

1 Baker Guidance Centre, *and not* Judge Baker Guidance Centre.

2 Heber College, *and not* Bishop Heber College.

3 Herzl Zion Club, *and not* De Herzl Zion Club.

4 Srinivasa Sastri Entertainment Committee, *and not* Rt Hon'ble Srinivasa Sastri Entertainment Committee.

5 Walter Raleigh Monument Association *and not* Sir Walter Raleigh Monument Association.

A reader, who remembers the name including the omitted initial epithet, knows the Substantive Word coming after it and prescribed as the Entry Word. But every reader who knows this Entry Word may not remember the omitted initial epithet. In course of time, the initial epithet has a great chance to fade out of memory. Therefore, both classes of readers will be able to locate their sought headings—the latter in the first attempt and the former in the second attempt—if the name is rendered according to this Rule.

It may not even be necessary to use the forms as the Heading for a Cross Reference Index Entry, though it is not prohibited.

15 Numeral at the Beginning

In rendering the name of an Institution beginning with a Numeral Figure, the Numeral is to be spelt out in the Lnaguage of the rest of the words in the name of the Institution.

Examples:

Twenty-Eighth January 1948 Memorial Society, *and not* 28 January 1948 Memorial Society.

16 Uniformised Name

In rendering the name of an Institution, in whose name trivial variants occur in different documents, the Uniformised Name is to be used.

See Sec FA91.

2 Individualising Element

If the bare name of an Institution does not individualise it, the Individualising Element to be used for resolving the Homonym is to be the term denoting its

1 Place, if it is a localised Institution;

2 Country, if it has a national status;

3 Constituent state, county, district, taluk, etc if it is a State, County, District, Taluk, etc, Institution; and

4 Headquarters, if it cannot be individualised conveniently by any of the terms mentioned in 1, 2, and 3 above.

Examples:

1 Great Western Railway (Great Britain).
2 Great Western Railway (United States).
3 Labour Party (Canada).
4 Labour Party (Great Britain).
5 National Research Council (Canada).
6 National Research Council (Japan).
7 Landholders' Association (Madras).
8 Landholders' Association (Tanjavur).
9 Landholders' Association (Tanjavur) (Taluk).
10 Provincial Congress Committee (Bombay).
11 Provincial Congress Committee (Madras).
12 Teachers' Guild (Salem).
13 Teachers' Guild (Tanjavur).
14 General Post Office (Bombay).
15 General Post Office (Calcutta).
16 General Post Office (London).
17 Hindu High School (Sirkali).
18 Hindu High School (Triplicane).
19 Linnean Society (London).
20 Linnean Society (New South Wales).
21 Linnean Society (New York).
22 State Bank of India (Madras) (City).
23 State Bank of India (Salem) (Town).
24 State Bank of India (Tanjavur) (Town).

The Rule prescribes the name of the place as an Individualising Element only and not as the Entry Word for resolving the Homonym, even in the case of recurring institutional names such as Post Office and State Bank of India, because the Name of a Place has been prescribed as the Heading for the Government of the place. The Homonym caused by the use of the same Geographical Name as the Entry Element or First Heading for Government as well as an Institution will be one made by the Catalogue Code itself. The drafting of a Catalogue Code should not thus create Homonyms on its own initiative.

21 Year of Foundation

If the Individualising Element prescribed in Sec JD2 and/or the presence of the name of a place or of a person as an integral part of the name of the Institution does not completely resolve the Homonym, the Year of Foundation of the Institution is to be used as a Second Individualising Element.

Examples:

1 Cincinnati Medical Society (1819).
2 Cincinnati Medical Society (1837).
3 Cincinnati Medical Society (1851).
4 State Agricultural Society (South Carolina) (1839).
5 Statf [illegible]ltural Society (South Carolina) (1855).

3 Organ of an Institution

The Rendering of the name of an Organ of an Institution is to be made on the analogy of the Sec JC2 to JC8.

4 Related Institutions

The summary in Sec GD8 will be of use in determining whether the name of an Institution is to be rendered as if it were an Organ of a Parent Body or as an Independent Corporate Body. That summary covers Institutions related to other Corporated Bodies as Affiliated, or Branch, or in any other way.

5 Change of Name

Change in the name of an Institution is looked after by the Canon of Ascertainability and the Rules on Cross Reference Index Entry.

CHAPTER JE

CONFERENCE

1 Introduction

The rendering of the name of a Conference is to be on the analogy of the Sec of Chap JD and in accordance with the following additional Sec.

2 Individualising Element

The name(s) of the place(s) of a Conference and its year are to be added as Individualising Elements to the name of a Conference which is not held periodically.

A periodical conference is to be catalogued in accordance with the Rules for a Periodical Publication given in Part 7.

Examples:

1 BESANT MEMORIAL MEETING (Madras) (1933).
2 CONFERENCE OF ORIENTALISTS (Simla) (1911).
3 INTERNATIONAL PEACE CONFERENCE (The Hague) (1899).
4 POLITICAL SUFFERERS' CONFERENCE (Gauhati) (1933).
5 TAMIL BOOK-LOVERS CONFERENCE (Madras) (1933).

3 Diplomatic Conference

The name of the place of a Diplomatic Conference is to be prefixed to the name of the Conference not held periodically, so as to form a word-group, if it is not already in the name of the Conference; and the year(s) of the Conference is (are) to be added as Individualising Element.

Examples:

1 GENEVA SUMMIT CONFERENCE (1956).
2 PARIS PEACE CONFERENCE (1919).
3 VIENNA CONGRESS (1814-15).

The name of the place has to be made part of the word-group, since it would mean the Government of the Place if it is made an independent Main Heading and thus a Homonym will be created by cataloguing convention itself.

4 Without Specific Name

The name of a Conference without a Specific Name and not held periodically is to be made of the name of the Class of Persons meeting together as Conference, such as Citizens, Indian Residents, Ladies, Merchants, and Musicians.

41 Name of Place

The name of the place of Meeting is to be added as Individualising Element to the name of a Conference rendered as specified in Sec JE4.

42 Year, Month, Date

If two or more names rendered as specified in Sec JE4 and JE41 are the same, the Year or the Year along with the Month or the Date of the Conference is to be added as a Second Individualising Element.

Examples:

1 Citizens (Madras).
2 Indian Residents (Cape Town) (1948).
3 Indian Residents (Cape Town) (1958).

5 Organ Conference

If a Conference is the Organ of another Corporate Body, it is to be given a Multiple Corporate Heading (*See* Sec FR57).

51 Parent Body

The Heading in which the name of the Conference is rendered is to be preceded by the Heading(s) specifying its Parent Body which may itself be an Organ.

52 Joint Parent Bodies

If the Parent Body of an Organ Conference consists jointly of two or more Corporate Bodies, the name of each Parent Body is to precede the name of the Conference. The names of the Parent Bodies are to be connected by a conjunction.

Examples:

1 Madras, Collector's Conference (Ootacamund) (1918).

2 Madras, Instruction (Department of Public—), Educational Officer's Conference (Madras) (1929).

3 Madras, Engineer (Chief—) and Mysore, Engineer (Chief—), Palar River Conference (Mysore) (1956).

CHAPTER JF

TITLE

1 Entries of Occurrence

The Title has to be rendered compulsorily in the

1 Title Section of the Main Entry (*See* Sec FQ93);

2 Second Section of the Book Index Entry (*See* Sec FQ92);

3 Heading of the Title Index Entry;

4 Referred-to-Section of a Cross Reference Entry (*See* FQ32); and

5 Heading of the Main Entry if neither the name of the Author nor any other Substitute for it is available for use as its Heading.

The rendering of a title will be the same in cases 1 and 5. It will be the same in cases 2, 3 and 4, but shorter than the former whenever warranted.

2 Language

The Language in which the Title is to be rendered is to be decided in accordance with the Sec of Part M.

3 Initial Article and Honorifics

In rendering the title in the Title Section or in the Heading of a Main Entry, the initial article and honorifics are to be omitted; and the remaining words are to be written in the sequence in which they occur in the Title-Page.

Examples:

1 BHAGAVATAM, and not SRIMAD BHAGAVATAM, as "Srimad" is an honorific.

2 BIBLE, and not either THE BIBLE or THE HOLY BIBLE or HOLY BIBLE, as "Holy" is an honorific and "The" is an article.

3 LIFE OF Samuel Johnson and not THE LIFE OF Samuel Johnson.

4 Entry Element

When the Title occurs in the Heading, the First two Words are to be deemed to form the Entry Element.

See examples under Sec JF6.

5 Puff

In rendering the Title in the Title Section or in the Heading of a Main Entry, **Puff,** if any, at the middle or at the end of the Title, is to be omitted and is to be replaced by three dots if in the middle and by "etc", if in the end.

Examples:

In the following titles, the words shown within circular brackets may be conveniently replaced by " . . . " or by "etc", as the case may be, and the portion italicised is to be ignored altogether, as it designates the author of the document and, as such, contributes to the Heading:

1 "The Travels *of Sig Pietro della Valle, a noble Roman* into East-India and Arabia Deserta. (In which, the several countries, together with the customs, manners, traffique, and rites both religious and civil, of those oriental princes and nations, are faithfully described:) in familiar letters to his friend Signior Mario Schipano."

2 "The life of Samuel Johnson, (LL.D., comprehending an account of his studies and numerous works, in chronological order: a series of his epistolary correspondence and conversations with many eminent persons; and various original pieces of his composition, never before published; the whole exhibiting a view of literature and literary men in Great Britain for near half a century, during which he flourished) *by James Boswell, Esq.*"

3 "In Ashanti and beyond (the record of a resident magistrate's many years in tropical Africa, his arduous and dangerous treks both in the course of his duty and in pursuit of big game, with descriptions of the people, their manner of living and the wonderful ways of beasts and insects) *by A. W. Cardinall, F.R.G.S.F.R.A.I., District Commissioner, Gold Coast; author of Natives Northern Territories of the Gold Coast*", etc. (*with illustrations and maps*).

50 Entries Omitting Puff

Such verbose titles are nowadays going out of fashion. The Main Entries of these books are to be as shown hereunder:

1 U8. 4K'3 K64

Valle (Pietro della) (1586).

Travels into East India and Arabia Deserta . . . in familiar letter to his friend Signior Mario Schipano.

5705

2 O,6L09w M87
BOSWELL (James) (1740).
Life of Samuel Johnson etc.
3314

3 U8. 655'N3 N27
CARDINALL (Allan Wolsey) (1887).
In Ashanti and beyond etc.
45315

As Cutter puts it, "Many a title a yard long does not convey as much meaning as two well-chosen words." That is the import of Sec JF5.

51 Abbreviation not a Licence

This is not to be interpreted, however, as giving the cataloguer a licence to show scant courtesy to the title. It must be remembered that the title is the name of the book and "should not be changed but by act of legislature" as Cutter puts it in his inimitable way. "Our necessities oblige us to abbreviate it, but nothing obliges us to make additions to it or to change it without giving notice to the reader that we have done so."

52 Art of Abbreviation

The art of abbreviation and addition is a matter of skill and experience. No cut and dry instruction can be given. The utmost a beginner may be told by word of mouth is put pithily by Cutter: "Omit puffs[1] and many *descriptive words* which are implied either by the rest of the title[2] or by the custom of books of the class under treatment[3], and those descriptive phrases which, though they add to the significance of the title, do not give enough information to pay for their retention[4]. Omit all other unnecessary words" [C5].

1 *Ex.* A (plain) treatise on; an (exact and full) account.

2 In "compendious pocket dictionary", either compendious or pocket is superfluous.

3 *Ex.* Nekrolog, 1790-1800 (enthaltend Nachrichten von dem Leben merkwurdiger in diesem Jahre verstorbener Personen).

4 "By an American not by birth but by the love of liberty".

It may be stated explicitly that the omission of the name of the author or authors or of the imprint or of the name of series or of the printer's devices, or of the mottoes or of the quotations, if any, need not be indicated as provided in this Rule as those do not form part of the title of the book.

6 Short Title

In rendering the Title in the Second Section or in the Heading of a Book Index Entry or in the Referred-to-Section of a Cross Reference Entry, the Short Title is to be used; and the words in it are to be written in the sequence in which they occur in the Title-Page.

Examples:

For the three titles given as examples in Sec JF5, the rendering of the Title in the Heading Section of any Book Index Entry is to be respectively:

1 TRAVELS IN East India and Arabia Deserta.

2 LIFE OF Samuel Johnson.

3 IN ASHANTI and beyond.

In the Second Section of a Book Index Entry, the first two words will not be in block letters.

2 In the Second Section of a Book Index Entry and the Referred-to-Section of a Cross Reference Entry, the rendering of the title,

"Some aspects of literary criticism in Sanskrit or the theories of Rasa and Dhvani"

should be as follows:

"Some aspects of literary criticism in Sanskrit."

3 In the Second Section of a Book Index Entry and the Referred-to-Section of a Cross Reference Entry, the rendering of the title,

"William Shakespeare: A study of facts and problems"

should be as follows:

William Shakespeare.

If the book is to be given a Title Entry, its Heading is to be

WILLIAM SHAKESPEARE.

7 Words Supplied by Cataloguer

If the Title-Page of a book does not mention the Title, or if any addition is to be made to make the Title intelligible, the Title or the Words to be so added are to be supplied by the cataloguer and enclosed in square brackets.

Example:

One of the volumes in the 'Mermaid series' gives only the following information on its title page:

"Thomas Otway with an introduction, notes,/by/the Hon. Roden Noel"

In this case, the Main Entry has to be as follows, but for the note portion.

1 O,2K52*x* M88

OTWAY (Thomas) (1652).

[Best plays] ed by Roden Noel.

2792

8 Homonym in Title Heading

If two or more Book Index Entries have the same Title as

Heading, the Homonym is automatically resolved by the Second Section in most cases.

81 Individualising Element

If two or more Book Index Entries have the same Title as Heading and if the Homonym is not resolved by the Second Section; the Individualising Element for resolving the Homonym is to be in the sequence of preference, the

1 Author, if the name of the author is known;

2 Year of its first publication, if the year is known;

3 Name of the version;

4 Class to which it belongs, the class being of sufficient degree of intension to resolve the Honomym, if 1 or 2 is not applicable.

Example:

1 Genesis (Anglo-Saxon poem).
2 Genesis (Middle High German poem).
3 Genesis (Old Saxon peom).

91 Alternative Titles

If the title page contains two or more alternative titles, they are all to be given in the title portion of the Main Entry, connected by the word "or" or by the symbol ":" or in any other suitable manner.

Example:

1 Eνl'N3 N28
Jones (T W) (1898).
Hermes [or] the future of chemistry.
51070

CHAPTER JG

SERIES

1 Entries of Occurrence

The Name of a Series may have to be rendered in the

1 Note Section of a Main Entry (*See* Sec FQ4) and
2 Heading of a Book Index Entry.

2 Uniformised Name

If the Name of a Series occurs in Variant Forms in several pages of a book or in several books of the Series, that which gives the maximum information in the shortest form is to be used as the **Uniformised Name** for rendering.

3 Assertainability Violated

If the Name of a Series does not occur anywhere in a book, but occurs in some other book of the Series, it is to be taken from that book.

This Rule amounts to a deliberate deviation from the Canon of Ascertainability.

Example:

The volume "Library movement" was published by the Madras Library Association in 1929. It did not mention the name of any Series. But in the second volume, "Five laws of library science" published by the same Association, the half-title page mentioned the name "publication series" and gave these two titles the serial numbers 1 and 2 respectively.

4 Article and Honorific Word

In rendering the Name of a Series in the Note Section or in the Heading, the initial article and honorific word, if any, are to be omitted; and the remaining words are to be written in the sequence in which they occur in the document.

5 Individualising Entry

If the Name of the Series is not individualising—for example, English series, Publication series, Translation series—its name is to be preceded by the name of an Individualising Entity with which it is associated—such as publisher, sponsor, university —followed by a comma.

51 Name of Individualising Entity

The name of the Entity used as the Individualising Entity is to be rendered as prescribed by the Rules for the Entities of its kind.

Examples:

1 Broadway oriental library.
2 Cambridge tracts in mathematics and mathematical physics.
3 Sammlung Schubert.
4 Wiley farm series.
5 Wiley social science series.
6 Madras Library Association, bibliographical series.
7 Madras Library Association, legislative series.
8 Madras Library Association, publication series.
9 Patna University, readership lectures.
10 Ranganathan series in library Science.
11 University of Chicago, supplementary educational monographs.
12 University of Delhi, library science series.
13 University of Illinois, studies in language and literature.
14 Bombay, Agriculture (Department of—), bulletin.
15 Institute for Medical Research (Federated Malay States), bulletin.

In the example 14, the sponsor of the series is an Administrative Department of a Government. Its name has been rendered as prescribed in Chap JC.

In the example 15, the sponsor of the series is an Institution. Its name has been rendered as prescribed in Chap JD.

52 Author's Name as Individualising Element

If the Entity used for Individualising a Series is the Author of the Book, the name of the Individualising Entity is to be replaced by the term *'Its' 'His'* or *'Her'* in italics, in the Series Note of the Main Entry and in the Second Section of the Series Entry.

Example:

1 L:42:2:(G91) *c*1N56
MEDICAL RESEARCH COUNCIL (Great Britain).
National collection of type cultures catalogue of species. Rev ed.
(*Its* memoranda, 35)
200375

2 MEDICAL RESEARCH COUNCIL (Great Britain), MEMORANDA.
35 *Its* National collection of type cultures catalogue of species.
L:42:2:(G91) *c*1N56

6 Major and Minor Series

If the Name of a Series consists of two distinct parts—viz those denoting a Major Series and a Minor Series respectively and if the name of the Minor Series is not sufficient to individualise it, the rendering is to consist successively of the Name of the Major Series, a comma, and the Name of the Minor series.

7 Individualising Element

If two or more series have the same proper name, a suitable Individualising Element is to be used for resolving the Homonym.

Examples:

1 Gifford Lectures (University of Edinburgh).
2 Gifford Lectures (University of St Andrews).

CHAPTER JH

PSEUDO SERIES

1 Entries of Occurrence

The name of a Pseudo Series may have to be rendered in the

1 Note Section of a Main Entry;

2 Heading of a Book Index Entry.

The name of a Pseudo Series will not be given by the publisher, as in the case of a regular publisher's series. But, it has to be established artificially by a Catalogue Code. In this, it resembles the name of a Government (*See* Sec JC1)

2 Edition with Distinctive Name

The rendering of the Name of a Pseudo Series of Kind 1 (*See* Sec FH2) is to consist successively of

1 Name of the Author, rendered as prescribed in Chap JA;

2 Comma; and

3 Name of the Edition in Sense 2 (*See* Sec FK2).

Examples:

1 Sankara, memorial ed.

2 Shakespeare (William), varioum ed.

3 Tolstoy (Leo), centenary ed.

3 One Author and a Common Generic Title

The rendering of the Name of a Pseudo Series of Kind 2 (*See* Sec FH3) is to consist successively of

1 Name of the Author, rendered as prescribed in Chap JA;

2 Comma;

3 Common Generic Title; and

4 Name(s) of Collaborator(s), if any, preceded by the word(s) describing the role(s) of the collaborator(s).

Examples:

1 Grimsehl (E), textbook of physics, ed by R Tomaschek.

2 Hertzler's monographs on surgical pathology.

4 Different Authors and a Common Generic Title

The rendering of the Name of a Pseudo Series of Kind 3 (*See* Sec FH3) is to consist successively of

1 Common Generic Title; and

2 Name(s) of Collaborator(s) if any, preceded by the word(s) describing the role(s) of the collaborator(s).

Examples:

1 British empire, a survey, ed by Hugh Gunn.
2 History of England, ed by Charles Oman.

PART K

CLASS INDEX ENTRY

Note: The Class Numbers used for illustration in this Part are Colon Numbers, unless otherwise stated.

CHAPTER KA

TERMINOLOGY OF CLASSIFICATION

1 Basic Class

10 **Subject.**—An assumed term.

This term will be used only in discussion in the Verbal Plane.

11 **Class.**—The term used to denote "Subject", in discussion in the Idea Plane.

12 **Class Number.**—The term used to denote "Subject", in discussion in the Notational Plane.

13 **Focus.**—The generic term used to denote "Class" in the Idea Plane, "Subject" in the Verbal Plane, and "Class Number" in the Notational Plane.

Other uses of the generic term "Foucs" will be found in the succeeding Sections.

14 **Main Class=Main Subject=Main Class Number=Main Focus.**—Any focus enumerated in the schedule of Main Classes in the Scheme of Classification used.

Examples:

In Colon Classification: B Mathematics, R Philosophy, T Education, X Economics, Z Law.

In Decimal Classification: 1 Philosophy, 2 Religion, 4 Linguistics, 7 Fine Arts, 8 Literature.

15 **Canonical Class=Canonical Subject=Canonical Class Number=Canonical Focus.**—Any focus enumerated as a Canonical Class of a Main Class in the Scheme of Classification used.

Examples:

In Colon Classification: B1 Arithmetic, B2 Algebra, B3 Analysis, R1 Logic, R2 Epistemology, R3 Metaphysics.

In Decimal Classification: 51 Mathematics, 52 Astronomy, 53 Physics, 61 Medicine, 62 Engineering, 63 Agriculture.

16 **Basic Class = Basic Subject = Basic Number = Basic Focus.**—Any Main Class or any Canonical Class.

2 Isolate and Facet

20 **Isolate** (generic term)=**Isolate Idea** (in the Idea Plane)= **Isolate Term** (in the Verbal Plane)=**Isolate Number** (in the National Plane)=**Isolate Focus.**—Any of the Divisions of a Basic Class based on a characteristic or a succession or Train of (homogeneous) Characteristics and enumerated in the Scheme of Classification used, as Foci in a **Facet.**

Here the terms Isolate and Facet are defined together in relation to each other. A more detailed discussion will be found in the *Colon classification.*

21 A Basic Focus can be a Subject by itself. But an Isolate Focus cannot be a Subject by itself. A Subject is formed only when it is attached to a Basic Focus.

For example, "Gold" by itself is not a Subject. It is only an Isolate. But a subject can be formed by attaching it to a Basic Class—e g Chemistry of Gold, Mineralogy of Gold, Sculpture in Gold, Mining of Gold, Economics of Gold.

In the schedules of Decimal Classification, we do not find Isolates enumerated. We find only combinations of Basic Class and Isolates enumerated. However, they are separable in the Idea Plane, the Verbal Plane, and the Notational Plane. Therefore, it need not be believed that the concepts of Basic Class, Isolate, and Facet are peculiar to the Colon Classification. These concepts belong to the Idea Plane. They therefore hold good universally in all Schemes of Classification. The only difference is that the Colon Classification consciously and explicitly recognises them, and enumerates them as such in separate schedules. A scheme which does so is called an **Analytico-Synthetic Classification.** In the Decimal Classification, the Basic Foci and the Isolate Foci are not given in separate schedules. It is only Subjects formed by their combination, that are enumerated in its schedules. A scheme of this kind is called an **Enumerative Classification.**

22 **Digit.**—Each one of the distinct symbols in a Class Number.

221 **Connecting Digit.**—Digit used in an Analytico-Synthetic Classification to connect Isolate Numbers to Basic Number or to another Isolate Number.

In the Colon Number X415:6.44'N57 (which means "Financing Railways in India in 1957", the colon, the full-stop) and the inverted comma are connecting digits. Thus the Basic Number X and the respective Isolate Numbers 415 and 6, and 44 and N57 stand out physically separated and are visually recognisable as distinct. By a certain convention stated in Rule 6503 of Colon Classification, the connecting digit between the Basic Class Number X and the first facet number 415 is omitted.

In an Enumerative Classification, there is no Connecting Digit provided. Therefore, the Basic Numbers and the Isolate Numbers will not be visibly recognisable. But, while interpreting the meaning of the several digits and combinations of digits in the Idea Plane, the Facets, the Basic Numbers. and the Isolate Numbers can be mentally separated.

See Sec KA31, KA41, KA51, KA61, KA73, and KA82.

A **Quasi Digit** may be called a **Fused Number**. It may be a Fused Chronological Number, a Fused Geographical Number, a Fused Subject Number etc.

222 **Quasi Digit.**—Group of Digits to be treated as if they together formed a single digit.

23 **Compound Focus = Compound Class = Compound Class Number.**—Focus consisting of one Basic Focus and one or more Isolate Foci.

3 Chronological Device

30 **Chronological Device.**—Device of using the appropriate Chronological Number for the formation or the subdivision of an Isolate, which is capable of chronological formation or subdivision, or when the individualisation of the isolates or sub-isolates may be made to depend conveniently on the period of origin or birth, or on the year of first investigation, or discovery, or initiation or commencement or occurrence, or on the year that may be definitely associated with the respective isolates in any other manner or for any other reason. Some of the cases where this device may be employed are generally indicated either in the Schedules or in the Rules of the Scheme of Classification used.

Examples:

O111,2J64 denotes "William Shakespeare". Here O is the Basic Number meaning "Literature";

111 is an Isolate Number meaning "English";
, is a Connecting Digit;
2 is an Isolate Number meaning "Drama"; and
J64 is the Isolate Number got by Chronological Device.
It means an English dramatist born in 1564; i e "William Shakespeare".

31 The part of a Class Number, got by Chronological Device, should be treated as a whole, as if it were a single digit.

4 Geographical Device

40 **Geographical Device.**—Device of using the appropriate Geographical Number (that is, of continent, country, state, district etc, as the case may be) for the formation of the subdivision, or when the individualisation of the isolates, or sub-isolates may be made to depend conveniently on the place of origin or prevalence or habitation or one that may be definitely associated with the respective foci in any other manner or for any other reason. The cases where this device may be applied are generally indicated either in the Schedules or in the Rules of the Scheme of Classification used.

3141 In some Class Numbers, to be determined by context, the part of a Class Number, got by Geographical Device, may have to be treated as a whole, as if it were a single digit.

5 Subject Device

50 **Subject Device.**—Device of using the appropriate Class Number for the formation or the subdivision of an isolate which is capable of such formation or subdivision, or when the individualisation of the isolates or sub-isolates may be made to depend conveniently on a Class Number that may be definitely associated with the respective classes in any manner or for any reason. The cases where this Device may be applied are generally indicated either in the Schedules or in the Rules of the Scheme of Classification used. The Subject Device part of an Isolate Number is to be enclosed in circular brackets; and it is called **Packeted Number.**

Example:

T9(Y31) denotes Rural Education.
Here T is the Basic Number meaning "Education";

9 is an Isolate Number meaning "other educands" and
(Y31) is the Number got by Subject Device. It means "Rural Social Group" or simply "Rural". It is put within brackets to show that it is got by Subject Device. It is a Packeted Number.

In Decimal Classification also, Subject Device is often used. But the number got by Subject Device is not packeted. There is nothing to make it visible to the eye that it is got by Subject Device. The Committee on the General Theory of Classification (FID/CA) of the International Federation for Documentation has recommended that the Universal Decimal Classification will do well to adopt Packeted Notation as illustrated by the Colon Classification.

51 The part of a Class Number, got by Subject Device—that is the Packeted Part of a Colon Number—should be treated as a whole, as if it were a single digit.

6 Alphabetical Device

60 **Alphabetical Device.**—Device of using the first or the first two, or the first three, etc, initial letters of the name of an entity, existential or conceptual, for the formation of the subdivision of an isolate.

Examples:

D5125H = Hind cycle.
D5125HU = Hudson cycle.
D5125HUM = Humber cycle.

61 The part of a class number, got by Alphabetical Device, should be treated as a whole, as if it were a single digit.

7 Phase Relation

71 Complex Class and Inter-Class Phase Relation

710 **Complex Class.**—Class formed by combining two or more classes, by a device other than Subject Device.

Example:

B0*b*D Engineering Mathematics, which means "Mathematics for those primarily interested in Engineering".
Here B means "Mathematics";
0 is a Connecting Digit;
b means "Inter-Class Bias Relation"; and
D means "Engineering".

711 **Inter-Class Phase.**—Each of the Classes whose combination forms a Complex Class,

Example:

In the example given under KA710

B Mathematics is the First or the Basic Phase.

D Engineering is the Second Phase. It is a Biasing Phase as the relation is Bias Relation.

712 **Inter-Class Phase Relation.**—The relation between the Component Classes of a Complex Class.

713 The Class Number forming the second or any other later Phase should be treated as a whole, as if it were a single digit.

72 Complex Isolate and Intra-Facet Phase Relation

720 **Complex Isolate.**—Isolate formed by the combination of two or more Isolates of the same Facet by other than Superimposition Device, on the basis of their mutual relation.

Example:

X555.440*k*1N48 Commonwealth preference in India's commerce.

Here X555 means "Foreign Commerce";

. is a Connecting Digit;

44 means "India";

0 is Connecting Digit;

k means "Intra-Facet Bias Relation";

1N48 means "The Commonwealth";

440*k*1N48 is a Complex Isolate.

721 **Intra-Facet Phase.**—Each of the Isolates whose combination forms a Complex Isolate.

722 **Intra-Facet Phase Relation.**—The Relation between the Components of a Complex Isolate.

723 In a Complex Isolate, the Isolate Number of each Component Isolate should be read as a whole, as if it were a single digit.

73 Complex Array Isolate and Intra-Array Phase Relation

730 **Complex Array Isolate.**—Array Isolate formed by the

combination of two or more Array Isolates of the same array by other than Superimposition Device on the basis of their mutual relation.

Example:

Y310w35 Which means "Difference between rural folk and city folk."
Here Y means "Sociology";
31 means "Rural folk";
0 is Connecting Digit
w means "Intra-Array Relation of Difference";
35 means "City folk";
310w35 is a Complex Array Isolate.

731 **Intra-Array Phase.**—Each of the Array Isolates whose combination forms a Complex Array Isolate.

9 Complicated Cases

90 Array and Chain

901 **Array.**—A sequence of Coordinate Classes of Isolates.

902 **Immediate Universe.**—A Class or Isolate of which the Classes or Isolates of an Array are Sub-classes or Sub-isolates respectively.

Examples:

1 Among the Isolates forming the Natural Group of Plants in Botany, the Isolates Algae, Fungi, and Lichen form an Array, with Thallophyta as the Immediate Universe.

2 Among the Isolates forming the Systems of Philosophy, the Isolates Advaita, Visishtadvaita and Dvaita form an Array with Vedanta as the Immediate Universe.

3 Among the Isolates forming the Social Groups in Sociology, Rural, Urban, and City Residents form an Array with Groups-by-Residence as the Immediate Universe.

905 **Chain.**—A modulated sequence of Subordinate Classes or Isolates.

Examples:

1 Thallophyta, Fungi, Basidiomycetes, and Mushroom form a Chain of Isolates.

2 Vedanta, Advaita, Pratyabhijna, and Virasaiva Schools of Indian Philosophy form a Chain of Isolates.

3 Social Activity, Ceremonial, Ceremonial of Childhood, and Ceremonial of Naming form a Chain of Isolates.

91 Telescoped Array

91 **Telescoped Array.**—An Array of Isolates in a Schedule of Classification, made of an Isolate and its Sub-isolates, as viewed from the Idea Plane, but whose Isolate Numbers appear to be Co-ordinate ones, as viewed from the Notational Plane.

Example:

R5 Vedanta, R6 Advaita, R7 Visishtadvaita, R8 Dvaita form a Telescoped Array in the Schedules of the Colon Classification.

911 **Isolate-at-Telescoping-Point.**—The Isolate in a Telescoped Array, of which succeeding Isolates in the Array are Sub-isolates.

Example:

In the Telescoped Array given as example in Sec KA91, R5 Vedanta is the Isolate-at-Telescoping-Point.

92 Chain-with-Gap

92 **Chain-with-Gap.**—A Chain of Isolates in a Schedule of Classification, in which an Intermediate Isolate is not given, as a result of failure to conform to the Canon of Modulation.

Example:

In Decimal Classification 2 Religion, 22 Sacred Books, 225 New Testament, is a Chain-with-Gap, as the Isolate "Christianity" is missing between 2 Religion and 22 Sacred Books.

921 **Missing Isolate.**—The Isolate missing in a Chain-with-Gap.

Example:

In the Chain-with-Gap given as example in Sec KA92, "Christianity" is the Missing Isolate. Its Isolate Number may, as the last resort, be written as 22/28.

CHAPTER KB

TERMINOLOGY OF CHAIN PROCEDURE

Examples are given in Chap KC

0 **Chain and Link.**—Represent a class number in the form of a chain, according to the following procedure treating Quasi Digit as a Digit

1 Make

11 the First Link, out of the first digit;

12 the Second Link, out of the first two digits;

13 the Third Link, out of the first three digits, and so on, up to the Last Link which is to be made of all the digits.

2 Write the Links one below the other in succession;

21 Write against each link its translation into natural language—i e the name of the class of which the link is the class number;

22 Connect each link with its translation by an "=" sign.

3 Join the "=" sign of each link with that of the next succeeding link by a downward arrow.

Putting the arrow is merely a means to make the suggestion of Chain visible to the eye.

In the above Rule, the terms "Chain" and "Link" get defined in relation to each other, by the context in which they are used.

1 **Last Link.**—Link occurring last in the Chain produced by a Class Number.

2 **False Link.**—Link which is

1 Not a Class Number—that is, it is not a concatenation of digits, intelligible according to the Rules of Classification—that is, it has no meaning; or

2 The last link of a Compound Class Number and does not have a name in the verbal plane, in common usage in a natural language—in other words, does not represent a subject with a definite name.

For example, a link is a False Link if it ends with a

1 Connecting symbol; or

2 Digit representing a Phase Relation; or

3 Digit representing an Intra-Facet Relation: or

4 Digit representing an Intra-Array Phase Relation; or

5 Time-Isolate representing Time itself in the Time Facet of the class, and not representing any other Fundamental Category —Space, Energy, Matter, or Personality—in their respective facets in the Class Number.

3 **Unsought Link.**—Link which

1 Ends with a part of the Isolate Focus in a Facet of a Class Number; and

2 Represents a subject on which reading material is not likely to be produced or sought or which is not likely to be looked up by any reader seeking materials on the Specific Subject forming the Last Link of the full Class Number.

This Rule admits of Local Variation in its application. In the light of the reading materials organised, the interest of the readers served, and the nature of the service attempted, each library may define in an exact way suited to itself the links which should be deemed to be Unsought Links. This more precise local definition should be consistently followed. A similar local definition may also be made by an organisation engaged in the production of Inter-National or National Bibliographies, of Union Catalogue of Books and/or of Periodical Publications. *See* Examples 5 and 6 in Chap KC.

4 **Sought Link.**—Link which is neither False, nor Fused nor Unsought, and Link ending with an After-Time Anteriorising Common Isolate Digit.

5 **Upper Link.**—Link other than the last Link.

6 **Lower Link.**—This term is a relative one when two links are engaging attention. Lower link is that one of the two links which occurs lower in a chain than the other of the two links.

91 Complicated Cases

91 **Link-at-Telescoping-Point.**—A Link in a Telescoped Chain, whose Class Number ends with a digit representing an Isolate-at-Telescoping-Point.

911 In representing a Class Number in the form of a Chain, every Link-at-Telescoping-Point is to be inserted at the proper place, whenever it occurs.

Example:

See Example 1 in Sec KH1.

92 Missing Link

92 **Missing Link.**—A Link in a Chain-with-Gap, corresponding to the Missing Isolate in the Chain.

921 In representing a Class Number in the form of a Chain, every Missing Link is to be inserted at the proper place whenever there is need.

Example:

In representing the Decimal Class Number "22 Sacred Books," the Missing Link "22/28 Christianity" should be inserted between the links "2 Religion" and "22 Sacred Books"

CHAPTER KC

EXAMPLES OF CHAIN AND LINK

1 L45:421 = Tuberculosis of lungs.

L = **Medicine.**
(Sought Link)

L4 = **Medicine of respiratory system.**
(Sought Link)

L45 = **Medicine of lungs.**
(Sought Link)

L45: = (*False Link*)

L45:4 = **Disease of lungs.**
(Sought Link)

L45:42 = **Infectious disease of lungs.**
(Sought Link)

L45:421 = **Tuberculosis of lungs.**
(Sought Link)

2 O111,2J64,52 = Othello

O = **Literature.**
(Sought Link)

O1 = Indo-European literature.
(*Unsought Link*)

O11 = Teutonic literature.
(*Unsought Link*)

O111 = **English literature.**
(Sought Link)

O111, = (*False Link*)

O111,2 = **English drama.**
(Sought Link)

O111,2J64 = **Shakespeare.**
(Sought Link)
↓
O111,2J64, = *(False Link)*
↓
O111,2J64,P = **Othello**
(Sought Link)

3 XM,8(J):51.73'N3 = Co-operative marketing in agriculture in U S A, brought upto 1930's.
↓
X = **Economics.**
(Sought Link)
↓
XM = **Co-operation.**
(Sought Link)
↓
XM, = *(False Link)*
↓
XM,8(A) = **Co-operative industries.**
(Sought Link)
↓
XM,8(J) = **Co-operative agriculture.**
(Sought Link)
↓
XM,8(J): = *(False Link)*
↓
XM,8(J):5 = **Co-operative trade in agriculture.**
(Sought Link)
↓
XM,8(J):51 = **Co-operative marketing in agriculture.**
(Sought Link)
↓
XM,8(J):51 = *(False Link)*
↓
XM,8(J):51.7 = **Co-operative marketing in agriculture in America.**
(Unsought Link)
↓
XM,8(J):51.73 = **Co-operative marketing in agriculture in U S A.**
(Sought Link)
↓
XM,8(J):51.73. = *(False Link)*
↓
XM,8(J):51,73'N = **Co-operative marketing in agriculture in U S A. brought upto 1900's.**
(False Link)
↓
XM,8(J):51.73'N3 = Co-operative marketing in agriculture in U S A, brought upto 1930's.
(False Link)
↓
4 V56;2:(Z)'N5 = British constitutional law brought upto 1950's.

V	=	History. (Sought Link)
V56	=	British History. (Sought Link)
V56:	=	(*False Link*)
V56:2	=	British constitutional history. (Sought Link)
V56:2:	=	(*False Link*)
V56:2:(Z)	=	British constitutional law. (Sought Link)
V56:2:(Z)	=	(*False Link*)
V56:2:(Z)'N	=	British constitutional law brought upto 1900's. (*False Link*)
V56:2:(Z)'N5	=	British constitutional law brought upto 1950's. (*False Link*)

5 BxM87:*g* = Evaluation of Ramanujan's works.

B	=	Mathematics. (Sought Link)
B*x*	=	Works in mathematics. (*Unsought Link*)
BxM87	=	Works of Ramanujan. (Sought Link)
BxM87:	=	(*False Link*)
BxM87:*g*	=	Evaluation of Ramanujan's works. (*Unsought Link*)

Note: 1 It is a matter of judgment that readers will not look for the above class under the Common Isolate "Evaluation" followed by "Ramanujan". That is why the last link has been marked as Unsought Link.

2 It is not totally wrong to mark it as Sought Link.

3 See Example 6, where the Last Link ending with the common Isolate "Evaluation" is marked Sought Link.

6 O111,2J64:*g*	=	Shakespearean criticism.
O	=	**Literature.** (Sought Link)
O1	=	Indo-European literature. (*Unsought Link*)
O11	=	Teutonic literature. (*Unsought Link*)
O111	=	**English literature.** (Sought Link)
O111,	=	(*False Link*)
O111,2	=	**English drama.** (Sought Link)
O111,2J64	=	**Shakespeare.** (Sought Link)
O111,2J64:	=	(*False Link*)
O111,2J64:g	=	**Shakespearean evaluation** (Sought Link)

Note: 1 It is a matter of judgment that readers may look for the above class under the Common Isolate "Evaluation" followed by "Shakespeare". That is why the Last Link has been marked as Sought Link.

2 See example 5 where the Last Link ending with the Common Isolate "Evaluation" is marked Unsought Link.

3 A Link ending with a Common Isolate calls for exercise of judgment. This is one of the cases where mechanical consistency cannot be insisted upon in arriving at Class Index Entries.

7 T9(Y31).44'N3*s*	=	Statistics of rural education in India brought upto 1930's.
T	=	**Education.** (Sought Link)
T9	=	(*False Link*)
T9(Y31)	=	**Rural education.** (Sought Link)
T9(Y31).	=	(*False Link*)

T9(Y31).4	=	**Rural education in Asia.** (Sought Link)
T9(Y31).44	=	**Rural education in India.** (Sought Link)
T9(Y31).44'	=	(*False Link*)
T9(Y31).44'N	=	(*False Link*)
T9(Y31).44'N3	=	Rural education in India brought upto 1930's. (*False Link*)
T9(Y31).44'N3s	=	**Statistics of rural education in India brought upto 1930's.** (Sought Link)

Note: 1 The Last Link ends with the Common Isolate "Statistics". It is a matter of judgment that readers will look for the above class under the Common Isolate "Statistics" followed by other Subheadings. That is why the Last Link has been marked as Sought Link.

2 As for the Subheadings, see Example 7.1 in Chap KG.

8 O111,2J64:*g*xM66:*g* = Criticism of Croce's works on Shakespearean criticism.

The first eleven Links of the above Class Number are the same as the Links in Example 6. In what follows, the first ten Links are to be taken as understood. The Chain is shown only from the eleventh Link.

O111,2J64:g	=	**Shakespearean evaluation.** (Sought Link)
O111,2J64:*gx*	=	Works on Shakespearean evaluation. (*Unsought Link*)
O111,2J64:gxM66	=	**Croce's works on Shakespearean evaluation.** (Sought Link)
O111,2J64:*g*xM66:	=	(*False Link*)
O111,2J64:*g*xM66:*g*	=	Evaluation of Croce's works on Shakespearean evaluation. (*Unsought Link*)

Note: Unlike in the case of an evaluation of Shakespeare, an Evaluation of a Shakespearean critic is not likely to be sought under the main heading "Evaluation". This illustrates the play of judgment in deciding whether a link of this kind should be treated as sought or as unsought.

9 B0*b*D	=	Engineering mathematics.
B	=	**Mathematics.** (Sought Link)
B0	=	(*False Link*)
B0*b*	=	(*False Link*)
B0bD	=	**Engineering mathematics.** (Sought Link)

10 F550*b*M5	=	Fuel technology for glass manufacturers.
F	=	**Technology.** (Sought Link)
F5	=	Organic technology. (*Unsought Link*)
F55	=	**Fuel technology.** (Sought Link)
F550	=	(*False Link*)
F550*b*	=	(*False Link*)
F550bM5	=	**Fuel technology for glass manufacturers.** (Sought Link)

11 Z44,30*b*X:545	=	Indian law of contract for exporters.
Z	=	**Law.** (Sought Link)
Z44	=	**Indian law.** (Sought Link)
Z44,	=	(*False Link*)
Z44,3	=	**Indian law of contract.** (Sought Link)
Z44,30	=	(*False Link*)
Z44,30*b*	=	(*False Link*)

Z44,30bX:545 = **Indian law of contract for exporters.** (Sought Link)

12 C0cE = **Comparison of physics and chemistry.**

C = **Physics.** (Sought Link)

C0 = *(False Link)*

C0c = *(False Link)*

C0cE = **Physics Compared with chemistry.** (Sought Link)

13 W0gU = **Geopolitics.**

W = **Political science.** (Sought Link)

W0 = *(False Link)*

W0g = *(False Link)*

W0gU = **Geopolitics.** (Sought Link)

14 X:3.44'N50gZ = **Influence of law on distribution of wealth in India.**

X = **Economics.** (Sought Link)

X: = *(False Link)*

X:3 = **Distribution of wealth.** (Sought Link)

X:3. = *(False Link)*

X:3.4 = **Distribution of wealth in Asia.** (Sought Link)

X:3.44 = **Distribution of wealth in India.** (Sought Link)

X:3.44. = *(False Link)*

X:3.44'N = (*False Link*)
↓
X:3.44'N5 = Distribution of wealth in India brought upto 1950's.
(*False Link*)
↓
X:3.44'N50 = (*False Link*)
↓
X:3.44'N50*g* = (*False Link*)
↓
X:3.44'N50*g*Z = **Influence of law on distribution of wealth in India.**
(Sought Link)

15 Y310*w*5:72 = Difference between the intelligence of rural and city people.
↓
Y = **Sociology.**
(Sought Link)
↓
Y3 = Sociology of groups based on residence.
(*Unsought Link*)
↓
Y31 = **Rural Sociology.**
(Sought Link)
↓
Y310 = (*False Link*)
↓
Y310*w* = (*False Link*)
↓
Y310*w*5 = **Difference between rural and city people.**
(Sought Link)
↓
Y310*w*5: = (*False Link*)
↓
Y310*w*5:7 = **Difference in personality between rural and city people.**
(Sought Link)
↓
Y310*w*5:72 = **Difference in intelligence between rural and city people.**
(Sought Link)

16 G:30*r*2 = Influence of anatomy on physiology.
↓
G = **Biology.**
(Sought Link)
↓
G: = (*False Link*)

G:3 = **Physiology.**
(Sought Link)

G:30 = (*False Link*)

G:30r = (*False Link*)

G:30r2 = **Influence of anatomy on physiology.**
(Sought Link)

CHAPTER KD

CHOICE OF CLASS INDEX HEADING

1 Choice

A Class Index Entry is to be given using as Heading the term represented by the last digit of each of the Sought Links of the Chain representing the Class Number of each Main Entry and each Cross Reference Entry.

The object of Class Index Entries is to inform the reader about the Class Number under which he can find reading materials on the specific subject in which he is interested. The reader often fails to mention his specific subject in exact terms. He may mention only a subject of greater extension. This may be due to his own way of thinking or to his believing that the Library Catalogue may not have provided entries under such minute specific subjects as he is thinking of. Whatever the reason, the fact remains that it is subjects of greater extension, than the one needed, that are often looked up by readers. It is to meet this contingency that this Rule provides for a Class Index Entry, not only corresponding to the Last Sought Link of a chain, but also to each of the Upper Sought Links.

2 Main Heading

If the term derived for the Heading by Sec KD1 does not by itself individualise it, it is to be taken as the Main Heading in a Multiple Subject Heading as defined in Sec FR56.

21 Subheadings

The Subheadings necessary to secure individualisation are to be derived, with the aid of the Canon of Context [RP7], from the last digit of one (or more) of the upper sought Links in the Chain.

22 Minimum Number

The Minimum Number of such links, necessary and sufficient for individualisation, are to contribute the Subheadings.

23 NOMINATIVE CASE

Each Heading or Subheading is to be a single noun in nominative case except when a qualifying adjective is necessary as in "Algebraic equations", "Digestive system", and "Social sciences".

3 **Proper Name or Single Word**

If it happens that the whole Class Number or a part of it, made up of the Basic Number and/or, one or more of its Isolate Numbers, represents a proper name or can be translated into a single word in popular usage, it is to be used as the Heading.

4 **No Duplication**

If the Class Number of the Main Entry or of a Cross Reference Entry of a document is already found in any other entry of the Classified Part of the catalogue, Class Index Entry is not to be written for any of its Sought Links.

41 If Sec KD4 is not operative, a Class Index Entry is to be written for the Last Sought Link.

42 If Sec KD41 is operative and if a Class Number with the Next Upper Sought Link as its own Last Sought Link is already found in any Entry of the Classified Part of the catalogue, Class Index Entry is not to be written for it or for any of its Upper Sought Links.

43 If Sec KD42 is not operative, Class Index Entry is to be written for the Upper Sought Link in question.

44 The other Upper Sought Links are to be dealt with on lines analogous to Sec KD4 to KD43.

The purpose of the procedure prescribed by. Sec KD4 and its Subdivisions is to secure that no Class Index Entry occurs more than once in the catalogue.

It may be mentioned, however, that the back of the Main Card should contain the Heading of the Class Index Entry suggested by a book, though an Index Card is not to be written as a result of Sec KD4 to KD44. That is because the back of the Main card must give a thoroughly reliable key to all the Class Index Entries in the catalogue that can be related to the book.

As a trivial but important practical detail, mention may be made of the following as a possible device. Such of the Headings on the back of the Main Card, as have already received a Class Index Entry in the library catalogue in connection with an earlier book, are distinguished for the guidance of the typist and the amanuensis by a pencil dot placed just to the left of the Heading on the back of the Main Card.

The procedure prescribed in Sec KD4 and its Subdivisions secures the purpose mentioned in paragraph 1 of the commentary, by working through the Classified Part of the catalogue. It is possible to secure the same purpose by working through the Alphabetical Part also.

Before writing the Class Index Entry for the Last Sought Link, the Alphabetical Part may be looked up. If the entry is already found there, it need not be written again.

In a case of this kind there is nothing to choose between working through the Classified Part or through the Alphabetical Part.

On the other hand, if the Class Index Entry of the Last Sought Link has not already been made, we have yet to decide which of the Upper Sought Links call for their own Class Index Entries to be written out. To decide this, we have to look up again and again the Classified Part or the Alphabetical Part, as the case may be.

In the Classified Part, the Class Numbers forming the Upper Links will occur in entries lying close to one another. But in the Alphabetical Part, the entries to be verified will lie scattered from A to Z. Therefore, the Law of Parsimony would prefer working through the Classified Part of the catalogue.

CHAPTER KE

RENDERING OF CLASS INDEX HEADING

1 Standard Term

The terms used as Headings or Subheadings are to be the standard ones given in the Classification Scheme in use.

2 Rendering

If the term used as Heading or Subheading is the name of a Person, or a Geographical Entity, or a Corporate Body, or the Title of a Work it is to be rendered according to Chap JA to JF.

3 Other Multiworded Terms

If the term used as Heading or Subheading consists of more than one word and Sec KE 2 is not applicable, the words are to be written in their natural sequence.

4 Inter-Class Phase

If the Class Number has two or more Inter-Class Phases, the terms of the different phases are, wherever necessary, to be linked up by an appropriate connecting word such as "influencing", "biasing", "compared with" etc, which is the standard equivalent of the Phase Relation Digit as given in the Classification Scheme used.

5 Intra-Facet or Intra-Array Phase

If the Class Number comprehends Intra-Facet or Intra-Array Phase Relation, the rendering is to use an appropriate connecting word on the analogy of Sec KE4.

6 Individualising Element

When warranted, Individualising Element(s) is(are) to be added, as prescribed in Part J, either to the Heading as a whole or to any block in the Heading.

See Chap KG for examples.

7 Canon of Currency

The terms used as Headings are to be watched and as they become obsolete, fresh entries are to be made with their current equivalents in the Headings, and the old ones may be removed ultimately, though not immediately.

71 Evolution of Words

This rule relates to a factor which makes the Class Index Entry a source of trial for cataloguers. One of the basic principles in Classification is that the term used to denote a Class in the Schedule of Classification should have a fixity of meaning. In deference to this principle, individuals, that have to do with the administration of libraries, may use the same term with the same meaning at all times. But there are forces, beyond the control of individuals, which change the meaning of terms in course of time. The vicissitudes in the meaning of terms such as Philosophy, Philology, Anthropology, Sociology and so on, are cases in point. Nobody in the world, much less the classifier and the cataloguer, can arrest this semasiological change and evolution of the words in human use. Apart from the changes that come through ages—a library catalogue, being a permanent entity, has no doubt to take note of these—the publication of the supplementary volume of the New Oxford Dictionary demonstrates the extraordinary rate at which new terms are born and old terms change their colour and meaning even in a single generation.

72 Internal Repair

What cannot be prevented must be met with suitable adjustments. It is here that the Canon of Currency's call for repair of the catalogue comes—internal repair [RP6] as distinct from the repair of the physical card. As the terms used as Headings of Class Index Entries become obsolete, cards should be added having their more up-to-date equivalents as Headings. This process requires constant vigilance and industry. Otherwise instead of the catalogue helping the people, it may prove to be harmful and misleading.

73 Why of Card Form

The need for such insertion of entries from time to time makes it imperative that the physical form of the catalogue should be such that any given entry can be removed, or corrected, or replaced, or added without disturbing the other entries. This would rule out the ledger or book form of the catalogue and make the Card Catalogue, the form PAR EXCELLENCE.

CHAPTER KF

CLASS INDEX ENTRY

0 Sections

A Class Index Entry is to consist successively of the following Sections:

1 Leading Section; and

2 Second Section followed by the Index Number.

The only Part of this Code, whose Sec may not be of direct detailed application irrespective of the Scheme of Classification used, is this Part dealing with Class Index Entries.

Its Sec are applicable with ease if the Scheme of Classification used satisfies the Canons of Modulation [RP5], Relativity [RP8], and Expressiveness [RP9].

In particular, the Chain Procedure prescribed in the Rules of this Part gives satisfactory results if the Colon Classification is used. The *British national bibliography* has demonstrated the applicability of the Chain Procedure with satisfactory results if the Decimal Classification is used with a few improvised devices.

All the other Sec of this Code are applicable whatever be the Scheme of Classification used.

1 Leading Section

The Leading Section is to consist of the Class Index Heading appropriate to the Class Index Entry.

11 Choice and Rendering

The Choice and Rendering of the Class Index Heading are to be made in accordance with the Rules of Chap KD and KE respectively.

2 Second Section

The Second Section of a Class Index Entry is to consist of the following Directing Words:

For documents in this Class and its Subdivisions see the Classified Part of the catalogue under the Class Number.

20 No Underlining

Notwithstanding Sec ED52, the Directing Element prescribed in Sec KF2 is not to be underlined.

21 Class Index Card

The Class Index Entries will appear more elegant and readable if the cards used for them have the Directing Words printed on them in a convenient position leaving three lines at the top for inserting the Heading. Printing the directing words in a distinctively coloured ink such as red ink has been found to be helpful.

22 Class Index Entry in A Catalogue in Book Form

The Directing Words prescribed in Sec KF2 are found to be too long, for use in a catalogue in book form. The usual practice appears to be to omit the Second Section altogether. Under the pressure of this practice, it was omitted in the card catalogue also in the Madras University Library in the earlier years. But when the Second Section was introduced later, it was found that the readers had a greater satisfaction.

The fact of the Directing Words giving satisfaction makes one think of what can be done in the case of a catalogue in book form, as considerations of space and cost would rule out the insertion of three lines of Directing Words in every one of the Class Index Entries.

23 Separate Sequence for Class Index Entries

A possible solution is to put all the Class Index Entries together in a separate Alphabetical Sequence. In that case, the directing words can be printed at the top of each page in a suitably modified form. Of course this method will split up the Alphabetical Part of the Catalogue into two sub-parts. Some investigation should therefore be made about the desirability or otherwise of adopting this suggestion.

24 Class Index Entry in National Bibliography

This problem may not be serious in the case of a library catalogue, because a library catalogue is seldom made now-a-days in a book form. But the production of National Bibliography in book form is now rightly becoming common in several countries. The Rules for a National Bibliography closely follow the Rules for a Library Catalogue. In fact, whatever information is given in an entry of a library catalogue is also given in the corresponding entry of a National Bibliography. The latter merely contains some additional information. The problem of Class Index Entries discussed above is therefore a real one in a National Bibliography. That is why an investigation of the problem and of the relative merits of the two methods is suggested.

3 Index Number

The Index Number in a Class Index Entry is to consist of the Class Number representing the term in the Heading Section.

CHAPTER KG

EXAMPLES OF CLASS INDEX ENTRIES

The Class Numbers, whose Chains are given as examples in Chap KC, will call for the following Class Index Entries:

Example 1 *of Chap* KC

1.1 TUBERCULOSIS, LUNGS.
For documents in this Class and its Subdivisions see the Classified Part of the catalogue under the Class Number L45:421

1.2 INFECTION, DISEASE, LUNGS.
For documents in this Class and its Subdivisions see the Classified Part of the catalogue under the Class Number L45:42

1.3 DISEASE, LUNGS.
For documents in this Class and its Subdivisions see the Classified Part of the catalogue under the Class Number L45:4

1.4 LUNGS, MEDICINE.
For documents in this Class and its Subdivisions see the Classified Part of the catalogue under the Class Number L45

1.5 RESPIRATORY SYSTEM, MEDICINE.
For documents in this Class and its Subdivisions see the Classified Part of the catalogue under the Class Number L4

1.6 MEDICINE
For documents in this Class and its Subdivisions see the Classified Part of the catalogue under the Class Number L

Example 2 *of Chap* KC

2.1 OTHELLO, SHAKESPEARE (William).
For documents in this Class and its Subdivisions see the Classified Part of the catalogue under the Class Number O111,2J64,P

2.2 SHAKESPEARE (William) (1564), DRAMA.
For documents in this Class and its Subdivisions see the Classified Part of the catalogue under the Class Number O111,2J64

2.3 DRAMA, ENGLISH.
For documents in this Class and its Subdivisions see the Classified Part of the catalogue under the Class Number O111,2

2.4 ENGLISH, LITERATURE.
For documents in this Class and its Subdivisions see the Classified Part of the catalogue under the Class Number 0111

2.5 LITERATURE.
For documents in this Class and its Subdivisions see the Classified Part of the catalogue under the Class Number O

Example 3 *of Chap* KC

3.1 UNITED STATES, MARKETING, AGRICULTURE, CO-OPERATION.
For documents in this Class and its Subdivisions see the Classified Part of the catalogue under the Class Numbet XM,8(J):51.73

3.2 MARKETING, AGRICULTURE, CO-OPERATION.
For documents in this Class and its Subdivisions see the Classified Part of the catalogue under the Class Number XM,8(J):51

3.3 TRADE, AGRICULTURE, CO-OPERATION.
For documents in this Class and its Subdivisions see the Classified Part of the catalogue under the Class Number XM,8(J):5

3.4 AGRICULTURE, CO-OPERATION.
For documents in this Class and its Subdivisions see the Classified Part of the catalogue under the Class Number XM,8(J)

3.5 INDUSTRY, CO-OPERATION.
For documents in this Class and its Subdivisions see the Classified Part of the catalogue under the Class Number XM,8(A)

3.6 CO-OPERATION, ECONOMICS.
For documents in this Class and its Subdivisions see the Classified Part of the catalogue under the Class Number XM

3.7 ECONOMICS.
For documents in this Class and its Subdivisions see the Classified Part of the catalogue under the Class Number X

Example 4 *of Chap* KC

4.1 LAW, CONSTITUTION, GREAT BRITAIN.
For documents in this Class and its Subdivisions see the Classified Part of the catalogue under the Class Number V56:2:(Z)

4.2 CONSTITUTION, GREAT BRITAIN.
For documents in this Class and its Subdivisions see the Classified Part of the catalogue under the Class Number V45:2

4.3 GREAT BRITAIN, HISTORY.
For documents in this Class and its Subdivisions see the Classified Part of the catalogue under the Class Number V56

4.4 HISTORY.
For documents in this Class and its Subdivisions see the Classified Part of the catalogue under the Class Number V

Example 5 *of Chap* KC

5.1 RAMANUJAN (Srinivasa) (1887), WORKS.
For documents in this Class and its Subdivisions see the Classified Part of the catalogue under the Class Number BxM87

5.2 MATHEMATICS.
For documents in this Class and its Subdivisions see the Classified Part of the catalogue under the Class Number B

Example 6 *of Chap* KC

6.1 CRITICISM, SHAKESPEARE (William) (1564).
For documents in this Class and its Subdivisions see the Classified Part of the catalogue under the Class Number O111,2J64:*g*

Example 7 *of Chap* KC

7.1 STATISTICS, INDIA, RURAL, EDUCATION.
For documents in this Class and its Subdivisions see the Classified Part of the catalogue under the Class Number T9(Y31).44'N3*s*

7.2 INDIA, RURAL, EDUCATION.
For documents in this Class and its Subdivisions see the Classified Part of the catalogue under the Class Number T9(Y31).44

7.3 ASIA, RURAL, EDUCATION.
For documents in this Class and its Subdivisions see the Classified Part of the catalogue under the Class Number T9(Y31).4

7.4 RURAL, EDUCATION.
For documents in this Class and its Subdivisions see the Classified Part of the catalogue under the Class Number T9(Y31)

7.5 EDUCATION.
For documents in this Class and its Subdivisions see the Classified Part of the catalogue under the Class Number T

Example 8 *of Chap* KC

8.1 CROCE (Benedetto) (1866), CRITICISM, SHAKESPEARE (William) (1564).
For documents in this Class and its Subdivisions see the Classified Part of the catalogue under the Class Number O111,2J64:*gx*M66

Example 9 *of Chap* KC

9.1 ENGINEERING biasing MATHEMATICS.
For documents in this Class and its Subdivisions see the Classified Part of the catalogue under the Class Number B0*b*D

9.2 MATHEMATICS.
For documents in this Class and its Subdivisions see the Classified Part of the catalogue under the Class Number B

Example 10 *of Chap* KC

10.1 GLASS MANUFACTURE biasing FUEL, TECHNOLOGY.
For documents in this Class and its Subdivisions see the Classified Part of the catalogue under the Class Number F550*b*M5

10.2 FUEL, TECHNOLOGY.
For documents in this Class and its Subdivisions see the Classified Part of the catalogue under the Class Number F55

10.3 TECHNOLOGY.
For documents in this Class and its Subdivisions see the Classified Part of the catalogue under the Class Number F

Example 11 *of Chap* KC

11.1 EXPORT biasing CONTRACT, INDIA, LAW.
For documents in this Class and its Subdivisions see the Classified Part of the catalogue under the Class Number Z44,30*b*X:545

11.2 CONTRACT, INDIA, LAW.
For documents in this Class and its Subdivisions see the Classified Part of the catalogue under the Class Number Z44,3

11.2 INDIA, LAW.
For documents in this Class and its Subdivisions see the Classified Part of the catalogue under the Class Number Z44

11.4 LAW.
For documents in this Class and its Subdivisions see the Classified Part of the catalogue under the Class Number Z

Example 12 *of Chap* KC

12.1 CHEMISTRY compared with PHYSICS.
For documents in this Class and its Subdivisions see the Classified Part of the catalogue under the Class Number C0*c*E

12.2 PHYSICS.
For documents in this Class and its Subdivisions see the Classified Part of the catalogue under the Class Number C

Example 13 *of Chap* KC

13.1 GEOPOLITICS.
For documents in this Class and its Subdivisions see the Classified Part of the catalogue under the Class Number W0*g*U

13.2 GEOGRAPHY.
For documents in this Class and its Subdivisions see the Classified Part of the catalogue under the Class Number U

Example 14 *of Chap* KC

14.1 LAW influencing INDIA, DISTRIBUTION, ECONOMICS.
For documents in this Class and its Subdivisions see the Classified Part of the catalogue under the Class Number X:3.44'N50*g*Z

14.2 INDIA, DISTRIBUTION, ECONOMICS.
For documents in this Class and its Subdivisions see the Classified Part of the catalogue under the Class Number X:3.44

14.3 ASIA, DISTRIBUTION, ECONOMICS.
For documents in this Class and its Subdivisions see the Classified Part of the catalogue under the Class Number X:3.4

14.4 DISTRIBUTION, ECONOMICS.
For documents in this Class and its Subdivisions see the Classified Part of the catalogue under the Class Number X:3

14.5 ECONOMICS.
For documents in this Class and its Subdivisions see the Classified Part of the catalogue under the Class Number X

Example 15 *of Chap* 33

15.1 INTELLIGENCE, CITY PEOPLE difference from RURAL PEOPLE.
For documents in this Class and its Subdivisions see the Classified Part of the catalogue under the Class Number Y310*w*5:72

15.2 PERSONALITY, CITY PEOPLE difference from RURAL PEOPLE.
For documents in this Class and its Subdivisions see the Classified Part of the catalogue under the Class Number Y310*w*5:7

15.3 CITY PEOPLE difference from RURAL PEOPLE.
For documents in this Class and its Subdivisions see the Classified Part of the catalogue under the Class Number Y310*w*5

15.4 RURAL, SOCIOLOGY.
For documents in this Class and its Subdivisions see the Classified Part of the catalogue under the Class Number Y31

15.5 SOCIOLOGY.
For documents in this Class and its Subdivisions see the Classified Part of the catalogue under the Class Number Y

Example 16 *of Chap* KC

16.1 ANATOMY influencing PHYSIOLOGY.
For documents in this Class and its Subdivisions see the Classified Part of the catalogue under the Class Number G:30*r*2

16.2 PHYSIOLOGY.
For documents in this Class and its Subdivisions see the Classified Part of the catalogue under the Class Number G:3

16.3 BIOLOGY.
For documents in this Class and its Subdivisions see the Classified Part of the catalogue under the Class Number G

CHAPTER KH

CLASSIC

1 Names of Work and of Author

If a work—say a Classic, a Sacred Work, a Literary Work, or a Commentary on any of these—is a Quasi-Class and has

1 A proper name of its own;

2 An author whose name is known; and

3 The same digit to represent itself and its author,

there is to be a Class Index Entry using as Heading each of the following:

1 Name of the Work as Main Heading and Name(s) of the Author(s) as Subheading;

2 Name(s) of Author(s) as Main Heading and Name of the Work as Subheading; and

3 In the case of Multiple Author, the Names of the Authors in every cyclic permutation of them as Main Heading and the Name of the Work as Subheading.

The cyclic permutation will ensure one entry with the name of each author as the first name in the Heading.

11 RENDERING

The rendering of the names of authors and titles should be according to Part J.

2 Example 1

21 CHAIN

R66,5x1,B,B,K,P	=	Appayya Dikshita: Parimala
R	=	Philosophy. (Sought Link)
R6	=	Indian philosophy. (Sought Link)
R65	=	Vedanta (Link-at-Telescoping-Point) (Sought Link)

R66,	=	**Advaita.** (Sought Link)
R66	=	(*False Link*)
R66,5	=	**Brahma-sutra.** (Sought Link)
R66,5*x*	=	Commentary on Brahma-sutra. (*Unsought Link*)
R66,5x1	=	**Sankara on Brahma-sutra.** (Sought Link)
R66,5*x*1,	=	(*False Link*)
R66,5x1,B	=	**Sankara: Brahma-sutra-bhashya.** (Sought Link)
R66,5*x*1,B,	=	(*False Link*)
R66,5x1,B,B	=	**Vacaspatimisra: Bhamati.** (Sought Link)
R66,5*x*1,B,B,	=	(*False Link*)
R66,5x1,B,B,K	=	**Amalananda: Kalpa-taru.** (Sought Link)
R66,5*x*1,B,B,K,	=	(*False Link*)
R66,5x1,B,B,K,P	=	**Appayya Dikshita: Parimala.** (Sought Link)

22 CLASS INDEX ENTRIES

1 PARIMALA, APPAYYA DIKSHITA.
For documents in this Class and its Subdivisions see the Classified Part of the catalogue under the Class Number R66,5*x*1,B,B,K,P

2 APPAYYA DIKSHITA, PARIMALA.
For documents in this Class and its Subdivisions see the Classified Part of the catalogue under the Class Number R66,5*x*1,B,B,K,P

3 KALPA-TARU, AMALANANDA.
For documents in this Class and its Subdivisions see the Classified Part of the catalogue under the Class Number R66,5*x*1,B,B,K

4 AMALANANDA, KALPA-TARU.
For documents in this Class and its Subdivisions see the Classified Part of the catalogue under the Class Number R66,5*x*1,B,B,K

5 BHAMATI, VACASPATI MISRA.
For documents in this Class and its Subdivisions see the Classified Part of the catalogue under the Class Number R66,5*x*1,B,B

6 VACASPATI MISRA, BHAMATI.
For documents in this Class and its Subdivisions see the Classified Part of the catalogue under the Class Number R66,5x1,B,B

7 BRAHMA-SUTRA-BHASHYA, SANKARA.
For documents in this Class and its Subdivisions see the Classified Part of the catalogue under the Class Number R66,5x1,B

8 SANKARA, BRAHMA-SUTRA-BHASHYA.
For documents in this Class and its Subdivisions see the Classified Part of the catalogue under the Class Number R66,5x1,B

9 BRAHMA-SUTRA, ADVAITA.
For documents in this Class and its Subdivisions see the Classified Part of the catalogue under the Class Number R66,5

10 ADVAITA.
For documents in this Class and its Subdivisions see the Classified Part of the catalogue under the Class Number R66

11 VEDANTA.
For documents in this Class and its Subdivisions see the Classified Part of the catalogue under the Class Numbers R65 to R68

12 INDIAN PHILOSOPHY.
For documents in this Class and its Subdivisions see the Classified Part of the catalogue under the Class Number R6

13 PHILOSOPHY.
For documents in this Class and its Subdivisions see the Classified Part of the catalogue under the Class Number R

3 Example 2

31 CHAIN

P35,ExM60,1 = Sankara Rangayya and Venkatarama Sastri: **Bala-vyakarana-guptartha-prakashika.**

P = **Linguistics.**
(Sought Link)

P3 = **Dravidian linguistics.**
(Unsought Link)

P35 = **Telugu linguistics.**
(Sought Link)

P35, = ***(False Link)***

P35,E = **Modern Telugu linguistics.**
(Sought Link)

P35,E*x* = Works on modern Telugu linguistics.
(*Unsought Link*)

P35,E*x*M60 = **Chinnaya Suri (Paravastu): Bala-vyakaranamu.**
(Sought Link)

P35,E*x*M60, = (*False Link*)

P35,E*x*M60,B = **Sankara Rangayya and Venkatarama Sastri: Bala-vyakarana-guptartha-prakasika.**
(Sought Link)

CLASS INDEX ENTRIES

1 BALA-VYAKARANA-GUPTARTHA-PRAKASHIKA, SANKARA RANGAYYA AND VENKATARAMA SASTRI.
For documents in this Class and its Subdivisions see the Classified Part of the catalogue under the Class Number P35,E*x*M60,B

2 SANKARA RANGAYYA AND VENKATARAMA SASTRI, BALAVYAKARANA-GUPTARTHA-PRAKASHIKA.
For documents in this Class and its Subdivisions see the Classified Part of the catalogue under the Class Number P35,E*x*M60,B

3 VENKATARAMA SASTRI AND SANKARA RANGAYYA, BALAVYAKARANA GUPTARTHA-PRAKASHIKA.
For documents in this Class and its Subdivisions see the Classified Part of the catalogue under the Class Number. P35,E*x*M60,B

4 BALAVYAKARANAMU, CHINNAYA SURI (Paravastu).
For documents in this Class and its Subdivisions see the Classified Part of the catalogue under the Class Number P35,E*x*M60

5 CHINNAYA SURI (Paravastu), BALA-VYAKARANAMU.
For documents in this Class and its Subdivisions see the Classified Part of the catalogue under the Class Number P35,E*x*M60

6 MODERN, TELUGU, LINGUISTICS.
For documents in this Class and its Subdivisions see the Classified Part of the catalogue under the Class Number P35,E

7 TELUGU, LINGUISTICS.
For documents in this Class and its Subdivisions see the Classified Part of the catalogue under the Class Number P35

8 LINGUISTICS.
For documents in this Class and its Subdivisions see the Classified Part of the catalogue under the Class Number P

CHAPTER KJ

COMMISSION REPORT

1 Two Entries for the Last Link

In the case of a Commission Report, which is a Quasi-Class, there is to be a Class Index Entry using as heading each of the following:

1 The words in the heading of the Main Entry (omitting the information about the Chairman of the Commission), as Main Heading; and

The term, such as 'Report,' forming the title, as Subheading; and

2 The word-group consisting of the entry element in the name of the Chairman followed by the word 'Commission' or its equivalent and the year used in the Main Entry as the individualising element, as Main Heading; and

The term, such as 'Report,' forming the title, as Subheading.

The need for this prescription was brought to our notice by N K Goil [G2].

11 Authority in the Main Entry

To help in the derivation of the second of the above Class Index Entries, provision has been made in Sec JC72 for the addition of the name of the Chairman of the Commission after the individualising element as if it were another individualising element.

2 Example

21 Chain

X79E0*t*F.44'N51*t*	=	Report of the Indian Finance Commission (1951).
X	=	**Economics.** (Sought Link)
X7	=	**Public finance.** (Sought Link)
X79	=	(*False Link*)

X79E = **State finance.** (Sought Ling)

X79E0 = (*False Link*)

X79E0*t* = (*False Link*)

X79E0*t*F = **Federal in relation to State finance.** (Sought Link)

X79E0*t*F. = (*False Link*)

X79E0*t*F.44 = **Federal in relation to State finance in India.** (Sought Link)

X79E0*t*F.44' = (*False Link*)

X79E0*t*F.44'N = (*False Link*)

X79E0*t*F.44'N5 = (*False Link*)

X79E0*t*F.44'N51 = (*False Link*)

X79E0*t*F.44'N51*t* = **Report of the Indian Finance Commission (1951)** (Sought Link)

Note: This Commission is Known as Neogy Commission as Kshitish Chandra Neogy was its chairman. (*See* Example 1 in Sec JC7).

22 Class Index Entries

17.1 INDIA, FINANCE (Commission) (1951), REPORT.
For documents in this Class and its Subdivisions see the Classified Part of the catalogue under the Class Number X79EO*t*F.44'N51*t*

17.2 NEOGY COMMISSION (1951), REPORT.
For documents in this Class and its Subdivisions see the Classified Part of the catalogue under the Class Number X79E0*t*F.44'N51*t*

17.3 INDIA, FEDERAL in relation to STATE, PUBLIC FINANCE.
For documents in this Class and its Subdivisions see the Classified Part of the catalogue under the Class Number X79E0*t*F.44

17.4 FEDERAL in relation to STATE, PUBLIC FINANCE.
For documents in this Class and its Subdivisions see the Classified Part of the catalogue under the Class Number X79E0*t*F

17.5 **State, Public Finance.**
For documents in this Class and its Subdivisions see the Classified Part of the catalogue under the Class Number X79E

17.6 **Public Finance.**
For documents in this Class and its Subdivisions see the Classified Part of the catalogue under the Class Number X7

17.7 **Economics.**
For documents in this Class and its Subdivis ons see the Classified Part of the catalogue under the Class Number X

Note: The authority for entry 17.2 is Sec KD31.

CHAPTER KK

HOMONYM IN CLASS INDEX HEADINGS

1 Genesis

Homonyms are fatal as much in the headings of catalogue entires as among the class numbers themselves. Though two class numbers may be entirely different from each other, it is possible for the Class Index Headings yielded by them to be homonyms. This may be due to many causes.

11 Homonym between Common Isolate and Basic Class

One of the causes, detected so far, for the incidence of homonyms in Class Index Headings is the incidence of homonyms between Anteriorising Common Isolates on the one side and Basic Classes on the other side.

Here are some examples:

Example 1:

1	2:51*v*	History of Classification
2	2:51,9(V)	Classification of History

These two class numbers yield the following Chains and Class Index Headings:

1	2	= Library Science	= 2
		↓	
2	2:51	= Classification	= 2:51
		↓	
3	2:51*v*	= History, Classification	= 2:51,9(V)

The above chain shows that the Class Index Heading "History, Classification" is a homonym. This homonym should be resolved. There appears to be no way of resolving it without violating the rule prescribing that the terms in a Class Index Heading should be only nouns. Therefore, this problem had been for long left unsolved till now.

Example 2:

1	2:55*m*	Periodical on Cataloguing
2	2:55,9Y4	Cataloguing of Periodical

These two class numbers yield the following Chains and Class Index Headings:

1	2	= Library Science	= 2
		↓	
2	2:55	= Cataloguing	= 2:55
		↓	
3	2:55*m*	= Periodical, Cataloguing	= 2:55,9Y4

The above chain shows that the Class Index Headings "Periodical, Cataloguing" is a homonym. This homonym should be resolved. There appears to be no way of resolving it without violating the rule prescribing that the terms in a Class Index Heading should be only nouns. Therefore, this problem had been for long left unsolved.

The following Sec prescribe a way out of this difficulty:

2 Insertion of Auxiliary Word

When an Anteriorising Common Isolate term and the term denoting a Class are homonyms, in the Class Index Heading having the former as a Heading or a Sub-Heading, an appropriate auxiliary word such as '*in*' '*of*' and '*on*' is to be inserted before the succeeding Sub-heading.

3 Semantic Value

The auxiliary word so inserted is to have its usual semantic value.

4 No Ordinal Value

The auxiliary word inserted is to have no ordinal value.

5 Circular Brackets

As a signal for depriving it of its ordinal value, the auxiliary word is to be enclosed within circular brackets.

This amounts to saying that the auxiliary word should be ignored in the arrangement of the entries.

Example 1:

HISTORY, CLASSIFICATION	2:51,9(V)
HISTORY, (of) CLASSIFICATION	2:51*v*

Example 2:

PERIODICAL, CATALOGUING	2:55,9Y4
PERIODICAL, (on) CATALOGUING	2:55*m*

6 Inflectional Language

In the language where the result of the addition of the auxiliary word is got by morphological change in the noun form, the

Sub-Heading should be written as a noun and the inflectional element should be written as a separate word after it. The Sec KJ 3 to KJ 6 apply to them.

Examples:

(English)	HISTORY, CLASSIFICATION	2:51,9(V)
(Hindi)	ITIHAS, VARGIKARAN (ka)	2:51,9(V)
(Marathi)	ITIHASA, VARGIKARAN (aca)	2:51,9(V)
(Bengali)	ITIHAS, BARGIKARAN (er)	2:51,9(V)
(Tamil)	CARITRAM, PAHUPADU (udaiya)	2:51,9(V)
(Telugu)	CARITA, VARGIKARANAMU (yokka)	2:51,9(V)

7 Arrangement

As a result of the auxiliary word having no ordinal value, the arrangement of the homonymous Class Index Headings is to be determined by the ordinal values of the digits in the respective index numbers with the proviso that Roman Small need not be given anteriorising value.

CHAPTER KL

FEATURE HEADING

1 Guide Cards

In the Classified Part of the card catalogue, it is helpful to insert guide cards with their top tabs projecting above the level of the cards having regular entries. Such a tab carries the Class Number and the name of the subject covered, in the succeeding cards. The legends in the guide cards catch the eye of the reader. They guide him to spot out the particular subject of his interest at the moment. The Class Number and the name of the subject, written on the tab of the guide card, taken together is called Feature Heading.

2 Printed Catalogue

If the catalogue is printed, these Feature Headings will be of even greater help. They are usually provided in distinctive types. They are, moreover, shorter than the entries themselves. Therefore, they are picked up by the eye in its first sweep of the pages.

3 Derivation

The Feature Headings can be got by Chain Procedure. They are got by translating each successive digit in the class number into its equivalent term in the natural language, proceeding from left to right. This is just the reverse of what we do in using Chain Procedure to arrive at the sequence of Headings and Sub-headings in the Class Index Entry. A Feature Heading is to consist of the part of the Class Number ending with the digit contributing to the Feature Heading followed by the equivalent term in the Favoured Language.

31 Single Term

When consecutive Feature Headings stand together without being separated by entries, the term corresponding to the last digit in the Class Number may be sufficient.

Example:

The Class Index Heading derived from the class number, V2,21:3 will be, Functions, President, India. On the other hand, this will yield the following successive Feature Headings:

V	=	History
V2	=	India
V2,21	=	President
V2,21:3	=	Functions

These Feature Headings will clutter together if there is no entry in any of the classes History, or Indian History, or Organs of the Government of India, or President of India.

32 Additional Terms

When consecutive Feature Headings are separated out so much that the Feature Headings cannot be comfortably picked up by the eye in association with one another, it may be necessary to add the terms contributed by the earlier digits to the term contributed by the last digit, to the extent necessary for easy intelligibility.

Examples:

In the example given in Sec KL31 the following cases may occur:

1 If there is no entry between the Feature Headings "President" and "Functions," there will be no need to add another term after the term "Functions." On the other hand, if there is a sufficient number of entries between these two Feature Headings, it may be necessary to make the last of the Feature Headings

Either

1 President, Functions

Or

2 Functions of President.

Which form should be adopted and what is the number of entries that will make the addition of the term "President", necessary is a matter of judgement. No objective rule can be laid down.

2 There will be a greater chance for several entries separating out the Feature Headings "India" and "President" than in the first case. Therefore, the Feature Heading "President" should necessarily be followed by "India."

3 This will get even more pronounced in respect of the Feature Headings "History" and "India." In almost every case it may be necessary to add the term "History" after the term "India."

4 Number of Feature Headings

Theoretically there may be a Feature Heading for every Sought Link in the Chain. But it may not be wise to blindly follow the indications of theory in determining the number of Feature Headings to be given. This is a matter of judgement. This is determined by the size of the catalogue, the entries under different headings, and what will be really helpful to a reader who scans through the Feature Headings to pick up the subject needed by him at the moment.

5 Effectiveness

The Feature Headings are found to be effective if the classification scheme is based on the postulates concerning the Five Fundamental Categories,

PMEST—Personality, Matter, Energy, Space, and Time. They are helpful even when other schemes of classification are used, except that difficulties arise when the structure of the class number fails to follow the pattern of PMEST. In DC for example, difficulties arise when Anteriorising Common Isolates are indiscriminately mixed up with the isolates special to Basic Class.

For example, 770.2 has been used as generic for many energy isolates in "770 Photography," while the remaining energy isolates come after the common isolates which occupy the numbers 770.4 to 770.9—that is, they appear against the numbers 771 to 779. To illustrate the improvisations that have to be made to face this situation, a few of the Feature Headings occurring in page 449 of the BNB of 1963 are given below:

770	Photography. General works
770.28	General photo-processes
770.284	Positives
770.2842	Printing
770.2843	Finishing
770.2843[1]	Toning
770.5	Periodicals on Photography.

If "Photography" is not added in the last feature heading, it would read as "Periodicals on Toning."

When we came across such problems in our early days, we were not sure whether these problems were inherent in Chain Procedure or were caused by the defective structure of the DC. Experience has shown us that the latter is the cause in every such case [W1].

CHAPTER KZD

MODIFICATIONS FOR DICTIONARY CATALOGUE

1 Terminology of Classification

All the terms defined in the Sec of Chap KA are applicable to the Dictionary Catalogue also. In addition, we need to borrow from the discipline of classification the term "Common Isolate."

191 Common Isolate

Common Isolate.—An Isolate Idea in the idea plane denoted by the same Isolate Term in the verbal plane and represented by the same Isolate Number in the notational plane, to whatever Basic Class it is attached.

Any Geographical Isolate is a Common Isolate. The Isolates denoted by the following terms are also Common Isolates:

Anthology	Cyclopedia	Report of Conference
Bibliography	Directory	Serial
Biography	History	Syllabus
Collection	Periodical	

2 Terminology of Chain Procedure

All the terms defined in Chap KB are applicable to the Dictionary Catalogue also. In addition, we need also the terms defined in the succeeding Sec.

291 First Part of a Chain

First Part of a Chain.—The part of the Chain of a Class Number, ending with the digit just preceding the digit representing a Common Isolate, if any.

292 Common Isolate Part

Common Isolate Part of a Chain.—The Part of the Chain of a Class Number beginning with the digit representing a Common

Isolate, if any, and ending with the digit just preceding the digit representing the second Common Isolate, if any. It may also be called **Second Part of a Chain.**

293 Further Parts of a Chain

Further Parts.—The Parts of the Chain of a Class Number beginning with a digit representing a Second or a Third etc Common Isolate, if any. They may be respectively called **Third, Fourth,** etc **Parts of a Chain.**

294 Kinds of Links

In each Part of a Class Number there may be all kinds of links such as False Link, Unsought Link, Sought Link, First Link, Upper Link, and Lower Link.

295 Later Phases

Each Phase is also to be regarded as a Part.

3 Examples

The Chains of Examples 3, 7, and 10 of Chap KC are now presented as for a Dictionary Catalogue. To save space, only the Sought Links are shown in the Chain.

Example 3:

XM,9J:51.73'N3 = Co-operative marketing in agriculture in USA brought up to 1934's.

Part 1 *of the Chain begins*

X = Economics.
↓
XM = Co-operation.
↓
XM,8(A) = Co-operative industries.
↓
XM,8(J) = Co-operative agriculture.
↓
XM,8(J):5 = Co-operative trade in agriculture.
↓
XM,8(J):51 = Co-operative marketing in agriculture.
↓
Part 2 *of the Chain begins*

XM,8(J):51.73 = Co-operative marketing in agriculture in USA.

Example 7:

T9(Y31).44'N3*s* = Statistics of rural education in India brought up to 1930's.

Part 1 *of the Chain begins*

T = Education.

↓

T9(Y31) = Rural education.

↓

Part 2 *of the Chain begins*

T9(Y31).4 = Rural education in Asia.

↓

T9(Y31).44 = Rural education in India.

↓

Part 3 *of the Chain begins*

T9(Y31).44'N3*s* = Statistics of rural education in India brought up to 1930's.

Example 10:

F550*b*M5 = Fuel technology for glass manufacturers.

Part 1 *of the Chain begins*

F = Technology.

↓

F55 = Fuel technology.

↓

Part 2 *of the Chain begins*

F550*b*M5 = Fuel technology for glass manufacturers.

4 Choice of Subject Heading

The Choice of Subject Heading in a Dictionary Catalogue is to be according to Chap KD, using as the basis of Chain Procedure the Class Number of the Document and of each of the subjects calling for a Subject Analytical Entry.

40 Alternative Choice

The above Sec will give Subject Entries suitable for a truly Alphabetical Catalogue, which a Dictionary Catalogue is, without any Classified Pocket at any of its points.

401 Classified Pockets and Neural Necessity

But, in the current practice of Subject Headings in a Dictionary Catalogue, Classified Pockets are produced, though it is against the avowed principle implicit in its very name. This is no doubt due to the inexorable hold that classified arrangement has on the human mind. I have shown in my *Prolegomena* [RP10] that classified arrangement is a neural necessity. That is why a pure dictionary arrangement has to be adulterated by some element of classified arrangement.

402 CORRECT WAY

The correct way of meeting this neural necessity for classified arrangement is to adopt the Classified Catalogue, whose Classified Part meets the neural necessity in full measure and the Alphabetical Part satisfies the needs of the inevitable alphabetical approach in an equally full measure. The virtue of the Classified Catalogue is this holistic combination of classified as well as alphabetical arrangement, enabling each to do its best in the sphere in which it can do its best, without encroachment into the sphere of each other.

403 PRESSURE OF OLD SUBJECT HEADING

Since its foundation, the *British national bibliography* has been adopting the Chain Procedure. It represents the first large scale, systematic, and continued, general application of the procedure. Its editorial staff has had an unusually rich chance to observe the reaction of librarians and users alike to its value. Though the BNB is a Classified Catalogue, its staff had been observing also the reaction of those accustomed to the Dictionary Catalogue. When I visited the office of the BNB in June 1953, A J Wells, the Editor, and his colleague E J Coaes told me that those who use the Dictionary Catalogue would like to have the benefit of deriving the Subject Headings mechanically and consistently from Class Numbers, but that they would like to retain some kinds of entries they had been accustomed to when they depended on Dictionaries of Subject Headings.

404 CLASSIFIED POCKETS AND HABIT

The problem, thus presented, was formulated in an article in the *Annals of library science* [RC1]. It had been simmering in the mind all along. Probably, Classified Pocket is one of the major features of the traditional Dictionary Catalogue for whose retention there is a longing in those who had been accustomed to its use. This longing is perhaps the result of habit.

405 VERSATILITY OF CHAIN PROCEDURE

The question then is: "Can there be an alternative set of Rules of Chain Procedure so as to retain such Classified Pockets in the Dictionary Catalogue ?" I now find that the answer is "Yes." In fact, the Rules of Chain Procedure can be so framed as to yield several alternative patterns of arrangement of Subject Headings. Indeed the versatility of the Chain Procedure is greater than what has been realised during the early years of its use. If any pattern of arrangement whatever is clearly defined, a corresponding set of Rules of Chain Procedure can be framed. All that the Chain Procedure does is to mechanise the process of deriving the kind of Subject Headings implied by the pattern and to secure consistency in the pattern.

406 RESEARCH TO BE TAKEN UP

The following Rules on the Choice of Subject Headings along with the other additional Rules of this Chap form a tentative sample of one set of

Alternative Rules of Chain Procedure capable of retaining one variety of Classified Pockets in a Dictionary Catalogue. It is worth attempting to construct other sets of Alternative Rules so as to secure other prescribed results. Perhaps, research into the Psychology of the Use of Catalogue and all the various possible Alternative Rules of Chain Procedure will eventually lead us to a more improved form of Entries in the Alphabetical Part of the Catalogue.

49 Specific Subject Heading

491 Main Heading

The Main Heading of the Specific Subject Entry or a Subject Analytical Entry, as the case may be, contributed by a Class Number, is to be the term represented by the Last Digit of the Last Sought Link of its First Part.

492 to 4944 Similar to Sec KD2 to KD44.

495 Subheading due to Second Part

If the Chain of the Class Number has a Second Part, the term represented by the Common Isolate forming the First Link of that Part, or the link formed by Second Phase as the case may be, is to be added as a further Subheading.

496 Lower Link Subheadings

If the Link ending with the Common Isolate has Sought Lower Links, the term represented by the Last Digit of each such Link is to be added successively as a further subheading to the extent needed for Resolution of Homonyms.

497 Subheading due to Later Parts

Further subheadings from the Second and the Later Parts of the Chain are to be had on the analogy of Sec KZD495 and KZD496.

499 *See also* Subject Heading

4991 Choice

There is to be a *See also* Subject Entry corresponding to each of the Sought Links of the Chain, upper or lower to the Link contributing the Main Heading of Specific Subject Entry or the Subject Analytical Entry as the case may be.

It can be seen that the Lower link can be contributed only by Part 2 of the Chain and by the later Parts.

49911 Main Heading

The Main Heading of a *See also* Subject Entry contributed by a Sought Link is to be the term represented by its Last digit.

4992 to 49944 Similar to Sec KD2 to KD44.

5 Rendering of Subject Heading

The Rendering of a Subject Heading in a Dictionary Catalogue is to be according to Chap KE.

6 *See also* Subject Entry

A Specific Subject Entry or a Subject Analytical Entry is a Book Index Entry. The Rules for these entries will therefore be given in Sec MZD2 and its subdivisions. The only General Subject Entry, falling within the purview of this Chap, is the *See also* Subject Entry. The Rules for such an entry are given in the succeeding Sec.

60 Sections

A *See also* Subject Entry in a Dictionary Catalogue is to consist successively of the following Sections:

1 Leading Section;
2 Second Section; and
3 Referred-To Heading.

61 Leading Section

The Leading Section is to consist of the Referred-From Heading concerned.

611 referred-from heading

The Choice and Rendering of the Heading of a *See also* Subject Entry of a Dictionary Catalogue are to be made respectively in accordance with the Sec KZD4 and its subdivisions and Sec KZD5. Each Catalogue should exercise the option to elect Sec KZD4 or KZD49 to KZD4994. The alternative chosen should be consistently followed.

62 Second Section

The Second Section of a *See also* Subject Entry in a Dictionary Catalogue is to consist of the Directing Words "*See also.*"

63 Referred-To Heading

631 choice

The Referred-To Heading of a *See also* Subject Entry in a Dictionary Catalogue is to be the same as the Heading of the Specific Subject Entry or the Subject Analytical Entry as the case may be, determined by the Chain contributing the *See also* Subject Entry.

632 rendering

The Rendering of the Referred-To Heading is to be as it is in the Heading of the Specific Subject Entry or the Subject Analytical Entry mentioned in Sec KZD63.

7 Examples

For Example 3 of Sec KZD3

Specific Subject Heading

3.1 Marketing, Agriculture, Co-operation, United States.

See also Subject Entries

3.2 Trade, Agriculture, Co-operation.
See also
Marketing, Agriculture, Co-operation, United States.

3.3 AGRICULTURE, CO-OPERATION.
See also
MARKETING, AGRICULTURE, CO-OPERATION, UNITED STATES.

3.4 INDUSTRY, CO-OPERATION.
See also
MARKETING, AGRICULTURE, CO-OPERATION, UNITED STATES.

3.5 CO-OPERATION, ECONOMICS.
See also
MARKETING, AGRICULTURE, CO-OPERATION, UNITED STATES.

3.6 ECONOMICS.
See also
MARKETING, AGRICULTURE, CO-OPERATION, UNITED STATES.

FOR EXAMPLE 7 OF SEC KZD 3

SPECIFIC SUBJECT HEADING

RURAL, EDUCATION, INDIA, STATISTICS.

See also SUBJECT ENTRIES

7.1 STATISTICS, INDIA, RURAL, EDUCATION.
See also
RURAL, EDUCATION, INDIA, STATISTICS.

7.2 INDIA, RURAL, EDUCATION.
See also
RURAL, EDUCATION, INDIA, STATISTICS.

7.3 ASIA, RURAL, EDUCATION.
See also
RURAL, EDUCATION, INDIA, STATISTICS.

7.4 EDUCATION.
See also
RURAL, EDUCATION, INDIA, STATISTICS.

FOR EXAMPLE 10 OF SEC KZD3

SPECIFIC SUBJECT HEADING

FUEL, TECHNOLOGY biased TO GLASS MANUFACTURE

See also SUBJECT ENTRIES

10.1 GLASS MANUFACTURE biasing FUEL, TECHNOLOGY.
See also
FUEL, TECHNOLOGY biased to GLASS MANUFACTURE.

10.2 TECHNOLOGY.
See also
FUEL, TECHNOLOGY biased to GLASS MANUFACTURE.

PART L

CROSS REFERENCE INDEX ENTRY

CHAPTER LA

STRUCTURE AND TYPES

1 Sections

A Cross Reference Index Entry is to consist successively of the following Sections:

1 Leading Section;
2 Second Section; and
3 Referred-To Heading.

11 Leading Section

The Leading Section is to consist of the Referred-From Heading concerned.

111 REFERRED-FROM HEADING

As defined in Sec FN452, a Referred-From Heading consists of the word or word-group, which is usually an alternative name of the person, the geographical entity, the series, or the document respectively, mentioned in the Referred-To Heading.

The Referred-From Heading is likely to be brought up by some readers while looking up the catalogue.

12 Referred-To Heading

Referred-To Heading is usually that name of a person, a geographical entity, a series, or a document, which has been preferred for use in the Main Entry or Book Index Entry concerned.

It will also be seen in Chap LE and LF that the Referred-From Heading can also be something other than an Alternative Name.

13 Purpose

The purpose of a Cross Reference Index Entry is to invite the attention of a reader from the term he brings up to the catalogue to its equivalent term or some other term under which he can find his information. For, the catalogue uses in all Specific Entries only the term found on the title-page and its overflow of the document catalogued. The Canon of Ascertainability forces such a course on the catalogue. In the cases covered by Chap LE and LF, the Law of Parsimony prescribes Cross Reference Index Entries.

14 Deviation from Canon of Ascertainability

It will be seen later in Chap LB and LD respectively that in certain prescribed cases, the Canon of Ascertainability may be slightly deviated from. In such a case, the Referred-To Heading will be a Uniformised Version of the terms involved, be it the name of a Sacred Work (*See* Sec FA5) or a Classic (*See* Sec FA7), or a Work of Literature (*See* Sec FA6), or a Pedestrian Work (*See* Sec FA91).

2 Second Section

The Second Section is to consist of the directing term "*See*" or "*See also*", as the case may be.

If each of two or more alternative terms is used as the Heading of a Book Index Entry, when the Referred-From Heading is one of these, the Directing Word should be "*See also.*" If, on the other hand, a Referred-From Heading is never used as the Heading of a Book Index Entry, the Directing Word should be "*See.*" Occasions may arise when the directing term "*See*" has to be changed into "*See also.*"

See the examples given in the later chapters of this Part.

3 Type of Cross Reference Index Entry

A Cross Reference Index Entry may be one of five types, namely

1 Alternative Name Entry;
2 Variant-Form-of-Word Entry;
3 Pseudonym-Real-Name Entry;
4 Editor-of-Series Entry; and
5 Generic-Name Entry.

Each of these types will be dealt with in Chap LB to LF respectively.

4 Avoidance of Duplication of Entry

Care is to be taken not to write a Cross Reference Index Entry suggested by a document, if an identically similar entry is already found in the catalogue.

CHAPTER LB

ALTERNATIVE NAME ENTRY

1 Choice of Referred-From Heading

There is to be an Alternative Name Entry, using as Referred-From Heading each of all the possible Alternative Names by which any person, any corporate body, any geographical entity, any series, or any document respectively, whose name has been used as the Heading for a Main Entry or a Book Index Entry, is known or is likely to be known.

It is difficult to make an exhaustive list of all likely Alternative Names which should be used as Headings of Cross Reference Index Entries.

The name of a Person may be changed for various reasons, such as marriage, peerage, change of religion, change of "asrama" or status in some of the religions of India and also in some other religions, and even a fanciful desire for change. A Usage Name may develop in course of time. A person may have different names in different languages.

The name of a Corporate Body may also be changed for various political, administrative, or other reasons.

Name of a Country, City or any other Geographical Entry may be changed for political, sentimental, or other reasons.

There are also some Series which have alternative names.

So also, the title of a document may change. The same document may be given different titles in different editions. The same document may also appear in different countries with different titles.

In the case of a person, a corporate body, a series, or a document, alternative name may be created by popular usage, without its being formally adopted.

In the case of an Institution, in addition to change of name either in official usage or in popular usage, there may be need to permute the words in the name so as to bring a certain significant word to the beginning of the name, since the Institution may be remembered under that catchword.

In the case of an Institution, the correct official or statutory name may be either too long or too unfamiliar. In such a case, it would be convenient to use such an unused official or statutory name as the Heading of a Cross Reference Index Entry, referring from it to the form of the name actually occurring on the title-page of the documents concerned.

It may be remarked here that the causes giving rise to Cross Reference Index Entry are many; and new causes may appear from time to time. The choice of the Alternative Names to be used as Cross Reference Index Entry Headings is not determined by the definite Canon of Ascertainability. The cataloguer has to fish for them in the market place as it were. This contingency is likely to bring in a violation of the Canon of Consistency. But there appears to be no remedy. The Choice of Alternative Names has to be left to the selective instinct of the cataloguer for what is worthwhile. Indeed this flair distinguishes an efficient cataloguer from an unimaginative plodder. But it may be stated that the frequency of the demand for Cross Reference Index Entry is ordinarily small.

For convenience, the Cross Reference Index Entry cards may ha red top-edges.

2 Rendering of the Referred-From Heading

The rendering of the Referred-From Heading of an Alternative Name Entry is to be according to Part J.

3 Choice of Referred-To Heading

The Referred-To Heading of an Alternative Name Entry is to be the Heading of the related Main Entry or Book Index Entry, as the case may be.

4 Rendering of Referred-To Heading

The rendering of the Referred-To Heading of an Alternative Name Entry is to be the same as the one actually used in the related Main Entry or Book Index Entry, as the case may be.

The following examples of Cross Reference Index Entry relate to the Main Entries and the Book Index Entries given as examples in Part M.

Examples:

1.1 COUCH (Arthur Quiller-) (1863).
See
QUILLER-COUCH (Arthur) (1863).
Q.

1.2 QUILLER-COUCH (Arthur) (1863).
See also
Q.

1.3 QUILLER-COUCH (Arthur Thomas) (1863).
See
QUILLER-COUCH (Arthur) (1863).
Q.

The full name of the author to whom the above three Cross Reference Index Entries relate is Arthur Thomas Quiller-Couch. But it is seldom that the forename 'Thomas' occurs on the title page. Again in some cases, only the initial-name Q occurs on the title-page. Further as the surname is a compound name, it is desirable that a reference should be made from the second half of the compound name to the full name.

2 BIRD (Isabella) (1831).
See also
BISHOP (Isabella) (1831).

3 SALISBURY (1540).
See
HOWARD (Henry) (1540).

4.1 RONALDSHAY (1844)
See also
ZETLAND (1844).

4.2 ZETLAND (1844).
See also
RONALDSHAY (1844).

The last two Cross Reference Index Entries are both necessary since the author has written some books under one name and some other books under the other name.

5.1 PATTISON (Andrew Seth Pringle-) (1856).
See
PRINGLE-PATTISON (Andrew Seth) (1856).

5.2 PRINGLE-PATTISON (Andrew Seth) (1856).
See also
SETH (Andrew) (1856).

5.3 SETH (Andrew) (1856).
See also
PRINGLE-PATTISON (Andrew Seth) (1856).

The last three Cross Reference Index Entries require a word of explanation. We find from the *History of the University of Edinburgh* 1883-1933, that Professor Andrew Seth assumed the name of Pringle-Pattison on succeeding to the Haining Estate in 1898. In books written by him before that date his name occurs as Andrew Seth. But in later books it occurs as Andrew Seth Pringle-Pattison. Further, an additional Cross Reference Index Entry is necessitated by the newly assumed surname being a compound one.

6 ANANDA MATTEYYA.
See
BENNETT (Allan).

In this case Allan Bennett assumed the name Ananda Matteyya on embracing Buddhism.

7 DATTA (Narendra Nath) (1863).
See
VIVEKANANDA (1863).

In this case, N N Datta assumed the name Vivekananda, when he became a Sanyasin. In the latter asrama, he was familiarly known as Swami Vivekananda, the initial word "Swami" being an honorific prefix.

8 MARK TWAIN.
See
TWAIN (Mark).

9 MAHAJANA SABHA (Madras).
See
MADRAS MAHAJANA SABHA.

10 MADRAS UNIVERSITY.
See
UNIVERSITY OF MADRAS.

11 PATNA UNIVERSITY, SUKHRAJ RAY READERSHIP LECTURES IN NATURAL SCIENCE.
See
SUKHRAJ RAY READERSHIP LECTURES IN NATURAL SCIENCE.

In the case of an endowed University Lecture, which has a name which independently individualises it, it is desirable that a Cross Reference Index Entry be given with the name of the University in the Leading Section, as is illustrated in this case.

12 HARIDAS SANSKRIT GRANTHA MALA.
See
KASHI SANSKRIT SERIES.

CHAPTER LC

VARIANT-FORM-OF-WORD ENTRY

1 Choice of Referred-From Heading

There is to be a Variant-Form-of-Word Entry, using as Referred-From Heading each of all possible Variant Forms in which the word(s) in the name of a person or a corporate body or a geographical entity or a document, occurring in the Heading of a Main Entry or a Book Index Entry or an Alternative Name Index Entry, has (have) occurred or is (are) likely to occur.

Variant forms may be due to transliteration from one script or language to another, difference in usage in regard to archaic, modern and other forms of spelling, and preference of singular or plural forms, masculine or feminine forms, and similar alternative morphological forms [RT3].

It is even possible for the name of one and the same person to occur in different transliterated forms in different documents. Any one, attempting to look up the entries with the Entry Word "Muhamad" in catalogues of documents of Islamic culture, would easily realise the magnitude of this problem.

One way of saving the time of the reader and ensuring that he does not miss any of the relevant entries in such a case is to give a sufficient number of Cross Reference Index Entries, using the different variants as Headings, all the while making the Heading of the Main Entry and the relative Book Index Entry conform to the Canon of Ascertainability.

Another way is to use a Uniformised Form of the term for all the Main Entries and Book Index Entries and to refer from every variant form to the preferred Uniformised Form. Each library should prefer one of these alternatives and fix it in its Local Code.

2 Rendering of Referred-From Heading

The rendering of the Referred-From Heading of Variant-Form-of-Word Entry is to be according to Part J.

3 Choice of Referred-To Heading

The Referred-To Heading of a Variant-Form-of-Word Entry

is to be the Heading of the related Main Entry or Book Index Entry as the case may be.

4 Rendering of Referred-To Heading

The rendering of the Referred-To Heading of a Variant-Form-of-Word Entry is to be the same as the one actually used in the related Main Entry or the Book Index Entry or the Alternative Name Index Entry as the case may be.

Examples:

1.1 BRAUNE.
See also
BROWNE.
BROWN.

1.2 BROWN.
See also
BRAUNE.
BROWNE.

1.3 BROWNE.
See also
BRAUNE.
BROWN.

3 BANERJEE.
See also
BANDOPADHYAYA.

4 BANDOPADHYAYA.
See also
BANERJEE.

5 RANGANATHAN.
See also
RANGANADAM.
RANGANATHAN.
RANGANADHAM.
RANGANATHAN.
RUNGANATHAN.
and other similar variants.

CHAPTER LD

PSEUDONYM-REAL-NAME ENTRY

1 Choice of Referred-From Heading

There is to be a Pseudonym-Real-Name Entry in the case of every person whose Pseudonym alone or Pseudonym as well as Real name appears in the Main Entry concerned.

11 If the Pseudonym appears first in the Heading in the Main Entry, the Referred-From Heading in the Pseudonym-Real-Name Entry is to be the Real Name.

12 If the Real Name appears first in the Heading in the Main Entry, the Heading in the Pseudonym-Real-Name Entry is to be the Pseudonym.

2 Rendering of Referred-From Heading

The rendering of the Referred-From Heading of Pseudonym-Real-Name Index Entry is to be according to Part J.

3 Choice of Referred-To Heading

The Referred-To Heading of a Pseudonym-Real-Name Entry is to be the Pseudonym if the Heading is the Real Name and *vice versa*.

4 Rendering of the Referred-To Heading

The rendering of the Referred-To Heading is to be the same as the one actually used in the related Main Entry.

Examples:

1 RUSSELL (George) (1867).
See
A E, *Pseud.*

2 IBIN ARABI, *Pseud.*
See
MUHAMMAD IBIN ALI (Abu abdulla). al-Hatimi, al-Tai.

3 LAKE (Anne).
See
EKALENNA, *Pseud.*

CHAPTER LE

EDITOR-OF-SERIES ENTRY

1 Choice of Referred-From Heading

There is to be an Editor-of-Series Entry using as Referred-From Heading the name(s) of the Editor(s), if any, occurring in the Series Note in any Main Entry in the Catalogue.

11 In the case of Joint-Editors, an Editor-of-Series Index Entry is to be made for each of the permuted sequences of the names.

2 Rendering of Referred-From Heading

The rendering of the Referred-From Heading of an Editor-of-Series Entry is to be according to Part J.

3 Choice of Referred-To Heading

The Referred-To Heading of an Editor-of-Series Index Entry is to be the name of the Series, found in the Series Note of the Main Entry concerned.

4 Rendering of the Referred-To Heading

The rendering of the Referred-To Heading is to be the same as it is in the Series Note of the Main Entry concerned.

This type entry may be omitted under the Principle of local Variation.

Examples:

1 EGERTON (Clement) ( ), *Ed.*
See
BROADWAY ORIENTAL LIBRARY.
For the Main Entry concerned *See* Sec MF14, Example 13.

2.1 GETMAN (A K) (1887) and LADD (C E) (1888), *Ed.*
See
WILEY FARM SERIES.

2.2 LADD (C E) (1888) and GITMAN (A K) (1887), *Ed.*
See
WILEY FARM SERIES.

For the Main Entry concerned *See* Sec MF14, Example 6.

CAPPS (Edward) (1866) etc, *Ed.*
See
LOEB CLASSICAL LIBRARY.

For the Main Entry concerned *See* Sec MF14, Example 8.

CHAPTER LF

GENERIC-NAME ENTRY

1 Choice of Referred-From Heading

Corresponding to a Book Index Entry or a Class Index Entry with the name of an Institution or of a Conference as the Heading, there is to be a Generic-Name Entry using as Heading the appropriate Generic Term, such as "Botanical Garden," "College," "Conference," "Laboratory," "Library," "Museum," "School," "University," "Zoological Garden" etc.

This type of entry may be omitted under the Principle of Local Variation. The experience of the Reference Section is that entries of this type are of use in helping readers. This is due to the name of the Institution or the Conference consisting of several words and the first word not being always the same either in official use or in popular usage. The one piece of information about which one can be sure is the Type of the Institution or the fact that it is a Conference. If all the institutions of one Type are listed under the Generic-Name of the Type, a reader will have to look through only a limited number of consecutive entries, before he can spot out the name of the particular institution sought by him, though he may remember it only vaguely. The list of the names of the several institutions of the Type indexed will indicate the precise rendering, of the name sought by him, in the Book Index Entry or the Class Index Entry which will give the information sought by the reader. Otherwise the reader may have to look up several places in the catalogue, depending on the number of words in the name of the institution. If there are three words in the name, he may have to look up at least in the three places corresponding to each of the words. Perhaps, he may also have to look up some of the variant forms of these words, in which he may remember them. It may even happen that he may have to look up all the places which the possible permutations of the words and their variants in the name indicate. Therefore, a Cross Reference Index Entry with the Generic-Name as Heading would save the time of the reader. Thus the Fourth Law of Library Science will be satisfied.

Of course, another possibility is to repeat the Class Index Entry and each of the Book Index Entries with the name of the Conference or Institution as Heading, under each of the possible permuted forms of the name. This would violate the Law of Parsimony. Thus Cross Reference Index Entry with the Generic-Name as Referred-From Heading is a compromise between the Fourth Law of Library Science and the Law of Parsimony.

2 Number of Generic-Name Entries

Corresponding to any given Institution or Conference there are to be as many Generic-Name Entries as there are permuted forms of the name of the Institution or the Conference or other alternative names for it, likely to be sought by readers.

21 Of the several Generic-Name Entries prescribed in Sec LF2, one will be called the Basic Generic-Name Entry; and the others will be called Additional Generic-Name Entries.

3 Basic Generic-Name Entry

In a Basic Generic-Name Entry the rendering of the Referred-To Heading is to be the same as the one actually used in the Heading of the related Book Index Entry or Class Index Entry as the case may be.

4 Additional Generic-Name Entry

In an Additional Generic-Name Entry, the rendering of the Referred-To Heading is to be one of the permuted forms of the name of the Institution or Conference as the case may be, or one of its alternative names, or one of the permuted forms of an alternative name, likely to be sought by readers.

41 In an Additional Generic-Name Entry, there are to be two additional sections *viz* fourth section and fifth section respectively.

42 The Fourth Section of an Additional Generic-Name Entry is to consist of the directing word "*Indexed as.*"

43 The Fifth Section of an Additional Generic-Name Entry is to consist of the name of the Institution or Conference, rendered exactly as it is done in the Heading of the corresponding Book Index Entry or Class Index Entry, as the case may be.

Example:

Basic Generic-Name Entry

1.1 UNIVERSITY.
See also
UNIVERSITY OF MADRAS.

Additional Generic-Name Entry

12 UNIVERSITY.
See also
MADRAS UNIVERSITY.
Indexed as
UNIVERSITY OF MADRAS.

It may not be necessary to have an Additional Generic-Name Entry for some of the permuted forms of the name of an Institution or a Conference. These may not have any probability to be sought by any reader. These may naturally be ignored. No doubt, this means vesting of discretion in the cataloguer. This may lead to a violation of the Canon of Consistency. But this cannot be helped.

PART M

SINGLE-VOLUMED SIMPLE BOOK

CHAPTER MA

MAIN ENTRY: SOURCE

1 Title-Page As Source

The Main Entry is to be made up of a reproduction of a portion of the title-page modified according to prescribed Rules, utilising, if necessary, any relevant information given in the over-flow of the title-page.

2 Title-Page Absent

If the title-page had not been printed, or if it had been lost in the copy of the library and could not be copied from that of a sound copy elsewhere, the title-page of the book is to be reconstructed for the purpose of these Rules from the evidence available within the book and in outside sources.

3 Multiple Title-Pages

If there are two or more title-pages, the one to be chosen for cataloguing purposes is to be the earliest mentioned of the following, which is available:

1 That which is special to the document catalogued, i e, which is distinct from the generic title-page common to several documents;

2 That which is in the language of the dominant or distinctive work contained in the document catalogued; and

3 That which is in the language of the author of the work catalogued;

4 That which is in the Favoured Language of the library (*See* Sec EA1); and

5 That which is in the language occurring earliest in the Scale of Languages of the library (*See* Sec EA2).

4 Polyglot Title-page

If the title-page is polyglot, the portion to be chosen for cataloguing purposes is to be determined on the analogy of Sec MA3.

1 The only elements in the Main Entry which will be affected by this Sec are the Title-Portion and the Notes Section. For, the Leading Section made of the Call Number and the Heading Section made of the Name of the Author will be free from it.

2 If there is a title-page in the language of the original work as well as in that of its translation, the translation should be taken as the Distinctive Work.

3 If there is a title-page in the language of the basic work as well as in that of a Commentary deemed to be of greater value than the basic work, the Commentary should be taken as the Dominant work.

4 If the Commentary is not the dominant work, the title-page in the language of the author of the work catalogued is to be used.

CHAPTER MB

MAIN ENTRY: SECTIONS

0 Sequence

The Main Entry is to consist successively of the following Sections:

1 Leading Section;
2 Heading;
3 Title Section;
4 Note Section, if any;
5 Accession Number; and
6 Tracing Section.

As it has been stated already in Sec FM71, the Main Entry is the fullest entry for a document. It is also the basic entry which contains the data for all other entries. In fact, this Code goes even further and provides for an explicit statement in the Main Entry itself of all the entries that are made for a book. (*See* Chap MH)

1 Bibliographical Catalogue

It is by no means easy to decide what details should be given in the Main Entry. We have at the one extreme the practice of making the Main Entry the fullest possible bibliographical description of the book. Here is a specimen of such a full description of the 1922 edition of the *Forsyte saga* of John Galsworthy:

GALSWORTHY (John).
The Forsyte saga.

THE FORSYTE SAGA | BY | JOHN GALSWORTHY | 19 [*Publisher's device*] 22 | [*Line*] | LONDON: WILLIAM HEINEMANN, [1922].

Pp. xvi+1104, Cr. 8vo, consisting of:

A blank leaf, pp. [i, ii]; half-title, with a list of Works 'By the same Author' on verso, pp. [iii, iv]; title page (verso blank), pp. [v, vi]; dedication to the Author's wife (verso blank), pp. [vii, viii]; [Genealogical Table of the Forsyte family]; Preface, pp. ix-xii; contents, pp. xiii-xvi; divisional half-title, with dedication of *The Man of Property* on verso, pp. [1, 2]; and text, pp. [3]-1104 (Printers' imprint on p. 1104).

Issued in green grained cloth; lettering on spine, and, with monogram on front cover, all gilt, a line behind just inside edges of front cover. Publisher's device blind in lower right corner of back cover. Top edges green, fore and lower rough-trimmed.

CONTENTS

The Man of Property.
Indian Summer of a Forsyte.
In Chancery.
Awakening.
To Let.

Such an elaborate description may be of use in the case of the oldest printed books known as *incunabula*. But in modern books and for the ordinary service-libraries, it is unnecessary. Cutter's remarks [C4] on the influence of bibliography on library cataloguing are worth quoting: "Bibliographers have established a cult of the title-page; its slightest peculiarities are noted, it is followed religiously, with dots for omissions, brackets for insertions, and uprights to mark the ends of lines; it is even imitated by the facsimile type or photographic copying. These things may concern the cataloguer of the Lenox Library or the Prince Collection. The ordinary librarian, in general, has nothing to do with them."

2 Inventory Catalogue

We have at the other extreme the practice of making the Main Entry sufficiently meagre to be completed in a single line. This can happen only in an Inventory Catalogue.

3 Service-Library Catalogue

There are all imaginable intermediate positions taken up by the cataloguers in different libraries [RT2]. In this Code, Sec MB0 lays down the Sections that the Main Entry should have. The succeeding rules of this chapter elaborate the way in which each section is to be constructed.

4 Imprint

It will be noticed that two sections which are still lingering in Catalogue Codes are omitted, *viz*, collation and imprint. The persistence of these two sections is really due to the tradition of the printed catalogue. But in a modern open-access service-library, which is rightly compared to a workshop rather than a museum and which replaces the printed catalogue by the manuscript or type-written card catalogue, it is felt that the information contained in these two sections is seldom sought by the majority of readers and therefore is to be regarded as unnecessarily over-crowding the card. For the few that do want them, the published trade bibliographies or the Accession Register of the library may be made to furnish the requisite information.

5 Year of Publication

Further, with regard to the Year of Publication, it is contained in the Call

Number, if the Colon Classification is used. It is left to a L cal Code to prescribe the addition of the Year of Publication as an additional sentence at the end of the Title Section either when the Call Number does not indicate the Year of Publication or in all cases.

6 Format and Collation

With regard to collation, the exact size is not usually of prime importance to most of the readers. On the other hand, every reader would like to have some rough indication whether the book is of normal size or not—in particular, whether it is a pamphlet or a giant folio or whether it contains too many plates. A reference to Sec EE and its subdivisions will show the simple devices which can be used for conveying such information.

7 Accession Number

The insertion of the Call Number as the first section of the Main Entry needs no explanation in a Classified Catalogue. The provision for entering the Accession Number in the fifth sectioh of the Main Entry is, no doubt, unusual. It is not intended for the reader's eye. In fact Sec ED45 lays down that it is to be written at the left end of the bottom-most line of the card to reduce the chances of its catching the eye of the reader to a minimum. The reason for inserting it at all is purely administrative. It is to act as a link between the Accession Register and the Catalogue [RF7].

8 Tracing Section

The purpose of the Tracing Section is to facilitate the removal of all the related cards, when a book is weeded out from the library. This is of use to the Maintenance Section. It is also of help in co-ordinating the work of the Technical Section at the time of cataloguing. Some enter the Tracing Section in a separate slip called Process slip.

9 Annotation

An additional section entitled "Annotation" is sometimes added, explaining in a few words the importance or special features of the book, the status of the author, and so on, wi.hout introducing any critical opinion of the cataloguer [RT7].

CHAPTER MC

MAIN ENTRY: LEADING SECTION

1 Choice

The Leading Section is to consist of the Call Number of the document.

2 Source

The Call Number is to be taken from the back of the title-page [RL2].

The Call Number would have been assigned by the classifier in accordance with the Rules of Classification. If CC is used, the Call Number of a document will have necessarily two parts, *viz* Class Number and Book Number. It may also have a third part, *viz* Collection Number.

3 Book Number

The Book Number is to be written after the Class Number with a double space between them.

4 Collection Number

The Collection Number, if any, is to be written above the Book Number.

5 Style of Writing

The following Sec govern the writing of the Call Number:

SECTION	PURPORT
ED22	Instrument for writing (pencil)
ED23	Style of writing (library hand)
ED3	Position (start on the First Vertical)

CHAPTER MD

MAIN ENTRY: HEADING

1 Choice

The Heading is to consist of the earliest of the following which the document admits and the Part G prescribes as the Author:

1 The name of a Personal Author;

2 The names of Joint Personal Authors;

3 The name of a Corporate Author;

4 Names of a Joint Personal Author and of a Joint Corporate Author.

5 The names of Joint Corporate Authors;

6 A Pseudonym or two or more Pseudonyms;

7 The name of a Collaborator;

8 The names of Joint Collaborators; and

9 The Title of the Document.

2 Rendering

21 Name of Author

Names of persons and corporate bodies, pseudonyms with structure like that of a name-of-person, and titles of documents are to be rendered according to the Sec of the concerned Chap of Part J.

22 Pseudonym

A Pseudonym, not having the structure of a name-of-person, is to be written as it occurs on the title-page of the document, without any permutation of the elements constituting it.

23 Individualising Element

Whenever needed, the necessary Individualising Element is to be added to the name forming the Heading, as prescribed in the Sec of Part J.

24 Descriptive Element

Whenever needed, the Descriptive Element is to be added to the name forming the Heading, as prescribed in Sec MD41 and MD5.

25 Style of Writing

The following Sec govern the writing of the Heading:

Section	Purport
ED21	Writing fluid
ED23	Style of writing (library hand)
ED41	Position of first line (start on the Second Vertical)
ED42	Position of other lines (start on the First Vertical)
ED51	Block letters
ED53	Descriptive element
ED83	Individualising element

3 Joint Authors

32 Two Authors

If the title-page contains the names of two and only two Joint Authors, both the names are to be used as the Heading with the conjunction 'and' connecting them.

Examples:

1 Srinivasan (G A) and Krishnamachari (C).
2 Kuppuswami Sastri (S) and Chintamani (T R).
3 Harkness (James) and Morley (Frank).
4 American Library Association and Library Association (Great Britain).
5 Indian Standards Institution, Documentation (Section) and Insdoc, Technical (Committee).

For the use of semi-colon in the place of 'and' see Sec ED 84.

6 Bullens (DK) and Battelle Memorial Institute, Metallurgical (Staff).

33 Three or More Authors

If the title-page contains the names of three or more Joint Authors, the name of the first mentioned author alone is to be used as the Heading and the word 'etc' is to be added thereafter.

If there is provision for ignoring all but the first author in the case of joint authors, it may be asked why should not such a procedure be adopted uniformly in all cases of joint authorship even if the number of authors is two. The special treatment given to the number 'two' and denied to the number 'three' and the greater numbers, is purely out of deference to the habit of readers. It is found from experience that books by two authors are usually referred to by the names of both the authors, as 'Harkness & Morley,' 'Beaumont & Fletcher,' 'Jathar & Beri' and so on. But such a practice does not obtain when the number of authors is greater than two. But then, why not secure uniformity by mentioning the names of all the joint authors in all cases? Because, it becomes unwieldy and inconveniently crowds the card. And as it has been said, that readers do not, generally, remember all the names.

Example:

RANGANATHAN (Shiyali Ramamrita) (1892) etc is the Heading for the *Union catalogue of learned periodicals in South Asia* (1953), which has 20 other joint authors.

4 Pseudonym

41 Choice and Rendering

If the title-page gives only a Pseudonym in the place of the author's name, the Pseudonym is to be used as the Heading and it is to be followed by the Descriptive Element, '*Pseud.*'

It is to be remembered that the Descriptive Element is to be underlined and preceded by a comma, as prescribed in Sec ED53 and ED82 respectively.

Examples:

LIBRA, *Pseud.*
TWAIN (Mark), *Pseud.*
X Y Z, *Pseud.*

42 Real Name

421 If the title-page gives the Real Name of the author also in a subordinated manner, it is to be added in circular brackets

after the Descriptive Element '*Pseud.*' The Real Name of the author is to be preceded by the symbol '*i e.*' The bracket is to be preceded by a comma. The words in the Real Name are to be written in their natural sequence.

Example:
TWAIN (Mark), *Pseud*, (*i e* Samuel Langhorne Clemens).

422 If the title-page gives the Real Name of the author and adds the Pseudonym in a subordinated manner, the former is to be chosen for the Heading. The latter is to be added after it and enclosed in circular brackets. The Descriptive Element '*Pseud*' is to be added within the brackets. The bracket is to be preceded by a comma.

423 If the real name of the author can be found out from outside the work, it is to be added in square brackets after the Descriptive Element '*Pseud*'. The real name of the author is to be preceded by the symbol '*i e*'. The bracket is to be preceded by a comma. The words in the Real Name are to be written in their natural sequence.

424 If a Pseudonym represents two joint authors and if the Real Names of the joint authors be known, the symbol '*i e*' which comes after the Pseudonym is to be followed by the real names of both the authors. Their names are to be connected by the word 'and.' The words in each Real Name are to be written in their natural sequence.

425 If a Pseudonym represents three or more joint authors and if the Real Names be known, the symbol '*i e*' which comes after the Pseudonym is to be followed by the Real Name of one of the authors alone which itself is to be followed by the word 'etc.' The name to be written is to be chosen on the basis of some appropriate principle if available or otherwise arbitrarily.

Examples:
1 ABDUL HASAN, *Pseud*, [*i e* George Steele Seymour].
2 AN AMERICAN, *Pseud*, [*i e* James Fenimore Cooper].
3 A E, *Pseud*, [*i e* George Russell].
4 LIBRA, *Pseud*, [*i e* Shiyali Ramamrita Ranganathan].
5 ARTHUR (T C), *Pseud*, [*i e* Arthur Travers Crawford].
6 CONRAD (Joseph) *Pseud*, [*i e* Joseph Conrad Korzeniouski].

7 J—S G—Y, *Pseud*, [*i e* James Gray].
8 EKALENNA, *Pseud*, [*i e* Anne Lake].
9 CYCLA, *Pseud*, [*i e* Helen Clacy].
10 EHA, *Pseud*, [*i e* Edward Hamilton Aitken].
11 BELL (J Freeman), *Pseud*, [*i e* Israel Zangwill and L Cowen].
12 TWO BROTHERS, *Pseud*, [*i e* Alfred Tennyson and Charles Tennyson].

43 TWO OR MORE PSEUDONYMS

If there are two or more Pseudonyms occurring in the place of the authors' names, they are to be connected by the conjunction "and".

Example:
J K F R S and S A Sc, *Pseud*, [*i e* James Keir].

5 Collaborator Heading

51 CHOICE AND RENDERING

If the title-page does not give the name of a Personal Author or the names of Joint Personal Authors or indicate Corporate Authorship or give a Pseudonym or Pseudonyms in the Author Statement but contains the name of a collaborator, that name is to be used as the Heading and a Descriptive Element is to be added thereafter indicating the role of the person.

It is to be remembered that the Descriptive Element is to be underlined and preceded by a comma as prescribed in Sec ED53 and ED82 respectively.

Examples:
1 In the case of the book whose title-page reads "The | Oxford Book | of English prose | chosen & edited by | Sir Arthur Quiller-Couch,"
the Heading is to be
QUILLER-COUCH (Arthur) (1863), *Ed*.
2 In the case of the book whose title-page reads "Selected Russian | short stories | chosen and translated by | A E Chamot,"
the Heading is to be
CHAMOT (A E) (1855), *Comp* and *Tr*.
3 In the case of the book whose title-page reads "Nineteenth | century life | *Selected by* Kathleen Tracey,"
the Heading is to be
TRACEY (Kathleen), *Comp*.

52 Many kinds of Collaborators

If the title-page gives the name of each of two or more of the kinds of collaborators enumerated in the definition in Sec FD1, the name belonging to one and only one kind is to be chosen as Heading. The name of the one making a more important contribution than the others is to be chosen.

Examples:

1 In the case of the book whose title-page reads "The | Vedanta sutras | with the commentary of | Ramanuja | translated by | George Thebaut," the Heading is to be

RAMANUJA, *Comm.*

2 In the case of the book whose title-page reads "Norway's | best stories | an introduction to modern | Norwegian fiction | translations by Anders Orbeck | A selection of short stories by | . . . | edited by Hanna Astrup Larsen,"
the Heading is to be

LARSEN (Hanna Astrup) (1873), *Ed.*

53 Commentator

In the case of commentaries with the text complete, it is to be remembered that if the commentary is of primary importance and not the text, the name of the commentator is to be used as the Heading, notwithstanding Sec MD1.

Example:

In the case of the book whose title-page reads "Vedanta Darsana | with commentary, | Brahmamritavarsini | by | Sri Ramananda | Saraswati Swami | edited by | S Vyankataramana Aiyar, B.A., B.L."
the Heading is to be

RAMANANDA SARASWATI, *Comm.*

It may be stated here that the initial word 'Sri' and the final word 'Swami' are omitted from the name of the author as they are merely honorific "puffs".

54 Joint Collaborators

If the title-page gives two or more names of the category contributing to the Heading in accordance with Sec MD51 and its subdivisions, the Heading is to be written on the analogy of Sec MD3 and its subdivisions.

Examples:

1 In the case of the book whose title-page reads "Chief British poets | of the fourteenth and | fifteenth centuries | selected poems | edited with explanatory | and biographical notes | by | W A Neilson | *Professor of English*/and K G T Webster | *Assistant Professor of English* | Harvard University,"
the Heading is to be
NEILSON (William Allan) (1869) and WEBSTER (Kenneth Grant Tremayne) ( ), *Ed.*

2 In the case of the book whose title-page reads "The | Cambridge | ancient | history | edited by | J B Bury, M.A., F.B.A. | S A Cook, Litt. D | F E Adcock, M.A."
the Heading is to be
BURY (John Bagnell) (1861) etc, *Ed.*

3 In the case of the book whose title-page reads "Vinaya texts | translated from the Pali | by T W Rhys Davids | and | Hermann Oldenberg,"
the Heading is to be
DAVIDS (Thomas William Rhys) (1843) and OLDENBERG (Hermann) ( ), *Tr.*

6 Title of the Document

61 CHOICE

If a book is a general biographical dictionary or an encyclopaedia belonging to the class Generalia, or Science General or Useful Arts or Social Science, or if the Heading cannot be chosen in accordance with any of the other Rules of this Chapter, the Title of the document, excluding an initial article or an initial honorific word, if any, is to be used as the Heading.

The words in the Title are to be written in their natural sequence (*See* Sec JF3). The first two words in the Title are to be written in Block Letters (*See* Sec JF4).

62 AUTHOR'S NAME

621 FROM WITHIN THE DOCUMENT

If the name of the author can be found out from any other part of the work, it is to be added after the Title within circular brackets and is to be preceded by the word 'by'.

Example:

WILLIAM ERNEST Johnson (by C D Broad).

In this case, the title page-reads only as
"William Ernest | Johnson | 1858-1931."
But the author's name occurs at the end of the book
For another example, *see* Example 1 under Sec MF14.

622 FROM OUTSIDE THE DOCUMENT

If the name of the author can be found out from outside the work, it is to be added, after the title, within square brackets and is to be preceded by the word 'by'.

Example:

LIZZIE LEIGH [by E C Gaskell].

CHAPTER ME

MAIN ENTRY: TITLE SECTION

0 Parts

The Title Section is to consist of one, two, or three sentences, according to the nature of the information contained on the title-page and its back, giving successively in a single paragraph:

1 The title;

2 Information regarding the edition; and

3 Information regarding collaborator(s).

The title-page of a book usually contains one or more of the following items:

1 The name of the series to which it may belong;

2 The name(s) of the editor(s) of the series;

3 The title of the book;

4 The name(s) of the author(s) and their qualifications, positions etc;

5 The name(s) of the collaborator(s) including writers of subsidiary parts such as the preface, introduction, appendix etc with their respective qualifications etc, and a description of their respective roles;

6 The specification of the edition;

7 Information about illustrations;

8 Mottoes and the printer's or publisher's device; and

9 The imprint.

The specification of the edition may also be found on the back of the title-page.

The *Anglo-American code* would reproduce in the Title Section all the above items except "1" and "8" and indicate the omission of even these by " . . . ". This is largely traceable to the influence of the full bibliographical description, referred to in the commentary on Sec MB1. A slightly greater divergence from the bibliographical ideal is to omit "4" also and indicate its omission by " . . . ". A further simplification is to omit also the names of writers of subsidiary parts of the book, unless the subsidiary portion covered by it is particularly important.

But except in *Incunabula* and other books of exceptional rarity or oddity, this superstitious veneration of the title-page and the halting and partial deviation from the tradition of descriptive bibliography must give place to a bold assertion of the cataloguer's independence of the rule for descriptive bibliography. If the purpose of a library catalogue is borne in mind, it is bound to be conceded that, other things being equal, that title-portion is best which can be taken at a glance. With this in view and in view of what has been said about "9" in Sec MB4 this code would confer the right of contribution to the Title Section on "3", "5", and "6" only. It would throw off the yoke of bibliographical tyranny by refusing, further, to indicate the omissions of the other parts, by dots or in any other way.

1 Title

The first part of the first sentence is to be in accordance with the Sec of Chap JF.

2 Edition

21 Choice

Information regarding edition is to be given only in the case of the second and later editions and editions having special names.

22 Rendering

If the edition is to be described numerically, the appropriate number is to be written after the word 'Ed'.

See Examples 1 to 3 under Sec ME31.

221 Special Name

If the edition has a special name, initial article and honorific word, if any, are to be omitted.

Example:
Centenary ed.

3 Collaborator

Subject to the subdivisions of this Sec, the second part of the first sentence is to be a transcription or transliteration as the case may be, of that part of the title-page which gives the information mentioned in category '2' of Sec ME0.

Only the Pure Name (*See* Sec HE4) of each collaborator is to be given. There should be no permutation of the words in the name.

301 TRANSLATION

In the case of a translation, the edition or other specification of the original, if any, is to be mentioned.

See Example 6 under Sec ME31.

31 NAME CONTRIBUTING TO HEADING

The names, which occur in this part of the title-page but have been used to contribute to the Heading, are to be ignored.

Examples:

1 *a*X 113N30
SCHNEIDER (Georg) (1876).
Handbuch der bibliographie. Ed 4.
62168

2 A.56,*f*,9K*v*N3 N12
ROYAL SOCIETY OF LONDON.
Record. Ed 3.
15449
In this book, the title-page reads,
"The record | of | the Royal Society | of London | third edition | entirely revised and enlarged."
The Heading is supplied by the cataloguer and the words in the last line are ignored.

3 A*v*5'G5 N27
HASKINS (Charles Homer) (1870).
Studies in the history of mediaeval science. Ed 2.
59915
In this example, the official position of the author, though mentioned on the title-page, has been ignored.

4 B 122N14
ZORETTI (Ludovic) (1880).
Lecons de mathematiques generales etc.
13617

In this case, the designation of the author, *viz*, "Professeur a la faculte des sciences de Caen," given on the title-page, has been ignored. Further, the words "avec une preface de P. Appell" have been replaced by "etc" as the preface is not of great importance.

5 C30*b*NA,2 N27

DAVIS (A H) and KAYE (George William Clarison) (1880).
Acoustics of buildings.
44654

In this example the academic distinctions and the official positions of the authors have been ignored though given on the title-page and the initials of one of them have been expanded.

6 F N04

WAGNER (Rudolf Von) (1805).
Manual of chemical technology. Tr and ed by William Crookes from the thirteenth German ed rev by Ferdinand Fischer.
11752

The title-page of this book reads as follows:

"Manual | of | chemical technology | by | Rudolf Von Wagner | translated and edited by | Sir William Crookes, FRS | past pres. C. S, pres. Inst. E E | from the thirteenth enlarged German edition as remodelled by | Dr. Ferdinand Fischer | with 596 illustrations | reprinted 1904."

Fischer's preface makes it clear that the revision is substantial but not sufficient to replace the name of Wagner by that of Fischer in the heading.

7 H N28

BRIGHAM (Albert Perry) (1855).
Geology. Rev by Frederick A Burt.
52141

In this book, the title-page is as follows:

"Geology | by | Albert Perry Brigham, SC.D., L.H.D., LL.D., | Professor of Geology in Colgate University | revised and expanded by Frederick A Burt, B.S., F.A.A.S., | Associate Professor of Geology in the Agricultural | and Mechanical College of Texas."

8 O-,6*x*M8 N25

QUILLER-COUCH (Arthur) (1863), *Ed*.
Oxford book of English.
35282

A copy of the title-page of this book has been given as Example 1 under Sec MD 51. This is a case of Collaborator Heading for Main Entry.

9 P N32

GARDINER (Alan Handerson) (1879).
Theory of speech and language.
74793

In this book, the title-page is as follows:

"The theory of | speech and | language | by | Alan H. Gardiner fellow of the British Academy."

10 R66,5x3,1 15N16

RAMANANDA SARASWATI (1300 ?), *Comm.*

Vedanta darsana with comm Brahmamritavarsini. Ed ˙y S Vyankataramana Aiyar.

17392

The title-page of this book is both in Sanskrit and in English and the English portion has been transcribed in the example under Sec MD53.

11 T:64p441,N32 N32

HEALTH PROPAGANDA BOARD (Madras), MEDICAL INSPECTORS (Conference of—)

Proceedings etc.

73882

The title-page of this book reads:

"Proceedings of the conference of | medical inspectors of schools with a foreword | by | W E Smith, Esq., M.A. | Director of Public Instruction, Madras. | Health Propaganda Board. | Madras."

The foreword is not of sufficient importance and hence the portion of the title-page relating to it is replaced by "etc".

12 T3:2(A) N27

GREAT BRITAIN, EDUCATION (Board of—), ADULT EDUCATION (Committee).

Natural science in adult education.

46399

In this case, the title-page contains the tittle only. The heading had to be re-constructed from the information contained in the book.

13 V44,11xN10 N17

INDIA, VICEROY AND GOVERNOR GENERAL (Hardinge).

Speeches.

50398

In this case, the title-page reads as follows:

"Speeches of | His Excellency, the Right Hon'ble | Baron Hardinge of Penhurst, | G.C.B., G.M.S.I., G.C.M.G., G.M.I.E., G.C.V.O., I.S.O., C.V.O., Viceroy and Governor General of India, | 1910-1916."

14 V441'N3 N33

MADRAS.

Madras Presidency, 1881-1931.

74723

15 X N29

TURNER (John Roscoe) (1882).

Introduction to economics.

34459

In this example the only words ingnored are those giving the official position of the author, *viz*, "Professor of Economics and Dean of Washington Square College, New York University."

16 Y N33
COOLEY (Charles Horton) (1864) etc.
Introductory sociology.
74751

The title-page of this book reads as follows:

INTRODUCTORY SOCIOLOGY

CHARLES HORTON COOLEY

Late Professor of Sociology in the University of Michigan

LOWELL JUILLIARD CARR and ROBERT COOLEY ANGEL

Assistant Professor of Sociology in the University of Michigan.

Associate Professor of Sociology in the University of Michigan.

32 TWO COLLABORATORS

Subject to Sec ME31, if two Names occur under any one kind of collaborator, both the names are to be written out.

Example:

1 ND44,C N17
FOUCHER (Alfred) (1865).
Beginnings of Buddhist art etc. Tr by L A Thomas and F W Thomas.
9216

In this book, the title-page reads:
"The beginnings of | Buddhist art | and other essays | in Indian and Central-Asian archaeology | by | A Foucher | of the University of Paris | revised by the author and translated by | L A Thomas and F W Thomas | with a preface by the latter."

33 THREE OR MORE COLLABORATORS

Subject to Sec ME31, if three or more names occur under any kind of collaborator, the first name alone is to be written followed by the word 'etc'.

Example:

BxM87 N27

RAMANUJAN (Srinivasa) (1887).

Collected papers. Ed by G H Hardy etc.

46878

In this book, the title-page reads:

"*Collected papers of* | Srinivasa Ramanujan | *edited by* | G H Hardy P V Seshu Aiyar | *and* | B M Wilson."

CHAPTER MF

MAIN ENTRY: NOTE

0 Choice

The following is a list of the kind of notes likely to be available for choice:

1 Series note;
2 Multiple series note;
3 Extract note;
4 Change of title note;
5 Extraction note; and
6 Associated book note.

There has been always some difference of opinion with regard to the utility of mentioning the series to which a book belongs and with regard to giving a series index entry to a book. Quinn seems, for example, to suggest a compromise:

"Experience goes to prove that such entries have little practical value and are sometimes dispensed with altogether. The statement in the main entry showing that the book belongs to a particular series, is found to be sufficient for most purposes, especially in such a series as the *International Scientific* where the subjects are so varied as to have no unity, no relation to one another, or characteristics in common. There is something to be said in favour of a series-entry in the case of a bibliographical or similar series where the various volumes are more or less akin or connected in subject, though it is seldom that people either want to read through a series systematically or wish to know what volumes are contained in it.

"Probably it is more desirable to enumerate under a series-heading the works published in connection with lecture trusts like the Bampton, Boyle, Gifford, Hibbert, Hulsean, Swarthmore, and others as they are usually founded to advocate some special purpose, and therefore each book in the series has some underlying similarity" [Q1].

01 Sequence

If two or more kinds of Notes are admitted by a document, they should be written as separate sections in the sequence given in Sec MF0.

The following Sec governs the style of writing the Note Section.

SECTION	PURPORT
ED21	Writing fluid
ED23	Library hand
ED54	Typography
ED41	Position (start on the Second Vertical)
ED42	Position of other lines (start on the First Vertical)
ED55	Serial Number

1 Series Note

11 RENDERING

A Series Note is to consist successively of

1 The name of the series, omitting the initial article or honorific word, if any;

11 A full stop

2 The words "Ed by", followed successively by the name(s) of the editor(s) of the series, if the series has editor(s);

21 A full stop; and

3 The serial number.

See Chap FH for definition of 'Series'.

111 NAME OF SERIES

See Chap JG for rendering of the Name of the Series.

12 EDITOR

If there are two editors, the names of both are to be written with the conjunction 'and' connecting them.

See Example 8 under Sec MF14.

121 MORE THAN TWO EDITORS

If there are three or more editors, the name of the first editor alone is to be written followed by the word, 'etc'.

See Examples 10 and 12 in Sec MF14.

13 Serial Number

The Serial Number is to be the Number indicating the position of the book in the series, as is given by the publisher

See Examples 2-5, 13, and 14 in Sec MF14.

131 ABSENCE OF SERIAL NUMBER

If the publisher has not assigned serial numbers, the books are to be given serial numbers in the sequence of the accession or in any other convenient sequence.

See Examples 1, 8, 10, 15, and 16 in Sec MF14.

132 SUBSTITUTE FOR SERIAL NUMBER

If more appropriate, the serial number may be replaced by a year or a year and a number or any other similar entity appropriate to the book.

See Examples 6, 7, 9, 11, and 12 in Sec MF14.

14 Examples of Series

1 2 *p*7N29
Library Movement, a collection of essays by divers hands etc.
(Madras Library Association, publication series. 1).
42008

Information about foreword and message, contained in the title-page is replaced by "etc" as they do not form a substantial part of the book.

2 2 N57
Ranganathan (Shiyali Ramamrita) (1892).
Five laws of library science. Ed 2.
(Madras Library Association, publication series. 23).
166519

3 2:51N3 qN52
RANGANATHAN (Shiyali Ramamrita) (1892).
Colon classification. Ed 4.
(Madras Library Association, publication series. 19).
166666

4 2:55N3 qN58
RANGANATHAN (Shiyali Ramamrita) (1892).
Classified catalogue code with additional rules for dictionary catalogue code. Ed 4.
(Madras Library Association, publication series. 24).
167000

In the above four examples, the bare name of the series, *viz* "Publication series" is not sufficient to individualise it. Hence, the name of the Corporate Body publishing the series is prefixed, as required in Sec JG5.

The name of the series is not given on the title-page, but is given on the half-title page in the last three books, and the serial number also occurs there.

But in the case of Example 1, the name of the series does not occur anywhere in the book. However, the later publications forming examples 2 to 4 definitely refer to this book as the first volume of the series. Hence, the series note is added in its case also. This is an extreme example of the cataloguer having to use information outside the book to form the note. But such cases will be only very occasional.

5 B 113N10
SCHUBERT (Hermann) (1848).
Elementare arithmetik und algebra. Ed 2.
(Sammlung Schubert. 1).
54497

In this book the name of the series is printed as the first line of the title-page and the serial number also is printed along with it.

6 C9B2 N31
SAHA (Megh Nad) (1893).
Six lectures on atomic physics.
(Patna University, readership lectures. 1928).
74937

In this book, the information about the name of the series is given on the title-page in the form "Readership lectures delivered before the Patna University, 1928". The name of the University has to be prefixed to the name of the series, in accordance with Sec JG5, as the name of the series does not get individualised without this addition.

In a case like this, it is more convenient to replace the serial number by the year number as provided for in Sec MF132.

7 E:2131:(C9D8:47) N31

SEN (Hemendra Kumar) ( ).

High temperature flames and their thermodynamics.

(Sukhraj Ray readership lectures in natural science. 1926 | 1927).

749397

In this book, the title-page gives the additional information that this readership lecture series is of the Patna University. But, the name of the series gets individualised even without prefixing the name of the university. Hence Sec JG5 is not applicable.

But it will be seen in Sec LB1 that the name of the series with the name of the University prefixed to it is to be treated as an alternative name of the series for cross-reference purposes.

In this case also, the year may well take the place of the serial number in accordance with Sec MF132.

8 J;1 N30

WORTHEN (Edmund L) (1882).

Farm soils, their management and fertilisation.

(Wiley farm series. Ed by A K Getman and C E Ladd. 2).

55145

The names of the series and of its joint editors are given on the half-title page. As there are only two editors for the series, the names of both of them are given in the note in accordance with Sec MF12.

Although the volumes of the series are not actually numbered by the publisher, the verso of the half-title page gives a list of the volumes of the series, in which the name of this book occurs as the second. Hence the serial number of the book is fixed as "2" in accordance with Sec MF131.

In ed 7 of *Colon Classification*, 'Soil' is treated as Matter Facet instead of as Energy Facet as was done in earlier editions. Therefore J:1 is changed to J;1.

9 L35:42381:4 N30

LEWTHWAITE (Raymond) ( ).

Experimental tropical typhus in laboratory animals.

(Institute for Medical Research (Federated Malay States), bulletin. 1930, 3).

7069

In this case, the name of the series occurs on the title-page. The numbering of the volume is also given there. Each year, a varying number of volumes is published. The volumes published each year are numbered amongst themselves serially. Hence the serial number is given as "1930, 3" in accordance with Sec MF132.

10 O13,5C58x 111N27

ISAEUS.

[Works] Tr by Edward Seymour Forster.

(Loeb classical library. Ed by E Capps etc. 202).

53421

The names of three editors are mentioned under the name of the series, which is given on the half-title page. Hence the name of the first mentioned editor alone is given in accordance with Sec MF121.

The serial number is not given anywhere inside the book but it is blind-tooled near the lower back-corner of the cloth cover of the end board forming the publisher's case.

11 R3,(Q:368) N22
PRINGLE-PATTISON (Andrew Seth) (1856.)
Idea of immortality.
(Gifford lectures (University of Edinburgh), 1922).
40001

In this case, although the name of the series contains a personal name, it does not individualise the series, as by the will of Lord Gifford, there are four sets of Gifford lectures delivered in the four Scottish University centres. Hence, the name of the centre has to be added, within brackets, to the name of the series to individualise it.

It is easily seen that, in a case like this, it is more convenient to use the year of delivery of the lecture instead of the serial number, *i e*, to follow MF132.

12 O:g(S:43)H1 N27
BUNDY (Murray Wright) ( ).
Theory of imagination in classical and mediaeval thought.
(University of Illinois, studies in language and literature. Ed by William A Oldfather etc. V 12, N 2-3).
60507

In this case, the names of three editors are mentioned on the half-title page, which gives the name of the series. Hence, the name of the first-mentioned editor alone is given in the note, in accordance with Sec MF121.

This series consists of a number of monographs, normally issued four per annum. All the volumes published in a single year receive the same volume number. The individual monographs belonging to a given volume are normally numbered serially as 1, 2, 3, and 4. However, when a monograph is beyond a certain size, it appears to take the place of two issues and receives two serial numbers, as it happens in the example given above. Thus the series number of this book takes the peculiar form "V 12, N2-3" as provided for in Sec MF132.

13 T15:3(B1):(S) N27
JUDD (Charles Hubbard) (1873).
Psychological analysis of the fundamentals of arithmetic.
(University of Chicago, supplementary educational monographs. 32).
45498

The name of the series as well as the publications of the series with their respective serial numbers is given in the inside and outside of the end cover.

The list is headed by the words "Publications of the Department of Education, the University of Chicago". As the name of the series does not by itself individualise it, the name of the university is prefixed to the name of the series in accordance with Sec JG5.

The name of the University by itself is sufficient to individualise the name of the series. But, the name of the department is not by itself sufficient to do so. If it is inserted, there is need to prefix to it the name of the University also. Thus, the prefixing of the name of the University is the minimum that is sufficient.

14 V4462'L9 N31

ASPINALL (A) ( ).

Cornwallis in Bengal etc.

(University of Manchester, publications, historical series. 60).

69578

In this example, the bare name of the series *viz* "Historical series" is not sufficient to individualise it. Hence the name of the major series to which this belongs is prefixed as required in Sec JG6. The books do not receive separate serial numbers in the major series.

The name of the series occurs in the half-title page. The serial number also is found in the half-title page.

The "etc" represents five lines of the title-page omitted in writing the title-portion.

15 Wv41'C5 N32

HSU (Leonard Shihlien) (1901).

Political philosophy of Confucianism etc.

(Broadway oriental library. Ed by Clement Egerton. 3).

7474

The name of the series occurs on the half-title page but not on the title-page. The half-title page does not give the serial number. But the verso of the half-title page gives a list of the volumes belonging to the series. This book appears third in that list.

The "etc" represents three lines of the title-page, omitted in writing the title portion of the catalogue. The omitted lines read "an interpretation of the social and political ideas of Confucius, his forerunners, and his early disciples."

16 Y35 N32

DAVIE (Maurice R) (1893).

Problems of city life etc.

(Wiley social science series. Ed by Henry Pratt Fairchild. 1).

74753

The name of the series occurs only on the verso of the half-title page. That page contains also a list of the volumes belonging to the series, without assigning serial numbers to them. As this book occurs as the first item in the list, it has been given the serial Number "1".

15 Examples of Pseudo-Series

1 C5 N33

Grimsehl (E) (1861).

Optics . . . Tr. . . by L A Woodward.

(Grimshel (E), Textbook of physics. Ed by R Tomaschek. 4).

81379

The title-page of each of the 5 V of the set, of which the above book is the 4th, contains the generic title given in the series note. The volumes have no common index. The Laws of Library Science will be better satisfied if each volume is treated, *i e* classified, catalogued, and shelved on the basis of its own specific subject. And yet the catalogue should help the reader to collect all the volumes of the set readily and to take all the titles at a glance. To this end, the Pseudo-Series note is given so that an Added Entry may be given in the Alphabetical Part under the name of the series featuring all the volumes together in their serial sequence.

2 O142,3M28,1 111N28

Tolstoy (Leo) (1828).

Childhood, boyhood and youth.

(Tolstoy (Leo). Centenary ed. 3).

49834

The binder's title of each of the 21 V of the set, of which the above book is the 3rd, contains the generic specification 'Works of Leo Tolstoy, Centenary Edition' and the serial number. The serial numbers of the several volumes are also given on P505 of the last volume. The set has no common index and it covers the biography, the dramas, the novels, and the prose pieces of Tolstoy. The Laws of Library Science will be better satisfied if the volumes of the set are treated, *i e* classified, catalogued and shelved, on the basis of their respective specific subjects. And yet the catalogue should help the reader to collect together readily all the volumes of the set. This it can do by giving the Pseudo-Series note mentioned, so that an Added Entry may be given in the Alphabetical Part under the name of the series featuring all the volumes of the set entered in their serial sequence. Further, it will be helpful if a Cross Reference Index Entry is given with "Works, Tolstoy (Leo)" as the Referred-From Heading and "Tolstoy (Leo). Centenary ed" as the Referred-To Heading.

3 R66,5*x*1,1 15N10.1 to 15N10.3

Sankara.

Brahmasutra bhashya. 3 V.

(Sankara. Vani Vilas Press ed. 1-3).

17375-7

Each of the 20 V of the collected works of Sankara brought out by the Vani Vilas Press has in addition to its specific title-page a generic title-page with the words "Works of Sri Sankaracharya" and the appropriate serial or volume number. Further, it may be helpful if a Cross Reference Index

Entry is given with "Works, Sankara" as the Referred-From Heading and "Sankara. Vani Vilas Press ed" as the Referred—To Heading.

4 V561'K0 N18

INNES (Arthur D) (1863).
England under the Tudors. Ed 5.
(History of England. Ed by Charles Oman. 4).
5012

5 T.1-3'N3 N24

NEWTON (Arthur Percival) (1873).
Universities and educational systems of the British Empire.
(British Empire, a survey. Ed by Hugh Gunn. 10).
45846

It is difficult to decide whether Example 4 is a case of series or pseudo-series. It is on the border line.

6 L17:47:4 N37

HERTZLER (Arthur E) (1870).
Surgical pathology of the diseases of the neck.
(Hertzler's monographs on surgical pathology. 9).
98523

16 Thesis

Publications of theses submitted to a university or any other body are to be deemed to belong to a series, whose name is to consist successively of the following:

1 The name of the university or body;
2 A comma; and
3 The word "theses".

Example:

1 O15:gvK5 111N29

SANKARAN (A) ( ).
Some aspects of literary criticism in Sanskrit or the theories of rasa and dhvani.
(University of Madras, theses. 1925, 1).
58166

The title-page contains the information that it is a research thesis. The year of the thesis is inferred from the preface and, in the absence of any other information to the contrary, it is marked as 1 of the published theses presented in 1925.

2 Multiplicity of Series

20 Kinds

If a book belongs to two or more series, the notes corresponding to them are to be called

1 Independent, if the individualisation of the name of each series is independent of the names of the other series; otherwise

2 A sequence of inter-dependent series notes; and

3 Alternative name note if the same series has two or more names.

21 Independent Series Notes

Each independent series note is to be constructed in accordance with Sec MF1 and its subdivisions, and written in separate sections.

Example:

1 NR44x3,1 15N28

MATANGAMUNI.

Brhaddesi. Ed by K Sambasiva Sastri.

(Trivandrum sanskrit series. 94).

(Setu Laksmi prasadamala. 6).

51608

In this case, the book gets a serial number in two series and the name of either series is individualised by itself, without the help of the other. Hence, the two series notes are independent and they are enclosed in separate brackets of their own and written as separate sections.

It may also be added, that the name of the second series, as it is given on the title-page, begins with the honorific word "Sri". It is omitted in the catalogue entry in accordance with Sec MF11.

22 Interdependent Series Note

In the case of a sequence of interdependent series notes, the primary series note is to be constructed in accordance with Sec MF1 and its subdivisions. This note is to be followed by

1 A semi-colon;

2 The name of the secondary series;

3 A full stop;

4 The serial number of the book in the secondary series, constructed in accordance with Sec MF13 or MF131 or MF132, as the case may be;

5 A semi-colon;

6 The name of the ternary series;

7 A full stop;

8 The serial number of the book in the ternary series; and so on.

Example:

1 O-,2J96:g(Y35) N14

PARLIN (Hanson T) (1879).

Study in Shirley's comedies of London life.

(University of Texas, bulletin. 371; humanistic series. 17; studies in English. 2).

72005

This is a case of three interdependent series notes forming a sequence. The second and the third do not get individualised unless the first is given.

221 SERIAL NUMBER NOT GIVEN IN EARLIER SERIES

If the books are not numbered by the publisher in a member of such a sequence of series, other than the last sub-series, that member is not to be given a note of its own in the sequence of interdependent series notes, but its name is merely to be used to individualise the name of the succeeding subseries in accordance with Sec JG6.

222 SERIES NUMBER NOT GIVEN IN LAST SECTION

If the publisher has not given serial numbers in the last sub-series, they are to be given by the cataloguer in accordance with Sec MF13 or MF131 or MF132 as the case may be.

Example:

1 X8(M7):9F.42'N3 N31

MATSUOKA (Asa) (1893).

Labour conditions of women and children in Japan.

United States, Labour Statistics (Bureau of—), bulletin. 558; industrial relations and labour conditions series. 10.

This is obviously a case of interdependent series note. The volumes get numbered in the first-mentioned series, but not in the second. However, the end pages give the lists of the volumes belonging to the various secondary series that are included in the major series. From that number it is inferred that this volume is the tenth in its secondary series.

It may be remarked here also that the work is a pamphlet and its Book Number should, therefore, be underlined.

The subject is a very specialised one and hence its call number is proportionately long. Further the book deals only with the textile industry.

23 Alternative Names of Series

If a series has alternative names, the names are to be written one after the other, with an intervening "or".

Example:

1 O15,1D40,M N31

Kalidasa.

Meghaduta, with three commentaries, the Sanjivini by Mallinatha, Charitravardhini by Charitra Vardhanacharya, and Bhavaprabodhini by Narayan Sastri Khiste. Ed by Narayan Sastri Khiste.

(Kashi Sanskrit series or Haridas Sanskrit granthamala. 88; kavya section. 14).

72098

3 Extract Note

31 Rendering

An Extract Note is to consist successively of the

1 Descriptive words "*Extract from*" or "*Supplement to*", as the case may be or other appropriate ones; and

2 Specification of the work from which it is an extract.

It is to be remembered that a Note of this Kind is to be put within inverted commas.

32 Extract from a Periodical Publication

If the extract is from a Periodical Publication, the specification is to consist successively of

0 The Call Number of the volume of the periodical, if and only if the library has a copy of the volume;

1 The name of the Periodical Publication;

2 A colon; and

3 The term "V"; and

4 The number or the year or both of the volume of the

Periodical Publication, the number and the year being separated by a semi colon,

or any other appropriate sepcification of the locus.

Example:

1 2.7362,*d* N21

SWANTON (W I) (1869), *Comp.*

Libraries in the District of Columbia etc.

(National Research Council, reprints and circular series, 20).

"*Extract from* Special libraries. V 12; 1921".

54855

This is a case in which the book is an extract from a periodical and at the same time forms a volume of a series. Hence, there are two independent notes; firstly the Series Note and secondly the Extract Note.

33 EXTRACT FROM A BOOK

If the extract is from a book, the specification is to consist successively of

0 The Call Number of the book, if and only if the library has a copy of the book;

1 The Heading of that book;

2 A full stop;

3 The short title of that book the first word of the title beginning with capital letter;

4 A full stop; and

5 If possible and necessary, the parts, chapters of pages of the book from which it is extracted.

Provided that 2 and 3 are to be omitted if the Heading is the Title.

Example:

1 2:(Z44) *q*N57

RANGANATHAN (Shiyali Ramamrita) (1892).

Union library act.

"*Extract from* Ranganathan (Shiyali Ramamrita) (1892). Five laws of library science. Ed 2. Sec 43".

40003

Note: The Note in the above example implies that the library has no copy of the original book.

If the library has a copy of the original book, the Note will be as follows:

"*Extract from* 2 N57 Ranganathan (Shivali Ramamrita) (1892). Five laws of library science. Ed 2."

4 Extraction Note

An Extraction Note is to consist successively of

1 The directing words "*For extracts see*" and
2 The Call Number of the Extract;
3 The Heading of the Extract;
4 The Title of the Extract, and
5 Information on the Editions, if other than ed 1.

The Extraction Note for each Extract should be given as a separate section.

It is to be remembered that a Note of this Kind is to be put within inverted commas.

Example:

1 2 N57
RANGANATHAN (Shiyali Ramamrita) (1892).
Five laws of library science. Ed 2.
(Madras Library Association, publication series. 23).
"*For extracts see*
2:(Z44)*t*7 *q*N57 Ranganathan (Shiyali Ramamrita) (1892). Union library act.
2.1'N3 N57 Ranganathan (Shiyali Ramamrita) (1892). Library movement and legislation abroad."

5 Change of Title Note

51 RENDERING

A Change of Name Note is to have successively the sections consisting of

1 The directing words such as "*Published previously as*" or "*Published later as*" or "*Published in U S A as*" as the case may be; and
2 Each of the titles under which it has appeared.

It is to be remembered that a Note of this Kind is to be put within inverted commas.

Example:

1 Y31:1:7.44'N3 N29

BRAYNE (Frank Lugard) (1882).
Remaking of village India.
"*Published previously as*
Village uplift in India".
54137

52 DIFFERENT EARLIER AND LATER NAMES

If the book has different earlier as well as different later names, the Change of Name Note is to consist of two notes, one for the earlier names and another for the later ones.

6 Note for Other Kinds of Related Books

The Note for other kinds of Related Books is to consist successively of

1 An appropriate phrase indicating the nature of the association such as

"*For an associated book on theory*";
"*For an associated book on practice materials*";
"*For an associatied book of maps*";
"*For an abridgment*";
"*For a merger book*";
"*For merged books*";

2 The directing word "*see*"; and

3 The Call Number(s) of the Associated Book(s) written in separate section(s).

Examples:

1 V1-56'N3 N34

ANDERSON ( ) ( ) and
MARSDEN ( ) ( ).
Short history of the British Empire.
"*For an associated book on teaching technique see*
T:3(V1-56'N3 N34) N35".
39563

2 T:3(V1-56'N3 N34) N35

WREN (F C) (1885).
Teachers' handbook to Anderson and Marsden's Short history of the British Empire.
"*For the associated text book see*
V1-56'N3 N34".
39564

3 C N38

BLACK (Newton Henry) (1874) and DAVIS (Harvey Nathaniel) (1881).

Elementary practical physics.

"*For an associated book on experiment see* C:3 N38".

39565

4 C:*f*3 N38

BLACK (Newton Henry) (1874).

Laboratory experiments in elementary physics: To accompany Black and Davis's Elementary practical physics.

"*For an attached book on theory see*
C N38"

39566

5 O-,2J64*w* N33

WILLIAMS (Charles) (1886).

Short life of Shakespeare with the sources.

"*Abridged from*
O-,2J64*w* N30.1 to N30.2."

43242

6 O-,2J64*w* N30.1 to N30.2

CHAMBERS (Edmund Kerchiver) (1866).

William Shakespeare: A study of facts and problems.

"*For abridgement see*
O-,2J64*w* N33."

21162

7 X.436'N5 N53

BOEK (J H).

Economics and economic policy of dual societies as exemplified by Indonesia.

"*For merged books see*
X.436'N5 N42
X.436'N5 N46".

180943

8 X.436'N5 N42

BOEK (J H).

Structure of the Netherlands Indies economy.

"*For the merger book see*
X.436'N5 N53"

205392

9 X.436'N5 N46

BOEK (J H).

Solutions of the Netherlands Indies economy.

"*For the merger book see*
X.436'N5 N53"

2537452

CHAPTER MG

MAIN ENTRY: ACCESSION NUMBER

1 Choice

The Accession Number is to be taken from the back of the title page.

If there is no title page for a document the Accession Number is to be taken from the top of the first page.

The Accession Number would have been assigned by the accessioner [RL1].

2 Style of Writing

The following Rules govern the writing of the Accession Number:

SECTION	PURPORT
ED21	Writing fluid
ED23	Style of writing (library hand)
ED45	Position
ED451	Two or more Accession Numbers (sequence of the numbers)
ED910	Inclusive notation
ED913	Non-consecutive numbers

According to Sec ED45 the Accession Number is to be written on the bottom most line of the card. This is because the Accession Number is not for the notice of the reader. It is given in the Main Entry for administrative purposes to facilitate tracing certain information about the book in other records in the library.

Sec ED45 also recommends that the Accession Number be written from the First Vertical. In the case of multivolumed documents a number of Accession Numbers may have to be accommodated on the last line of the Main Entry card. It is to provide as much space as possible in such cases that the Accession Number section commences at the First Vertical.

CHAPTER MH

MAIN ENTRY: TRACING SECTION

1 Purpose

The back of the Main Entry card is to furnish information as to what additional entries have been made for the book, *viz*,

1 Cross Reference Entry;
2 Class Index Entry;
3 Book Index Entry; and
4 Cross Reference Index Entry.

2 Organization of the Back

The back of the Main Entry card is to be imagined to be divided into two halves by a line drawn parallel to its shorter sides. The two halves are to be called the Left Half and the Right Half respectively.

3 Organization of the Right Half

The Right Half is to be imagined to be divided into three convenient parts by two imaginary lines drawn at convenient distances parallel to the longer sides of the card. The parts are to be called the Upper Part, the Middle Part, and the Lower Part.

4 Cross Reference Entry

One line of the Left Half is to be devoted to each Cross Reference Entry (*See* Chap MJ). It is to contain successively the:

1 Class Number which forms the Leading Section of the Cross Reference Entry; and, if necessary,

2 Word "P" followed by the pages of reference or the

word "Sec", or "Chap", or "Part" etc followed by the Number(s) concerned.

5 Class Index Entries

The lines of the Upper Part of the Right Half are to contain successively the Heading of each of the Class Index Entries, contributed by the chains of the Class Numbers of the book and of the Cross Reference Entries, beginning from the last link and ending with the upper-most link (*See* Part K).

6 Book Index Entries

The lines of the Middle Part of the Right Half are to contain successively the Heading of each of the Book Index Entries of the book, in the sequence in which they are treated in Chap MJ.

7 Cross Reference Index Entries

The lines of the Lower Part of the Right Half are to contain successively the Heading of each of the Cross Reference Index Entries of the book in the sequence in which they are treated in Part L.

91 Style of Writing

All the words should be in ordinary hand subject to the rules of grammar on the use of capitals. (*See* Sec ED54).

92 Continuation Line

A continuation line is to be indented by two spaces.

93 Punctuation

A full stop is to be inserted at the end of each of the Headings, and at the end of each of the Items corresponding to each Cross Reference Entry.

Example:

1 BwM87 P*xi-xix*

RAMANUJAN (Srinivasa) (1887), Works, Mathematics.

Ramanujan (Srinivasa) (1887), Biography

Hardy (G H) etc, *Ed.*

See Example 1 in Sec ME23 for the Main Entry.

It must remembered that in passing from the front side to the back side, the card is to be turned through two right angles with the bottom edge as the axis. Therefore, the writing on the back of the card should begin on the first line near the bottom of the card as it stands in the cabinet tray. The other lines should be written successively after it.

CHAPTER MJ

CROSS REFERENCE ENTRY

0 Sections and Their Sequence

A Cross-Reference Entry of a Simple Book is to consist successively of the following Sections:

1 Leading Section;
2 Second Section; and
3 to 5 Locus Section.

01 Sections of a Locus Statement

The Locus Statement is to consist successively of the following Sections:

3 Call Number of the Book;
4 Heading of the Main Entry of the Book; and
5 Title of the book and place of occurrence.

1 Leading Section

11 Choice

The Leading Section is to consist of the Class Number of the subject from which the document is referred.

12 Source

The Class Number of the Specific Subject for which the book is cross-referred is to be furnished by the Classifier.

These Class Numbers will be found in the Tracing Section of the Main Card. The Classifier may write these numbers in a process slip for incorporation in the Tracing Section by the Cataloguer.

About the specific subjects to be chosen for Cross Reference Entry, *See* Sec FM72.

2 Second Section

The Second Section is to consist of the Directing Element "*See also*"

3 Call Number of the Book

The Call Number of the book is to be the same as in its Main Entry.

4 Heading of the Book

The Heading of the book is to be the same as in its Main Entry, omitting the Secondary and other Individualising Elements in the case of the name of a person. It is to be written in ordinary hand (*Sec* See ED54).

5 Title of the Book

The Short Title of the book is to be used.

51 Whole Book

If the reference is to the whole book, the place of occurrence is not to be given.

52 Place of Occurrence

If the reference is not to be the whole book, the Short Title of the book is to be followed successively by

1 A full stop; and

2 Specification of the place of occurrence in the form of "p", or "Sec", or "Chap" or "Part", or any other appropriate term, followed by the number concerned.

6 Cross-Reference Card

To distinguish the Cross-Reference cards from the Main cards easily, a differentiation in colour may be used, *e g* the Main cards may be white and the Cross-reference cards, light red.

Example:

1 BwM87

See also

BxM87 N27

Ramanujan.

Collected papers. P *xi—xix.*

See Example 1 under Sec ME23 for the Main Entry.

This was the only biography of Ramanujan to be published. Unless it is brought out by the Cross-Reference card, it may be missed by readers. But, if the above card is written out, such a contingency and waste of time will be eliminated for ever.

2 L.44'D5

See also

V440r51'D5 N20

Banerjee.

Hellenism in ancient India. P 186-207.

3 LBaN1

See also

V440r51'D5 N20

Banerjee.

Hellenism in ancient India. P 206-7.

7 Value

It can be easily seen that few readers could be expected to think of Banerjee's book in tracing material on the history of medicine in India. Nor could they expect a good bibliography of the Ayurvedic system of medicine in this book. But for these Cross-Reference cards, even the reference staff of the library may not get scent of these references, except with repeated loss of time. Further, it may even happen that this is the only book in the library bearing on the subject. If these Cross-references are not given, many a reader may go disappointed, while the information they sought is lying hidden in the printed pages, heaped unanalysed in the library.

Multifocal books are quite common. Classification, as it has been developed till now, is unable to deal with them and looks to the catalogue to make up for the deficiency [RF7]. Reference service cannot be efficient unless the catalogue gives Cross-Reference Entries, that is, Subject Analyticals [RT5]. However, this type of entries leads to civil war, as it were, among the Laws of Library Science and a compromise is to abstain from giving such entries in the case of the books which have been analysed in published bibliographies [RT5].

8 Need for Cooperation

Generally speaking, Cross-Reference Entry is largely a matter of judgment. In this the classifier, the cataloguer, the reference librarian, the periodicals librarian, and even specialist readers may have to cooperate with one another.

This is apart from the play of the Principle of Local Variation.

CHAPTER MK

BOOK INDEX ENTRY

0 Sections and their Sequence

A Book Index Entry is to consist successively of the following sections:

1 Leading Section;
2 Second Section;
3 Index Number; and
4 Note Section, if any.

01 Consolidation

If two or more entries are alike in the Heading and the Second Section and differ only in the Index Number, they may be consolidated into one entry, the different Call Numbers being added in succession, one below the other in one or more columns.

1 Leading Section

A Book Index Entry is to be given using as Heading each of such of the following as the Main Entry of the Book admits of:

1 *Derived from Heading*

11 Heading, provided it is not, as such, eligible to be used as the Main Heading of a Class Index Entry appropriate to the Book; and

12 Permutation of the names in the Heading, if it is one of two Joint Authors or two Collaborators of the same kind; and in the case of a Joint Organ or Conference of two bodies, permutation of the names of the two Corporate bodies in the Main Heading; and in the Case of a personal author and a Corporate author, permutation of the name of the personal author and of the corporate author.

2 *Derived from Title Section*

211 Name of each Collaborator mentioned in the Title portion in case there is only one Collaborator of that kind;

212 Permutation of the names of Joint Collaborators of any kind mentioned in the Title portion, in case there are only two Joint Collaborators of that kind;

213 Name of the first Collaborator of any kind mentioned in the Title portion, followed by the word "etc", in case there are three or more Collaborators of that kind.

214 Name of the Sponsor in the case of a Bill or set.

22 Title of the book;

1 If it is fanciful; or

2 If it contains a proper non ; or

3 If it is treated in usage as a proper noun; provided that

1 It has not been used as the Heading of the Main Entry; or

2 It is not, as such, eligible to be used as the Main Heading of a Class Index Entry of the book;

3 *Derived from Note Section*

31 Name of the Series occurring in each Independent Series Note;

32 Name of each of the Series occurring in an Interdependent Series Note;

33 The Heading of the Work mentioned in the Extract Note;

34 Heading, for each of the Alternative Titles of the book.

2 Second Section

The Second Section of a Book Index Entry is to depend on the nature of the Heading, as prescribed by the succeeding Rules.

20 Edition

The Second Section is to specify the edition also, if it is other than ed 1. The information about the edition is to be preceded by a full stop.

211 HEADING AS IN MAIN ENTRY

If the Heading is of the kind 11 or 12 enumerated in Sec MK1, the Second Section is to consist of the Short Title of the book.

Examples:

Example 1 in Sec JF7 is not to be given an Author Index Entry as the book demands a Class Index Entry with the name of the Author as the Main Heading.

Example 1 in Sec ME31 is to be given the following Author Index Entry:

1 Schneider (Georg) (1876).
Bibliographie. Ed 4. *a*X 113N30

Example 5 in Sec ME31 is to get the following Joint Authors Index Entries:

2 Davis (A H) (1892) and Kaye (George William Clarison) (1880).
Acoustics of buildings. C30*b*NA,2 N27

3 Kaye (George William Clarison) (1880) and Davis (A H) (1892).
Acoustics of buildings. C30*b*NA, 2 N27

Example 16 in Sec ME31 may get the following Author Index Entry:

4 Cooley (Charles Horton) (1864) etc.
Introductory sociology. Y N33

Example 8 in Sec ME31 is to get the following Editor-Heading Index Entry:

5 Quiller-Couch (Arthur) (1863), *Ed.*
Oxford book of English prose. O-,6*x*M8 M25

Example 3 in Sec MD51 is to get the following Compiler and Translator-Heading Index Entry:

6 Chamot (A E) (1855), *Comp* and *Tr.*
Select Russian short stories. O142,3*x*M7 111N25

Example 1 in Sec MD54 is to get the following Joint-Editors-Heading Index Entries:

7 Neilson (William Allan) (1869) and Webster (Kenneth Grant Tremayse) ( ), *Ed.*
Chief British poets of the fourteenth and fifteenth centuries.
O-,*x*19 N16

8 WEBSTER (Kenneth Grant Tremayse) ( ) and NEILSON (William Allan) (1869), *Ed.*
Chief British poets of the fourteenth and fifteenth centuries.
O-,x19 N16

The example in Sec MD621 is to get the following Title-Heading Index Entry:

9 WILLIAM ERNEST Johnson. RwM58 N31

221 NAME OF COLLABORATOR AS HEADING

If the Heading is of the kind 21 enumerated in Sec MK1, the Second Section is to consist successively of

1 The Heading of the Main Entry of the book, along with the Descriptive Element, if any, with the provision that, in the case of a name-of-person, it is sufficient if the Entry Element alone is used;

2 A colon; and

3 The Short Title of the book, with the initial letter in capital.

Examples:

Example 6 in Sec ME31 is to get the following Reviser Index Entry:

1 FISCHER (Ferdinand) (1843), *Rev.*
Wagner: Chemical technology. F N04

It should also get the following Translator and Editor Index Entry:

2 CROOKES (William) (1832), *Tr* and *Ed.*
Wagner: Chemical technology. F N04

Example 10 in Sec ME31 is to get the following Editor Index Entry:

3 VYANKATARAMANA AIYAR (S), *Ed.*
Ramananda Saraswati, *Comm:* Vedanta darsana with comm Brahmaritavarsini. R66,5x3,1 15N16

222 TITLE AS HEADING

If the Heading is of the kind 22 enumerated in Sec MK1, the Second Section is to consist successively of the

1 Connecting word "by" or other similar suitable term; and

2 Heading of the Main Entry of the book, along with the Descriptive Element, if any, with the provision that, in the case of a name-of-person, it is sufficient if the Entry Element alone is used.

Examples:

1 The fanciful title' Meghaduta' in Example 1 in Sec MF23 is not to be given Title Index Entry as it demands a Class Index Entry.

2 The book whose title page is "Next Five Years / An Essay / in / Political Agreement" has no doubt, for its effective title, "Next Five Years." But this does not show forth what its subject is; it thus amounts to a fanciful title. And yet it should not be given Title Index Entry, as its Main Entry itself has it as Heading. Thus, "NEXT FIVE YEARS" will take the place of the Heading-of-Author Index Entry.

3 Example 1 in Sec JF91 is to be given the following Title Index Entry:

1 HERMES.
By Jones. Evl'N3 N28

231 NAME OF INDEPENDENT SERIES AS HEADING

If the Heading is of the kind 31 enumerated in Sec MK1, the Second Section is to consist successively of

1 The Serial Number of the book, or the entity by which it is replaced;

2 The Heading of the Main Entry of the book, along with the Descriptive Element, if any, with the provision that in the case of a name-of-person, the Secondary Element is omitted ;

3 A colon; and

4 The Short Title of the book, with the initial letter in capital,

provided that if the Heading is the Title, 2 and 3 are to be omitted.

Examples:

Example 5 in Sec MF14 is to get the following Series Index Entry:

1 SAMMLUNG SCHUBERT.
1 Schubert: Arithmetik und algebra. Ed 2. B 113N10

Example 6 in Sec MF14 is to get the following Series Index Entry:

2 PATNA UNIVERSITY, READERSHIP LECTURES.
1928 Saha: Atomic physics. C9B2 N31

Example 9 in Sec MF14 is to get the following Series Index Entry:

3 INSTITUTE FOR MEDICAL RESEARCH (Federated Malay States), BULLETIN.
1930, 3 Lewthwaite: Experimental tropical typhus.
L35:42381:4 N30

Example 15 in Sec MF14 is to get the following Series Index Entry:

4 BROADWAY ORIENTAL LIBRARY.

3 Hsu: Political philosophy of Confucianism. Wr41'C5 N32

Example 8 in Sec MF14 is to get the following Series Index Entry:

5 WILEY FARM SERIES.

2 Worthen: Farm soils. J;1 N30

Example 12 in Sec MF14 is to get the following Series Index Entry:

6 UNIVERSITY OF ILLINOIS STUDIES IN LANGUAGE AND LITERATURE.

V 12, N 2-3 Bundy: Theory of imagination in classical and medieval thought. O:g(S:43)H1 N27

2311 Consolidation of Series Entries

All entries with the same Heading of the kind 31 enumerated in Sec MK1, are to be consolidated into a single entry, the different Second Sections being written in separate paragraphs in their serial sequence; sufficient space is to be left for gaps, if any, in the serial numbers.

Example:

The Series Index Entries of Examples 2 to 4 given in Sec MF14 are to be consolidated as follows:

1 MADRAS LIBRARY ASSOCIATION, PUBLICATION SERIES.

19 Ranganathan: Colon classification. Ed 4. 2:51N3 qN52

23 Ranganathan: Five laws of library science. Ed 2. 2 N57

24 Ranganathan: Classified catalogue code. Ed 4. 2:55N3 qN58

If the different books in a Series are to be arranged in the Series Index Entry alphabetically by the name of the author, the consolidation of Series Entry would become wasteful if the Series is in progress. On the other hand if the volumes in a Series are arranged in the serial sequence as provided in this Sec, consolidation is possible; and thus some saving can be effected.

232 NAME OF INTERDEPENDENT SERIES AS HEADING

If the Heading is of the kind 32 enumerated in Sec MK1, the Second Section is to be constructed on the analogy of Sec MK231 and MK2311.

Examples:

Example 1 in Sec MF22 is to get the following Series Index Entries:

1 UNIVERSITY OF TEXAS. BULLETIN.

371 Parlin: Study in Shirley's comedies of London life. O-,2J96:g(Y35) N14

2 UNIVERSITY OF TEXAS, BULLETIN, HUMANISTIC SERIES.

17 Parlin: Study in Shirley's comedies of London life. - O-,2J96:g(Y35) N14

3 UNIVERSITY OF TEXAS, BULLETIN, HUMANISTIC SERIES, STUDIES IN ENGLISH.

2 Parlin: Study in Shirley's comedies of London life. O-,2J96:g(Y35) N14

Example 1 in Sec MF 222 is to get, in addition to the Author Index Entry, the following two Series Index Entries:

4 UNITED STATES, LABOUR STATISTICS (Bureau of-), BULLETIN.

588 Matsuoka: Labour conditions of women and children in Japan. X8(M7):9F.42'N3 N31

5 UNITED STATES, LABOUR STATISTICS (Bureau of-), INDUSTRIAL RELATIONS AND LABOUR CONDITIONS SERIES of the Bulletin

10 Matsuoka: Labour conditions of women and children in Japan. X8(M7):9F.42'N3 N31

2321 Direction to Published List

Government and other series of this type have long names and they include hundreds of publications. In such cases, it may be conducive to economy to replace a whole set of series cards by a single card, directing attention to the printed list of the volumes of the series, if such a list could be found in any of their publications. Such a direction may take the following form:

1 UNITED STATES, LABOUR STATISTICS (Bureau of-) BULLETIN.

See list in P of

(give here the exact reference, whether in office file or in a trade list or in some book.)

Of the various types of Book Index Entries, there is some difference of opinion about the Series Index Entry. The remarks that have been made in the preceding para justify the despair into which some Series Index Entries are likely to drive cataloguers. It is particularly long series like those of some governments with a number of secondary and ternary series that have made the cataloguers stand at bay.

At the same time, we have to examine whether there is no value whatever in Series Index Entries. In University and Scientific libraries and other libraries catering to the special needs of research workers, it is found that the Series Index Entry is of some value. How they help every reader to get his book and every book to get its reader is discussed in the *Five laws of library science* [RF5].

Further, they are of great help both in book-selection and in book-ordering. Some cataloguers, who realise this, propose a compromise and leave it to the discretion of the cataloguer to decide whether a Series is worth being given a Series Index Entry.

This is the direction of the Principle of Local variation.

One method of economy is indicated in the first para.

233 EXTRACT INDEX ENTRY

If the Heading is of the kind 33 enumerated in Sec MK1, the Second Section is to consist successively of

1 The title of the work mentioned in the Extract Note;
2 A full stop;
3 Specification of the portion extracted followed by
4 A descriptive term such as "*printed as*" or "*bound as*";
5 The Heading in the Main Entry of the Extract along with the Descriptive Element, if any, with the provision that, in the case of a name-of-person, the Secondery Element is omitted;
6 A colon; and
7 The short title of the Extract

provided that, if the Heading is Title, 5 and 6 are to be omitted.

Example:

Example 1 in Sec MF33 is to get the following Extract Index Entry:

1 RANGANATHAN (Shiyali Ramamrita) (1892).
Five laws of library science. Ed 2.
Sec 43 *printed as*
Ranganathan: Union library act. 2:(Z44) *q*N57

2331 Consolidation of Extract Index Entries

All entries with the same Heading of the kind 33 and the same Second Section may be consolidated in a single entry on the analogy of Sec MK2311.

Example:

1 RANGANATHAN (Shiyali Ramamrita) (1892).
Five laws of library science. Ed 2.
Sec 43 *printed as*
Ranganathan: Union library act. 2:(Z44) *q*N57
Chap 3 *bound as*
Library movement and legislation abroad. 2,1'N3 N57

234 AUTHOR INDEX ENTRY FOR ALTERNATIVE ENTRY

In the case of the heading of the kind 34 enumerated in Sec MK1, the Second Section is to consist of the Alternative Title followed by a description as prescribed in Sec MF41 and MF42.

The Call Number of each version in the library should be

given an Index Number at the end of the section giving the title of that version.

Example 1 in Sec MF51 is to get the following Author Index Entries corresponding to the two alternative titles:

1 BRAYNE (Frank Lugard) (1882).
Remaking of village India.
"*Published previously as*
Village uplift in India." Y31:1:7.44'N3 N29

2 BRAYNE (Frank Lugard) (1882).
Village uplift in India.
"*Published later as*
Remaking of village India." Y31:1:7.44'N3 N29

Index Entries of the kinds 33 and 34 enumerated in Sec MK1 are found to be necessary to avoid unintended duplication in book-selection and book-ordering, in addition to their reference value.

CHAPTER MZD

DICTIONARY CATALOGUE

1 Main Entry

10 Difference

The Main Entry of a book in the Dictionary Catalogue differs from that in the Classified Catalogue only in

1 The Sequence of the Sections:

4 The Note concerning Related Books, other than those belonging to Series; and

6 The Tracing Section.

11 Sections

In the Entry of a book in the Dictionary Catalogue, the Heading occupies the Leading Section; and the Call Number occupies the Index Number Section and it precedes the Accession Number Section.

Example:

The Main Entry given as Example 9 in Sec MF31 will appear in the Dictionary Catalogue as follows:

1 Gardiner (Alan Henderson) (1879).
Theory of speech and language. P N32
74793

14 Note on Related Book

In a Note relating to a Related Book in the Main Entry of a book in the Dictionary Catalogue, the Call Number is to give place to the Heading and Short Title, wherever Call Number is prescribed in the Rules for the Classified Catalogue.

16 Tracing Section

Chap MH on Tracing Section are applicable with the following modifications:

161 One line of the Left Half is to be devoted to the Specific

Subject Entry and to each of the Subject Analyticals. It is to contain successively:

1 The Heading which forms the Leading Section of the Subject Entry concerned; and, if necessary,

2 The term "P" followed by the pages of reference or the term "Section", or "Chap", or "Part" etc followed by the number concerned.

62 The lines of the upper part of the Right Half are to contain successively the Headings of the *See also* Subject Entries, arising out of the Specific Subject Entry as well as each of the Subject Analyticals.

2 Specific Subject Entry and Subject Analyticals

In structure, the Specific Subject Entry and the Subject Analyticals in the Dictionary Catalogue, resemble the Cross Reference Entry in a Classified Catalogue with the omission of the Section containing the Directing Element.

21 The Name of the Specific Subject concerned is to be put in the Leading Section.

The derivation of the Name of the Specific Subject from the Class Number by Chain Procedure has been prescribed in Chap 3D. The classifier is to furnish the Class Number of the book and of the classes contributing to Subject Analyticals. The Chain Procedure is to be applied to each of these Class Numbers.

23 The Locus Section of a Specific Subject Entry or a Subject Analytical is to be constructed on the analogy of Chap MJ with the following modifications:

32 The Secondary and the other Individualising Elements in the Name of a Person are to be retained.

Examples:

1 MATHEMATICS, BIOGRAPHY, RAMANUJAN (Srinivasa).
Ramanujan (Srinivasa) (1887).
Collected papers. P *xi-xix*. BxM87 N27

2 LIBRARY SCIENCE.
Ranganathan (Shiyali Ramamrita) (1892).
Five laws of library science. Ed 1 and 2. 2 N31 and N57

3 Book Index Entry

31 It should be realised that the Dictionary Catalogue

can not have a Book Index Entry corresponding to the Author Index Entry, or rather the Heading-of-Main-Entry Index Entry of the Classified Catalogue.

32 Wherever the Sec of Chap MK prescribe the Heading of the Main Entry of the book for incorporation in the Second Section, omit the following provision "with the provision that in the case of name-of-person, it is sufficient if the entry element alone is used".

Example:

Example 1 in Sec MK221 will figure as follows in the Dictionary Catalogue:

1 FISCHER (Ferdinand), *Rev.*
Wagner (Rudolf Von): Chemical technology. F N04

A Book Index Entry of a book in the Dictionary Catalogue has to differ from that in the Classified Catalogue in the way indicated above. This difference arises from the fact that the Link between a Book Index Entry and the Main Entry in the Dictionary Catalogue is the Name of the Author or the Title of the Book, whichever is the Heading of the Main Entry. On the other hand, in the Classified Catalogue the Call Number is the Link. In the Dictionary Catalogue the Call Number is virtually impotent in the Main Entry. In the Classified Catalogue on the other hand the name of the author is impotent in the Main Entry. This difference accounts for the difference in the prescription made for the Second Section in a Book Index Entry in the two kinds of Catalogue.

This difference in Book Index Entry between Dictionary Catalogue and Classified Catalogue does not arise when the Heading of the Main Entry of the book concerned is a Corporate Author, a Pseudonym, or a Title.

PART N

COMPOSITE BOOK AND MULTI-VOLUMED BOOK

CHAPTER NA

ORDINARY COMPOSITE BOOK

1 Main Entry

An ordinary Composite Book is to be dealt with as a Simple Book ignoring the names of the contributors of the constituent parts except for Index Entries (*vide* Sec NA3 and its subdivisions).

Examples:

In the case of the book whose title-page reads

"The happy baby / editorial adviser: / Dr L Emmett Holt / contributors: / Dr L Emmett Holt Dr Ralph Lobenstine / Dr Harvey J Burkhart Dr Henry L K Shaw,"

the Main Entry is to be as follows:

1 L9C:75 N26

HOLT (Luther Emmett) (1855), *Ed.*

Happy baby.

46411

Here is a case where the title-page contains no other information, except the title and the imprint.

2 R3,(Q)0*g*A *p*7N31

SCIENCE AND religion, a symposium.

68340

In the case of the book whose title-page reads

"Psychological elements / in speech / by / Emill Fröschels / in company / with Professor Dr Octmar Dittrich / *and* / Frau Dr Ilka Wilhelm / translated from the German by / Nils Ferre,"

the Main Entry is to be as follows:

3 S:682 N32

FRÖSCHELS (Emil) (   ).

Psychological elements in speech. Tr by Nils Ferre.

74308

In the case of the book whose title-page reads

"The modern state / by / Leonard Woolf / Lord Eustace Percy / Mrs Sydney Webb / Professor W G S Adams / Sir Arthur Salter / *edited by* / Mary Adams."

the Main Entry is to be as follows:

4 W *p*7N33

ADAMS (Mary) (1898), *Ed.*

Modern state.

74736

Here is another example of a symposium.

5 A *p*77N11

M'INTOSH (William Carmichael) (1838) etc, *Ed.*

University of Saint Andrews, five hundredth anniversary: Memorial volume of scientific papers.

32405

In the case of the book whose title-page reads

"Science in World War II / Office of Scientific Research and Development / Applied physics / Electronics. A History of Divisions 13 and 15 and the Committee on Propagation NDRC, edited by C G Suits. With a foreward by Karl T Compton / Optics. A History of Divisions 16 and 17, NDRC, by H Kirk Stephenson and Edgar L Jones, edited by George R Harrison / Metallurgy. A History of Division 18, NDRC, by Louis Jordan / With illustrations / An Atlantic Monthly Press Book / Little, Brown and Company, Boston / 1948,"

the Main Entry is to be as follows:

6 A.73'N5 N48

APPLIED PHYSICS etc.

(Science in World War II, 7).

12345

2 Cross Reference Entry

20 The Cross Reference Entries of an Ordinary Composite Book are to be of two types:

1 Special; and

2 Chain.

21 Special Cross Reference Entry

A Special Cross Reference Entry is to consist successively of the following sections:

1 Leading Section, consisting of the Class Number of the contribution Cross Referred;

2 Its Heading omitting Individualising Elements;

3 Its short Title;

4 The Directing Element "*See*"

5 Call Number of the Host Book;

6 Heading of the Host Book omitting Individualising Elements; and

7 Title of the Host Book, a full stop, specification of the place of occurrence of the Referred-from Document in the

form of "P", or "Chap", or "Part", or in any other appropriate form, followed by the number concerned.

Example:
2:97(X:9)y7
Kaula.
Documentation in social sciences.
See
2:97 N63
Ranganathan, *Ed.*
Documentation and its facets. Chap F6.

22. Chain Cross Reference Entry

For convenience,

1 The Document Referred-from may be called the Document of Remove 2; and

2 The contribution in the Host Book containing the Document of Remove 2, may be called Document of Remove 1.

A Chain Cross Reference Entry is to consist successively of the following sections:

1 Leading Section, consisting of the Class Number of the Document of Remove 2;

2 The Directing Element "*See also*";

3 Heading of the Document of Remove 1;

4 Title of the Document of Remove 1, a full stop, specification of the place of occurrence of the Document of Remove 2 within the Document of Remove 1 in the form of "P", or "Chap", or "Part", or in any other appropriate form, a comma, followed by the number concerned;

5 The descriptive term "*Forming*", followed by the specification of the place of occurrence of the Document of Remove 1 in the Host Book in the form of "P", or "Chap", or "Part", or in any other appropriate form, the number concerned, and the term "*of*";

6 Call Number of the Host Book; and

7 Heading of the Host Book Omitting individualising elements, a full stop, and its Short Title.

Example:
In the example given in Sec NA 21 let us assume that the portion "Schedule

of classification of wages" appearing as Sec 9 of the Referred-from Document has to be cross-referred. This will be done as follows:

2:519(X:93)
See also
Kaula (PN)
Documentation in social sciences, Sec 9.
Forming Chap F6 *of*
2:97 N63
Ranganathan, *Ed.* Documentation and its facets.

3 Class Index Entry

An Ordinary Composite Book is to be given Class Index Entries as prescribed in Part K.

It may be stated explicitly that the Class Index Entries, arising out of the Class Number, of each of the Contributions, are also to be given.

4 Cross Reference Index Entry

An Ordinary Composite Book is to be given Cross Reference Index Entries as prescribed in Part L and, in addition, for the alternative terms for "Festschrift."

5 Book Index Entry

An Ordinary Composite Book is to be given Book Index Entries as prescribed in Chap MK.

6 Contribution Index Entry

An Ordinary Composite Book, other than encyclopaedias and memorial volumes, is to be given Book Index Entries for each of the **contributions** contained in it.

61 For convenience of reference, a Book Index Entry of a **contribution** in an Ordinary Composite Book is to be called a "**Contribution Index Entry**".

611 A Contribution Index Entry may be a **Contributor-Index Entry** or a **Collaborator-to-Contributor Index Entry**.

62 Contributor-Index Entry

620 SECTIONS

A Contributor Index Entry of an Ordinary Composite Book is to consist successively of the following sections:

1 Leading Section;
2 Title Section;
3 Descriptive term such as "*Forming part of*";
4 Heading of the Host Book, a full stop, its Short Title, a full stop; and
5 Index Number.

621 LEADING SECTION

The Leading Section is to consist of the Heading of the Contribution as determined by Sec MK1 (category 1).

622 TITLE SECTION

The Title Section is to be that of the Contribution as determined by Sec MK2 and its subdivisions.

624 HEADING OF HOST BOOK

The Heading of the Host Book is to be that in its Main Entry modified as follows:

The Secondary Element in a Name-of-person is to be omitted.

625 INDEX NUMBER

The Index Number is to be the Call Number of the Host Book.

63 Collaborator-To-Contributor Index Entry

630 SECTIONS

The Collaborator-To-Contributor Index Entry of an Ordinary

Composite Book is to consist successively of the following sections:

1 Leading Section;

2 Second Section;

3 Descriptive terms such as "*Forming part of*";

4 Heading of the Host Book, a full stop, its Short Title, a full stop; and

5 Index Number.

631 LEADING SECTION

The Leading Section is to consist of the Heading made of the name(s) of the collaborator(s) as determined by Sec MK1 (category 211).

632 TITLE SECTION

The Title Section is to be that of the contribution as determined by Sec MK221.

634 HEADING OF THE HOST BOOK

Same as in Sec NA624.

635 INDEX NUMBER

Same as in Sec NA625.

Examples:

1 WEBB (Sydney) (1859).
Diseases of organised society.
Forming part of.
Adams, *Ed*. Modern state. W *p*7N33

2.1 SUITS (C G) (1905), *Ed*.
Electronics.
Forming part of
Applied physics. A.73'N5 N48

2.2 STEPHENSON (H Kirk) ( ) and JONES (Edgar L) ( ).
Optics. Ed by George R Harrison.
Forming part of
Applied physics. A.74'N5 N48

2.3 JONES (Edgar L) ( ) and STEPHENSON (H Krik) ( ).
Optics. Ed by George R Harrison.
Forming part of
Applied physics. A.73'N5 N48

2.4 HARRISON (George R) (1898), *Ed.*
Stephenson and Jones. Optics.
Forming part of
Applied physics. A.73'N5 N48

2.5 JORDAN (Louis) (1895).
Metallurgy.
Forming part of
Applied physics. A.73'N5 N48

64 AUTHOR ANALYTICAL

This type of entry is called an Author Analytical. Composite books calling for them are becoming common. Author Analyticals are beyond doubt of help to readers and to the reference staff. However, they lead to civil war, as it were, among the Laws of Library Science under the instigation of the Law of Parsimony; and a compromise is to abstain from giving such entries in the case of books which have been analysed in published bibliographies [RT4].

7 Festschrift Index Entry

A Festschrift is to be given a Book Index Entry consisting successively of the following Sections:

1 Leading Section consisting of the term "FESTSCHRIFT."

2 Second Section consisting of the Name of the Person or Institution or any other entity felicitated, rendered as prescribed in Part J; and

3 Index Number consisting of the Call Number of the book forming the festschrift.

Example:
Example 5 in Sec NA1 is to be given the following Festschrift Index Entry:

1 FESTSCHRIFT.
University of Saint Andrews. A *p*77N11

71 DEDICATEE INDEX ENTRY

A festschrift is to be given a Book Index Entry to be called

Dedicatee Index Entry, consisting successively of the following sections:

1 Leading Section consisting of the name of the Dedicatee rendered in accordance with the Sec of Part J, followed by a comma, and itself followed by the descriptive element "*Ded*";

2 Second section consisting of the term "FESTSCHRIFT"; and

3 Index Number consisting of the Call Number of the book forming the Festschrift.

Example:

Example 5 in Sec NA1 is to be given the following Dedicatee Index Entry:

1 UNIVERSITY OF ST ANDREWS, *Ded.*
FESTSCHRIFT. A *p*77N11

CHAPTER NB

ARTIFICIAL COMPOSITE BOOK

1 Main Entry

In the case of an Artificial Composite Book, the Main Entry is to be constructed as if it were the Main Entry of the First constitutent work except that to this is to be added a section for each later constituent work. Further, the descriptive term "*Composite book*" is to be added after the Call Number at the end of the Leading Section.

12 Sections

The section giving the entry for the Second Constituent Work is to consist of

1 The number "2";

2 The Heading appropriate to it;

3 A colon;

4 Its Title-portion with the initial letter in capital;

5 A full stop;

6 Notes, if any (subject to Sec NB14); and

7 Its Call Number, written at the right end of the last line of the section.

121 The various parts of the section are to be constructed as prescribed in Part M.

13 The paragraph giving the entry for any later Constituent Work is to be similar to the entry for the Second Constituent Work, except that the appropriate serial number is to take the place of "2".

14 Note

If all the Constituent Works belong to the same Series, a note need not be written in the section for each Constituent Work. It is sufficient if a single note is added as the final section, the serial number part of the section consisting of the successive serial numbers.

Example:

1 B633:23 N11 *Composite book*
HENDERSON (Archibald) (1877).
Twenty-seven lines upon the cubic surface.
2 Wood (P W): Twisted cubic with the cubical hyperbola.
B6363:23 N13
(Cambridge tracts in mathematics and mathematical physics. 13, 14).
6060

2 Cross Reference Entry

The Cross Reference Entries of an Artificial Composite Book are to be of two types:

1 Special; and
2 Ordinary.

21 SPECIAL CROSS REFERENCE ENTRY

A Special Cross Reference Entry is to be given from the Call Number of each of the second and the succeeding Constituent Works.

211 SECTIONS

A special Cross Reference Entry is to consist successively of the following sections:

1 Leading section consisting of the Call Number of the Constituent Work cross-referred;

2 Its Heading;

3 Its Title;

4 The descriptive term such as "*Bound as part* 2 *with*" or "*Printed as part* 2 *with*" as the case may be;

5 the Call Number in the Leading Section of the Main Entry; and

6 the Heading of the Main Entry, as prescribed in Chap MJ, the short title of the First Constituent Work, and a full stop.

Example:

1 B6363:23 N13.
WOOD (P W) ( ).
Twisted cubic with the cubical hyperbola.
Bound as part 2 *with*
B6363:23 N11
Henderson: Twenty-seven lines upon the cubic surface.

See Example 1 in Sec NB41 for the Main Entry.

22 ORDINARY CROSS REFERENCE ENTRY

An Ordinary Cross Reference Entry is to be given from every topic in each of the Constituent Works, which may call for it.

221 An Ordinary Cross Reference Entry is to be constructed as prescribed in Chap MJ, with the following modifications:

1 The Call Number, the Heading and the Short-title are to be those of the First Constituent Work;

2 Instead of page reference only, the part and the pages of reference, if any, are to be given; and

3 The descriptive term "*Composite book*" is to be added after the Call Number.

3 Class Index Entry

All the Class Index entries appropriate to each Constituent Work are to be given as prescribed in Part K.

4 Cross Reference Index Entry

All the Cross Reference Index Entries appropriate to each Constituent Work are to be given as prescribed in Part L.

5 Book Index Entry

All the Book Index Entries appropriate to each Constituent Work are to be given as prescribed in Chap MK, with the modification that, for the second and later constituent works, the Third and the Fourth Sections are to be as follows:

3 The Descriptive term such as "*Bound as part* 2 *with*" or "*Printed as part* 2 *with*," as the case may be; and

4 The Index Number of the First Constituent Work.

Example:

1 Wood (P W) ( ).
Twisted cubic.
Bound as part 2 with B6363:23 N11
See Example 1 in Sec NB44 for the Main Entry.

CHAPTER NC

MULTI-VOLUMED BOOK

0 Types

Two types of Multi-volumed Books are to be recognized, *viz:*

1 The Type in which the constituent volumes do not have a special title other than the common title of all the volumes and do not have any difference in the other factors that are capable of contributing to the title-portion of a Main Entry; and

2 Others.

1 Type 1

A multi-volumed book of the first type is to be catalogued like a simple book with the additional provisions given in the sub-divisions of this Sec.

13 Completed Set

If all the volumes of the book have been published, an additional sentence is to be added to the Title Section of the Main Entry. This additional sentence is to consist successively of the

1 Number representing the number of volumes constituting the book; and

2 Term "V" or its equivalent in the language of the title-page.

131 UNCOMPLETED SET

If all the volumes of the book have not yet been published, the additional sentence to be added is to consist successively of the

1 Term "V"; and

2 Numbers of the volumes published so far and a dash.

This additional sentence is to be in pencil.

In this case, the entry is said to be **Open.**

1311 As soon as all the volumes are received, the pencil portion of the Title Section is to be replaced in accordance with Sec 13.

132 INCOMPLETE SET

If all the volumes of the book, which have been published, are not possessed by the library, a further sentence is to be added to the Title Section, in square brackets. This sentence in brackets is to consist successively of the

1 Term "V";
2 Numbers representing the volumes not in the library; and
3 Term "not in library."

14 CROSS REFERENCE ENTRY

In the Cross Reference Entries the volume number is to be added whenever necessary.

15 BOOK INDEX ENTRY

In the Book Index Entries, the additional sentence prescribed in Sec 131 is to be repeated with the short title used in such Entries.

2 Second Type

A multi-volumed book of the second type is to be catalogued like the books of the first type with the additional provisions given in the subdivisions of this Sec.

21 ADDITIONAL PARAGRAPHS

Additional paragraphs are to be added in the Title Section of the Main Entry—one paragraph to correspond with each volume that has extra specific information in its title-page.

22 Content of Additional Paragraph

Each paragraph is to consist successively of the following:

1 The term "V";

2 The number of the volume;

3 A full stop;

4 The special title of the volume;

5 The term "by" followed by the names of the distinctive author(s) of the volume, if any;

51 A Full stop;

6 Term indicating the kind of collaboration followed by the names of distinctive collaborator(s), if any;

7 A full stop; and

8 A note in circular brackets, if necessary, to indicate any other special features.

221 NUMBERING OF VOLUMES

If the numbering of the volumes is not normal, the corresponding portions of the paragraphs are to follow what is given in the book.

222 COMMON SPECIAL TITLE

If two or more, but not all the volumes of a set, have a common special title, they are to be given only a single paragraph in common, in the additional section of the Main Entry, the numbers of all such volumes being written after the term "V" or its equivalent.

23 Book Index Entry

The Book Index Entries of the Book are to include all such additional Entries as are relevant to the special Title Section of the different volumes, given in the Main Entry.

3 Call Number

The Call Numbers of the volumes of a Multi-volumed Simple Book are to consist of their common Class Number, followed by their successive Book Numbers. If the publication is in progress, the last Book Number is to be followed by a dash.

32 In Cross Reference Entry

If a Cross-Reference is to some and not to all the volumes of the set, the third section of the corresponding Cross Reference Entry is to give only the Book Numbers of the volumes to which reference is made.

37 Abnormal Size

If some and not all of the volumes of a set are undersized or oversized or abnormal, the underlining, etc, is to be made to the Book Numbers of those volumes only.

Examples:

1 X XN20.1—N20.2
TAUSSIG (Frank William).
Principles of economics. Ed 2. 2V.
10101; 10013

2 O-,3L71*w* N32.1-N32.4—
SCOTT (Walter) (1771).
Letters. Ed by H J C Grierson, etc V 14—
V 1. 1787-1807.
V 2. 1808-1911.
V 3. 1811-4.
V 4. 1814-7.
73352-4; 73778

It is assumed that this publication is still in progress. The last Book Number is, therefore followed by a dash and the corresponding volume part of the Title-Portion is to be in pencil.

It is obvious that the detailed information about the contents of each volume given above will be of help to readers.

3 E1*a*N1 N12.1-N12.4
HOFFMANN (M K) (1878), *Ed.*
Dictionary of the inorganic compounds.
3V in 4.
V 1. Part 1. Introd etc and water to silver, N 1-31.
Part 2. Mercury to boron, N 32-55.
V 2. Aluminium to xenon N 56-58. Bibliographies.
V 3. Calculation table, index, etc. (This volume has A Thiel as additional editor).
11520—11523

In this case, the book has its title in four languages, *viz*, English, German, French, and Italian. Hence, the entry is made as if English were the favoured language of the library. It may be noted that the name of an additional joint editor appears on the title page of the third volume and that this information is conveyed in the entry by an appropriate note. A Thiel would give rise to a Joint Editor Entry.

It is obvious that the detailed information about the contents of each volume given above will be of help to readers.

PART P

PERIODICAL PUBLICATION

Note: The examples given in this Part are as they were in the First Edition of this book. That is, the changes in the Complexities of the Periodicals, which occurred after 1933 are not indicated in the sections recording the complexities. But this does not affect their value as mere examples.

CHAPTER PA

COMPLEXITIES

1 Introduction

The definition of the term "Periodical Publication" has been given in Sec FF11. Periodical Publications form one of the sources of perplexity in cataloguing practice. Their vagaries may transcend all imagination and anticipation. It looks as if nothing relating to a Periodical Publication can escape the sport of caprice—sponsor, name, periodicity, format, pagination, excrescential attachments to all or stray volumes, and, last but not least, span of life and resurrection.

11 For convenience, Chap PB confines itself to Periodical Publications of the simple type, *i e* those that are free from vagaries of any kind. The later chapters will be devoted to the additional treatment that must be given to Periodical Publications presenting complexities of different kinds.

2 Kinds of Complexity

Periodical Publications may present one or more of the following kinds of complexities.

20 Irregularity in Volume-Number

21 Change in volume-periodicity.

22 Volumes being numbered in two or more sequences, the sequences being termed New Series, First Series, Second Series, etc, or by similar names.

23 Volumes being numbered simultaneously in two or more sequences.

30 Irregularity in Publication

31 Non-publication of volumes in certain periods, but the sequence of volume numbers being continuous.

32 Break in the sequence or irregularity in the numbering of volumes due to non-publication or other causes.

33 Two or more volumes published as a single volume or bound as a single volume.

40 Change of Title and Sponsor

41 Change of title, or of sponsor, or of both, but the numbering of the volumes being continued in the original sequence.

42 Change of title, or of sponsor or of both, with change in the sequence of volume numbers.

50 Amalgamation

51 Amalgamation of two or more Periodical Publications under the title of one of the amalgamated Publications, and the numbering of the volumes continued in its original sequence.

52 Amalgamation of two or more Periodical Publications under the title of one of the amalgamated Publications but with change in the sequence of volume numbers.

53 Amalgamation of two or more Periodical Publications under a new title with its Class Number the same as that of one of the Publications amalgamated.

54 Amalgamation of two or more Periodical Publications under a new title and with its Class Number different from that of any of them.

60 Splitting

61 Splitting up into two or more Periodical Publications with one of them having the original Class Number.

62 Splitting up into two or more Periodical Publications, the original Class Number not being borne by any of them.

63 Multiple Periodical of which the issues contain two or more periodicals, with or without a Generic Title, but has to be split into independent periodicals, either associated or not, on the completion of a volume.

70 Supplement

71 Having monograph supplements or book supplements without separate pagination and title-page.

72 Having monograph supplements or book supplements with separate pagination and title-page.

73 Having a sequence of supplementary or extra volumes having separate pagination and title-page, and each capable of being regarded as a Periodical Publication by itself.

74 The supplements of the kinds 72 and 73 being covered by the cumulative indexes of the main Periodical Publication.

8 Plan of Work

Following the example of Mathematicians we shall first confine ourselves to each kind of complexity by itself—that is, uncomplicated by association with other kinds of complexity. We shall consider and develop the technique necessary to meet each individual complexity. We shall illustrate in the final chapter—Chap PJ—how a combination of complexities is to be treated.

CHAPTER PB

SIMPLE PERIODICAL PUBLICATION

1 Main Entry

10 SECTIONS

The Main Entry of a simple Periodical Publication is to consist successively of Sec giving the following:

1 Leading Section;
2 Heading;
3 Periodicity;
4 Series Note, if any;
5 Holdings; and
6 Tracing.

11 LEADING SECTION

The Leading Section is to consist of the Class Number of the Periodical Publication.

111 SOURCE

The Class Number is to be taken from the back of the title-page.

It will be seen from Sec MC1 that the Leading Section of the Main Entry of a book consists of its Call Number. But in the case of a Periodical Publication, the Leading Section is to consist only of the class number. It is so because the main entry of a Periodical Publication stands, not for one volume, but for an indefinite number of its volumes to be added from time to time. *See* Sec PB15.

12 HEADING

The Heading of the Main Entry of a simple Periodical Publication is to consist successively of

1 Its title proper, omitting the name of its sponsor, if any, occurring in continuation of its title proper;

2 A comma; and

3 The name of its sponsor, if any.

121 NAME OF THE SPONSOR

The name of the sponsor, if any, is to be put within circular brackets, if it does not occur in continuation of the title proper on the title-page.

The first two words of the title proper are to be written in block letters, as prescribed in Sec JF4.

1211 Nominative Case

The name of the sponsor, if any, is to be written in the nominative case.

122 INDIVIDUALISING ELEMENT

If the title proper of a Periodical Publication taken along with the name of the sponsor, if any, does not individualise it, an Individualising Element is to be added.

The Individualising Element is to be written in ordinary hand and enclosed within circular brackets, as prescribed in Sec ED83.

1221 Choice

The Individualising Element in the Heading of a Periodical Publication is to be the name of its country, state, province, district, county, taluk, city, or town—that one of these areas which has the greatest extension and is sufficient for individualisation.

Examples:

1 EDUCATIONAL REVIEW (India).
2 EDUCATIONAL REVIEW (United States of America).
3 FREE PRESS (Bombay).
4 FREE PRESS (Madras).

123 CONFERENCE PROCEEDINGS

If a Periodical Publication consists of the Proceedings of a Conference held periodically, the place and the year of the Conference, prescribed by Sec JE2 for inclusion in the Heading, are to be omitted.

13 SECTION ON PERIODICITY

The Section on Periodicity is to consist successively of

1 Statement of Periodicity as prescribed in Sec 131, 132, and 133 of this Chap.

2 A fullstop;

3 The term "V";

4 The number of the first volume (which will usually, but not necessarily in all cases, be 1);

5 A dash;

6 Some space and a semicolon;

7 The year of commencement; and

8 A dash.

130 The Section on Periodicity is to be enclosed in square brackets.

131 If the period is one year or less, the Statement of Periodicity is to consist successively of

1 The number indicating the number of volumes per year;

2 The term "V per year";

3 A semicolon;

4 The number of separately bound parts in a volume, if more than one;

5 The term "parts per volume" if it is operative; and

6 A fullstop.

132 If the period is greater than one year, the Statement of Periodicity is to consist successively of

1 The term "1 V for";

2 The number indicating the number of years;

3 The term "years";

4 A semicolon;

5 The number of separately bound parts in a volume, if more than one;

6 The term "parts per volume" if it is operative; and

7 A fullstop.

133 If the Periodical Publication is irregular, the Statement of Periodicity is to begin with the term "Irregular."

134 If the Periodical Publication continues to be published whether taken in the library or not, no figure is to be added after the dashes within the square brackets.

1341 If Sec PB134 is applicable, the entry is said to be **"Open for the Publication."**

135 If the Periodical Publication has ceased to be published, the number of the volume and of the year of the last published volume are to be inserted after the respective dashes, within the square brackets.

1351 If Sec PB135 is applicable, the entry is said to be **"Closed for the Publication."**

This Volume Periodicity Note may have to get its information from outside the publication itself. That is why it is directed to be enclosed in square brackets. It may not be possible to get at the year of commencement of some periodical publications. But the cataloguer should spare no efforts to hunt for the information in all possible bibliographical sources and should not rest until he has succeeded in his effort. The chapter entitled "Bibliographical suggestions" in the *Guide to the cataloguing of the serial publications of societies and institutions* published by the Library of Congress maps out for him the regions where he must hunt for information. No doubt this process may often take an indefinite length of time. That does not mean that the cataloguing should be postponed and the periodical publication should be held up in the cataloguer's unsolved heap, until the information sought is obtained. Such a procedure would go quite against all the Laws of Library Science. On the other hand, what should be done is to release the publication for public use, leaving the space, within the square brackets in the catalogue card, blank. A list of such incomplete cards should be maintained so that they may not be forgotten. The blank space is to be filled in as and when the necessary information is obtained.

14 Series Note

The Series Note, if any, is to be enclosed in circular brackets and is to be constructed in accordance with Sec MF1 and its subdivisions, except that the serial numbers of all the volumes of the Periodical Publication are to be given in succession at the end of the note. Further, if the first volume of the set does not belong to the series, the volume number or in its absence the year number of the earliest volume of the set which belongs to the series is to be written as the denominator under its corresponding Serial Number. If any of the later volumes of the set happen to go off the series, the volume number, or in its absence the year, of the next earliest volume that belongs to the series is to be written as a denominator under its corresponding Serial Number; and so on.

15 Holdings Section

In the case of the Library having a continuous set of volumes of the Periodical Publication, the Holdings Section is to consist successively of

1 The term "This library has";

2 The term "V";

3 The numbers of the volumes available in the library, if the volumes of the Periodical Publication are numbered;

4 A semicolon; and

5 The years of the volumes available in the library.

By the "year of the volume" is meant, the year covered by the volume which may not necessarily be the year of publication of the volume. See, for instance, Example 2 under Sec PB21.

153 The statement of the number of volumes available in the library is to consist successively of

1 The number of the earliest volume available in the library;

2 A dash; and

3 The number of the latest volume available in the library.

155 The statement of the years of the volumes available in the library is to consist successively of

1 The year of the earliest volume available in the library;

2 A dash; and

3 The year of the latest volume available in the library.

156 If the Periodical Publication is current in the library, the numbers of the latest volume and of its year are to be written in pencil.

1561 If the Periodical Publication is current in the library, the entry is said to be "Open for the Library."

157 If the Periodical Publication is discontinued in the library, the numbers of the last available volume and of its year are to be inked.

1571 If the Periodical Publication is discontinued in the library, the entry is said to be **"Closed for the Library."**

The idea in writing the numbers of the volume and of the year of the latest volume in pencil, if the Periodical Publication is current in the library, is that they will be changed into the succeeding numbers as soon as the succeeding volume gets completed and accessioned. Some libraries do not write these numbers even in pencil, but leave their places blank. Knowing as we do, the notorious impunctuality of the periodicals, it is seldom possible to guess the number and the year of the last completed volume. The simple device suggested in these Rules has been found to be a source of great relief both to the reference staff and to the readers.

158 In the case of the library having a discontinuous set of the Periodical Publication, for each continuous block of the set, the information covered by the categories 2 to 5 of Sec 15 of this chapter is to be written as a single block.

1581 The blocks of information so given are to be in the increasing sequence of the numbers of their respective volumes or year.

1582 Each block of information so given is to be separated from its succeeding block by a fullstop.

1583 *Examples*

See Example 1 among the following *Examples:*

Note: In the examples of this Part, the numbers to be written in pencil as per Sec PB156 are shown in antique type.

1 *n*1,M

STATESMAN'S YEAR book, etc.

[1 V per year. V1—; 1864—].

This library has V1-21; 1864-84. V23-30; 1887-93. V65-70; 1928-33.

The term "etc" represents the term "statistical and historical annual of the states of the world."

The library has a broken set of this Serial. But it is current in the library.

2 *w*73*n*M9

WHO'S WHO in America, etc.

[1 V for 2 years. V1—; 1899/1900-].

This library has V 16; 1930/31

The term "etc" represents the term "a biographical dictionary of notable living men and the women of the United States."

The library has got only one volume of this Serial. But it continues to be published. This entry is "closed for the library," but is "open for the publication."

3 *z*.4411,t41,M*n*

CALENDAR, Presidency College (Madras).

[1V per year. -].

This library has 1926/27-1933/34

The volumes of this Serial are not numbered. The 'year of the volume' is the only factor distinguishing the volumes from one another. The information about the year of commencement of the serial is not available. Therefore, its space within the square brackets is left blank. It is to be filled up as soon as the information is got.

This Serial is current in the library.

4 *z*.73,*g*,C*r*

YEAR BOOK, Carnegie Institution of Washington.

[1 V per year. V1- ; 1902-].

This library has V1-31; 1902-32.

The library has an unbroken set of this Serial. It is also current in the library.

5 *z*44*m*44,M7

INDIAN ANTIQUARY etc.

[1 V per year. V 1-62; 1872-1933].

This library has V 3-62; 1874-1933.

The term "etc" represents the term "a journal of oriental research in archeology, epigraphy, ethnology, geography, history, folklore, languages, literature, numismatics, philosophy, religion, etc, etc."

This entry is both "closed for the publication" and "closed for the library."

6 I*m*56,M8

ANNALS OF botany.

[1 V per year. V 1- ; 1887-].

This library has V 1-47; 1887-1933.

This Periodical continues to be published. The library has an unbroken set. It is current in the library.

7 W,6*m*44,N3

LOCAL SELF-GOVERNMENT quarterly, (Madras Chamber of Local Boards).

[1 V per year. V 1- ; 1931/32-].

This library has V 1-2; 1931/32-1932/33.

In this example and in example 3, the "year of the volume" is not a calendar year, but an artificial year spread over two calendar years. But in example 2, a similar notation stands for two full calendar years. This homonym in notation has not yet been resolved. However the Statement of Periodicity makes this difference clear.

8 Z438y7m438,N
INDIAN LAW reports, Rangoon series etc, (Burma, High Court).
[1 V per year. V 1- ;1923-].
This library has V 1-11; 1923-33.

16 TRACING SECTION

161 The Tracing Section of the Main Entry—that is, the back of the Main Card—of a Periodical Publication is to furnish

1 On the left half

the Number, the Year Number, the Book Number, and the Accession Number, of each volume, in a tabular form using inclusive notation, wherever possible; and

2 On the right half

21 The Call Number used for each Cross Reference Entry, along with the indication of its locus;

22 The Heading used for each Class Index Entry; and

23 The Heading used for each Class Index Entry arising out of each Cross Reference entry.

162 In the case of the Proceedings of a Periodical Conference, the information to be furnished about each volume of the Conference, in the left half, is to include the Name of the Place of the Conference between the Number of the Year and the Book Number.

163 In case the number of lines in Tracing Section exceeds the capacity of the back of the Main Card, the information is to be continued both in the front and the back of the necessary number of Continuation Cards.

Examples:

1 For Example 6 in Sec PB1583, the Tracing Section will need two continuation cards. It should be written as follows:

1	1887	M87	2345	Botany,
2	1888	M88	2987	Periodical, Botany
3	1889	M89	3424	Great Britain, Periodical, Botany
		etc		Annals of botany

Note 1: The second of the Class Index Entries implied in the above, will be useful in answering the question, "In what subjects has the library Periodicals ?"

Note 2: The third of the Class Index Entries, implied in the above, will be useful in answering the question, "In what subjects has the library British Periodicals ?"

Note 3: The two above-mentioned Class Index Entries are subject to the Principle of Local Variation.

2 Cross Reference Entry

20 No Cross Reference Entry is to be given for a Periodical Publication, except for a volume of it, containing only a single work or a Festschrift or forming a special volume in any other sense, admitting of its being looked upon as a Simple or Ordinary Composite Book.

21 A Cross Reference Entry for a Periodical Publication is to consist successively of the following sections:

1 The Leading Section consisting of the volume would get, if classified as an independent work (Leading Section);

2 The Directing Element "*See*"; and

3 The Locus Section consisting successively of sections giving

31 The Class Number of the Periodical Publication;

32 The Heading of the Periodical Publication; and

33 The Locus Section in the form;

331 The term "V"; and

332 The Number of the volume or its year or both, according to the information available.

Examples:

1 B *p*77N30
See
B*m*44,N0
BULLETIN, Calcutta Mathematical Society.
V 20; 1928.

The title-page of this volume reads as follows:

"Commemoration volume | on the occasion of the | twentieth anniversary | of the foundation of | the Calcutta Mathematical Society in 1928 | bulletin | Vol. XX."

It may be stated here that the volume was actually published only in 1930, as shown in the imprint. But, 1928 is the "year of the volume," as prescribed by the commentary on Sec PB15.

2 P15,25A*x*1,T M71
See
*z*4*m*73,M
JOURNAL, American Oriental Society.
V 9; 1871.

This ninth volume is made of a single work *Taittiriyapratisakhya*. In fact, the title of the work appears on the first page of the volume as follows:

"The Taittirīya-prātiśākhyā with the commentary, the Tribhaṣyaratna text, translation, and notes, by William D Whitney, professor of Sanskrit in Yale College."

3 Class Index Entry

31 Sought Link

The Last Link contributed by the Class Number of a Periodical Publication is a Sought Link.

32 Unsought Link

If a Periodical Publication is one associated with another, the Link forming the Class Number of the Host Periodical Publication is to be taken as an **Unsought Link.**

See Rule 21*m*3 of the *Colon classification* for an explanation of the term Associated Periodical Publication.

Example:

1 B*m*44,N Journal, Indian Mathematical Society; and

2 B*m*44,N,1 Mathematics Student, (Indian Mathematical Society)

are Associated with each other. The former is the Host and the latter is the Associated Periodical.

In the Chain derived from the Class Number of the latter, B*m*44,N is an Unsought Link.

33 Heading for Last Link

In accordance with Sec KD3, the Heading of the Class Index Entry contributed by the Last Link of the Class Number of a Periodical Publication is to be the same as that of its Main Entry.

34 Additional Class Index Entries

Corresponding to the Last Link of the Class Number of a Periodical Publication, a Class Index Entry is to be written, using as Heading each of the following also:

1 Every Alternative Name, including contracted name or initionym, by which the Periodical Publication is popularly referred to among its users;

2 In the case of a sponsored Periodical Publication, the Heading got by interchanging the name of the Sponsor and the Title of the Periodical Publication; and

3 Every variation got by substituting every Alternative Name of the Sponsor in the Heading prescribed in category 2.

341 PUNCTUATION MARK

When the Heading is one prescribed by kind 2 or 3 of Sec PB4 a Comma is to be inserted between the name of the Sponsor and the Title-Proper, unless the whole Title of the Periodical Publication begins with the name of the Sponsor.

35 OMISSION OF DIRECTING SECTION

In a Class Index Entry of a Periodical Publication having a Heading either as shown in commentary PB33 or as prescribed in Sec PB34, the Directing Section, prescribed by Sec KF2, is to be omitted.

Examples:

Note: In the following example, the Class Index Entries for the Upper Links are omitted.

Example 2 under Sec PB 1583 is to get the following Index Entry:

1 WHO'S WHO in America. *w73n*M9

The Zeitschrift der Deutschen morgenlandischen Gesellschaft is to get the following Main and Class Index Entries:

2 *z4m55*,M

ZEITSCHRIFT, Deutschen Morgenlandischen Gesellschaft.

The third and the later Sections are omitted in the above Main Entry.

3 ZEITSCHRIFT, Deutschen Morgenlandischen Gesellschaft *z4m55*,M

4 Z D M G *z4m55*,M

The last is the familiar name by which this Periodical is asked for by the students of Asian culture.

5 DEUTSCHEN MORGENLANDISCHEN GESELLSCHAFT, Zeitschrift. *z4m55*,M

The Journal of the Indian Mathematical Society is to get the following Main and Class Index Entries

6 Bm44,N
JOURNAL, Indian Mathematical Society.

The third and the later Sections are omitted in the above Main Entry.

7 JOURNAL, Indian Mathematical Society. Bm44,N

8 INDIAN MATHEMATICAL SOCIETY, Journal Bm44,N

The Journal für die reine und angewandte Mathematik is to get the following Main and Class Index Entry:

9 Bm55,M
JOURNAL FÜR die reine und angewandte Mathematik.

The third and the later Sections are omitted in the above Main Entry.

10 JOURNAL FÜR die reine und angewandte Mathematik. Bm55,M

11 CRELLE's JOURNAL Bm55,M

This is the name by which it is familiarly asked for by the students of mathematics.

Example 3 in Sec PB1583 is to get the following Class Index Entries:

12 CALENDAR, Presidency College (Madras). z.4411,t41,Mn

13 PRESIDENCY COLLEGE (Madras), Calendar. z.4411,t41,Mn

Example 7 in Sec PB1583 is to get the following Class Index Entries:

14 LOCAL SELF-GOVERNMENT quarterly, (Madras Chamber of Local Boards). W,6m44,N3

15 MADRAS CHAMBER OF LOCAL BOARDS, Local self-government quarterly. W,6m44,N3

Example 8 in Sec PB1583 is to get the following Class Index Entries:

16 INDIAN LAW reports, Rangoon series, (Burma, High Court). Z438y7m438,N

17 RANGOON LAW reports, (Burma, High Court). Z438y7m438,N

18 BURMA LAW reports, (Burma, High Court). Z438y7m438,N

19 BURMA, HIGH COURT, Indian law reports, Rangoon series. Z438y7m438,N

36 LOCAL VARIATION

The following Sec allow of Local Variation.

37 GENERIC CLASS INDEX ENTRY

1 Generic Class Index Entry with the Heading "Periodical" or "Serial," as the case may be, may be written for the Periodical Publication, corresponding to each of its Specific Class Index Entries.

371 The Second and the Third Sections of a Generic Class Index Entry of a Periodical Publication are to consist, respectively of:

2 The Heading of the Specific Class Index Entry to which it corresponds; and

3 The Class Number of the Periodical Publication.

Example 6 in Sec PB35 may get the following Generic Class Index Entries:

1 PERIODICAL.
Journal, Indian Mathematical Society. Bm44,N

2 PERIODICAL.
Indian Mathematical Society, Journal. Bm44,N

Example, 12 in Sec PB35 may get the following Generic Class Index Entries:

3 SERIAL.
Calendar, Presidency College (Madras). z.4411,t41,Mn

4 SERIAL.
Presidency College (Madras), Calendar. z.4411,t41,Mn

38 OPTIONAL CLASS INDEX ENTRIES

Class Index Entries may be given for a Periodical Publication corresponding to the Links of its Class Number ending with the Common Isolate Digit and the Geographical Isolate Number respectively.

Example:

Example 6 in Sec PB35 may get the following Optional Class Index Entries:

1 INDIA, PERIODICAL, MATHEMATICS. Bm44

2 GERMANY, PERIODICAL, MATHEMATICS. Bm55

3 PERIODICAL, MATHEMATICS. Bm

Example 16 in Sec PB35 may get the following Optional Class Index Entries:

4 BURMA, REPORT, BURMA, LAW. Z438y7m438

5 REPORT, BURMA, LAW. Z438y7m

4 Cross Reference Index Entry

No Cross Reference Index Entry is necessary for a Periodical Publication.

Its purpose—*viz* to provide entries to link up alternative names of a Periodical Publication—is served by the Class Index Entries prescribed in Sec PB33 and PB34.

5 Book Index Entry

50 No Book Index Entry is to be given to a Periodical Publication, as such.

51 Any book, contained in a Periodical Publication and given a Cross Reference Entry as prescribed in Sec PB2 and PB21, is to be given its Book Index Entries.

52 A Book Index Entry given according to Sec PB51 is to have a Locus Section as prescribed in Sec PB21, instead of the Index Section prescribed in Sec MK0.

6 Cumulative Index

In the case of a volume constituting a cumulative index of a Periodical Publication, there is to be only a Main Entry consisting of the following Sections written in accordance with the earlier rules appropriate to them:

1 The Leading Section consisting of the Call Number;

2 Heading, which is to be the same as for the Periodical Publication to which it relates; and

3 Extract from the title-page, indicating the nature and scope of the index.

Example:

1 l*m*56,M8 *b*N01
Annals of botany.
Index to V 1-10; 1887-96.

CHAPTER PC

IRREGULARITY IN VOLUME-NUMBER

1 Change in Volume-Periodicity

In the case of complexity of kind 21 enumerated in Sec PA2, a separate Main Card is to be made for each Volume-Periodicity.

11 The Class Number in each such card being the same, all such cards are to be treated as a set of 'continued cards' as per Chap EF.

12 The entry in all but the last card of the set is to be 'closed for the publication' as provided in Sec PB1351.

2 Volume Number in Different Sequences

In the case of complexity of kind 22 enumerated in Sec PA2 a separate Main Card is to be made for each sequence with the name of the series extra-polated before the term "V" in the the Volume-Periodicity Section and the Holdings Section.

21 The Class Number in each such card being the same, all such cards are to be treated as a set of 'continued cards' as per chap EF.

22 The entry in all but the last card of the set is to be 'closed for publication' as provided in Sec PB1571.

See Examples 3.3 to 3.12 given in Sec PJ6.

3 Volume-Number Simultaneously in many Sequences

In the case of complexity of kind 23 enumerated in Sec PA2, Sec PC2 and its subdivisions are to be applied with the following modification:

Wherever the numbering of volumes occurs, the number in the alternative sequence is to be inter-polated after the one in the other sequence in circular brackets as in examples 2.1 to 3.16 given in Sec PJ6.

Which sequence is to be shown within brackets is a question to be decided according to the circumstances of each case,—according to the prominence given in the publication itself to one or other of the sequences.

CHAPTER PD

INTERRUPTED PUBLICATION

1 Suspension without Break in Volume Number

In the case of complexity of kind 31 enumerated in Sec PA2, an additional section is to be added in crooked brackets, after the Holding Section, consisting successively of the

1 Term "No V in"; and
2 Year(s) corresponding to which there is no volume.

This complexity is of frequent occurrence. For example, the *Annual report* of the American Bison Society, which started in 1905 as volume 1, is still continued, but there were no issues in 1921 and 1922.

Many periodicals seem to have suffered an interruption during the World War. For example, the *Journal* of the Association of Official Agricultural Chemists (Washington D C), which started in 1915, has been regularly coming out as one volume per year except for the interruption during the years 1917-1919; with the result, the number of the volume for 1920 is 3 and not 6. Again the *Isis*, started by the History of Sciences Society (Washington D C) in 1913, had to be suspended from July 1914 to August 1919; with the result, while the 1913 volume is numbered as 1, the volume for 1920 is numbered as 2 instead of 8. So also the *Carolina journal of pharmacy* started by the North Carolina Pharmaceutical Association in 1915 was suspended from 1918 to 1921; with the result, the volume for 1922 is numbered 4 instead of 8.

Here is a case of infantile mortality. The *Journal* of the Portland Society of Natural History whose first number of the first volume came out in 1864 has not till now sent out a second number. Further, in the case of another Periodical emanating from the same body under the title *Proceedings*, 4 volumes have come out between the years 1862 and 1930. But the Society still continues to be active and nobody can prophecy that further volumes will not come.

Another case of what appears to be one of a long drawn out infantile mortality was characterised by actual resurrection a century later. "The Connecticut Academy of Arts and Sciences was organised and chartered by the State in the year 1799. In 1810 it issued the first part of Vol 1 of the *Memoirs* of the Academy ... Part 2 of this volume appeared in 1811, Part 3 in 1813, and 4 in 1816 ... Since 1816 papers read before the Academy have, to a considerable extent, found their way to be published through the *American journal of science* the first number of which was issued in August 1818."

[A2]. As a matter of fact the very first article in N 1 of V 1 of the *American journal of science* is the *Essay on musical temperament* by Prof Fisher of Yale College, which is published with the following note: "From the MS papers of the Connecticut Academy, now published by permission." The career of the *Memoirs* of the Connecticut Academy of Arts and Sciences, which took seven years to complete its first volume, was believed to have come to an end. As has been indicated in the passage already quoted, the *Memoirs* was published in the *American journal of science* from 1818 to 1865. In 1866, the Academy commenced its second Periodical under the title of *Transactions* and the *Memoirs* was published in it from 1866 to 1909. But to the surprise of all and even while the *Transactions* was still in progress and after an interval of nearly a century, V 2 of the *Memoirs* came out in 1910, thereby establishing a record in suspended animation. Unfortunately, however, it was not able to keep to time; and since the seventh volume came out in 1920 instead of 1915, nothing is yet known whether it is actually dead or has gone into another spell of suspended animation, though its younger sister, the *Transactions*, from which it broke away in 1910, still appears to be progressing quite normally.

Here are some examples of Main Entries relating to complexity of this kind:

Examples:

1 A*vm*73,N

ISIS, (History of Science Society) (Washington D C).

[1 V per year. V 1—; 1913-].

This library has V 1-15 1913-23.

{No V in 1914-19}.

2 J:(E)*m*73,N

JOURNAL, Association of Official Agricultural Chemists (Washington D C).

[1 V per year. V 1—; 1915-].

This library has V 1-16; 1915-33.

{No V in 1917-9}.

2 Suspension with Break in Volume Number

In the case of complexity of kind 32 enumerated in Sec PA2, an Additional Note is to be added in crooked brackets, after the Section on Periodicity, consisting successively of the

1 Term "V"; *Either*

21 Number(s) of the volume(s) not published; *or*

22 Term "for the year(s)"; and

221 Number(s) of the Year(s) of the volume(s) not published; and

3 Term "not published."

This complexity does not occur as frequently as complexity of kind 31. But it is by no means absent. The *Transactions* of the American Laryngological, Rhinological and Otological Society exist only from volume 2 published in 1896. It appears that volume 1 was never published. Another case of this type is that of the *Proceedings* of the Certified Milk Producers' Association of America whose published volumes number from 3, dated 1910, volumes 1 and 2 not having been published.

Here is another queer case. In the case of the *Transactions* of the American Otological Society, the first number of the first volume was issued only in manuscript and V 2 was published with the *Proceedings* of the American Ophthalmological Society, with the result, the set of the *Transactions* does not have the second volume, and the first volume is incomplete. Again volumes 2 and 5-7 of the *Proceedings* of the Potato Association of America have not been published, though the other volumes have been coming out regularly.

In the case of the irregular Periodical called *Percolator* and published by the Chemists' Club (New York City), the first five volumes were published in 1909-1922. From 1922-1925, numbers 56-62 of the publication came out without being grouped as volumes at all. But the numbers of 1926 claimed to form part of volume 8 of the publication. Similarly, the *Engineers bulletin* published by the Colorado Society of Engineers sent out its first 55 numbers between the years 1918 and 1922 and made no attempt to group them into volumes. But from 1923 onwards, the numbers coming out in a year are made into a volume, the 1923 volume being numbered 7.

Here is an example of the Main Entry for complexity of this type.

Example:

1 KX31*m*73,N
PROCEEDINGS, Certified Milk Producers' Association of America.
[1 V per year. V 3—; 1920-].
{ V 1-2 not published }.
This library has V 3-16; 1920-33.

3 Clubbed Volumes

In the case of complexity of kind 33 enumerated in PA2, an Additional Note is to be added in crooked brackets after the Section on Periodicity, consisting successively of:

1 The term '*Published together*' or *Bound together*,' as the case may be;

2 Specification of each set of volumes published or bound together, prescribed by; *either*

211 The term 'V' followed by the numbers of the volumes forming the set;

212 Semicolon; and

213 The years of the volumes forming the set; *or*

22 The years alone if the volumes are not numbered; and

3 A fullstop between the successive blocks of such information about the respective sets, if there are two or more sets.

See Examples 2.1 and 2.2 in Chap PJ.

CHAPTER PE

CHANGE OF TITLE AND SPONSOR

1 Without Change in Sequence of Volume Number

In the case of complexity of kind 41 enumerated in Sec PA2 a separate Main Card is to be made for each different title and heading.

11 The Class Number in each such card being the same, the cards are to be treated as a set of 'continued cards' as per Chap EF.

12 The entry in all but the last card of the set is to be 'closed for publication' and also 'closed for the library' as provided in Sec PB135 and PB157.

Both the change of name of a Periodical Publication and the change of name of the sponsoring body occur rather frequently. Very few publications escape this complexity. A case is reported of a Society changing its name 41 times in 14 years. Sometimes the change of title is such as to tempt the classifier even to give a different Class Number. But the fact that the volumes are consecutively numbered or that there is a cumulative index covering all the titles prevents one from changing the Class Number to suit the change of title. This is illustrated in the examples given at the end of this chapter, and in the examples given at the end of these remarks.

Here are some less serious changes. The year 1905 saw the foundation of the National Association of Cement Users at Detroit, Machigan. In 1913, it had its name changed as American Concrete Institute. It has been responsible for a Periodical, called *Proceedings* from 1905 to 1913, *Journal* from 1914 to 1915 and again *Proceedings* since 1916. The numbers of all the volumes run, however, in one continuous sequence.

Again the American Electro-therapeutic Association, founded in 1890, took over the Periodical *Medical library* which had been running its course from 1883 without a 'learned' god-father, changed its name to *Journal of electro-therapeutics*, but continued the old sequence in numbering the volumes. Thus the first volume of the *Journal of electro-therapeutics* came out in 1890 as volume 8. In 1902, the Publication was given another name and so volumes 20 to 33 (1902-1915) appeared under the more high sounding name *Journal of advanced therapeutics*. The way in which this name came to be adopted is told [P1] by its editor in the following words:

"At the annual meeting of the American Electro-therapeutic Association, held in Buffalo in 1901, as prospective Editor of the Journal and with the consent of the Publisher, the Association accepted the Journal under the

Editor's management, as the Official Organ of the Association. Under that arrangement and with the co-operation of the leading members of the American Electro-therapeutic Association the first issue was prepared for January first, 1902. It was first decided that the Journal should appear thereafter as the American Journal of Electrology and Radiology, and an issue was prepared under that title. At the urgent request of the publisher, however, who wished to combine the Journal with another publication of his own, the name adopted and appearing in a second issue of the first volume was the Journal of Advanced Therapeutics."

However, the original idea, which seems to have been simmering in the mind of the Association, ultimately gained the upper hand and from 1916 to 1925, volumes 34 to 43 came out under the long title *American journal of electro-therapeutics and radiology.* But with volume 44 which came out in 1926, a further change in name led to the title *Physical therapeutics*, the name of the Association itself having been changed later in October 1929 into American Physical Therapy Association as if in conformity with this title, as a result of merging itself with the Western Association of Physical Therapy. God alone knows what further nomenclative future is lying hidden in the womb of time for this Periodical. The April issue of 1932 was the last number of this Periodical. A circular about it said: "PHYSICAL THERAPEUTICS, the official journal of the American Physical Therapy Association, will hereafter be incorporated by the ARCHIVES OF PHYSICAL THERAPY, X-RAY, RADIUM, the official journal of the American Congress of Physical Therapy, since the American Physical Therapy Association has merged its interests with those of the American Congress of Physical Therapy . . . The unexpired part of your subscription is now assumed by the ARCHIVES OF PHYSICAL THERAPY, X-RAY, RADIUM and you will, commencing with the February, 1933 issue, receive the ARCHIVES for the unexpired term of your subscription to PHYSICAL THERAPEUTICS." All honour, however, for the consistency in the volume periodicity and the persistence in one and only one uninterrupted sequence of volume numbers.

Here is a more chequered career. The year 1895 saw the birth of the *New Jersey forester*. Even before the first volume was completed its name was changed as *Forester*. This name was allowed till the seventh volume came out in 1901. The hospitality of its pages was thrown open in 1898 to accommodate the *Proceedings* of the American Forestry Association. This Association had as its old name American Forestry Congress. This name was assumed in 1882. But it was changed to American Forestry Association in 1889. With volume 8 which came out in 1902, the Periodical was given the longer name *Forestry and irrigation*. But in the middle of volume 14 and the middle of year 1905, while only 8 of the issues of volume 14 had come out, it appears to have been paralysed. It was revived in 1908 under the title *Conservation*. But when it was revived it recollected its previous existence exactly and insisted that the first issue of the *Conservation* should be brought out as volume 14 number 9. However, this incarnation was but shortlived. It had to change again in 1910 and have its back gilted as

American forestry. This name continued for V 16-29; 1910-23. Again volume 30 which came out in 1924 brought with it another life for our many-lifed publication under the more comprehensive appellation *American forests and forest life*. We wish this hardy fellow many more births coupled with the correct memory of his sequence of volume numbers.

Sometimes the change in the name is very slight and imperceptible. For example, the Periodical, known as *Journal of abnormal psychology and social psychology* from 1906, changed its name in 1926 to *Journal of abnormal and social psychology*.

Sometimes the learned societies themselves appear to be subject to slip of memory. For example, the Illinois State Academy of Science which started its career in 1907 began its *Transactions* even in its first year of life and is still continuing it. But from 1911 to 1917 it appears to have forgetfully named them as *Transactions* of the Illinois Academy of Science. It is not known who reminded it of the propriety of reinstating the 'State' at the proper place in 1918.

A more quixotic forgetfulness, on the part of a learned body, of its own name and a more vagarious change of the name of its only Periodical is illustrated by the following: The Medical Association of Georgia saw the light of day in 1849. Immediately it started its Periodical and is, since then, sending out its volumes regularly at one per year. But look at the plethora of names appearing on the title pages of its volumes. Volumes 1 and 2 were called *Minutes of the proceedings* of the Medical Association of Georgia. Volumes 3 and 4 were called *Transactions* of the Medical Society of the State of Georgia. Volume 5 was given the name of the first born. Volumes 6 to 19 came out as the *Proceedings* of the Georgia Medical Association. Volumes 20 to 23 were called the *Transactions* of the Georgia Medical Association, while volumes 24 to 61 came out one after another regularly for 38 years under the uniform name *Transactions* of the Medical Association of Georgia and reached volume 61. As if this uniformity was too good to be continued any longer the Association changed the name of the Periodical to *Journal* in 1911 and further started a new sequence for numbering the volumes. Surely this idiosyncrasy would justify one crying out "Physician, heal thyself". But, for the poor cataloguer these vagaries mean writing no less than 7 Main instead of one and perhaps no less than 9 Index Cards instead of two. Thus, the cataloguer's work is increased fivefold. Are the managements of libraries sensitive to such woes of the librarian and disposed to increase the cataloguing staff fivefold? Their present attitude, however, appears to be one born of blissful ignorance of the complexities of cataloguing. Due to an unfortunate tradition, cataloguing is still looked upon by them as a feminine job for semi-literate persons. Perhaps, it is worth quoting the following from the *Five laws of library science* [RF2], "But the superior arrogance of those, who can more than read books, who feel competent to criticise literary style or have gained some acquaintance with a special department of knowledge, is more annoying. They imagine that anything in a library beyond their (own), scholarship, is manual, clerical, and rather beneath their efforts, not knowing that they are yet only good material out of which librarians might be made. Not infrequently one comes across a bumptious upstart who has the cheek to say, 'What is there in *indexing* ?,' meaning by 'Indexing,' 'Cataloguing.' One only wishes that he was allowed to try his hand at 'Indexing' for a couple of months to discover for himself what a mess he is capable of making."

We shall conclude these remarks with the Main entries in the case of a Periodical which has seen changes in its own name as well as in the name of its learned god-father.

Examples:

1 L:4:7*m*73,M9

TRANSACTIONS, National Association of Railway Surgeons (United States of America).

[1 V per year; 1891-3].

This library has 1891-3.

continued in the next card.

2 L:4:7*m*73,M9 *continued* 1.

RAILWAY SURGEON, (National Association of Railway Surgeons) (United States of America).

[1 V per year. V 1-4; 1894-7].

This library has V 1-4: 1894-7.

continued in the next card.

3 L:4:7*m*73,M9 *continued* 2.

RAILWAY SURGEON, (International Association of Railway Surgeons) (United States of America).

[1 V per year. V 5-10; 1898-1903].

This library has V 5-10; 1898-1903.

continued in the next card.

4 L:4:7*m*73,M9 *continued* 3.

RAILWAY SURGICAL journal, (American Association of Railway Surgeons).

[1 V per year. V 11-27; 1904-20].

This library has V 11-27; 1904-20.

continued in the next card.

5 L:4:7*m*73,M9 *continued* 4.

SURGICAL JOURNAL, (American Association of Railway Surgeons).

[1 V per year. V 28-; 1921-].

This library has V 28-40; 1921-33.

2 With Change in Sequence of Volume Number

Cases of complexity of kind 42 enumerated in Sec PA2 are to be treated on the analogy of Sec PE1 and its subdivisions.

This complexity is as frequent as the preceding one. Here are some examples. What was organised in 1859 as the Entomological Society of Philadelphia has come to be known as the American Entomological Society since 1867; with the result, one of its Periodicals appears as *Proceedings* of the Entomological Society of Philadelphia from 1861 to 1867 and, since the latter date, is still coming out as the *Transactions* of the American Entomological Society, but with a different sequence of volume numbers.

Again the American Geographical and Statistical Society founded in 1854 changed its name in 1871 to the American Geographical Society of New York. The metamorphosis in the name of one of the Periodicals commenced by it in 1859 is very interesting. The first two volumes were called the *Journal* of the American Geographical and Statistical Society. The third volume was published as the *Annual report* of the Society. The numbers of volumes 4 to 32 appeared as *Bulletin* but were to be called *Journal* when bound. However, volumes 33 to 47 were permitted to have the same name as their constituents, viz *Bulletin*. This was till 1915. But in 1916 this Periodical came to be known as the *Geographical review* and as if in recognition of this drastic change in name, a new sequence was begun in numbering the volumes.

We may conclude this rule with the Main Entries of a Periodical with the complexity covered by this rule.

Examples:

6 Lm73,M8

PROCEEDINGS, Chicago Medical Society.
[1 V per year. V 1-3 N10; 1888-91].
This library has V 1-3 N10; 1888-91.
{ V 3 not completed. }

continued in the next card

7 Lm73,M8 *continued* 1.

CHICAGO MEDICAL record, (Chicago Medical Society).
[1 V per year. V 1-2; 1891-2].
This library has V 1-2; 1891-2.

continued in the next card.

8 Lm73,M88 *continued* 2.

CHICAGO MEDICAL recorder, (Chicago Medical Society)
[1 V per year. V 3-; 1893-].
This library has V 3-43; 1893-1933.

CHAPTER PF

AMALGAMATION

1 Continuation of Title and Volume Number

In the case of complexity of kind 51 enumerated in Sec PA2, the title, which is continued, is to be given a new Main Card.

11 The Class Number in the new Main Card being the same as in the earlier Main Card with the same title, they are to be treated as a set of "continued cards" as per Chap EF.

12 The entries in the Main Cards of all the amalgamated Publications including the earlier one of the continued title are to be 'closed for publication' and 'closed for the library' as provided in Sec PB135 and PB137.

13 In the new Main Card an Additional Note is to be added after the Holdings Section and written within inverted commas, consisting successively of the

1 Term "*Amalgamates*"; and

2 Class Numbers and names of the other Periodical Publications amalgamated with it, the information about the different Publications being put in separate lines.

14 In the last Main Card of each of the Periodical Publications mentioned in the Additional Note of the new Main Card, an additional note is to be added after Section on Periodicity, consisting successively of the

1 Term "*Amalgamated with*"; and..

2 Class Number and the name of the Publication with which it is amalgamated.

2 Continuation of Title but not of Volume Number

Cases of complexity of kind 52 enumerated in Sec PA2, are to be treated on the analogy of Sec PF1 and its subdivisions.

Examples:

1 T*m*73,M9

EDUCATIONAL REVIEW (United States of America).
[2 V per year. V 1-76; 1891-1928).

This library has V 1-76; 1891-1928.
{ V 76 lacks the last two issues. }
"*Amalgamated with*
Tm73,N1 SCHOOL AND SOCIETY."

2 Tm73,N1
SCHOOL AND SOCIETY.
[2 V per year. V 1-27; 1915-28].
This library has V 1-27; 1915-28.

continued in the next card.

continued.

3 Tm73,N1
SCHOOL AND SOCIETY.
[2 V per year. V 28- ; 1928-].
This library has V 28-33; 1928-33.
"*Amalgamates*
Tm73,M9 EDUCATIONAL REVIEW (United States of America)"

Amalgamations occur fairly frequently. Sometimes they occur without notice and suddenly. Sometimes due notice is given. Or the amalgamation is explicity brought to the notice of readers at least after the event. In some cases no such clue is given except for a slight change in the title. In the example given above, a long standing Periodical like the *Educational review* which had run its course over 76 volumes was put to the necessity, all on a sudden, of getting into alliance with another youngster even while it was in the middle of a volume. The merging of this veteran with the comparatively youngster *School and society* has been described with a sigh of sorrow by Dr Frank Pierrepont Graves, New York State Commissioner of Education and President of the University of the State of New York who once nourished the *Educational review* for a few years [S2].

"Does it not seem an unhappy circumstance that such a magazine should lose its identity ?... Since, however, it has been decreed that the name and form should vanish, it is most fortunate that the spirit and substance are to be preserved in a journal that has so clearly won its way to educational leadership as SCHOOL AND SOCIETY."

This capacious *School and society* has absorbed also other educational periodicals, viz *School journal* established in 1874 and the *Teachers' magazine* established in 1878. This information is not shown in the entries as the years of their amalgamation are not known.

Examples:

4 Tm73,M97
AMERICAN EDUCATION.
[1 V per year. V 1-32; 1897-1928].
This library has V 1-32; 1897-1928.
{ V 32 had only four issues }.
"*Amalgamated with*
Tm73, M8 EDUCATION."

5 Tm73,M8
EDUCATION.
[1 V per year. V 1-48; 1880/81—1927/28].
This library has V 1-48; 1880/81—1927/28.
continued in the next card.

6 Tm73,M8 *continued.*
EDUCATION.
[1 V per year. V 49-; 1928/29—.]
This library has V 49-52; 1928/29—1932/33.
"*Amalgamates*
Tm73,M97 AMERICAN EDUCATION."

In this case, the necessity for amalgamation seems to have arisen by the time the *American education* had issued the first four numbers of volume 32. But the fourth number of volume 32 had an explicit announcement in the following terms [A1].

"With this December issue, AMERICAN EDUCATION ceases to exist as a separate magazine and is merged with EDUCATION. All unexpired subscriptions to AMERICAN EDUCATION will be filled to the end of the subscription date with copies of EDUCATION. Since the list price of EDUCATION is just twice that charged for AMERICAN EDUCATION we feel sure that our subscribers will appreciate this bargain in educational literature."

There are even more queer types of amalgamation and merging. Instead of the constituent periodicals giving up their identity, as has happened in the two preceding examples, the continuing periodical acts as a host and the amalgamated periodicals are treated as guests with their own individuality persisting in some form or another. Here are some examples: The Appalachian Mountain Club founded in 1876 is conducting three Periodical Publications, viz, *Appalachia* commenced in 1876, *Register* commenced in 1879, and *Bulletin* commenced in 1907. The *Appalachia* had its independent existence from 1876 to 1921. From 1922 it appears merely as a number of the *Bulletin*. For instance the 1922 volume is N 5 of V 16 of the *Bulletin*. The *Bulletin* has also begun to play the host to the *Register*, by vacating another of its numbers for it.

Another example is that of the Periodical Publications published by the Ohio Academy of Science organised on 31 December 1891. It started its *Proceedings* in 1892 and this Periodical still continues regularly. The *Annual reports*, which appeared as an independent Serial from 1892 to 1902 and had its volumes numbered as 1-11, became part of *Proceedings* from 1903 onwards. So also the *Special papers*, whose first seven volumes appeared independently in the years 1899 to 1902, has now become a guest and the volumes of this guest, beginning from the eighth, are now to be found within the hospitable covers of the *Proceedings*.

Still another interesting case of amalgamation is that of *Journal*, *Bulletin*, and *Ceramic abstracts* of the American Ceramic Society which are all published under one cover but separately paged. Another complication in this case is that they together constitute the continuation of the *Transactions*. The

Society was founded in 1899. From 1899 to 1917, it published the 19 volumes of this *Transactions*. In 1918 the *Transactions* was replaced by the *Journal*. In 1922 the *Bulletin* and the *Ceramic abstracts*, came into existence but agreed to live as members of a joint family under the same cover as their elder sister, *Journal*, each signifying its individuality by having its own pagination. Long live this happy family free from any fratricidal propensity !

3 New Title and Old Class Number

In the case of complexity of kind 53, enumerated in Seç PA2, the new title is to be given a new Main Card.

31 If its Class Number be the same as for the earlier title whose numbering of volumes is continued under the new title, it is to be treated on the analogy of the subdivisions of Sec PF 1.

311 If the Class Number is different, it is to be treated on the analogy of the subdivisions of Sec PF4.

4 New Title and New Class Number

In the case of complexity of kind 54, enumerated in Sec PA2, the new title is to be given a Main Card.

41 An Additional Note is to be added in it, within inverted commas, consisting successively of the

1 Term "*Amalgamates*"; and

2 Class Numbers and the titles of the Periodical Publications amalgamated in it, the information about the different Publications being put in separate lines.

42 The Entries in the Main Cards of all the amalgamated publications are to be 'closed for the publication' and also 'closed for the library' as provided in Sec PB135 and PB157.

43 An Additional Note is to be added, within inverted commas in the last Main Card of each of the Amalgamated Publications, consisting, successively of the

1 Term "*Amalgamated in*"; and

2 Class Number and the title of the Publication Amalgamating it.

Examples:

1 Gam73,N

BIOLOGICAL ABSTRACTS.

[1 V per year. V 1-; 1927-].
This library has V 1-7; 1927-33.
"*Amalgamates*
G91*am*73,N ABSTRACTS OF bacteriology; and
I*am*73,N BOTANICAL ABSTRACTS."

2 G91*am*73,N
ABSTRACTS OF bacteriology.
[1 V per year. V 1-10; 1917-26].
This library has V 1-10; 1917-26.
"*Amalgamated in*
G*am*73,N BIOLOGICAL ABSTRACTS."

3 I*am*73,N
BOTANICAL ABSTRACTS.
[1 V per year. V 1-7; 1912-26].
This library has V 1-7; 1920-26.
"*Amalgamated in*
G*am*73,N BIOLOGICAL ABSTRACTS."

CHAPTER PG

SPLITTING UP

1 Class Number Continued by One

In the case of complexity of kind 61 enumerated in Sec PA2, each of the Publications into which the original is split is to be given a new Main Card.

11 The old Main Card and the Main Card of the Publication continuing the old Class Number are to be treated as a set of "continued cards" as per Chap EF.

12 The Entry in the old Main Card is to be 'closed for publication' and also 'closed for the library' as provided in Sec PB135 and PB157.

13 An Additional Note is to be added within inverted commas, in its old Main Card, consisting successively of the

1 Term "*Split partially into*"; and

2 Class Number and the title of each of the Publications, other than the one continuing the old Class Number, into which it is split, the information about each publication being given in a separate lines.

14 In the Main Card of each of the Publications, other than the one continuing the old Class Number, into which it is split, an Additional Note is to be added within inverted commas, consisting, successively of the

1 Term "*Split partially from*"; and

2 Class Number and the title of the original Publication.

See examples 1.5 and 2.3 in Sec PJ6.

2 Class Number Continued by None

2 Complexity of kind 62 enumerated in Sec PA2, is to be treated on the analogy of Sec PG1, and its subdivisions, with the modification that the term "Split" is to be substituted for the term "Split partially" wherever it occurs.

Examples:

1 A*m*42,M

JOURNAL, College of Science, Imperial University of Tokyo.
[Irregular. V 1-45; 1887-1925].
This library has V 1-45; 1887-1925.
"Split into
BZ*m*42,N2 JOURNAL, Faculty of Science, Imperial University of Tokyo, Section 1, etc.
H*m*42,N2 JOURNAL, Faculty of Science, Imperial University of Tokyo, Section 2, etc.
I*m*42,N2 JOURNAL, Faculty of Science, Imperial University of Tokyo, Section 3, etc.
K*m*42,N2 JOURNAL, Faculty of Science, Imperial University of Tokyo, Section 4, etc.
Y7*m*42,N2 JOURNAL, Faculty of Science, Imperial University of Tokyo, Section 5, etc.

2 BZ*m*42,N2

JOURNAL, Faculty of Science, Imperial University of Tokyo, Section 1 Mathematics, astronomy, physics, chemistry.
[Irregular. V 1-; 1925/29—].
This library has V 1-; 1925/29—
"Split from
A*m*42,M JOURNAL, College of Science, Imperial University of Tokyo."

The second volume of this Periodical had not been completed in 1934. That is why the number of the volume and the year of the second volume are not shown in the last line.

3 H*m*42,N2

JOURNAL, Faculty of Science, Imperial University of Tokyo, Section 2, Geology, mineralogy, geography, seismology.
[Irregular. V 1-; 1925/27—].
This library has V 1-2; 1925/27—**1926/30.**
"Split from
A*m*42,M JOURNAL, College of Science, Imperial University of Tokyo."

4 I*m*42,N2

JOURNAL, Faculty of Science, Imperial University of Tokyo, Section 3, Botany.
[Irregular. V 1-; 1925/27—].
This library has V 1-4; 1925/28—**1932/33.**
"Split from
A*m*42,M JOURNAL, College of Science, Imperial University of Tokyo."

5 K*m*42,N2

JOURNAL, Faculty of Science, Imperial University of Tokyo, Section 4, Zoology.
[Irregular. V 1-; 1925/29—].
This library has V 1-2; 1925/29—**1919/31.**

"*Split from*

Am42,M JOURNAL, College of Science, Imperial University of Tokyo."

6 Y7m42,N2

JOURNAL, Faculty of Science, Imperial University of Tokyo, Section 5, Anthropology.

[Irregular. V 1*-; 1925—].

The library has V 1 -; 1925—.

"*Split from*

Am42,M JOURNAL, College of Science, Imperial University of Tokyo."

*Even the first volume of this Periodical had not yet been completed. After the completion of the first volume the asterisk will be rubbed off. (The above note is, as it was added in 1934, to state the position then prevailing).

3 Splitting into Independent Periodicals

Complexity of kind 63 enumerated in Sec PA2 is to be treated on the analogy of Sec PG2 with the modification that the term "*Split on completion of each volume into*" is to be substituted for the term "*Split*".

31 The entry of the original periodical will not have the Holdings Section.

In fact the original periodical will cease to exist when the volume is completed.

32 In the Main Entries for the periodicals into which the original periodical is split, an Additional Note is to be added, consisting of the

1 Term "*Originally published as part of*", and

2 Class Number and the title of the publication of which it was originally a part.

Example 1:

On the completion of a volume, the *Abgila* (=*Annals, bulletin, granthalaya*, Indian Library Association), gets totally split up into

1 *Annals*, Indian Library Association;

2 *Bulletin*, Indian Library Association; and

3 *Granthalaya*, (Indian Library Association).

The title page and the index are not issued so as to cover the whole of the *Abgila*. On the other hand, each of its constituents is provided with an independent title page and index.

The following will be the entries:

2m44,N4

LIBRARY BULLETIN (Indian Library Association)
[1 V per year. V 1-5 N2; 1942, April-1946, July]
This library has V 1-5 N2; 1942, April-1946, July.

2m44,N4,1

{ No V in 1946, August-1948, December }
"*Continued as*

2m44,N4,1 ABGILA, etc, (Indian Library Association)"
ABGILA etc (Indian Library Association).
[1 V in 2 years. V 1-2; 1949-52]

continued in the next card.

2m44,N4,1 ***continued* 1.**

ABGILA, etc (Indian Library Association).
[1 V per year. V 3; 1953]
"*Split on completion of each volume into*
2m44,N4,2 ANNALS, Indian Library Association.
2m44,N4,3 BULLETIN, Indian Library Association.
2m44,N4,4 GRANTHALAYA, (Indian Library Association)."

2m44,N4,2

ANNALS, Indian Library Association.
[1 V in 2 years. V 1-2; 1949-52]
This library has V 1-2; 1949-52

continued in the next card.

2m44,N4,2 ***continued* 1.**

ANNALS, Indian Library Association.
[1 V per year. V 3-; 1953]
This library has V 3; 1953.
"*Originally published as part of*
2m44,N4, 4 ABGILA, (Indian Library Association).

2m44,N4,3

BULLETIN, Indian Library Association.
[1 V in 2 years. V 1-2; 1949-52]
This library has V 1-2; 1949-52.

continued in the next card.

2m44,N4,3 ***continued* 1.**

BULLETIN, Indian Library Association.
[1 V per year. V 3, N2; 1953, March, June].
This library has V 3 N 2; 1953, March, June.
"*Originally published as part of*
2m44,N4 ABGILA, (Indian Library Association)."

2m44,N4,4

GRANTHALAYA, (Indian Library Association).
[1 V in 2 years. V 1-2; 1949-52]

This library has V 1-2; 1949-52.

continued in the next card.

2*m*44,N4,4 *continued* 1.

GRANTHALAYA, (Indian Library Association).
[1 V per year. V 3 N2; 1953, March, June].
This library has V 3 N2; 1953, March, June.
"*Originally published as part of*
2*m*44,N4 ABGILA, (Indian Library Association).

Example 2:

On the completion of a volume, the *All India reporter* gets totally split up into the 21 constituent periodicals:

Z2*an*N1
All India reporter: Statute and article referencer.

Z2*m*2,N1
All India reporter: Journal.

Z2*y*7*n*N1
All India reporter: Supreme Court

Z2,928*n*N1
All India reporter: Indian acts.

Z211*y*7*n*N1
All India reporter: Madras.

Z212*y*7*n*N1
All India reporter: Kerala.

Z213*y*7*n*N
All India reporter: Mysore.

Z216*y*7*n*N1
All India reporter: Andhra Pradesh.

Z231*y*7*n*N1
All India reporter: Bombay.

Z237*y*7*n*N1
All India reporter: Rajasthan.

Z243*y*7*n*N1
All India reporter: Punjab.

Z245*y*7*n*N1
All India reporter: Himachal Pradesh.

Z247*y*7*n*N1
All India reporter: Jammu and Kashmir.

Z252*y*7*n*N1
All India reporter: Allahabad.

Z255*y*7*n*N1
All India reporter: Madhya Pradesh.

Z2791y7nN1
All India reporter: Tripura.

Z2792y7nN1
All India reporter: Manipur.

Z271y7nN1
All India reporter: Orissa.

Z237y7nN1
All India reporter: Patna.

Z275y7nN1
All India reporter: Calcutta.

Z277y7nN1
All India reporter: Assam.

The number of constituent periodicals was 11 in 1914 and 1915. The maximum number of constituent periodicals was 29. This occurred in 1954. In 1960 the number was 20 [RZR].

CHAPTER PH

SUPPLEMENT

1 Without Separate Pagination

In the case of complexity of kind 71 enumerated in Sec PA2, the Supplements are to be given Cross Reference Entries on the analogy of Sec PB2.

The right side of the back of the Main Card, will indicate all the monographs and books that are caught up as part of the Periodical Publication.

2 With Separate Pagination

In the case of complexity of kind 72, enumerated in Sec PA2, each monograph supplement or book is to be separated from the Periodical Publication and dealt with as an independent book.

21 In the appropriate Main Card of the Periodical Publication, an Additional Note is to be added within inverted commas, consisting successively of the

1 Term "*For supplements see*"; and

2 Call Numbers of the separated books, written as separate sentences.

22 In the Main Cards of the separated books, an appropriate Extract Note is to be added, as provided in Sec MF3 and its subdivisions.

23 If a Supplement of this kind chances to be bound with a volume of the Periodical Publication, it is to be dealt with as if it were of kind 71.

3 Supplementary Periodical Publication

In the case of complexity of kind 73, enumerated in Sec PA2, the Supplements are to be treated as independent Periodical Publications.

31 In the corresponding Main Card of the main publication,

an Additional Note is to be added within inverted commas, consisting successively of the

1 Term "*Has as supplement*"; and

2 Class Numbers and the titles of the Supplements, the information about each Supplement being given in separate lines.

32 In the Main Cards of the Supplements, an Additional Note is to be added within inverted commas, consisting successively of the

1 Term "*Supplement to*"; and

2 Class Number and title of the main publication.

4 Cumulative Index

If the Supplements, treated as separate Periodical Publications or separate books, are covered by the Cumulative Indexes of the Main Periodical Publication, the appropriate volumes of the cumulative indexes are to be provided (in some convenient and prominent form, say, by the insertion in the supplements of a written or typed or printed slip), with the Class Numbers or the Call Numbers, as the case may be, of the separated supplements.

Examples:

1 z44m44,N27
JOURNAL OF oriental research.
[1 V per year. 1-; 1927-].
This library has V 1-7; 1927-33.
"*For supplements see*
P31,Dx1,1 N30.1
O15,2D35,V N31
R641x4,3 15N32."

2 P31,Dx1,1 N30.1
TOLKAPPIYAM .... Ed with comm in English by P S Subrahmanya Sastri. V 1. Eluttatikaram.
(Madras oriental series, 3).
"*Supplement to*
z44m44,N27 JOURNAL OF oriental research. V 2-4; 1928-30."
61618

3 O15,2D35,V N31
BHASA.
Vinavasavadattam with introd by S Kuppuswami Sastri.
(Madras oriental series. 2).

"*Supplement to*
z44m44, N27 JOURNAL OF oriental research V 1, 3-5; 1927, 1929-31."
61617

4 R641x4,V 15N32
MANDANA MISRA.
Vibhramaviveka. Ed by S Kuppuswami Sastri and T V Ramachaudra Dikshitar.
(Madras oriental series. 1)
"*Supplement to*
z44m44, N27 JOURNAL OF oriental research. V1; 1927."
61616

CHAPTER PJ

COMBINATION OF COMPLEXITIES

1 Introduction

We have so far followed the practice of pure mathematicians and dealt with each type of complexity in isolation, just for facilitating the development of the subject. But it is well known that, in actual life, it is seldom that difficulties come in such mathematical simplicity. So also it is seldom that a primary complexity occurs singly all by itself, in actual practice. Complexities appear, on the other hand, in all conceivable combinations. In such cases all the appropriate notes are to be added as indicated in the succeeding rules. It may be recalled here that the following kinds of sections and notes are possible:

1 Section on Periodicity, enclosed in square brackets;
2 Series Note, enclosed in circular brackets;
3 Holdings Section, not enclosed in any way;
4 Complexity Note, enclosed in crooked brackets; and
5 Notes relating to Amalgamation, Split up, and Supplement, each enclosed within inverted commas;

2 All the appropriate Sections and Notes are to be added in the first card and in each of the continued cards, as the case may be, to the extent warranted.

3 The Section on Periodicity is to be the First Section after the Title Section, in each card.

4 The Holdings Section is to be the Last Section, in each card.

5 The Notes on Complexities—Amalgamation, Split up, and Supplements—are to be written after the Holdings Section, in their chronological sequence.

6 Each Note is to be written as a Separate Section.

Examples:

1.1 Am56,K,1

ABSTRACTS OF the papers printed in the philosophical transactions, Royal Society of London.

[Irregular. V 1-4; 1800—1837/43].

This library has V 1-4; 1800/14—1837/43.

Continued in the next card.

1.2 Am56,K,1 *Continued* 1.

ABSTRACTS OF the papers, Royal Society of London.
[Irregular. V 5-6; 1843/50—1850/54].
This library has V 5-6; 1843/50—1850/54.

Continued in the next card.

1.3 Am56,K,1 *Continued* 2

PROCEEDINGS, Royal Society of London.
[Irregular. V 7-75; 1855/56—1904/05].
This library has V 7-75; 1856/57—1904-5.
"*Split into*
Azm56,k,1 PROCEEDINGS, Series A, Royal Society of London.
Gm56,K,1 PROCEEDINGS, SERIES B, Royal Society of London."

1.4 Azm56,K,1

PROCEEDINGS, SERIES A, Royal Society of London.
[Irregular,. V 76- ; 1905-].
This library has V 115-142; 1927-33.
"*Split from*
Am56,K,1 PROCEEDINGS, Royal Society of London.

1.5 Gm56,K,1

PROCEEDINGS, SERIES B, Royal Society of London.
[Irregular. V 76- ; 1905-].
This library has V 75-142; 1905/06-1927/33.
"*Split from*
Am56,K,1 PROCEEDINGS, Royal Society of London."

2.1 Bm44,N

JOURNAL, Indian Mathematical Club.
[1 V per year. V 1-2; 1908-10].
This library has V 1-2; 1908-10.
{ No V for 1909 }.
{ *Bound together* V 1-2 }.

Continued in the next card.

2.2 Bm44,N *Continued* 1.

JOURNAL, Indian Mathematical Society.
[1 V per year. V 3-14; 1911-22].
This library has V 3-14; 1911-22.
{*Bound together* V 3-4; 1911-2. V 5-6; 1913-4. V 7-8; 1915-6. V 9-10; 1917-8. V 11-12; 1919-20. V 13-14; 1931-2}.

Continued in the next card.

2.3 Bm44,N *Continued* 2.

JOURNAL, Indian Mathematical Society.
[1 V for two years. V 15- ; 1923/24-].
This library has V 15-19; 1923/24-1931/32.
"Each V from V 16 *has as supplement*

Bp44,N REPORT, Indian Mathematical Conference".
"*Split partially into*
Bm44,N,1 MATHEMATICS STUDENT, (Indian Mathematical Society)".

2.4 Bm44,N,1
MATHEMATICS STUDENT, (Indian Mathematical Society).
[1 V per year. V 1- ; 1933-].
This library has V 1- ; 1933-
"*Split partially from*
Bm44,N JOURNAL, Indian Mathematical Society".

2.5 Bp44,N
REPORT, Indian Mathematical Conference.
[1 V for two years. V 4- ; 1924-].
This library has V 5-7; 1924-31.
{ V 4 and 5 *bound with* Bm44,N JOURNAL, Indian Mathematical Society, V 15 and 16 respectively. }
{ V 1-3 not separately published, but included in Bm44,N JOURNAL, Indian Mathematical Society, V 9, 11, and 13. }
"*Supplement to*
Bm44,N JOURNAL, Indian Mathematical Society."

3.1 Cm55,L
ANNALEN DER physik.
[3 B per year. B 1-30, 31-60 (=Neue F: B1-30); 1799-1819].
This library has B 1-30, 31-60 (=Neue F: B1-30); 1799-1819.
Continued in the next card.

349 Cm55,L *Continued* 1.
ANNALEN DER physik und der physikalischen chemie.
[3 B per year. B 61-76 (=Neuste F:B1-16); 1819-24].
This library has B 61-76 (=Neuste F:B1-16); 1819-24.
Continued in the next card.

3.3 Cm55,L *Continued* 2.
ANNALEN DER physik und chemie.
[3 B per year. B 1-11 (=Ganzen F: 77-87); 1824-27].
This library has B 1-11 (=Gazen F: 77-87); 1824-27.
"Each of the V has an alternative title-page giving the title as ANNALEN DER physik".
Continued in the next card.

3.4 Cm55,L *Continued* 3.
ANNALEN DER physik und chemie.
[3 B per year. B 12-30 (=Ganzen F: 88-106); 1828-33].
This library has B 12-30 (=Ganzen F: 88-106); 1928-33.
Continued in the next card.

3.5 *Cm*55,L *Continued* 4.

ANNALEN DER physik und chemie.

[3 B per year. B 31-60 (=R:2: B 1-30=Ganzen F: 107-136); 1834-43].

This library has B 31-60 (=R:2: B 1-30=Ganzen F: 107-136); 1834-43.

"*Has as supplement*

*Cm*55,L,1 ANNALEN DER physick und chemie. Erganzungsband".

Continued in the next card.

3.6 *Cm*55,L *Continued* 5.

ANNALEN DER physik und chemie.

[3 B per year. B 61-90 (=R 3: B 1-30=Ganzen F: 137-166); 1844-53].

This library has B 61-90 (=R 3: B 1-30=Ganzen F: 137-166); 1844-53.

"*Has as supplement*

*Cm*55,L,1 ANNALEN DER physik und chemie, Erganzungsband".

Continued in the next card.

3.7 *Cm*55,L *Continued* 6.

ANNALEN DER physik und chemie.

[3 B per year. B 91-120 (=R 4: B 1-30=Ganzen F: 167-196); 1854-63].

This library has B 91-120 (=R4: B 1-30=Ganzen F: 167-196); 1854-63.

"*Has as supplement*

*Cm*55,L,1 ANNALEN DER physik und chemie, Erganzungsband".

Continued in the next card.

3.8 *Cm*55,L *Continued* 7.

ANNALEN DER physik und chemie.

[3 B per year. B 121-150 (=R 5: B 1-30=Ganzen F: 197-226); 1864-73].

This library has B 121-150 (=R 5: B 1-30=Ganzen F: 197-226); 1864-73.

"*Has as supplement*

*Cm*55,L,1 ANNALEN DER physik und chemie, Erganzungsband".

Continued in the next card.

3.9 *Cm*55,L *Continued* 8.

ANNALEN DER physik und chemie.

[3 B per year. B 151-160 (=R 6:B 1-10=Ganzen F: 227-236); 1874-77].

This library has B 151-160 (=R 6: B 1-10=Ganzen F:227-236); 1874-77.

"*Has as supplement*

*Cm*55,L,1 ANNALEN DER physik und chemie, Eganzungsband;"

C p77M74 Jubel band *Continued in the next card.*

3.10 *Cm*55,L *Continued* 9.
ANNALEN DER physik und chemie.
[3 B per year. Neue F: B 1-69 (=Ganzen F: 237-305); 1877-99].
This library has Neue F: B 1-69 (=Ganzen F:237-305); 1877-99.
"*Has as supplement*
*Cm*55;L,1 ANNALEN DER physik und chemie, Erganzungsband".
Continued in the next card.

3.11 *Cm*55,L *Continued* 10.
ANNALEN DER physik.
[3 B per year. F4: B 1-87 (=Ganzen R:306-392); 1900-28].
This library has F 4: B 1-87 (=Ganzen R:306-392); 1900-28.
Continued in the next card.

3.12 *Cm*55,L *Continued* 11.
ANNALEN DER physik.
[3 B per year. F 5: B 1-3 (=Ganzen R: 393-395); 1929].
This library has F 5: B 1-3 (=Ganzen R: 393-395); 1929.
Continued in the next card.

3.13 *Cm*55,L *Continued* 12.
ANNALEN DER physik.
[4 B per year. F 5: B 4-15; (=Ganzen R: 396-407); 1930-2].
This library has F 5: B 4-15; (=Ganzen R: 396-407); 1930-2.
Continued in the next card.

3.14 *Cm*55,L *Continued* 13.
ANNALEN DER physik.
[3 B per year. F 5: B 16-19; (=Gazen R: 408-411); 1933-].
This library has F 5: B 16-19; (=Ganzen R: 408-411); 1933-

3.15 *Cm*55,L,1
ANNALEN DER physik und chemie, Erganzungsband.
[Irregular. B 1-8; 1842-78].
This library has B 1-8; 1842-78.
"*Supplement to*
*Cm*55,L ANNALEN DER physik und chemie".

3.16 C p77M74
ANNALEN DER Physik und Chemie, Jubel band dem her J C Poggendorff, etc.
"*Supplement to*
*Cm*55,L ANNALEN DER physik und chemie".
5001

CHAPTER PZD

DICTIONARY CATALOGUE

1 Main Entry

The Main Entry of a simple Periodical Publication in the Dictionary Catalogue will differ from that in the Classified Catalogue only in one respect.

The Heading will occupy the Leading Section. The Class Number will form the penultimate Section, that is, the last section in the front side of the card.

Example:

1 ANNALS OF Botany.
[1 V per year. V 1- ; 1887-].
This library has V 1-47; 1887-933. Im56,M8

2 Subject Analytical Entry

The Rule for the Subject Analytical Entry of a volume of a Periodical containing only a single work or a Festschrift or forming a special volume in any other sense, admitting of its being looked upon as a Simple or Ordinary Composite Book, is analogous to Sec PB21.

Example:

1 COMMEMORATION VOLUME on the occasion of the twentieth anniversary of the foundation of the Calcutta Mathematical Society, in 1928.
See
BULLETIN, Calcutta Mathematical Society.
V 20; 1928. Bm44,N0 N28

2 TAITTIRIYA-PRATISAKHYA.
See
JOURNAL, American Oriental Society.
V 9; 1871. Z4m73,M M71

3 Other Matters

The Index Entries including the Alternative Name Entries are to be given on the analogy of Sec PB3 and its subdivisions. The Tracing Section of the Main Entry, and the Entry for Cumulative Index are to be on the analogy of Sec PB16 and PB6, with the usual adjustments demanded by the Dictionary Catalogue.

4 Complex Periodical

The only difference between a Dictionary Catalogue and a Classified Catalogue arises from the fact that the Leading Section is occupied by the Title of the Periodical Publication in the former and by its Class Number in the latter. Consequently the only Kind of Complexity which will call for a different rule in the Dictionary Catalogue is "Change of Title". In that case, the entries for the different titles assumed by the same Periodical Publication at different times will be scattered in the Dictionary Catalogue, whereas they will all be kept together in the Classified Catalogue by their having the same Class Number. The Classified Catalogue is, therefore, able to manage the complexity due to change of title, by merely providing for continued Cards. But in the Dictionary Catalogue, this simple procedure is not available. Therefore, the following set of alternative Rules are prescribed.

41 In the case of Complexity of Kind 41 enumerated in Sec PA2 or of change of title arising in any other way, the Basic Main Card for the Periodical Publication as a whole is to use its original Title as the Heading. It is to give the Periodicity of Volume Section, the full holdings of the library and the Class Number, ignoring all changes in Title. The right end of its last line is to contain the directing words "*For details see the next card.*"

411 The first 'Continued Card' is to be the Main Entry for those volumes which retain the original Heading and Title and it must be 'closed for publication.'

4111 The first 'Continued Card' is to give the following additional sections:

1 The Directing Element "*For continuation see*";

2 The Heading, a fullstop, and the specification of Holdings for the second Title with which the Periodical Publication was continued; and

3 A section similar to the above for each of the later Titles with which it was continued.

42 A Main Card is to be written for each different Title of the Periodical Publication, beginning with the second.

421 The entry for all but the last Heading and Title is to be 'closed for publication'.

422 Each of the Main Entries mentioned in Sec PZD42 is to be given the following additional sections:

1 The Directing Element "*For earlier Title(s) see*";

2 A Section for each of the earlier Titles written on the analogy of Sec PZD4111;

3 The Directing Element "*For continuation(s) see*"; and

4 A Section for each of the later Titles written on the analogy of Sec PZD4111.

Provided that 3 and 4 are to be omitted in the case of the last Title of the Periodical Publication.

Example:

BASIC MAIN ENTRY

1.1 TRANSACTIONS, National Association of Railway Surgeons (United States of America)
[1 V per year. 1891-].
This library has 1891-93; V 1-40; 1894-933. L:5:7m73,M9
For details see the next card.
{Volume-numbering began only in 1894}.

1.2 TRANSACTIONS, National Association of Railway Surgeons (United States of America).
[1 V per year. 1891-3]. L:4:7m73,M9
For continuation see
RAILWAY SURGEON, (National Association of Railway Surgeons) (United States of America). V 1-4; 1894-7.
RAILWAY SURGEON, (International Association of Railway Surgeons) (United States of America). V 5-10; 1898-903.
RAILWAY SURGICAL journal, (American Association of Railway Surgeons). V 11-27; 1904-20.
SURGICAL JOURNAL, (American Association of Railway Surgeons). V 28-40; 1921-33.

MAIN ENTRIES FOR CHANGED TITLES

1.3 RAILWAY SURGEON, (National Association of Railway Surgeons) (United States of America).
[1 V per year. V 1-4; 1894-7].
This library has V 1-4; 1894-7. L:4:7m73,M9
For earlier Title see
TRANSACTIONS, National Association of Railway Surgeons (United States of America). 1891-3.
For continuation see
RAILWAY SURGEON, (International Association of Railway Surgeons) (United States of America). V 5-10; 1898-903.
RAILWAY SURGICAL journal, (American Association of Railway Surgeons). V 11-27; 1904-20.
SURGICAL JOURNAL, (American Associations of Railway Surgeons). V 28-40; 1921-33.

1.4 RAILWAY SURGEON, (International Association of Railway Surgeons) (United States of America).

[1 V per year. V 5-10; 1898-903].

This library has V 5-10; 1898-903. L:4:7m73,M9

For earlier Titles see

TRANSACTIONS, National Association of Railway Surgeons (United States of America). 1891-3.

RAILWAY SURGEON, (National Association of Railway Surgeons) (United States of America). V 1-4; 1894-7.

For continuations see

RAILWAY SURGICAL journal, (American Association of Railway Surgeons). V 11-27; 1904-20.

SURGICAL JOURNAL, (American Association of Railway Surgeons). V 28-40; 1921-33.

1.5 RAILWAY SURGICAL journal, (American Association of Railway Surgeons).

[1 V per year. V 11-27; 1904-20].

This library has V 11-27; 1904-20. L:4:7m73,M9

For earlier Titles see

TRANSACTIONS, National Association of Railway Surgeons (United States of America). 1891-3.

RAILWAY SURGEON, (National Association of Railway Surgeons) (United States of America). V 1-4; 1894-7.

RAILWAY SURGEON, (International Association of Railway Surgeons) (United States of America). V 5-10; 1898-903.

For continuation see

SURGICAL JOURNAL, (American Association of Railway Surgeons). V 28-40; 1921-33.

1.6 SURGICAL JOURNAL, (American Association of Railway Surgeons)

[1 V per year. V 28- ; 1921-].

This library has V 28-40; 1921-33. L:4:7m73,M9

For earlier Titles see

TRANSACTIONS, National Association of Railway Surgeons (United States of America). 1891-3.

RAILWAY SURGEON, (National Association of Railway Surgeons) (United States of America). V 1-4; 1894-7.

RAILWAY SURGEON, (International Association of Railway Surgeons) (United States of America). V 5-10; 1898-903.

RAILWAY SURGICAL journal, (American Association of Railway surgeons). V 11-27; 1904-20.

CHAPTER PZY

DESIDERATA

1 The New World

It can be easily realised that the task of dealing with Periodical Publications is no light one. But it is the Periodical Publications that form the very breath of the research activities of a community. Hence, there has been a healthy co-operation in most countries among the library profession, the learned societies, the universities, and the government, in facilitating the work of individual libraries and securing that accuracy of information in the library catalogues, which is so essential to the advancement of research. Such a co-operation has resulted in the production of many bibliographical aids in several countries. A fairly long list of such bibliographical sources is to be found in P 76-119 of the *Guide to the cataloguing of the serial publications of societies and institutions*, ed 2, published by the Library of Congress in 1931. While some of these sources are of indifferent worth, there are some which are remarkable for their thoroughness and accuracy. One such example is the *Handbook of learned societies and institutions: America* published in 1908 as Number 39 of its publication series by the Carnegie Institution of Washington in co-operation with the Library of Congress. Another such example is the *Handbook of scientific and technical societies and institutions of the United States and Canada* published in 1930 as Number 76, of the Bulletin of the National Research Council of the United States.

2 India Then and Now

India is yet to produce a similar handbook. The absence of it is acting as a serious handicap in all libraries that aim at thoroughness in cataloguing, and promptness and efficiency in service. While some of the western countries had started quite an appreciable number of periodical publications even in the eighteenth century, India followed in their wake only in the nineteenth century; and this too due largely to the pioneering efforts of the western scholars working in India. But, during the present century, the fashion of floating periodical publications and forming learned bodies has passed into the hands of the sons of the soil and a very vigorous output is becoming the result. Since 1947, the year of independence, we are having a flood of periodical publications being floated from year to year. These are all prone to all the usual infanticides, marriages, divorces, paralytic strokes, deaths, resurrections and other ills that befall such publications. The work of libraries in dealing with them is further complicated by the slowness in the emergence of a well-organised library profession, publishing trade, and book-selling trade.

3 Help from Abroad

In every enlightened country men illustrious for talent, worth, and knowledge, professional organisations of librarians and bibliographers, associations of publishers and booksellers, the learned societies themselves, the universities, the State and certain quasi-governmental bodies, like National Research Councils, specially established to function as the nation's heralds of research and organisations like the Carnegie Institution of Washington and the Smithsonian Institution privately endowed for a similar purpose, are pooling their intellectual and material resources together and following a national programme to disentangle all such bibliographical knots. From their work, our country reaps and will for long continue to reap an abundant harvest of information; nor should any narrow national pride induce us to reject such an offering.

4 Help from Within

But can we offer nothing in return? How long is our international civic conscience to be satisfied with this oneway flow of bibliographical service? In activity of intellect, and fertility of resource and invention, producing a highly intelligent population, I believe, we have no reason to shrink from a comparison with any country. But devoted selfless workers, inspired by *esprit de corps* and characterised by an academic temperament, appear to be now comparatively few; they are, however, rapidly increasing in number; and notwithstanding the lower feelings and impulses fed by personal, linguistic, provincial, communal, and racial causes, signs are not altogether wanting of the emergence of a predisposition towards an amicable relation among fellow workers and a concentration of effort—witness for example the formation of an Indian Academy of Sciences and an Indian Library Association—to which will be attracted the efficient support of talent, knowledge and money, and from which we may hope for the happiest results, in the advancement both of our research and of our reputation in the world of learning.

5 First Effort

The Second Conference of the Indian National Commission for Co-operation with Unesco, held in New Delhi on 14 March 1951, adopted my resolution recommending the inclusion of a retrospective directory of Asian Periodical Publications in the agenda for the proposed Conference of National Commissions to be held at Bangkok in November 1951. This resolution was also adopted by the said Second Regional Conference of Unesco National Commissions in South Asia and South Pacific held at Bangkok from 26 November to 10 December 1951. This project was further approved by Unesco's Provisional International Committee on Bibliography and Documentation held at Paris from 21 to 25 April 1952. The project was divided into two parts—1 for Periodicals; and 2 for Serials. The former was assigned to me and the latter to P K Garde. Garde's *Directory* has been already published [G1]. My project was completed in March 1955. But Unesco has not yet published it. At its meeting held in Paris from 10 to 13 December 1957, the International Advisory Committee on Bibliography of Unesco, "discussed the as yet unpublished Retrospective bibliography of Asian learned periodicals. It heard with interest the Indian member's suggestion that the Library Association of his country might be able to publish this work. The Committee proposed that if the publication was not sponsored by the Indian Library Association or any other body, the work should be microfilmed and copies made available" [B1]. This *Retrospective bibliography of Asian learned periodicals* contains the results of the spade work done by me in the direction of the fulfilment of my own appeal made in 1934 and incorporated in Sec PZY4. If that book is printed and published, it may lead to a closer approximation being taken up by some enthusiastic worker. This important purpose will not be served, if it is merely microfilmed. From the point of view of the completion of the work for which an appeal has been made in Sec PZY4, it is necessary to print the *Retrospective directory*. I very much wish that the Indian Library Association carries out the suggestion contained in the proceedings of the Paris Meeting quoted above, as, for some strange reason, the International Bibliographical Committee appears to evade the publication of this retrospective bibliography and my report on Asian names.

PART Q

UNION CATALOGUE OF BOOKS

CHAPTER QA

COVERAGE

1 Holdings of Libraries

A Union Catalogue has been defined in Sec FM12. A Union Catalogue of Books available in the libraries of a country, or a zone, or a locality, should obviously mention in the Main Entry of a book the names of the libraries having a copy of it. This implies the addition of a new Section to the Main Entry of each book. We may call it the **Holdings Section**. This section should mention all the libraries having a copy of the book described in the Main Entry concerned. This is best done by having a Continuation Card, containing the Code Numbers of all the participating libraries. Some mark will have to be put against the Code Numbers of the libraries having a copy. Chap QE deals with this problem.

2 Need for Restriction

But the routine for keeping the Holdings Section up to date is by no means easy. Each participating library has to inform the Union Catalogue Centre of each of the new books accessioned and of the old books weeded out from time to time. This may be done either by sending to the Union Catalogue Centre periodical lists of them, or by sending duplicates of the Main Cards for the new books accessioned and lists for books withdrawn. The duplicates of the Main Cards may be photocopies if the context of the reporting library makes it cheaper. This information, furnished by the different participating libraries, should be incorporated in the Holdings Section of the Main Entry of the book in the Union Catalogue. It is usually found that the cost of this routine is out of proportion to the return it gives. Therefore, it is seldom that the Union Catalogue Centre is able to provide sufficient man-power to absorb all the information received from all the participating libraries from time to time. As a result, the Holdings Section is invariably left in arrears. Further, there can be no effective mechanism to make all the participating libraries prompt in sending their respective reports. For, the cost of preparing and sending the reports is also considerable. The National Central Library of Great Britain has had considerable experience in this matter. It is continuously trying to restrict the coverage of its Union Catalogue, both in respect of area, of the period of coverage, and of reading materials [F1]. The succeeding sections describe some possible ways of restriction.

3 Restriction by Area

The smaller the area, the greater the chance for the Union Catalogue to be kept up to date. Even more than area, it is the number of participating libraries that really counts. Therefore, the optimum area for a Union Catalogue of Books depends upon the state of the library development of a country. Though the area of India is many times greater than that of England, perhaps England will have to split up its National Union Catalogue into a greater number of Zonal Union Catalogues, than India will have to do at present. Some experimental study deserves to be made to arrive at the optimum conditions for the practicability and usefulness of a Union Catalogue. It will take us too far from the scope of this book to indicate the factors that should figure in such an experimental study. The Unesco took up this problem in 1952; but the work done was not thorough. However, the result of the project set up by it marks perhaps the first step in the direction. It gives a descriptive account of some of the current practices [B2].

4 Restriction by Type of Books

The smaller the quantity of different books to be covered by the Union Catalogue, the greater the chance for the Union Catalogue to be kept up to date. Various ways of restricting the quantity of books covered are possible.

The books covered may, for example, be restricted to

1 Costly books—that is, books with published price above a minimum;

2 Foreign language books—that is, books in languages, foreign to the country or the Zone;

3 Advanced books—that is, treatises, books classic in quality, and books likely to be only of occasional use and even that only to specialist readers and therefore uneconomical for many service libraries to own them;

4 Rare books—that is, books owned only by a few libraries and not procurable from the market—say incunabula and even later books not being republished; and

5 Books of value but produced only in limited edition.

5 Organisational Improvement

The need for restriction of coverage can be minimised considerably by a proper organisation at the national and international levels. During my visit to London in May 1957, I was very gratified to find an excellent experiment being set on foot by A J Wells, the editor of the *British national bibliography*. His organisation for the supply of printed catalogue cards is almost perfect. The master stencil he cuts for the catalogue card and the punched cards he produces for supplying printed cards to various libraries had given him a suggestion to make use of these materials in helping the Union Catalogue Centre with information for the Holdings Section, at nearly no cost [W3]. The only limiting factor will be the rate of growth of the size of the Union Catalogue. The size may soon reach a level which is by itself obstructive to efficient use. Then the restriction by type along lines outlined in Sec QA4 may have to begin. The results of this venture should be watched with interest. As soon as sufficient experience and quantitative data are available, it should be possible for many countries to profit by this British experience.

6 Pre-Natal Cataloguing

If Pre-Natal Cataloguing is practised by the National Central Library of a country with one language or by the Zonal or State Central libraries of a polyglot country, the maintenance of Union Catalogue will be made not only easy and prompt, but also cheap. However, the restriction called for by the size of the Union Catalogue will still be valid. If such Pre-Natal Cataloguing is practised by all countries, the Union Catalogue will be made equally easy even for foreign books. The organisation necessary for this has been described in the *Heading and canons* [RH5].

CHAPTER QB

MODIFICATION IN CATALOGUING RULES

1 Finding List

The primary function, if not the sole one, of a Union Catalogue of Books is to serve as Location List—that is, to show the names of the participating libraries having a copy of a specified book. This information is needed primarily for the purpose of Inter-Library Loan.

It is doubtful if it is practicable to make a Union Catalogue of Books perform any other function, such as co-ordinating book-selection or supplying bibliographical information or answering any other question usually asked of the catalogue of a service-library, enumerated in Chap DA. A Union Catalogue of Books is, therefore, best built as for a Location List.

2 Author and Title Approach

A Union Catalogue of Books is to be designed only for Author and Title Approach. It is so whether the enquirer is a reader or a service-library. It need not provide for any other approach. This is implied in the statements in Sec QB1. Therefore, the internal form of a Union Catalogue of Books has only to be that of a Dictionary Catalogue restricted to Author and Title Entries.

3 Result

These considerations indicate the need for drastic modifications of the rules of the normal Catalogue Code. This Part will restrict itself only to the indication of such modifications. These modifications concern the

1 Main Entry;
2 Prescription of the Holdings Section of the Main Entry; and
3 Design of Library Number to be used in the Holdings Section.

If there is Central Cataloguing, there is need to acquire for a Union Catalogue of Books only as many unit catalogue cards of a book as there will be Author and Title Entries for it.

4 Alphabetisation

The prepotent purpose of a Union Catalogue of books being that of a Finding List led to the preference of the Dictionary Form for the catalogue, and even there to its restriction to Author and Title Entries only. The same factor would press one still further in the direction of simplification. This lands one on the problem of alphabetisation. One simplification suggested by Ch W Brughoeffer of Frankfurt-on-Main was to ignore all the individualising elements in alphabetisation—ignoring not only year of birth and other elements, but even Secondary Element. It is claimed that the retention of the secondary element increases the time of filing by 55%. It is further claimed that the Secondary Element is not furnished by 15% of the enquirers. A further simplification is advocated by the Swiss Union Catalogue Centre even in respect of the Entry Element. It recommends the application of the Principle of Uniformisation in respect of all Variant Forms of an Entry Word arising out of transliteration or of cognate origin [E1]. For example, it is sought to equalise all the following words in alphabetisation:

Maier	Maiyer
Majer	Maiyer
Mayer	Maier
Mayr	

These steps in simplification really shift the potency in alphabetisation to the Title Section. The claim is that this happens inevitably if the enquiry fails to give the Entry Element accurately. What is the percentage of cases where it is not given accurately ? If it is not above 50, the result will be that the benefit of the greater potency of the Entry Word will be deliberately sacrificed in the majority of cases. Further, will the enquiring library give the title and particularly the first word of the title accurately ? Inaccuracy either in the name of the author or in the title necessarily causes delay in the location of the entry in the Union Catalogue. But the methods suggested above will cause equal delay even when accurate information is furnished. Surely this is not desirable. More of factual investigation is needed in respect of the optimum method for alphabetisation in a Union Catalogue of Books.

5 Card Form

The Fifth Law of Library Science and economic considerations rule out the book-form for a Union Catalogue of Books. Nor is there need for more than one copy. This copy is best kept and maintained at the Union Catalogue Centre. If at all, duplicate sets may be kept in certain regional centres. Even then, the number of sets will be small. A cheap method of duplication should prove sufficient. Thus the Card Form is indicated for a Union Catalogue of Books.

CHAPTER QC

MAIN ENTRY

0 Sections

The Main Entry of a book, in a Union Catalogue, is to consist successively of the following sections:

1 Leading Section;
2 Title Section; and
3 Holdings Section.

1 Leading Section

The Leading Section is to consist of the Heading chosen, rendered and written as prescribed in Chap MD for a Simple Book and the corresponding Sec of Part N for a Composite Book and for a Multi-Volumed Book.

2 Title Section

The Title Section is to be as prescribed in Chap ME for a Single-Volumed Simple-Book and the corresponding Sec of Part N for a Composite Book and for a Multi-volumed Book. The year of publication is to be added at the end.

3 Holdings Section

The Holdings Section is to give the Library Number (*See* Chap QD) for each of the participating libraries, arranged in columns with space between them for the mark mentioned in Sec QC31.

31 Report of Accession

A distinctive mark is to be put in pencil against the Library Number of the library reporting the accession of a copy of the book.

32 Report of Withdrawal

Whenever a library reports the withdrawal of a book, the mark against its Library Number is to be erased.

4 Artificial Composite Book

In the case of an Artificial Composite Book reported by a library, the Union Catalogue Centre is to prepare a separate Main Entry for each of the works contained in it.

5 Multi-volumed Book

In the case of a Multi-volumed Book, the Union Catalogue Centre is to prepare a separate Main Entry for each of its volumes.

CHAPTER QD

LIBRARY NUMBER

0 Functional Design

The Library Numbers are to be constructed according to the Principle of Geographical Contiguity [RP3] and so as to indicate the type of the library and its subject of specialisation, if any.

1 Zone Number

The First Digit of a Library Number is to represent the zone of the area of the Union Catalogue, in which the library is.

It may be called the **Zone Number.**

Here is a sample schedule of Zone Numbers for India:

A	Madras	L	Kashmir
B	Kerala	M	Uttar Pradesh
C	Mysore	N	Nepal
D	Andhra Pradesh	P	Bhutan
E	Maharashtra	Q	Bihar
F	Gujarat	R	Bengal
G	Madhya Pradesh	S	Assam
H	Rajasthan	T	Orissa
J	Delhi	U	Andamans
K	Punjab		

2 Sub-Zone Number

The Second Digit of a Library Number is to represent the Sub-Region, comprising one or more districts (counties), in which the Library is.

It may be called the **Sub-zone Number.**

This may be more or less in terms of the orientation zones such as:

1	East	5	West
2	South East	6	North West
3	South	7	North
4	South West	8	North East

This will have to be designed for each zone according to its shape, means of communication, and the nature of its terrain.

Here is a sample schedule of Sub-Region Numbers for the Zone "A Madras." :

1 Madras and Chingleput.
2 South Arcot and Tanjore.
3 Tiruchirappalli, Madura, and Ramnad.
4 Tirunelveli and Kanyakumari.
5 Coimbatore and Nilgiris.
6 Salem and North Arcot.

3 Locality Number

The Third Digit or Digit-Group of a Library Number is to represent the Locality in which the library is.

It may be called the **Locality Number.**

31 The Locality Number is to be got by the Alphabetical Device [RP4] using Capital for the initial letter and smalls for the second and later letters needed for use.

4 Type Number

The Fourth Digit is to represent the Status or the Subject of specialisation, if any.

This may be called the **Type Number.**

Here is a sample schedule of Status Number:

General Libraries :

1 State Central Library.
2 Public Library.
3 School Library.
4 College Library.
5 University Library.
6 Museum Library.
7 Research Institute Library.
8 Business or Departmental Library.

Specialising Libraries :

A to Z represented by their subjects of specialisation, as in the schedule of Main Classes of Colon Classification [RC12].

41 A library of any of the types 1 to 8, specialising in a subject should be treated as a specialising library.

5 Individualising Number

If there be more than one library with the same Library Number in the same locality, a further digit—say 1,2 . . —may be added to individualise them.

This further digit may be called **Individualising Number.**

Here is a selection from a Sample Schedule of Library Numbers:

A1M1	Madras State Central Library
A1M2	Madras City Central Library
A1M4	Madras Christian College Library
A1M41	Presidency College Library
A1M5	Madras University Library
A1M7	Servants of India Society Library
A1M8	Madras Legislature Library
A1MB	Indian Mathematical Society Library
A1MD	Madras Engineering College Library
A1ML	Madras Medical College Library
A1ML1	Stanley Medical College Library
A1MZ	Madras Law College Library
A1MZ1	High Court Library
A2A5	Annamalai University Library
A2NF	Neyveli Colliery Library
A3KB	Kodaikanal Solar Observatory Library
B1T5	Kerala University Library
C1BA	Bangalore Indian Institute of Science Library
C1BKX	Indian Dairy Research Institute Library.

6 Key to Library Numbers

The Union Catalogue Centre is to maintain a Key to Library Numbers in two Parts as follows:

1 The First Part is to serve as a dictionary to pass from the Library Number to the Name of the Library; and

2 The Second Part is to serve as a dictionary to pass from the Name of the Library to the Library Number.

Arrangement of the libraries in the Holdings Section according to the Library Numbers prescribed in this Chap will enable the Union Catalogue Centre to locate easily the most suitable library from which it can be borrowed for the library asking for inter-library loan. It is believed that this will be an advantage.

CHAPTER QE

CARD FOR UNION CATALOGUE

1 Material

The usual 125×75 mm card is to be used.

It is desirable to use strong durable card for a Union Catalogue.

2 Specification: Main Card

A card intended to take a Main Entry is to be printed as specified below:

1 The first four lines are to be left blank on one side to take the Heading and the Title Section.

2 Four columns of Library Numbers are to be printed in 8 point type below the space left vacant on that side.

3 Each of the above columns is to contain 7 Library Numbers with space at the bottom for interpolating one Library Number.

4 Four columns of Library Numbers are to be printed in 8 point type on the other side of the card.

5 Each of the columns is to contain 10 Library Numbers, with space in the middle and at the bottom for interpolating one Library Number in each space.

6 The commentary on Sec MH93 is to be borne in mind in printing the Library Numbers on the other side of the card.

7 Each Library Number is to be in antique type.

3 Example of a part of the Holdings Section

A1M1	A1M8	A1MZ	B1T3
A1M2	A1MB	A1MZ1	C1BA
A1M3	A1MD	A2A3	C1BA1
A1M4	A1ML	A2NF	C1BKX
A1M41	A1ML1	A3KX	C1BZ

4 Specification: Continuation Card

When the number of Library Numbers exceeds the capacity of one card, additional cards are to be written as Continued Cards.

41 A Continued Card is to have the Heading and the Title Section filled as in the original card.

42 A term such as "*Continued 1*" "*Continued 2*" is to be printed at the top right corner.

43 The term "*Continued in the next card*" is to be printed at the bottom of the Main Card and of all but the last of the continued cards.

44 The Library Numbers will, of course, be different in the different Continued Cards. This means that each continued card is to be printed separately.

PART R

UNION CATALOGUE OF PERIODICAL PUBLICATIONS

CHAPTER RA

COVERAGE

1 What to Include

Periodical Publications include periodicals as well as serials (*See* Sec FF11 and its subdivisions). Many serials are only of temporary value. Some kinds of directories may have more lasting value. Annual Reports—particularly of Departments of Governments—will have permanent value. Nor are all periodicals of permanent value. Some of them popularly called 'Magazines' are only of temporary value. It is usual to divide periodicals into Learned Periodicals and others. The cost of production of a Union Catalogue of Periodical Publications is high. Therefore, it is necessary not to allow it to cover all Periodical Publications. It is desirable to restrict it to serials of lasting value and to Learned Periodicals. In principle, this is a convenient method of restricting the coverage of Union Catalogue of Periodical Publications. But the application of the principle is by no means easy. In respect of serials, we can be certain of Annual Reports being worthy of inclusion. The others will require judgement on an *ad hoc* basis depending upon local conditions. In respect of periodicals, similarly, it is by no means easy to sort out periodicals into the learned ones and the others. One way of defining a Learned Periodical is that it is of value to research. Even this does not solve the problem. For, two difficulties are generally met with. In the first place, only a few contributions in each volume of a periodical may be of value to research. The others may be of impermanent value. Secondly, some periodicals may change their character with time. One starting as a Learned Periodical may not continue to be so throughout its career. On the other hand, there are periodicals which started with much humbler intention but have gained the status of Learned Periodicals in course of time. While compiling the *Union catalogue of learned periodicals in South Asia* (1953), I could easily spot out quite a number of periodicals definitely learned and permanently learned. On the other hand, there were several other periodicals about which this could not be said. Therefore, I started with the following definition:

A periodical is to be taken as a Learned Periodical if

1 Each issue of it contains at least one article of research value; and

2 At least one volume of a set is made of issues containing contributions of such value.

The above definition was over-simplified. It did not yield the desired result automatically. Greater difficulty was experienced in the field of periodicals of Social Sciences than of Natural Sciences. Even greater difficulty was felt in the field of Humanities. The difficulty was greater in Generalia. In the Natural Sciences, again, periodicals in applied fields gave much difficulty.

2 Value

From the point of view both of economy and of the conservation of the research-potential of a country, a Union Catalogue of Learned Periodicals is of even greater importance than one of books. Moreover, its area of coverage can be larger than for books. The routine of reporting to the Union Catalogue Centre is far less arduous.

3 Stability

A Union Catalogue of Periodical Publications comprehends fewer titles than the one for books. The number of new periodical publications taken in a participating library is far less than the number of new books. The frequency of the taking of new periodical publications is roughly one year, whereas that for new books may be as short as one week. The difference in respect of the discontinuance of periodical publications and of the withdrawal of books is also similar. Therefore, the task of the participating libraries in sending reports and of the Union Catalogue Centre in absorbing the reports is far less arduous. This gives a fair amount of stability to a Union Catalogue of Periodical Publications.

4 Elimination of Waste

If a Union Catalogue covers a rich collection so as to be a good approximation to a World List of Periodical Publications, it gives the answers to questions on world output of periodical publications, such as those enumerated in Sec RB4.

The answers on world output are needed particularly in regard to Abstracting and Indexing Periodicals, in order to eliminate wastage due to multiplication of effort in certain subjects and absence of any effort whatever in other subjects. The Unesco and the International Federation for Documentation made *ad hoc* investigations of this problem at a tremendous cost. This is a problem requiring continuous vigilance. It is best done at the least cost if the Union Catalogues of Periodical Publications are of the Classified Kind and give, in the Alphabetical Part, Class Index Entries of all kinds including those prescribed in Sec PB38.

CHAPTER RB

USERS

0 Multi-Purpose Approaches

Much of expenditure has to be incurred in printing a Union Catalogue of Periodical Publications. By spending an additional small percentage of it, the catalogue can be made to answer questions of all kinds of approaches, and serve not merely as a Finding List.

1 Subject Approach

Provision for Subject Approach calls for a Classified Part. This part will be of considerable help for the co-ordination of Selection Work in particular subject-areas, and the Work of Discontinuing particular titles, by the participating libraries. This co-ordination will ensure complete sets of more titles being available in the country or the region, than otherwise. This will be a great help to research-workers.

2 Conspectus-Effect

A comparison of the entries for a Periodical Publication with frequent changes of title—and such cases are many—given as examples in Chap PF and Sec PZD4 will show the far more effective and simpler presentation of a full conspectus by the Classified Catalogue than by a Dictionary Catalogue. The conspectus-effect is even more helpful in a catalogue in book-form than in a card catalogue. This factor also emphasises the value of the Classified Part.

3 Finding List

A Classified Catalogue implies the addition of an Alphabetical Part, as prescribed in Chap FP. The Alphabetical Part in a Classified Catalogue can be made very compact, virtually on the basis of one entry for a line. This will bring quite a large number of titles within a single sweep of the eye. And this is essential in a Finding List. On the other hand, in the Dictionary Catalogue, the alphabetical entry for each title will have to carry the full load of the Holding Section and the Sections setting forth the successive complexities in the career of the title, and the Section of Periodicity. A single sweep of the eye cannot take more than one title. This is a fault in a Finding List. Therefore, a Union Catalogue of Periodical Publications should be after the pattern of a Classified Catalogue.

4 Bibliographical Approach

It will be a great help to bibliographical research if the union catalogue can be made to give nearly ready-made answers to various bibliographical questions such as,

1 How many, and what, Periodical Publications in a given subject are available in the country or zone of the Union Catalogue ?

2 What are the subjects in which the Union Catalogue has entries of the Periodical Publications produced in a specific country or in a specific language ?

3 What are the weak areas of coverage, in terms of subjects and the countries of origin of the Periodical Publications, needing attention in the total holdings of the country or the region ?

4 What are the Abstracting and Indexing Periodicals available in the country and how is their subject-distribution ?

The answers to these questions will go a long way in pooling the Periodical Publications Fund of a country and getting the best return on it.

CHAPTER RC

PHYSICAL FORM

1 Card Form

The master Union Catalogue should be kept in cards to have all the advantages of the mobility of card-form and of their being thus kept perpetual. It will make the publications of successive editions less arduous than otherwise.

2 Printed Form

To facilitate use by libraries and others, the Union Catalogue of Learned Periodicals should also be printed in book form at convenient intervals. Therefore, this part is giving rules primarily for a Printed Catalogue in book form. It is based on experience gained from 1949 to 1953 in producing a Union Catalogue for the South Asian region [RZU].

3 Result

The Rules in Part P are sufficient to a large extent for the perpetual Card Catalogue to be maintained in the Union Catalogue Centre. But a Union Catalogue should have a Holdings Section. This calls for additional Rules. We have seen the additional Rules needed in this behalf in the case of a Union Catalogue of Books. But those Rules are not sufficient in the case of a Union Catalogue of Periodical Publication. Further, many of the Continued Cards prescribed for Card Technique will have to be represented only by additional sections in one and the same entry, if the catalogue is printed in book form. Such considerations indicate the necessity for modifications in the Rules of the normal Catalogue Code. This Part will restrict itself only to such modifications.

CHAPTER RD

MAIN ENTRY

1 Leading Section

The Leading Section of the Main Entry of a Periodical Publication is to contain successively of the Class Number and the Heading.

2 Change of Title

There is to be a separate Section for each Change of Title of the Periodical Publication.

21 The Sections due to Change of Titles are to be printed in their Chronological Sequence.

3 Volumes Published

The Section giving volumes published under each title is to follow the Section containing that Title.

31 The Section following a Title is to give successively all the information corresponding to all the complexities of the groups 2 and 3 enumerated in Chap PA.

4 Open for Publications

"Open for publication" is to be indicated by C instead of by a dash.

5 Cumulative Index

The first Section on Periodicity is to be followed by the Section on Cumulative Index, if any. It should begin with the term "*Index*". The specification of the indexes are to follow thereafter, in chronological sequence. Each specification is to give

1 Serial number such as 1, 2 etc;

2 Colon;

3 Numbers of the volumes covered in inclusive notation, if available;

4 Semicolon;

5 Numbers of the years covered, in inclusive notation; and

6 Full stop.

51 When a volume of a Cumulative Index does not have independent existence but forms a volume of the Periodical Publication itself or a part thereof, this information is to be given in crooked brackets, after the specification of the cumulative index concerned, with the introductory words "is contained in".

6 Complexity Section

Each Complexity Section is to be introduced by a term, so printed as to end at the right end of its line.

61 The introducing term of a Complexity Section is to consist successively of the

1 Term "From";

2 Number of the volume and/or the year of commencement of the complexity; and

3 Term in italics, indicating the nature of the Complexity.

62 The introducing line is to be followed by a Section for each of the other Periodical Publications involved in the Complexity.

63 The Section devoted to each such Periodical Publication is to mention its Class Number and the Title, or the Title only if its Class Number is the same as given in the Leading Section.

7 Holdings Section

The Holdings Section is to give the Library Number (*See* Chap QD) for each of the participating libraries in the sequence of the Library Numbers. Against the number of each library its holdings are to be given as prescribed in Sec PB15 and its subdivisions with the modification that 'Open for the Library' is to be shown by C instead of by a dash.

Example:

1 *Im*52,M **Nuovo botanico** italiano.
1-2; 1844-47.
Index. 1: (2) 1-25; 1869-93. {is contained in V (2) 25}.
From 1869 *continued as*
Nuovo giornale botanica italiano, (Societa Botanica Italiana).
(2) 1-25; 1869-93 Ns:1; 1894 C.
From 1892 *split partially into* and in 1927 *amalgamated*
*Im*52,M,1 **Bulletin,** Societa Botanica italiana.

A1M4 1-2	**A2A5** (2) Ns: 1 C
A1M5 1-2. (2) 1-25; Ns: 1-12, 32-40 C	**C1BA** (2) Ns: 32-40 C

CHAPTER RE

OTHER ENTRIES

1 Cross Reference Entry

No Cross Reference Entry is to be given in a Union Catalogue of Periodical Publications.

2 Class Index Entry

Class Index Entries in a Union Catalogue of Periodical Publications, corresponding to the part of each Class Number, preceding the Common Isolate Digit denoting "Periodical Publication", are to be given as prescribed in Chap K.

21 Class Index Entries are also to be given as prescribed in Sec LB3 and its subdivisions excepting Sec LB37 and LB371.

3 Cross Reference Index Entry

No Cross Reference Index Entry is to be given in a Union Catalogue of Periodical Publications.

4 Book Index Entry

No Book Index Entry is to be given in a Union Catalogue of Periodical Publications.

CHAPTER RF

ABBREVIATIONS

1 Scheme for Abbreviation

Abbreviations are to be used in the Alphabetical Part according to a definite scheme.

2 Guiding Principles

The entry in the Alphabetical Part should be short and brief—say, not more than 2 inches in length. This should be so in order to enable a single sweep of the eye to cover the largest possible number of entries.

To secure this, titles should be abbreviated by

1 Omitting articles, conjunctions, prepositions and other auxiliary words wherever they can be so omitted without causing unintelligibility;

2 Contracting generic oft-recurring words indicative of the periodical nature of the publication to the initial letter, wherever possible, and otherwise to the fewest possible, initial letters;

3 Contracting the names of subjects usually occurring in titles of periodical publications to as few letters as possible;

4 Contracting the names of countries, states and cities, usually occurring in titles of periodical publications to as few letters as possible; and

5 Contracting other words—nouns or adjectives—usually occurring in titles of periodical publications to as few letters as possible.

3 Omission of Auxiliary Words

The omission of auxiliary words will be of special advantage in looking up titles in unfamiliar languages. It is only the substantives in such titles that usually stick to memory. Even if some auxiliary words happen to be remembered, one is not sure of their morphological variations or of their variants in different languages. Many readers trip over mistakes made in this regard. When a reader looks up a Union Catalogue, it often happens that he is usually absorbed in his own thought. And therefore, tripping over such a trivial difficulty is quite common. Der, des, du, etc, form an example. So far as it can be seen, due weight does not seem to have been given to these psychological factors in the list of contractions set up in the *World list* or in the system of contractions promoted or recommended by ISO/TC 46.

4 Principles of Contraction

41 Single Word

It may not be necessary to abbreviate a title if it consists of a single word—particularly a short word.

42 Real Saving of Space

Abbreviations should not be used mechanically. They should be used only if there is real saving of space. In particular in an index, abbreviation need not be used unless there is a saving of a line.

43 Holistic Contraction

Contractions should not be attempted piece-meal. As whole a view as possible of the entire range of words to be contracted should be taken. The contractions should be so designed as to ensure ease of intelligibility and to secure maximum of abbreviation. Holism should be the guiding principle.

44 Cognate Words

While all this effort is worth making to secure shortness of entries, the abbreviations can be so designed as to serve a second useful purpose. Cognate words in diverse languages may be brought together whenever their first few letters are the same. Their reduction to the same contraction will be of particular value in the case of initial words of title. This second advantage also should be borne in mind in designing the system of contraction.

5 Resolution of Homonym

If two abbreviated titles are homonymous they should be individualised by adding the name of the language as the individualising term. Wherever this is not sufficient the name of the country also may be used. No doubt the Class Number of the periodical contains the number for the country. But we should not expect the reader to depend upon it.

6 Preservation of Sequence

Usually the words occurring as the entry words in title entries of periodicals are

1 Words denoting that a publication is a periodical one;
2 Names of subjects; and
3 Names of countries or languages.

It is therefore necessary that the contractions of such words should be such that the contractions will occur approximately in the same sequence in which the words themselves will occur if written in full. Any contraction, which involves elision of a letter in the middle of a word, like 'Bd' for 'Board', 'Enging' for 'Engineering', and 'Yrbk' for 'Year Book', will put the contraction in a place other than the one in which a reader will look for it. It is therefore necessary that the contraction of a word which is likely to be entry word should be made of the first few letters in the word written continuously without any elision.

7 Table of Contractions

This principle has been followed in the tables given below. For convenience of reference by the cataloguer, the contractions for the three classes of words mentioned above are given in separate tables. There is also a fourth table giving contractions of other words which commonly occur.

8 Indian Languages

The examples of contractions given hereunder do not include terms in any Indian Language. This is due to lack of experience. But the Documentation Committee of the Indian Standards Institution has taken up this problem.

CHAPTER RG

CONTRACTIONS FOR WORDS DENOTING 'PERIODICAL PUBLICATION'

Note:

1 The same contraction is to be used for all morphological forms of the words shown against it as well as for all its cognate forms in other languages in so far as the letters in the contractions are the first words in them.

2 Cognate forms in different languages differing in their initial letters should be linked up by cross reference (*See* Sec RG1 for examples).

3 In Germanic and Sanskritic languages words can be formed by coalescing several words together. In such cases each component word may be contracted and the contractions may be connected by hyphen.

Example:

1	Forsch-arb	= Forschungsarbeiten
2	M -ber	= Maandbericht
3	Q -schr	= Quartalschrift
4	Verb -nachr	= Verbandsnachrichten
5	Verb -z	= Verbandszeitschrift

2 Illustrative Abbreviations

Aarb Aarbog
Aarskr Aarskrift
Aarskat Aarskatalog
Abh Abhandlungen
Abstr Abstracts
Abt Abteilung
See also Afd
Act Acta
Administrative report
see Rep
Administrative
review *see* Rep
Afd Afdeeling
See also Abt
Afh Afhandlingar
Alm Almanac
Anecd Anecdota
An Annals
Annot Annotations
Annual report *see*
Rep
An Rep
Anz Anzeiger
Arb Arbeiten
Arch Archiv
Ark Arkiv
Beitr Beitraege
Beiw Beiwerke
Beretn Beretning
Bibliog Bibliography
Bibliot Biblioteca
Bijd Bijdragen
Bl Blaatter
Bol Boletin
Bul Bulletin
See also Bol
Cah Cahier

Chron	Chronicle
Circ	Circular
Col	Colecao
Com	Comment
Contrib	Contribution
Conv	Convention
Cor	Correio *See also* Cour
Corr	Correspondents
Cour	Courier *See also* Cor
Cro	Cronicon
Cur	Current
Diar	Diary
Dig	Digest
Disc	Discussion
Disk	Diskussionnyi
Diss	Dissertationes
Doc	Documentation
Dok	Dokumentation
Ecrit	Ecrits
Efem	Efemerides *See also* Ephem
Ency	Ecyclopaedia
Ephem	Ephemerides *See also* Efem
Ergeb	Ergebnisse
Estud	Estudios
Etud	Etudes
F	Fortnightly
Forsch	Forschung
Fortsch	Fortschritte
Gac	Gaceta
Gaz	Gazette
Ged	Gedichte
Ges	Gesellschaft
Gior	Giornale *See also* J and Zhur
Her	Herald
Intermed	Intermediare

J	Journal *See also* Gior and Zhur
Jahr	Jahrbuch
Jour *see* J and Zhur	
M	Monthly
Mag	Magazine
Meddel	Meddelanden
Mem	Memoires
Misc	Miscellaneous
Mit	Mitteilungen
Monog	Monograph
Nach	Nachrichten
Observ	Observations
Pam	Pamphlet
Per	Periodical
Prog	Progress
Progress Report *see* Rep	
Pub	Publications
Q	Quarterly
Rec	Record
Recu	Recueil
Rendic	Rendiconti
Rep	Report
Res	Research
Rev	Review
Ric	Ricerca
Rico	Ricordi *See also* Rec
Riv	Rivista *See also* Rev
Samm	Sammlung
Schr	Schriften
Scr	Scripta
Sel	Selections
Ser	Series
Skr	Skrifter
Souv	Souvenir

Stud	**Studies**	**Urk**	**Urkunden**
Sup	**Supplement**	**W**	**Weekly**
Surv	**Survey**	**Wirtsch**	**Wirtschaftliches**
		Wiss	**Wissen**
T	**Tijdschrift**	**Yearb**	**Yearbook**
Tab	**Tables**		
Tid	**Tidings**	**Z**	**Zeitschrift**
Trab	**Trabajos**	**Zei**	**Zeitung**
Trans	**Transactions**	**Zent**	**Zentral**
Trav	**Travaux**	**Zhur**	**Zhurnal**
Trib	**Tribune**		*See also* Gior *and* J

CHAPTER RH

CONTRACTIONS OF NAMES OF SUBJECTS

Note:

The same contraction is to be used for all morphological forms of the words shown against it as well as for all its cognate forms in other languages in so far as the letters in the contractions are the first words in them.

Contraction	Subject
Agric	Agriculture
Agron	Agronomy
Algol	Algology
Anthrop	Anthropology
Anthropos	Anthroposophy
Archaeol	Archaeology
Archit	Architecture
Astrol	Astrology
Astron	Astronomy
Astrophys	Astrophysics
Ayur	Ayurveda
Behav	Behaviorism
Biochem	Biochemistry
Biol	Biology
Biomet	Biometry
Biophys	Biophysics
Bot	Botany
Buddh	Buddhism
Chem	Chemistry
Coll	Colloids
Comm	Commerce
Crim	Crime
Cryst	Crystallography
Delinq	Delinquency
Derm	Dermatology
Ecol	Ecology
Econ	Economics *See also* Ekon
Educ	Education
Electr	Electricity
Electrochem	Electrochemistry
Ekon	Ekonomia *See also* Econ
Endocr	Endocrinology
Engin	Engineering
Entom	Entomology
Epigr	Epigraphy
Esth	Esthetics
Eth	Ethics
Ethn	Ethnology
Eugen	Eugenics
Farm	Farming
For	Forestry
Gard	Gardening
Geneal	Genealogy
Genet	Genetics
Geog	Geography
Geol	Geology
Geri	Geriatrics
Gyn	Gynecology
Harb	Harbour
Helminth	Helminthology
Highw	Highway
Hist	History
Homoeop	Homoeopathy
Hort	Horticulture
Hosp	Hospital
Hydr	Hydraulics
Hyg	Hygiene
Illum	Illumination
Insur	Insurance
Instrum	Instrument
Irrig	Irrigation
Jurisp	Jurisprudence
Lab	Labour
Legis	Legislation
Ling	Linguistics
Lit	Literature
Machin	Machine
Magn	Magnetism
Math	Mathematics
Mech	Mechanics

Med	Medicine	Psychoan	Psychoanalysis
Metaphys	Metaphysics	Psychomet	Psychometry
Meteorol	Meteorology	Psychosom	Psychosomatics
Metr	Metrology	Rad	Radio
Microbiol	Microbiology	Radioact	Radioactivity
Microsc	Microscopy	Railw	Railway
Mil	Military	Rel	Religion
Min	Mining	Rorsch	Rorschah
Minerol	Minerology	Sanit	Sanitation
Morph	Morphology	Sc	Science
Mus	Museum	Sch	School
Mycol	Mycology	Sculp	Sculpture
Myth	Mythology	Seism	Seismology
Nav	Naval	Sociol	Sociology
Nucl	Nuclear	Spectr	Spectroscopy
Nurs	Nursing	Statist	Statistics
Obst	Obstetrics	Stenog	Stenography
Opt	Optics	Surg	Surgery
Ophthal	Ophthalmology	Syph	Syphilis
Paras	Parasitology	Tax	Taxation
Parli	Parliament	Tech	Technology
Path	Pathology	Teleg	Telegraph
Ped	Pediatrics	Teleph	Telephone
Petr	Petrology	Telev	Television
Pharm	Pharmacology	Ter	Terrestrial
Phil	Philosophy	Theol	Theology
Philol	Philology	Theos	Theosophy
Phy	Physics	Therap	Therapeutics
Physiog	Physiography	Timb	Timber
Physiol	Physiology	Tr	Trade
Phyt	Phytology	Transp	Transport
Phytopath	Phytopathology	Tuber	Tuberculosis
Plast	Plastics	Vet	Veterinary
Polym	Polymer	Wiss	Wissenschaft
Psych	Psychology	Zoo	Zoology

CHAPTER RJ

CONTRACTIONS OF GEOGRAPHICAL NAMES AND NAMES OF LANGUAGES

Note:

The same contraction is to be used both for the name of a country and the name of a language if they are cognate and for all their morphological variations, in so far as the letters in the contractions are the first words in them.

Abys	Abyssinia	Egyp	Egypt
Afgh	Afghanistan	Eng	England
Afr	Africa	Equad	Equador
Alb	Albania	Esper	Esperanto
Alg	Algeria	Esthon	Esthonia
All	Allahabad	Eur	Europe
Alp	Alpine	Flem	Flemish
Amer	America	Fr	France
Arab	Arabia	Ger	Germany
Argen	Argentina	Guj	Gujarat
Asia	Asian	Holl	Holland
Austral	Australia	Hung	Hungary
Austr	Austria	Hyd	Hyderabad
Balt	Baltic	Ind	India
Belg	Belgium	Indo-Chin	Indo-China
Beng	Bengal	Ir	Ireland
Bih	Bihar	Ital	Italy
Bom	Bombay	Jap	Japan
Braz	Brazil	Kan	Kanarese
Br	British	Kash	Kashmir
Bulg	Bulgaria	Latv	Latvia
Burm	Burma	Lith	Lithuania
Can	Canada	Lond	London
Cey	Ceylon	Mal	Malayalam
Chil	Chile	Manch	Manchuria
Chin	China	Mang	Mangolia
Colomb	Colombia	Mex	Mexico
Cub	Cuba	Mys	Mysore
Czech	Czecho-Slovaka	Ned	Nederland
Dan	Danish	Neth	Netherlands
Denm	Denmark	Nied	Niederland
Deu	Deutsch	Nor	Norway

Oris	Orissa	Schweiz	Schweizerisch
Osterr	Osterreich	Scot	Scotland
Pak	Pakistan	Sind	Sindh
Palest	Palestine	Sinh	Sinhalese
Pers	Persia	Span	Spanish
Pol	Poland	Swed	Sweden
Port	Portugal	Switz	Switzerland
Punj	Punjab	Syr	Syria
Rum	Rumania		
Russ	Russia	Tam	Tamil
Sans	Sanskrit	Tel	Telugu
Scand	Scandinavia	Travan	Travancore
Schwed	Schwedisch	Turk	Turkey

CHAPTER RK

CONTRACTIONS FOR GENERAL WORDS

A	Annual
Abn	Abnormal
Acad	Academy
	See also Akad
Actu	Actuarial
Adm	Administration
Adv	Advancement
Advert	Advertisement
Akad	Akademi
	See also Acad
Alg	Algemein
Anal	Analytical
Anim	Animal
Antiq	Antiquarian
Appl	Applied
Artil	Artillery
Ass	Association
Atom	Atomic
Auto	Automobile
Aviat	Aviation
Biblioph	Bibliophile
Bayer	Bayerischen
Beibl	Beiblatten
Beih	Beihaft
Ber	Berichte
Cal	Calendar
Cat	Catalogue
Centr	Central
Cir	Circular
Civ	Civil
Civil	Civilisation
Clin	Clinical
Co	Company
Col	Collection
Colon	Colonial
Commis	Commission
	See also Kommis
Commit	Committee
	See also Kommit
Commun	Communication
Comp	Comparison
Conf	Conference
Cong	Congress
Const	Constitutional
Constr	Construction
Contr	Contribution
Co-op	Co-operation
Corp	Corporation
Corres	Correspondenza
Cott	Cotton
Crit	Critical
Cul	Cultural
D	Daily
Darst	Darstelling
Dep	Department
Diagn	Diagnosis
Dict	Dictionary
Diplom	Diplomatic
Dir	Direction
Dis	Diseases
Dist	District
Dram	Dramatic
E	East
Ed	Edition
Ele	Elementary
Exper	Experimental
	See also Sperim
Extr	Extract
Fac	Faculty
Fak	Fakultat
Fam	Family
Fed	Federal
Finan	Financial
For	Foreign
Formul	Formula
Found	Foundation
Fund	Fundamental
Gen	General

Gesh	Gechichte
Gesel	Gesellschaft
Gl	Glass
Gov	Government
Gr	Great
H	Halfyearly
Hebd	Hebdomadaire
Hist	Historical
Husb	Husbandry
Illus	Illustrated
Imp	Imperial
Impr	Imprint
Inc	Incorporated
Indep	Independent
Industr	Industrial
Inform	Information
Inorg	Inorganic
Inst	Institution
Intern	International
Juv	Juvenile
K	Koniglische
Kat	Katalog
Kommis	Kommission *See also* Commis
Kommit	Kommittee *See also* Commit
Korres	Korrespondence
Labor	Laboratory
Leg	Legal
Libr	Library
Linn	Linnean
Loc	Local
Man	Manual
Meth	Method
Mun	Municipal
N	North
Nach	Nachrichten
Nat	National
Natur	Natural
Nutr	Nutrition
Obs	Observatory
Occid	Occidental
Occup	Occupational
Off	Office
Opin	Opinion
Ordin	Ordinance

Org	Organic
Organ	Organisation
Orient	Oriental
Philat	Philatelic
Photo	Photographic
Pict	Picture
Plan	Planning
Pol	Political
Polytech	Polytechnic
Prac	Practical
Prak	Praktical
Prelim	Preliminary
Print	Printing
Prob	Problem
Prod	Production
Prog	Progress
Prov	Province
Pub	Public
Quell	Quellen
Quest	Questions
Quot	Quotation
R	Royal
Red	Redactor
Refl	Reflections
Reg	Register
Rej	Rejest-
Relat	Relation
Repos	Repository
Repr	Reprints
S	South
Samml	Sammlung
Sec	Secondary
Sect	Section
Sel	Selection
Sem	Semaine
Semest	Semestrialle
Serv	Service
Sits	Sitsung
Soc	Social
Spec	Special
Sperim	Sperimentale *See also* Exper
Stand	Standard
Tech	Technical
Tek	Teknisk
Termin	Terminology

Trien	Triennial	Vener	Veneral
Trop	Tropical	Ver	Verein
		Verb	Verband
Uber	Ubersicht	Vereinig	Vereinigung
Univ	University	Verz	Verzuhnis
Util	Utilities	Vet	Veterinary

CHAPTER RL

TYPOGRAPHY

1 Classified Part

It is helpful to have typographical distinction between the Leading Section, the Sections for Change of Titles, and the Holdings Sections on the one hand, and the Sections for Complexities on the other. The latter Sections may be subordinated to the former ones, by printing them in smaller type.

11 Leading Section

Perhaps, it is helpful to make the first two words in the Title of the Periodical Publication in the Leading Section more dominant than the other words in the Entry, say by printing them in antique capitals or in capitals and smalls.

2 Feature Heading

The Classified Part of a Union Catalogue of Periodical Publications is to be provided with Feature Headings on the analogy of the Rules in Sec SF1.

Examples:

The Chapter, headed "B Mathematics" will have Feature Headings as follows:

B MATHEMATICS

***Bam* Abstracting Periodical**

(Under this will be given all the Abstracting Periodicals in Mathematics, in the way shown below under "B9 Astronomy".)

***Bm* Periodical**

(Under this will be given all the Periodical Publications in Mathematics, in the way shown below under "B9 Astronomy").

B9 Astronomy

B9*m* Periodicals

B9*m*41 China

(Under this will be given all the Chinese periodicals in Astronomy).

B9*m*42 Japan

(Under this will be given all the Japanese periodicals in Astronomy).

B9*m*44 INDIA

(Under this will be given all the Indian periodicals in Astronomy).

3 Alphabetical Part

It may be of help to design a suitable typographical variation for the Titles, the Names of Sponsors and the Names of Specific Subjects, occurring as Heading in the alphabetical Entries. The following may be a suitable specification:

1 Title—Black face Capital and lower case letters to be used as in prose;

2 Sponsor Heading—Capital and small capitals; and

3 Specific subjects—Capitals and lower case letters.

4 Model

The above Rules on the lay-out and typography are based on the experience gained in publishing the *Union catalogue of learned periodical publications in South Asia* in 1953.

41 *See also* Sec SK2

CHAPTER RM

LAY OUT

0 Chapters

A printed Union Catalogue of Periodical Publications is to consist of the following six chapters:

1 To Find Out;
2 Key to Library Numbers;
3 Technical Note;
4 Conspectus of Specific Subjects;
5 Classified Part; and
6 Alphabetical Part

1 To Find Out

A sample draft of "To Find Out" is given hereunder:

11 If Name of Publication is Known

If you know the correct name of the periodical publication, look for it in the Alphabetical Part (Chap 6) in which the names of publications stand arranged alphabetically. Note the number entered against it. It is its Class Number.

Then turn to the Classified Part (Chap 5). The top-corners of its pages indicate the Class Numbers occurring in them. With their help, find out the page where the Class Number of what you seek lies.

There, you will find

1 Its Class Number;
2 Its name;
3 A specification of its published volumes:
4 Changes in its name and its other idiosyncracies; and
5 The holdings of the participating libraries. In each line of the holdings the number appearing at the beginning in black face—*e g* **L32**—represents a library. The succeeding numbers denote the volumes it has. For the name of the library represented by the number in black face, see the Key to Libraries (Chap 2). For further information see the Technical Note (Chap 3).

12 If Name is Not Known

If you do not know the correct first word in the name of the periodical publication, but remember its specific subject or some larger subject to which it belongs, look up the name of the subject in the Alphabetical Part (Chap 6). From it, pick out its Class Number. Then look up the Classified Part (as shown in Sec RM11) and arrive at the page or pages where the Class Number occurs. There, all the publications in the subject will follow one another in geographical sequence, and within a geographical group, in the chronological sequence. It will be easy for you to recognise the name of your periodical in this panorama.

The last section of the entry will show the libraries from where its volumes can be got (exactly as in Sec RM11).

13 Examples

1 Suppose you wish to know where the sixth volume of the *Annals of mathematical statistics* can be found. The Alphabetical Part (Chap 6) gives its number as B28*m*73,N. Look up this number in the Classified Part (Chap 5). The entry beginning with it gives all the libraries from where it can be had.

2 Suppose you did not remember the first word 'Annals'. Then look up 'Statistics' in the Alphabetical Part (Chap 6). It gives the class number B28. Look up this number in the Classified Part (Chap 5). It gives the periodicals on Statistics. Look down this list until you recognise the name you vaguely remembered. The last section of its entry gives all the libraries from where it can be had.

3 Even if you had looked up 'Mathematics' in the Alphabetical Part (Chap 6), it would have led you to the pages in the Classified Part (Chap 5) where Class Numbers begin with B. Looking through the list in those pages, you will be led to your periodical. Only you will have to scan a larger range of entries. But surely this range will be considerably smaller than the whole catalogue.

2 Key to Library Numbers

This chapter is to give a Key to Libraries to serve as a dictionary to pass from the Library Number to the Name of the Library.

21 Examples are to be given for the interpretation of Library Number.

3 Technical Note

The Technical Note is to feature and explain the following points:

1 The Classified Part—Information about the types of entries such as Cumulative Index Entry, and Main Entry, how they get themselves grouped, the structure of the Class Number, the rendering of the names of Periodical Publications, their idiosyncracies, and Holdings Section; and

2 The Alphabetical Part—Information about the types of entries, their uses and the abbreviation used.

4 Conspectus of Specific Subjects

The Conspectus of Specific Subjects is to be an exhaustive schedule, properly featured, of all the Class Numbers upto the beginning of a Common Subdivision digit—such as *m*, *n*, *p*, *r*.

Example:

B MATHEMATICS

B	Mathematics	B9:6	Astrophysics
		B93	Sun
B28	Statistics	B93:6	Solar physics
B31	Analysis	B96	Stars
B7	Mechanics	B963	Variable stars
B9	Astronomy		

C PHYSICS

C	Physics	C75	Terrestrial magnetism
C5	Radiation	C9B3	Nuclear physics
	etc	etc	etc

Under each of the above subjects, common subdivisions may occur as illustrated below:

B*a* Bibliography
B*e* Tables
B*w* Biography

The periodicals in these and in B (Mathematics proper) will stand arranged as shown below:

B*am* Abstracting periodical in Mathematics
B*en* Serial of Tables in Mathematics
B*m* Periodical in Mathematics
B*n* Serial in Mathematics
B*r* Administration Reports about Mathematics
B*wn* Who's who in Mathematics

CHAPTER RN

PAGINATION AND INCLUSIVE CAPTIONS

1 Pagination

The pagination is to be given at the outer end of the bottom of each page.

2 Classified Part

21 The left end of the top-line of a verso page is to give the Part of the Class Number ending with the geographical focus, pertaining to the entry occupying the first line of the page.

22 The right end of the top-line of a recto page is to give the part of the Class Number ending with the geographical focus, pertaining to the entry occupying the last line of the page.

3 Alphabetical Part

31 The left end of the top-line of a verso page is to give the first three letters pertaining to the first word of the entry to which the first line of the page belongs.

32 The right end of the top-line of a recto page is to give the first three letters pertaining to the first word of the entry to which the last line of the page belongs.

CHAPTER RP

CARD TECHNIQUE

1 Material

The usual 125×75 mm card is to be used.

It is desirable to use strong durable card for a Union Catalogue.

2 Specification: Main Card

The normal ruled Catalogue Card is to be used.

3 Continued Cards

The Continued Cards are to be added in accordance with the Rules in Part P.

4 Holdings Cards

The Holdings Card is to be inserted after all the Continued Cards of the entry.

41 Leading Section

The Leading line of the Holdings Card is to give the Class Number of the periodical.

42 Library Number

The Library Numbers are to be printed in a single column in their sequence.

43 Number of Library Numbers

The column is to contain ten Library Numbers, with place at the bottom for interpolating one Library Number.

44 Typography

Each Library Number is to be in Antique Type.

45 Number of Holdings Cards

If the Number of participating libraries is greater than twenty, Continued-Holdings Cards are to be used to the necessary extent.

PART S

NATIONAL BIBLIOGRAPHY

CHAPTER SA

DEFINITION OF NATIONAL BIBLIOGRAPHY

1 Definition

The term 'National Bibliography' may denote a list of all the documents with independent physical existence including Periodical Publications (which will hereinafter be denoted by the term 'Book'),

1 Produced within the country; or

2 In the language of the country whether produced within or outside the country; or

3 On the country, whether produced within or outside the country; or

4 By the nationals of the country, whether produced within or outside the country; or

5 On the country and on the nationals of the country, whether produced within or outside the country; or

6 On the thought created in the country, whether produced within or outside the country; or

7 All of the above or any combination of them.

2 Restricted Scope

Normally, a National Bibliography belongs to Category 1 mentioned in Sec 1. Even here, all the books are not included. Periodical Publications usually form an excluded category; if at all the first issue of a periodical gets included. In the National Bibliography of France, however, all the issues of the periodicals are included as and when they are published. Books below a certain value in money or below a certain number of pages in size, and below a certain standard are excluded in some National Bibliographies, though, the boundary line is not very definite. Some of the usually excluded types are:

1 Fleeting materials, such as minor works of only local interest such as reports on festivities and exhibition catalogues:

2 Pedlar songs;

3 Juvenile picture books;

4 Juvenile text-books and other practice materials;

5 Calenders of educational institution;

6 Instructions for workers, non-commissioned officers, and privates;

7 Recipes in home-management lacking scientific interest; and

8 Guides in know-how and other elementary knowledge.

Government Publications form another category which may not be included in a National Bibliography. However, as the Government is becoming the most prolific and influencial publisher in most of the countries, there is every chance that they will be included in future.

Maps, atlases, and theses are also not included by all National Bibliographies. Certain other bibliographies similar in status to National Bibliography, belong to the category 2 mentioned in Sec SA1. For example, *Cumulative book index* of H W Wilson and Co includes all books published in English whatever be the country of origin. So also *Deutsche Nationalbibliographie* published by Deutsche Bucherei of Leipzig covers all books published in German whatever be the country of origin. There are bibliographies belonging to the other four categories of Sec SA1 published retrospectively in respect of certain countries. But they are not continued bibliographies produced regularly year after year. The rules of this Part are applicable whatever be the kind of National Bibliography, though they are specially designed to suit National Bibliography of category 1.

CHAPTER SB

VALUE AND ITS IMPLICATIONS

1 International Cultural Contact

Bacon described books as "Messengers of Light". Books form a good agency in the promotion of International Understanding. It is not books written specially for consumption abroad that are of lasting value. It is books warbled out by the thinkers of a nation for the benefit of the people of the nation itself that will prove the best agency in establishing cultural contact between countries. To take advantage of this, each country should endeavour to know about the books written in every other country and to acquire them for the use of its own people. For this, the National Bibliographies of each country has to play a vital role. This is the international value of National Bibliographies.

2 Value to Posterity

National Bibliography, a country owes to its posterity. It is a cultural necessity. Viewed from this angle, a National Bibliography is a list or a catalogue of all the books produced in the country from time to time. It should be an exhaustive list of the entire intellectual deposit of the country all through time.

3 Current Value

National Bibliography has even greater current value than the deferred value to posterity. It forms the best and the most reliable source for book-selection for the libraries and for the reading public. It will be of similar service to the book-trade within the country and outside.

It has therefore to include in each Main Entry the format, the collation, the name of its place of publication, the name of the publisher, the year, the published price, and a serial number for facilitating the preparation of book-orders. In my visit to the office of the BNB (British National Bibliography) in 1956, I learnt that the book-sellers desire a title entry for each book included in the National Bibliography even for an expressive tell-tale title. To facilitate book-selection by either a library, or a book-seller, or a reader, it should be in the form of a classified catalogue. Such a form will also facilitate studies in book-survey.

4 Periodicity

To serve the current purposes mentioned in Sec SB3, it is necessary to publish a National Bibliography on a periodical basis. The period is to be determined on the basis of the economics of publication. If the annual book-production of a country or a state is not below 10,000, a weekly issue should be possible. If the annual out-put is below 10,000 but not below 3,000, a monthly issue should be possible. If it is below 1,000, a quarterly issue should be possible. If it is far below 1,000, only an annual issue or a half-yearly issue may be possible. In India there are now linguistic regions answering perhaps all the above periods of issue. Apart from the period of primary issue, there should also be periodical cumulations. They may have to be brought out every three months or at least every year. The BNB finds it worthwhile to cumulate the Index Part every month, though it cumulates the Classified Part only once in three months. It may be desirable to have also 5-yearly or 10-yearly cumulations. The British organisation for National Bibliography has some message on the organisation of the work along economical lines [W4].

5 Language and Script

To serve the purposes mentioned in Sec SB1 and SB2—*viz* service to libraries, the book trade and the readers in the country the favoured language and script for a National Bibliography should be the language and the script of the country. This is for a country with one language. On the other hand, in a polyglot country like India, the National Bibliography will have to be a composite one. It should be merely an assemblage of the different Linguistic Bibliographies. These should be published by the State Central Libraries of the different linguistic zones. These should be in the languages and the scripts of the respective zones. A considerable quantity of books is also produced in India in English and in Sanskrit. These are best listed in separate fascicules of their own, for India as a whole. These should be published by the National Central Library. Thus the Indian National Bibliography should consist of an assemblage of fascicules or volumes corresponding to each of the languages in which books are produced in the country. This is very much like an International Bibliography of Books being merely an assemblage of the National Bibliographies, each in its own language and script. The two pilot fascicules of Indian National Bibliography—one arranging the Main Entries by the Decimal Numbers and the other by the Colon Numbers, to facilitate comparative study by a wide circle of competent librarians—produced in 1957 are in Roman script. This is partly forced on them, as they seek to include the books in all the Indian languages in one fascicule and in one sequence. This is wrong, unhelpful, and wasteful. This problem has been discussed in detail in my *Indian National Bibliography* [RI1].

CHAPTER SC

PHYSICAL FORM

1 Printed Book Form

The immediate and dominant purpose of a National Bibliography is to serve the contemporary readers, the libraries, and the book-trade in the country or linguistic region or zone covered. These are many, and they lie scattered all through the area concerned. This indicates the printed book form as the most suitable physical form for the National Bibliography. For, it will be required by all the service-libraries and the entire book-trade. But unlike an Abstracting Periodical, a National Bibliography is not a 'frozen' catalogue though it has to be in printed book-form. For, the monthly, quarterly and annual cumulations will call for interpolation. This fact would call for certain features in the organization of the work on a National Bibliography.

2 Printed Cards

In the interest of national economy, the centre for National Bibliography should supply to service-libraries, copies of the Main Entry printed in cards, for use, as Main Entry and all the required Specific Added Entries. This calls for the Unit Card System described in Sec ED16. It has been shown in the *Heading and canons* [RH7] that this Card-Service will effect a saving of 79% in the total classification and cataloguing cost of a country. Since 1957, the BNB has been carrying out this Card-Service. Apart from saving in money, this has resulted in the virtual abolition of the time-lag between the receipt of a book in a Service-Library and its release for use by the public. For, the BNB has succeeded in supplying the catalogue cards within 48 hours of the order [W2]. This is only just short of the Prenatal Cataloguing described in Sec Q6. To enable a Service-Library to determine the number of unit-cards to be ordered for a book without spending time to calculate it, preferably to leave it to the National Centre itself to determine the number of cards to be supplied, the main entry in the printed bibliography should state the number of Unit-Cards required for the book concerned—for its Main Entry and all its Specific Added Entries.

CHAPTER SD

MODIFICATION OF CATALOGUING RULES

1 Book-Trade Section

The information needed for book selection by a Service-Library and the Book-Trade, calls for the addition of a new section in the Main Entry in a National Bibliography. This section may be called the Book-Trade Section. This Sec should give Collation, Imprint, and Published Price. It is best added immediately after the Title-Section.

2 Code Number Section

The Code Number Section should take the place of the Accession Number Section. This will be the last section in most of the Main Entries. In other cases, it will be the last in the part of the Main Entry printed in larger type. A properly designed System of Code Numbers will lead to considerable economy in a Service-Library, in ordering for a book and for its catalogue cards.

3 Number of Unit-Cards

Further economy can be effected in the order-work for the supply of the Unit-Cards, by including at the end of the Code Number the numeral representing the number of Unit-Cards required for the Main Entry and the Specific Added Entries of the book.

4 Additional Related-Book Note

A Service-Library and the Book-Trade will like to know

1 In the case of a new edition or a reprinting of a book, the Code Number of the next earlier edition or of the original printing; and

2 In the case of a new volume of a multi-volumed book, the Code Number of the next earlier volume published.

5 Annotation

It may be helpful to bring out in the Main Entry unusual features of a book such as

1 Peculiarity in type-face, say 'Type-writer Script';

2 Peculiarity in binding, say 'Sewed,' 'Loose-leaf,' 'In Slip-case';

3 Peculiarity in circulation, say 'Private Circulation,' 'Restricted Circulation,' 'Not Priced';

4 Peculiarity in title-page, say 'Title-page(s) in Sanskrit and English';

5 Name of Chairman of Commission; and

6 Periodicity in the case of a periodical publication, say 'Monthly,' Quarterly,' 'Irregular.'

The Annotation Section is best made the last section of the entry.

6 The Result

The succeeding sections of this chapter indicate the modifications necessary to adapt the Rules of Part M and Part N to the needs of a National Bibliography.

CHAPTER SE

MAIN ENTRY

0 Sections

The Main Entry in a National Bibliography is to consist of the

1 Main Section in larger type; and, if necessary;
2 Subsidiary Sections in smaller type.

The Class Number in the last feature heading immediately preceding the entry and the year of publication taken together form a virtual equivalent of the Call Number. If the form of exposition is not prose and if the language is not the favoured language, these may be indicated in the Annotation. Therefore, the Call Number Section is not necessary in a National Bibliography. Therefore, the Heading will occupy the Leading Position—corresponding to the Leading Section.

1 Main Section

The following items, which will occur successively as separate sections in a written or typed card-catalogue, are to be made separate sentences of the Main Section in a National Bibliography:

1 Heading;
2 Title Section;
3 Bibliographical Section;
4 Imprint Section; and
5 Code Number Section.

The Bibliographical Section and the Imprint Section taken together form the Book-Trade Section.

13 Bibliographical Section

The Bibliographical Section is to consist successively of

1 Format, giving the height and the breadth or the height alone of a page in centimetres;

2 Semicolon;

3 Collation, with a "+" inserted between the different paginations and the information about unpaginated plates, maps, and other items.

If paper-size follows international standard and conforms to the Principle of Aspect Ratio, the height will be $\sqrt{2}$ times the width. In such a case, the height alone will be sufficient to indicate the format.

14 Imprint Section

The Imprint Section is to consist successively of

1 Name(s) of place(s) of publication in abbreviated form wherever possible without prejudice to intelligibility, a comma separating the names if there be more than one name;

2 Semicolon;

3 Name(s) of publisher(s) in the shortest form consistent with intelligibility, a comma separating the names if there be more than one name;

4 Fullstop;

5 Month of publication if necessary and possible;

6 Year of publication;

7 Full stop; and

8 Published price, a comma separating the different currencies if there be more than one.

15 Code Number Section

The Code Number Section is to consist successively of

1 Code letter for the country;

2 Year of publication;

3 Full stop;

4 Serial number of the book in the sequence in which the book is included in the successive primary fascicules of the year;

5 Dash; and

6 Number indicating the number of Unit-Cards needed for the Main Entry and the Specific Added Entries of the Book.

151 The sequence of the Serial Number, given as category 4 in Sec SE15, is to start with '1' for each calendar year.

152 The first two digits of the Year of Publication are to be replaced by a Capital Letter in accordance with Schedule 3 of Part 2 of *Colon classification*, ed 6.

This will save one digit in the Code Number.

153 The Code Number Section is to be printed at the right end of the last line of the Main Section, and in case of there not being sufficient space in it, at the right end of the next line.

2 Subsidiary Section

The Subsidiary Section is to give in successive sentences the

1 Notes prescribed by part M and part N.

2 Additional Related-Book Notes, mentioned in Sec SD4; and

3 Annotation, mentioned in Section SC5.

22 Additional Related-Book Note

An Additional Related-Book Note is to be along the following lines:

1 See (insert Code Number) for Ed (insert the number of the earlier published edition); or

2 See (insert Code Number) for the original publication; or

3 See (insert Code Number) for V (insert the number of the volume of a multi-volumed book, published immediately earlier).

If it does not involve much increase of space, the different Notes and the Annotation may be printed as separate sections.

3 Tracing Section

Tracing Section is to be omitted in the Main Entry of a National Bibliography.

Its inclusion will increase the number of a pages and swell the cost of production. The BNB gives the tracing for Cross Reference Entries in a sparing way. It is difficult for it to be consistent.

The Library of Congress Cards contain the Tracing Section. But they are not reproduced in the Main Entry in the National Bibliography in printed book-form.

CHAPTER SF

OTHER ENTRIES

1 Cross Reference Entry

No Cross Reference Entry is to be given for a simple book in a National Bibliography.

The Principle of Local Variation (*See* Chap CF) has a great sway over the choice of Cross Reference Entries. The Canon of Context also (*See* Chap BF) has much to say on this. Therefore, it is desirable to leave the addition of Cross Reference Entries to each Service-Library. Even the National Central Library and the State Central Library preparing the fascicules of the National Bibliography will have to add the Cross Reference Entries to the Card Catalogues maintained by them.

The BNB inserts a few Cross Reference Entries here and there. But it should be difficult for it to enunciate a set of Rules ensuring consistency in practice.

11 Ordinary Composite Book

Notwithstanding Sec SF1, Cross Reference Entry *may* be given to each contribution in an Ordinary Composite Book.

In this case, it is possible to be consistent. But even here, this may prove to be too huge a task for a National Bibliography to undertake, as the number of Ordinary Composite Books is on the increase. It may be more economical to leave it to the care of Subject Bibliography rather than National Bibliography.

12 Artificial Composite Book

Notwithstanding Sec SE1, all the Special Cross Reference Entries, prescribed by Sec NB21 for an Artificial Composite Book, are to be given.

2 Class Index Entry

Class Index Entries are to be given in each fascicule and in each cumulation.

21 Class Index Entries are to be printed in an Alphabetical Sequence of their own.

22 The Second Section of the Class Index Entry is to be omitted in a National Bibliography; and the Heading and the Index Number are to form two sentences in a single section.

This means that the Class Index Entries should not be merged in one Alphabetical Sequence along with the Book Index Entries and the Cross Reference Index Entries. The proportion of Class Index Entries to the Book Index Entries decreases with the number of books included in the catalogue. The former dilute out the latter unless the number of books catalogued is well in excess of 50,000. The greater the number of books beyond the limit of 50,000, the less the chance for such a dilution to occur. In a National Bibliography, it is desirable that the Book Index Entries should not be diluted by Class Index Entries. And even the Annual Volume of a National Bibliography is not likely to list over 50,000 books. Sec SF21 is based on these considerations.

This feeling became dominant while consulting the Index Parts of the monthly issues, and the quarterly and annual cumulations of the BNB.

Perhaps, the 5-yearly or the 10-yearly cumulation may admit of the merging of the Class Index Entries and the Book Index Entries in one Alphabetical Sequence.

3 Cross Reference Index Entry

A National Bibliography is to give all the necessary Cross Reference Index Entries.

31 All the Sections of a Cross Reference Index Entry are to be made different sentences in a single section.

4 Book Index Entries

A National Bibliography is to give all the necessary Book Index Entries as prescribed in Chap M.

40 Except in a Series Entry, all the Sections are to be made different sentences in a single section.

41 Author Entry

An Author Entry is to give also the Name of the Publisher in an intelligible but abbreviated form—more abbreviated than in the Main Entry—and the Published Price.

42 Title Entry

A Title Entry is to give also the Name of Publisher and the Published Price, as prescribed in Sec SF41.

43 Series Entry

A Series Entry is to give also the Name of the Publisher and the Published Price, as prescribed in SF41.

CHAPTER SG

ARRANGEMENT OF ENTRIES IN CLASSIFIED PART

1 Fascicules and Volume of a Year

In each fascicule, in each cumulation, and in the volume of a National Bibliography pertaining to one year, the entries in one and the same Ultimate Feature Heading—that is, the entries with the same class number—are to be arranged among themselves Alphabetically.

All the books in them will have the same year of publication. Therefore, the Book Number using the year of publication as a facet will not differentiate them. It has been already stated in Sec SE10 that the purpose of the other possible facets in the Book Number is to be served by the 'Annotation.' Thus, Alphabetical Arrangement of the entries is the most helpful arrangement.

2 Cumulation Over Two or More Years

21 In a volume of a National Bibliography cumulating the publications of two or more years, all the books falling within one and the same Ultimate Class should be provided Book Numbers so as to individualise them.

22 The entries of the books in one and the same Ultimate Class are to be arranged by the Book Numbers.

23 As the book numbers will be prepotent in the arrangement, in each entry the Book Number is to form the entry element.

Implications of this prescription are:

1 The Heading of an entry will come only after the Book Number;

2 The Book Number will begin in the hanging indention part of the first line of the entry;

3 If the Colon Book Number is used, the Book Number will further sort out the entries on the basis of the form of exposition.

4 Another alternative arrangement would be pure Alphabetical Arrangement. In this case the picking out of the publications of a particular year, for book selection or for other purposes, will become a more difficult task. As against this, the method of individualising by Book Number will be a task for the compiler of the cumulation. It is a moot point whether the convenience of the user or the compiler should settle this issue;

5 Still another alternative method is possible. The Book Number can be inserted as if it were a Section Heading and all the books with the same Book Number may be arranged in it alphabetically.

The advantages here are:

1 The entries can begin with the Headings which are more intelligible to the user; and

2 There will be no need to provide Accession Facets to Book Numbers.

431 In a Series Entry, the Heading and the rest are to form two distinct sections.

432 The Name of the Publisher is to be given after the Name of the Series in the First Section.

433 The Price is to be given after the title in the Second Section.

The above six Rules are to facilitate the use of the National Bibliography, by the Book-Trade.

44 Index Number

The Index Number in a Book Index Entry in a cumulation of over two or more years is to consist of the first 4 digits of the Class Number of the book concerned.

The Code Number may be of use as Index Number in a primary fascicule and in cumulations within a year. But, it ceases to be of any use in bigger cumulations. The first 4 digits of the Class Number taken with the Heading will prove sufficient to locate the related Main Entry in the Classified Part. The BNB gives both the full Class Number and the Code Number of a book.

CHAPTER SH

PRINTED UNIT CARD

1 First Line

The Printed Unit-Card of a book should have the first line blank.

2 Reprint Only

It should be a reprint of the Main Entry of the book.

1 This will reduce the cost of production of the printed catalogue cards.
2 This would also imply the adoption of the rules of the Catalogue code as modified in the Part for a printed book form in place of the rules for card technique given in Parts M and N.

3 At the Service-Library

A Service-Library should prepare the Printed Unit-Cards for a book in the following way:

1 It should use one of the Printed Unit-Cards as the Main Entry Card after inserting the Call Number in the top line.

2 In all but the above one of the Printed Unit-Cards, it should insert in the top line the Heading appropriate to the respective Specific Added Entries.

3 It should insert the Call Number, in all the Printed Unit-Cards used for Specific Added Entries.

4 In the Main Entry Card, it should fill up the Accession Section and the Tracing Section.

5 It should prepare all the necessary Class Index Entries and Cross Reference Index Entries.

In the Printed Unit-Card of the Library of Congress, the Tracing Section is also printed. This is a help to the Service-Libraries. The Library of Congress is able to give this help, because it prints the Unit-Cards *ad hoc*. But the Unit-Card of the BNB is duplicated from the printed Weekly Issue of the Bibliography, printed in book-form. Probably it is this method which most National Bibliographies will have to adopt for reasons of economy. To introduce the Tracing Section into the book-form itself will unduly increase the size of the Classified Part. This in its turn will go against economy.

It is for investigation whether over-all economy would favour each Service-Library writing the Tracing Section on the back of the Main Card or the National Bibliography in printed book-form giving the Tracing Section at the bottom of the Main Entry in spite of the extra space required.

CHAPTER SJ

TYPOGRAPHY

1 Local Variation

The typography and lay-out of the printed book-form of a National Bibliography admit of much variation. They will depend on the type-faces available in the Favoured Script, the mode of printing in vogue, and the prevailing mental set of the users of the Bibliography. All these factors change—some suddenly and others gradually. The following are only suggestions. Even within the limits of these suggestions, many variations are possible.

2 Format

A4 (29.7 cm—21.0 cm). specified in the Indian standard IS: 1064-1957.

3 Columns

Two columns in the Classified Part and Three Columns in the Alphabetical Parts.

4 Spacing

41 Classified Part

411 The Feature Headings are to be set solid.

412 Each Feature Heading is to be in a separate line indented liberally, say 4 cm.

413 Each section of an entry is to be set solid.

414 Some space is to separate two consecutive entries.

415 The first line of an entry should have hanging indention.

As an example, if the Feature Heading has an indention of 4 cm, the first line of an entry may have an indention of 1 cm and its run-on lines an indention of 2 cm.

42 Alphabetical Part

421 The Alphabetical Parts are to be set solid.
422 The Index Number should be at the right end of the entry.

5 Type Face

51 Entry in Classified Part

In the Classified Part, the Entry Element of each Entry is to be in Caps and Sm Caps; and all the rest in Roman as in prose.

52 Feature Heading

Among the Feature Headings in the Classified Part,

1 The Main and the Canonical Classes are to be in Antique Caps;

2 Class of next Order is to be in Antique Caps and Lower Case;

3 Class of next Order is to be in Caps and Sm Caps;

4 The last Feature Heading covering an Entry is to be in Antique Caps and Lower Case.

5 All the other Feature Headings are to be in Roman Caps and Lower Case.

53 Alphabetical Part

In the Alphabetical Parts, Roman Cap and Lower Case are to be used throughout, except that Name of Publisher is to be in Italics Cap and Lower Case.

6 Type Size

61 Classified Part

1 In the Classified Part, 10 point type may be used for the Feature Headings and the Main Section of an Entry; and 8 point for the Subsidiary Section.

62 Alphabetical Part

In the Alphabetical Parts, 8 point type may be used.

The smallest possible readable type-size has to be used in the alphabetical parts, in order to bring into a Single Sweep of the Eye the largest possible number of entries of the alphabetical index.

CHAPTER SK

LAY-OUT

1 Parts

The following Lay-Out is recommended for each primary fascicule and cumulation of a National Bibliography:

1 To Find out;

2 Brief Outline of the Schedule of Classes of the Classification Scheme used;

3 Book Index Entries along with Cross Reference Index Entries;

4 Class Index Entries; and

5 Classified Part, made up of the Main and Cross Reference Entries.

For a sample draft for the Chap on 'To Find Out' *See* Sec RM1.

2 Sample Pages

The following sample pages illustrate the Rules on the construction of Entries in a National Bibliography. They also illustrate a possible choice of typography and lay out.

Note: 1 The year of birth of author, given in the entries, is imaginary. The actual year cannot be got in time. Therefore, imaginary years have been used to make the heading complete.

2 The Illustrator Entry for Perry is inserted, though not quite necessary, just to illustrate the omission of name of publisher and price in the case of a collaborator entry.

3 The BNB uses both Class Number and Code Number in full for Index Number. This is not necessary. Code Number can be of little use to one who consults the Index. The Class Number is necessary to direct the user to the Main Entry in the Classified Part. For this purpose, the full Class Number is not necessary. The first four digits of the Class Number will prove sufficient for the purpose. The Index Numbers given in the Book Index Entries are of this nature.

4 The BNB introduces many cross references in the Index Part. It is doubtful whether the resulting saving of space is sufficient to compensate for the inconvenience experienced by users in turning from one entry to another.

5 A comparative study should be made of the helpfulness of the lay-out of the BNB with the one suggested and illustrated in this section.

GRANTHA-JAGATH NATIONAL BIBLIOGRAPHY

PART 3

Book Index Entries

(*Examples* 374-387)

Black (George) (1902), *Ed.* Household doctor. New ed. *Ward, Lock.* 7*s.* 6*d.* L

Chronic bronchitis by National Association for the Prevention of Tuberculosis. *Author.* 6*s.* L44:4

Fishbein (Morris) (1896), *Ed.* Modern home medical adviser. *Bailey, S.* 40*s.* L

Household doctor ed by Black, *Ward, Lock.* 7*s* 6*d.* L

Marriott (Henry Joseph Llewellyn) (1908). Practical electrocardiography. *Bailliere, T C.* 40*s.* L32:4

Medical Research Council (Great Britian), Memoranda. *HMSO.* 35 *Its* National Collection of Type Cultures. Rev ed. 2*s* 6*d.* L:42

——. National Collection of Type cultures. Rev ed. *HMSO.* 2*s* 6*d.* L:42

Modern drug treatment in tuberculosis by Ross. *Nat Asso Preven Tuber.* 7*s* 6*d.* L45:4

—— home medical adviser ed by Fishbein. *Bailey, S.* 40*s.* L

National Association for the Prevention of Tuberculosis (Great Britain). Chronic bronchitis. *Author.* 6*s.* L44:4

National Collection of Type Culture by Medical Research Council (Great Britain). *HMSO.* 2*s* 6*d.* L:42

Perry (Maurice Ethridge), *Illust.* Marriott: Practical electrocardiography. L32:4

Practical electrocardiography by Marriott, *Bailliere, T C,* 40*s.* L32:4

Ross (John Donaldson) (1912). Modern drug treatment in tuberculosis. *Nat Asso Preve'n Tuber.* 7*s* 6*d.* L45:4

PART 4

Class Index Entries

(*Examples* 388-409)

Aetiology, Infection, L:42:2
Bronchi L44
Bronchitis L44: 415
Chronic bronchitis L44:4156
Circulatory system L3
Disease L:4
——, Bronchi L44:4
——, Heart L32:4
Disease, Lung L45:4
Drug, Tuberculosis, Lung, L45: 421:63
Electrocardiography L32:4:4206
Heart L32
Infection L:42
——, Lung L45:42
Lung L45
Medicine L
Pathology, Heart L32:4:4
Physical method, Pathology, Heart L32:4:402
Protista, Infection L:42:2:(G91)
Respiratory system L4
Therapy, Tuberculosis, Lung L45:421:6
Tuberculosis, Lung L45:421

PART 5

Classified Part

(*Examples* 410-415)

L MEDICINE

BLACK (George) (1902), *Ed.* Household doctor describing the diagnosis and treatment of diseases, first aid, and nursing. New ed. Feb 1958. 19cm; 256p. Lond; *Ward, Lock.* 7*s* 6*d.* GN57.2588-2
Earlier ed in 1948.

FISHBEIN (Morris) (1896), *Ed.* Modern home medical adviser, your health and how to preserve it. New rev ed. 24.5cm.; 3,34p. Lond; *HMSO.* 2*s* 6*d.* GN58.3592-3
Its memoranda 35. Sec BN52.86-3 for earlier ed. Earlier title was *List of species maintained in the National Collection of Type Cultures.* Sewed.

L3 Circulatory system
L32 HEART
L32:4 Disease
L32:4:4 Pathology

PART 5 (*Contd.*)

Nov 1957. 24cm; 4 col frontis, 35+902p, 18 plates. NY; Garden City Books. Lond; *Bailey and Swinton*. 40*s*. GN56.17084-2

L:4 Disease
L:42 INFECTION
L:42:2 Aetiology
L:42:2(G91) Protista

MEDICAL RESEARCH COUNCIL (Great Britain). National Collection of Type Cultures, catalogue of species. [Rev ed.]. Feb 1958.

L4 Respiratory system
L44 BRONCHI
L44:4 Disease
L44:415 Bronchitis
L44:4156 Chronic

NATIONAL ASSOCIATION FOR THE PREVENTION OF TUBERCULOSIS (Great Britain). Chronic bronchitis—an NAPT symposium, report of a meeting held in London 12 Dec 1956. Ed 2. Feb 1958. 20cm; 44p+4 plates. Lond; *Author*. 6*s*. GN58.3595-2
See GN57.4209 for earlier ed. Sewed.

L32:4:402 Physical method
L32:4:4026 Electrocardiography

MARRIOTT (Henry Joseph Llewellyn) (1908). Practical electrocardiography. Illus by Maurice Ethridge Perry. Ed 2. 1958.23.3cm; 16+226p. Lond; *Bailliere, Tindall and Cox*; 40*s*. GN58.3594-3
Earlier ed in 1954.

L45 LUNG
L45:4 Disease
L45:42 Infection
L45:421 Tuberculosis
L45:421:6 Therapy
L45:421:63 Drug

ROSS (John Donaldson) (1912). Modern drug treatment in tuberculosis, foreword by Geoffrey Todd. Feb 1958. 20cm; 47p. Lond; *Nat Asso Prev Tuber*. 7*s* 6*d*. GN58,3597-2.
Sewed.

CHAPTER SL

PAGINATION AND INCLUSIVE CAPTIONS

1 Pagination

Page numbers are to be printed at the bottom left end of a verso page and the bottom right end of a recto page.

2 Classified Part

In the Classified Part, the top left end of a verso page is to give not more than the first four digits of the Class Number of the Entry to which the first line of the page belongs; and the top right end of a recto page is to give not more than the first four digits of the Class Number of the Entry to which the last line of the page belongs.

21 Page Headings

In the Classified Part, the Page Heading of a verso page is to consist of the class number and the name of the Main Class or the Canonical Class to which the first line of the page belongs; and the Page Heading of a recto page is to consist of the class number and the name of the Main Class or the Canonical Class to which the last line of the page belongs.

3 Alphabetical Part

In the Alphabetical Parts, the top left end of a verso page is to give the first three letters of the Heading of the Entry to which the first line of the page belongs; and the top right end of a recto page is to give the first three letters of the Heading of the Entry to which the last line of the page belongs.

4 Class Index Part

In the Class Index Part each Page Heading is to be 'Class Index Entry.'

5 Book Index Part

In the Book Index Part each Page Heading is to be 'Book Index Entry.'

PART T

INDEXING PERIODICAL

CHAPTER TA

VALUE OF INDEXING PERIODICAL

1 Conservation of Research Potential

The enormous increase in the number of learned periodicals has made an Abstracting Periodical, or at least an Indexing Periodical, a necessity. Such a periodical goes a long way in conserving the research-potential of the world. It can help in the avoidance of the diversion of research ability into an unwanted and unintended duplication of effort in the pursuit of a problem. Thus we can have the benefit of Research-in-Series, instead of the wastage inevitable in Research-in-Parallel. There are already about 5,000 Abstracting and Indexing Periodicals in the world. Unesco is taking interest in co-ordinating the world-effort being spent on them. A discussion of the importance of Abstracting and Indexing Periodicals will be found in the *Depth classification* [RD1].

2 Effect of Large Number

A vast number of periodicals is now used for the communication of nascent thought. Their number is vast not only in the universe of knowledge taken as a whole, not merely in any single main class, but even in some classes of great intension.

3 Finance

In the first place their number takes their annual cost beyond the financial capacity of any individual. It takes them also beyond the capacity of a single library. Hardly any single library in the world takes even 25% of this form of medium of communication.

4 Individual Capacity

Secondly, let us assume that all the periodicals are made physically available in one library. Even then their use goes beyond the physical, mental, and time capacity of any individual.

5 Articles of Interest

Apart from sheer number causing this difficulty, no individual is likely to benefit by turning through every page of every periodical. To do it merely to locate articles of interest to him is by itself wasteful. To get a measure of this wastefulness let us make the following assumptions without loss of generality:

1	Number of learned periodicals current in the world ..	50,000
2	Average number of articles coming out each week ..	50,000
3	Average number of pages per article	10
4	Average number of index entries in a page of an Indexing Periodical	50
5	Number of pages in the Indexing Periodical of the week	1,000
6	Average number of articles in the week's Apupa Region of a reader	200
7	Number of pages to be turned through in the original periodicals to locate the 200 articles	500,000
8	Number of pages to be turned through in the Indexing Periodical to locate the 200 articles ..	1,000
9	Reduction ratio in the time for location of articles of interest if Indexing Periodical is used	$\frac{1}{50}$

The value of the Indexing Periodical arises out of this fact.

6 Classified Featuring

An arrangement of the indexes by the name of the author or by the title of the article will oblige a reader with a particular Umbra in his Apupa, to turn through all the 1,000 pages of the index. On the other hand, let us assume that the articles are minutely classified by an individualising, expressive, analytico-synthetic scheme of classification. Let us further assume that feature headings are added in a helpful way. We shall now assume without loss of generality that the Apupa Region of the reader will occupy only 1/10 of the Classified Indexing Periodical—that is, 100 pages. This makes it possible for the reader to skip out 900 pages in the Indexing Periodical and to look up only 100 pages of it. Thus the time for locating the articles of interest will be reduced to 1/500 of the time needed for turning through the pages of the original periodicals themselves. The value of a Classified Indexing Periodical arises out of this fact.

CHAPTER TB

COVERAGE

1 A Convention

In an informal way the following convention has developed in the production of periodical publications of bibliographical nature.

1 Periodical Bibliographies listing whole books or Macro Documents are produced on a national or linguistic basis. They are called National or State or Linguistic bibliographies as the case may be.

2 Subject Bibliographies or Documentation lists, commonly called Indexing Periodicals and Abstracting Periodicals, listing Micro documents particularly without independent physical existence, are produced on a subject basis.

The former covers all subjects within a single area. The latter covers all languages and all areas in which the documents are produced within a single subject. The problem of coverage does not present any difficulty in a National or State or Linguistic bibliography. For, their basis—*viz* Geographical Area or Language—is more or less definite. But 'What is the subject' does not get an equally simple answer.

2 Pressure of Nascent Micro Documents

World coverage—that is, World Bibliography—is neither practicable nor of help justifying the cost of production, in the case of macro documents or books. This came to be realised even within two centuries of the invention of printing. The case of subject bibliography of nascent micro documents is even worse. An all-subject bibliography is neither practicable nor of help justifying the cost of production—even more than in the case of bibliography of books.

The International Institute of Bibliography started in Belgium in the last years of the 19th century did not take long to demonstrate this. The venture of the *International catalogue of scientific literature* failed in spite of its fascicules specialising in specific areas of knowledge. This failure is due to its ambition to cover the entire universe of Natural Sciences though in seventeen separate fascicules. This was due to the rate of production of micro documents early in the present century. It has been estimated that the rate has by now increased thirty-fold. Such is the pressure of the down-pour of micro-documents.

3 Viable Subject Fields

The problem therefore is to find out viable subject areas for the economic maintenance of indexing and abstracting periodicals. In the past, generally speaking, the subject areas chosen were larger than what could be viable. For example, the *Biological abstracts* began in 1926 with the ambition of covering the entire field of Biological Sciences exclusive of clinical medicine. But by 1939 many of the subscribers found it to be beyond the capacity of their purse. Therefore, it had to present itself in nine different fascicules, each covering a smaller area of its own in the field of Biological Sciences. Even in the case of a mere indexing periodical, the entire area of Biological Sciences does not prove to be viable. For, in 1961, the Council of Management of Biological and Medical Abstracts Ltd, carried out an investigation of the viability of floating and *Index biologicus*. They have found that this would not be economically viable[S3]. Chemistry is another area where a large coverage has been attempted for several decades. But already the down-pour of the nascent documents claiming to be included in it has brought the lowest level of annual subscription offered to over Rs 1,000/—again absence of viavility. As the first step of fission they have jettisoned out the biochemical part to stand as an independent organ.

4 Intrinsic Difficulty

While the economic difficulty indicates that the subject coverage should be fairly small, the Apupa region of the user invariably extends over a considerable larger subject area. The unsolved problem is reconciliation of these two opposite demands.

5 A Possible Solution

The solution may perhaps be found along the following lines:

1 Each indexing or abstracting periodical should cover a subject field admitting of viability.

2 To meet the over-lapping of the Apupa regions of the different such subject fields, articles in one and the same periodical may have to be indexed or abstracted in more than one medium.

3 If it is an abstracting periodical, advantage may be taken of this by giving the appropriate slant to the abstracts.

4 The organisations responsible for the different subject fields should work in unison. For example, the articles in the periodicals covered by subject area A, either exclusively of interest to subject area B, or are likely to be of interest to both the areas should be brought to the notice of the organisation working in that area. And vice-versa.

5 Such a work should also be associated with reducing the number of agencies in the world working in one and the same subject area.

CHAPTER TC

NEED FOR MODIFICATION OF CATALOGUING RULES

1 Location Statement

Each Indexing or Abstracting Periodical generally catalogues micro documents not having an independent physical existence. They are all found in some host document or other. A Host Document is usually a periodical—a learned periodical. Therefore, the main entry in an Indexing or Abstracting Periodical should give the location of the micro document of which it is the entry. This is something new which does not arise in the Main Entry of a macro document or book which has independent existence.

2 Annotation

An Abstracting Periodical may include some of the important books in the field covered by it, appearing within the period covered by the Abstracting Periodical. It is usual for the Main Entry pertaining to it to give the Trade Section (*See* Sec Q) and also Annotation.

3 Physical Form

An Indexing or Abstracting Periodical should reach the hands of users. It is not prepared by an individual library. It is prepared by a national or an international central organization. It has to reach individual libraries also. Therefore, the production of the entries of an Indexing or Abstracting Periodical in cards is not convenient though it is not tc be ruled out altogether. The preferred physical form today is the printed book form even as it is with the national bibliographies. But some indexing or abstracting agencies issue printed cards as a subsidiary measure. It is the same practice in the production of card form as a subsidiary measure even as a national bibliography produces the entries in cards as a subsidiary measure.

4 Frozen Publication

We shall then proceed with the assumption that an Indexing or Abstracting Periodical is to be produced primarily in a printed book form. It is not usual to cumulate the issues of an Indexing or Abstracting Periodical on a quarterly, half-yearly, annual or quinquennial, etc basis, as is done in the case of a national bibliography. This is due to economic causes. The number of copies absorbed by the consumers is not sufficient to meet the cost of such cumulations. As a matter of fact, even the production of non-cumulating primary issues is often at a loss. This pattern of printed book form enables the freezing of the Classified Part. In other words, there will be no occasion to interpolate new entries among existing entries in the Classifie Part.

5 Serial Number

Therefore it is possible to give serial numbers to the Main Entries of an Indexing or Abstracting Periodical. These serial numbers can be used as the Index Numbers in the Alphabetical Parts, instead of class numbers being so used. The use of Serial Numbers as Index Numbers adds to comfort and elegance. These Serial Numbers do not arise in ordinary cataloguing.

6 The Result

There is therefore need for modifying the cataloguing rules mentioned in Part M, to the extent necessary. In most respects, the modifications are the same for an Indexing as well as an Abstracting Periodical. The later chapters of this part indicate modifications that will be common to Indexing and Abstracting Periodicals.

CHAPTER TD

MAIN ENTRY

0 Parts

Main Entry in an Indexing or Abstracting Periodical is to consist successively of the following parts written as separate sentences, except that a full stop is not necessary after the Serial Number:

1 Serial Number of the Entry;

2 Heading;

3 Title Section; and either

4 Specification of host document and locus in the case of a Micro Document without independent physical existence; or

5 Collation and imprint in the case of a Macro Document.

1 Serial Number

The Serial Number of Main Entry should begin with "1" for each volume.

2 Joint Authors

Notwithstanding Sec MD33, the Heading of the Main Entry of a Micro Document without independent physical existence is to give the names of all the joint authors even if their number exceeds two.

4 Location Part

Specification of the host document and the place of occurrence within it or the locus is to contain successively the following and is to be enclosed in circular brackets:

1 Title of the host periodical, in an intelligible abbreviated form in accordance with an accepted standard such as the one indicated in Chap RF;

2 **Fullstop;**
3 **Number of the volume of the host periodical;**
4 **Comma;**
5 **"N" followed by the number of the fascicule;**
6 **Number of the Fascicule of the host periodical;**
7 **Semicolon;**
8 **Year of the volume of the host periodical;**
91 **Comma;**
92 **Month or other specification of the fascicule of the host periodical;**
93 **Semicolon; and**
94 Number(s) of the page(s) of occurrence or locus in inclusive notation as prescribed in Sec ED91.

Note: Categories 5, 6, 91, and 92 may be unnecessary if the volume of the host periodical has continuous pagination.

5 Collation and Imprint

Specification of collation and imprint in the case of a Macro Document is to be as prescribed in Sec SE13 and SE14.

6 Tracing Section

Tracing Section is to be omitted in a Main Entry of an abstracting periodical.

7 Feature Heading

The Classified Part of an Indexing or Abstracting Periodical is to be provided with Feature Headings on the analogy of Sec SJ52 and its sub-sections.

CHAPTER TE

OTHER ENTRIES

1 Cross Reference Entry

The Classified Part of an Indexing or Abstracting Periodical is not to have any Cross Reference Entry.

11 MULTIFOCAL DOCUMENT

If a Micro Document without independent physical existence is multifocal, a separate Main Entry is to be given for it under the Class Number of each of its Foci.

2 Class Index Entry

Class Index Entries are to be given, as prescribed in Part K in a completed Volume of an Indexing or Abstracting Periodical as well as in each fascicule.

Whether Class Index Entries are to be given in each fascicule is a moot question. The answer will depend upon the size of the fascicule. For example, the BNB gives Class Index Entries only in quarterly cumulations. Though it is not an Indexing or Abstracting Periodical this practice has value in this context.

21 Class Index Entries are to be printed in an Alphabetical Part of their own.

22 The Second Section of a Class Index Entry is to be omitted in an Abstracting Periodical; and the Heading and the Index Number are to form two sentences in a single Section.

23 SERIAL NUMBER AS INDEX NUMBER

Against each Class Index Heading, the Serial Numbers of all the Main Entries under the Class Number concerned are to be given as Index Numbers in Inclusive Notation as prescribed in Sec ED91.

3 Cross Reference Index Entry

Cross Reference Index Entries are to be given, as prescribed in Part L, in a completed volume of an Indexing or Abstracting Periodical as well as in each fascicule.

31 Cross Reference Index Entries are to be printed in the same Alphabetical Part as the Book Index Entries.

32 All the Sections of a Cross Reference Index Entry are to be made different sentences in a single Section.

4 Book Index Entry

Book Index Entries are to be given as prescribed in Chap MK, in a completed volume as well as each of the fascicules.

41 Book Index Entries are to be printed along with Cross Reference Index Entries in an Alphabetical Part of their own.

42 Except in a Series Entry, all the Sections of the Book Index Entry are to be made different sentences in a single Section.

43 Serial Number as Index Number

In each Book Index Entry the Serial Number of the Main Entry concerned is to be given as the Index Number.

44 If a Book Index Heading admits of one and only one Serial Number, its second Section is to be omitted.

45 Each Author Entry is to consist only of the name of a single author in its Heading.

46 In the case of a Main Entry with two or more authors, each author is to be given an Author Entry, with his name followed by 'etc.'

CHAPTER TF

CLASSIFIED INDEX

1 In Completed Volume

A Classified Index to the Main Entries is to be given in every completed volume of an Indexing or Abstracting Periodical.

A Classified Index is necessary because there will be as many Classified Sequences as there are fascicules in a completed volume. This is the only means of taking away the unhelpfulness due to the scattering of the Main Entries in any given Class into several fascicules. Classified Index is not necessary in each fascicule, as there is no such scattering in it.

2 Double Purpose

The Classified Index is to serve the double purpose of the

1 Schedule of Classification; and
2 Classified Index to the Main Entries.

3 To Serve as Schedule

The Classified Index is to be printed as the Schedules of Classification are usually printed in Schemes of Classification with all helpful display, typographical variation, and variation in space between lines.

4 To Serve as Classified Index

Against each Class, the Serial Numbers of all the Main Entries occurring under the Class are to be given in Inclusive Notation as prescribed in Sec ED91.

CHAPTER TG

TYPOGRAPHY

1 General Prescription

The typography of an Indexing or Abstracting Periodical is to be analogous to that prescribed in Chap Q for a National Bibliography.

2 Serial Number

21 Class Index Entry

The Serial Numbers of the Main Entries, of which the Class Index Heading denotes their Ultimate Class, are to be in Antique Type.

22 Book Index Entry

The Index Number in each Book Index Entry is to be in Antique Type.

23 Classified Index

The Serial Numbers of the Main Entries of which the Class at the Head of the Classified Index Entry is the Ultimate Class, are to be in Antique Type.

CHAPTER TH

LAY-OUT

1 Parts

The following Lay-out is recommended for each annual volume of an Indexing or Abstracting Periodical:

1 To Find Out;

2 Book Index Entries along with Cross Reference Index Entries;

3 Class Index Entries;

4 Classified Index of the Entries; and

5 The Classified Part or the Text made up successively of the Text in the fascicules issued from time to time.

For a sample draft for the chapter on "To find out" *See* Sec RM1.

2 Index Aid

The Parts 2 to 4 constitute the Index-Aid to the Annual Volume.

3 In a Fascicule

In each Fascicule, it is sufficient if the Book Index Entries along with Cross Reference Index Entries, and the Class Index Entries are added to the text in separate sequences.

An example can be inferred from the examples given in Chap UF.

CHAPTER TJ

PAGINATION AND INCLUSIVE CAPTIONS

1 Pagination

Page numbers are to be printed at the bottom left end of the verso page and the bottom right end of the recto page.

2 Classified Part

In the Classified Part, the top left end of a verso page is to give the Class Number of the article to whose Entry the first line of the page belongs; and the top right end of the recto page is to give the Class Number of the article to whose Entry the last line of the page belongs.

21 Page Heading

In the Classified Part, the Page Heading of the verso page is to consist of the Class Number and the name of the Class to which the first line of the page belongs; and the Page Heading of a recto page is to consist of the Class Number and the name of the Class to which the last line of the page belongs.

3 Alphabetical Part

In the Alphabetical Parts, the top left end of the verso page is to give the first three letters of the Heading of the Entry to which the first line of the page belongs; and the top right end of a recto page is to give the first three letters of the Heading of the Entry to which the last line of the page belongs.

31 Page Heading

In the alphabetical part, each page heading is tc be "Index Entry."

PART U

ABSTRACTING PERIODICAL

CHAPTER UA

VALUE OF ABSTRACTING PERIODICAL

1 Conservation of Research Potential

In Sec TA6, it has been seen that the Reduction Ratio in the time of locating the articles of interest to a reader in a Classified Indexing Periodical as compared with locating them in the original periodicals themselves is 1/500. The next point to be sought is reduction of time needed for the actual perusal of all the original articles in the Apupa Region of the reader. It is here that a good Abstract effects a further saving. By the use of abstracts, it may be possible for the reader to eliminate many articles listed within the Apupa Region. The particular point sought by him might have been brought out by some of the articles listed. But abstracts may indicate that several of those articles do not have the quality or the information sought by the reader. He need not read those articles in the original. Let us assume that the number of articles to be perused in original is reduced to one half. Then, the Reduction Ratio in the time of the reader having an Abstracting Periodical for use is 1/1000. The value of an Abstracting Periodical arises out of this fact.

2 Quality

To give this measure of help, the quality of the Abstract should be of a high order. It should embody in it all the essential information contained in the original article. For example it should:

1 Indicate the exact boundary of the subject treated, to the extent to which it is not already indicated by the feature headings;

2 Indicate the new thought embodied;

3 Indicate new factual data recorded;

4 Indicate any new apparatus, diagram or other aid described; and

5 Relate it to any other work intimately associated with it.

3 Quantity

The incorporation in the Abstract of all the information demanded in quality will naturally increase the size of the Abstract—the number of words used. It is not desirable to print in the Abstract more words than can be taken within a comfortable sweep of the eye. The conflict thus arising between quality and quantity should be reconciled in the Abstract.

CHAPTER UB

CANONS FOR ABSTRACTING

1 Negative Canons

11 Don't provide any words in the Abstract to give information readily inferable from the feature headings and their sequences.

The Canons of Context and Enumeration should be fully relied upon. The feature headings stand arranged in helpful sequence by their class numbers. But the reader need not know the class numbers. The headings, which are in a natural language, will follow one another in more or less the sequence in which an expert in the subject would be familiar with and appreciate. This mere context of the entry amidst the feature headings carries with it a considerable information intelligible and valuable to an expert reader.

12 Don't provide, by words in the Abstract, information conveyed by the title of the article.

13 Don't give, by words in the Abstract, information going with the name of a well-known author of known standard.

The above canons amount to setting up symbiosis between classified arrangement with adequate feature-headings, the words in the heading and the title section of the entry on the one hand and the Abstract on the other.

14 Don't swell the Abstract with words describing in detail the sample used for study—the guinea-pig so to speak.

Normally this will neither be of interest nor necessary. The chief interest is normally only in the method used and the findings arrived at.

15 Don't attempt complete sentences. Use the so-called telegraphic language—without, of course, sacrifice of precision or clarity.

2 Positive Canons

21 If the range covered by the article is shorter than the

ultimate class under which it is entered, indicate in the Abstract the restricted boundary of the subject.

Classificatory technique has not been sharpened to produce co-extensive class numbers for newly emerging micro thought. Till a self-perpetuating scheme is properly designed, new micro thought will constantly outreach the capacity of classification. The extra intension of the new thought should be defined either by a 'verbal augmentation' of class numbers or by a statement in the Abstract. The former will be more economical.

22 State in the Abstract the primary advance in knowledge contained in the paper.

23 State in the Abstract any other secondary advances, if necessary.

It often happens that a paper may appear in the penumbral region of the Apupa of other disciplines. For example, a paper on the photographic method of studying viscosity may contain information on photographic technique or photographic materials. A Local Abstract, prepared for known clientele, can mask away all such secondary points. But an International Abstract, which has necessarily to be impersonal, cannot do any such masking.

24 Mention in the Abstract any new instrument or technique or nomograph or any other new aid used. Indicate their essential features, if practicable.

This is a very difficult part in the Abstract. It needs much judgement. This may swell the size of the Abstract. This must be guarded against.

25 Give in the Abstract the most outstanding factual data if they are not too many. Otherwise indicate the nature of the data provided.

This also requires considerable judgement. There are certain papers full of tabular statements which it is very difficult to abstract. In such cases, looking up the paper cannot be avoided.

3 Canon due to Time Factor

31 Pre-natal Abstracting should be done, to minimise time-lag.

Abstracting requires a careful reading of the article. Reading requires time. This time adds to the total time-lag between the release of an article and of its Abstract. A method of reducing the time-lag is for the publisher or the sponsoring authority to send a copy of the galley proof to the abstractor as and when it is ready. The page reference to the entry may be furnished by the latter at forme-proof stage. Therefore we add the above as a desirable canon to be worked upto.

4 Canons About Personnel

41 The author of an article should provide a Synopsis conforming as much as possible to the negative and the positive Canons of Abstracting.

42 A Co-ordinating Abstractor employed by the Abstracting Agency should establish the Abstract, taking the aid of the author's Synopsis.

43 The Abstracting Agency should also have an Expert in Classification. He and the Co-ordinating Abstractor should work in mutual consultation.

CHAPTER UC

ABSTRACTING PERSONNEL

0 Three Classes

There are three classes of personnel to consider:

1 Author;
2 Library expert; and
3 Subject expert.

1 Author

The author knows the subject matter of the article best. His only handicap is that he views the subject from his own personal angle. His abstract may not therefore be always impersonal. Secondly the author is too absorbed in his own speciality to get a mood either to absorb the spirit of the Canons for Abstracting or to implement them. The number of papers written by an author may not ordinarily justify his being asked to pick up sufficient knowledge of abstracting according to the Canons or to acquire facility in applying them correctly. Even if he does, he will not have occasion to exercise that knowledge sufficiently often to keep it alive. Even otherwise, the various articles will get scattered in regard to Abstracting Agency if the author is made the agency. There should, therefore, be in any case, a co-ordinating person to secure uniformity of standard in the Abstracts.

2 Library Expert

The Library Expert is perhaps best qualified to understand and implement the largest number of Canons of Abstracting. For it is he that serves the Abstracts to the readers. He knows the qualities expected in them. Even among librarians, one with experience in Reference Service and with a special knowledge of Depth Classification and Cataloguing is best suited to Abstracting Work. His handicap will be in regard to the newly forming specialised micro thought in a region already of very narrow extension. Often the thought will be too new to have been filtered down to a comprehensive book level, to enable the librarian to pick up sufficient familiarity.

3 Subject Expert

The Subject Expert has got all the handicaps of the author. Perhaps a full-timed abstractor drawn from subject experts can overcome the handicaps connected with the understanding of the spirit and the implementing of the

Canons of Abstracting. The only question is whether society can afford to release a really able man with capacity to do creative work in his own subject, to take up abstracting work.

4 Language

Language not familiar to the abstracting personnel will necessitate bringing in a translator. We are experiencing a great difficulty in this matter. Translation from the ordinary language used by the common man and current in common exposition is different from translation from the technical language used in a specialised subject. Indeed the two languages are quite different, though apparently the same. The risks thereby over-shadowing the province of the translator can perhaps be minimised if the abstracting is done by a subject expert with the language of the article as mother language and the translator translates only the abstract. This will also tie up helpfully with the Canon of Pre-Natal Abstracting mentioned in Sec UB3.

5 Interdependence

The Interdependence of Classification and Abstracting should be borne in mind. Many of the Negative Canons can best be observed if the Classification is done earlier. But if the Scheme of Classification admits of co-extensiveness even in the case of Micro Thought, the classifier may need the help of a Subject Expert to decide the last few digits of the Class Number. This will be specially so when the Classifier has to use his autonomy in constructing his own isolate numbers or in adding to their digits, consistent with the Canons of Classification. The Canons mentioned in Chap UB have taken all this into consideration.

6 Definition

Perhaps, it is desirable to give here the difference between a Synopsis and an Abstract. It is brought out by the following definitions:

61 **Synopsis.**—The author's summary of an article in a periodical, published simultaneously with the article itself. Usually, it might have had editorial scrutiny by the editor of the periodical.

62 **Abstract.**—The summary, usually by a professional other than the author, of the essential contents of a work, usually an article in a periodical, together with the specification of its locus—that is, its place of occurrence.

CHAPTER UD

MODIFICATION OF CATALOGUING RULES

1 Preliminary Communication

An Abstracting Periodical is thus a medium for the preliminary communication-in-brief of published nascent thought, to enable readers to choose the originals that they should read. It is a joint enterprise of three groups of specialists—classifiers, cataloguers, and abstractors. In Chap UB and UC we have dealt with the part to be played by the abstractors and classifiers. We have still to examine the part to be played by cataloguers.

2 Producers of the Past

Abstracting Periodicals are only about a hundred and fifty years old. Their number is still less than five hundred. They have been till now produced by specialists in their subjects of coverage, without any experience in Reference Service. Their production has not been based upon any special Catalogue Code. When able people are guided by their own instinct, the result is usually satisfactory. Its very satisfactoriness deters us from noting its faults. So it has been with the production of Abstracting Periodicals.

3 Consumers of the Past

Hitherto, the consumers of Abstracting Periodicals have been highly organised personalities. They could draw their help even from unhelpful sources. But, today world-wide team-work has become necessary in all fields of research. The team has to draw into itself many persons from the lower quartiles in the intellectual scale. To enable them to use Abstracting Periodicals with profit, these should be better produced. Mere dependence on instinct is not sufficient. Guidance by a carefully constructed Catalogue Code is necessary.

4 Non-Cumulation of Experience

Moreover, the discomfort and lack of helpfulness are experienced with an Abstracting Periodical, only at stray moments by stray individuals. There is no chance for these experiences to be cumulated by the readers themselves. The only persons on whom this experience is more frequently incident and who can cumulate them are the Reference Librarians. It is their duty to pass on to Cataloguers suggestions for improvement in the cataloguing aspect of Abstracting Periodicals. It is such empirical experience in Reference Service that has led to the Rules of this chapter.

CHAPTER UE

MAIN ENTRY

1 Section

The Main Entry in an Abstracting Periodical is to consist of a Main Section in bigger type and an Abstract Section in smaller type.

2 Abstract Section

The Abstract Section is to consist of the Abstract of the Micro Document or an Annotation on the Macro Document as the case may be.

3 Multifocal Document

If a Micro Document without independent physical existence is multifocal, a separate Main Entry is to be given for it under the Class Number of each of its Foci with an Abstract to suit the Class Number concerned.

CHAPTER UF

EXAMPLES

The typography, lay-out, pagination, and captions are to be as prescribed in Chap TG, TH, and TJ for Indexing Periodical with the addition that the Abstract Section in a Main Entry is to be in smaller type.

The following examples illustrate the Rules on the construction of Entries in an Abstracting Periodical. They also illustrate a possible choice of typography and lay-out.

Note: To fit in with the format of this book, the Index-Aids are printed in two columns and the Classified Part in a single column in the following examples.

PHYSICS ABSTRACTS

PART 2
Book Index Entries
(*Examples* 416-421)

Herzberg (G) **90**
Keshavamurthy (A) **112**
Molecular spectra and molecular structure
  2 Herzberg: Infra-red and Raman spectra of polyatomic molecules **90**
Thatte (R P) **112**
Venkiteshwaran (S P) **112**
Von Keussler (V) **66**

PART 3
Class Index Entries
(*Examples* 422-431)

Geography 108-118, 203-216
Instrument, Upper air **112, 216**
Line spectrum **66**
Molecule, Physics 70-110, 180-183
Physical geography 114-118, 214-216
Physics 12-108, 120-190
Radiation 38-85, 140-167
Raman effect, Infra-red, Molecule **90, 100**
Spectroscopy 65-70, 146-148-150
  Upper air 110-118, 203-216

PART 4
Classified Index
(*Examples* 432-441)

C Physics 12-108, 120-190
C5 Radiation 38-85, 140-167
U Geography 108-118, 203-216
U2 Physical Geography 108-118,

By Rule SJ52, Entry 110 has "Upper air" as its ultimate Class as it is in antique type. But, Entries 111-118, 203-216 are on subdivisions of "Upper air", as they are in Roman Type. Similarly, Entry 12 is on "Physics (general)" as it is in antique type. But, Entries 13-108, 120-190 are all on subdivisions of "Physics".

PART 5
Classified Part (Text)
(*Examples* 442-444)

C PHYSICS
C5 Radiation
C5:3 SPECTROSCOPY
C5:34 Line spectrum

66 VON KEUSSLER (V). Uber Angleichund der krummung von spektrallinien an eine Konstante Spaltkrummung. (On the adjustment of the curvature of special lines to a constant slit curvature.) (Z astrophys. 24; 1948; 252-262).

It is shown how a line of given curvature can be obtained by a suitable choice of slit curvature and geometrical conditions in prism and grating spectrometers.

C9B1 MOLECULE
C9B1:(C56:38N28) Infra-red Raman effect
90 HERZBERG (Gerhard). Infra-red and Raman spectra of polyatomic molecules 1950. N Y; D Van Nostrand. (Molecular spectra and molecular structure. 2).

Discusses molecular structure with the aid of the Raman Spectra of Infra-red Radiation.

U GEOGRAPHY
U2 Physical
U29 UPPER AIR
U29e Instrument
112 VENKITESHWARAN (S P), THATTE (R P) and KESHAVAMURTHY (A). Fan-type radio meteorography of the India Meteorological Department. (Sc notes, Ind Met Dep. 9; 1947; 127-159).

Describes a simple inexpensive radiometeorograph in which the driving mechanism for making successive contacts of the pressure, dry bulb and wet bulb temperature pens is provided by a paper fan which rotates as the meteorograph is carried up by the balloon. Describes the signaller, receiver and recorder and a receiving aerial with which signals can be received more satisfactorily at higher angles than with the usual vertical half-wave aerial. An inexpensive ht battery, that is assembled easily just before ascent, is described. Gives the method of computation with the necessary tables.

PART V

INCUNABULA AND NON-BOOK MATERIALS

CHAPTER VA

KINDS OF DOCUMENT FOR CONSIDERATION

1 The List

The rules in the earlier parts are all turned on the cataloguing of conventional books, periodical publications, and contributions in periodicals in the conventional physical form. But these do not exhaust the universe of documents. The following is a list of the other kinds of documents described in Chap FF.

1 Incunabula;

2 Document in non-conventional scripts such as

21 Braille;

22 Stenograph;

23 Music in notation; and

24 Cipher

3 Document similar to conventional book in physical appearance but using drawings, pictures, maps, and similar graphical media instead of phonetica symbols.

4 Manuscript in

41 Paper or cloth in codex form;

42 Paper or cloth in roll form;

43 Leaves;

44 Parchment;

45 Wood;

46 Metal;

47 Stone; and

48 Clay Tablets.

5 Reprographs of other than normal or near-normal size such as

51 Micro-film;

52 Microfiche; and

53 Micro-card.

6 Reprophonographs such as

61 Sound record of conventional books;

62 Speaking book or printed book with a companion attachment of the sound record of the letter-press in it; and

63 Conventional phonograph records.

7 Cinema reels including

71 Silent ones; and

72 Talkies.

8 Meta-documents or Instrument-record of phenomena.

2 Modification in Cataloguing Rules

All these categories will require specially framed rules to take care of the peculiarities arising out of their physical as well as internal form. This would affect the rules on the Bibliographical and Imprint Sections. But the categories, the Leading Section, the Heading, and the Title Section will all be governed by the normal rules of cataloguing. In category 7—that is Cinema Reels— there will in addition be need to provide special rules for the Heading Section. For, they are products of collaborators of diverse kinds not found in the book world. The relative claims of the different kinds of collaborators to occupy the Heading Section will call for careful consideration. There is another complication in this case. These are not used as physical documents by the general public, as books are. One has to study carefully how the limited circle of people, calling for them, approach such materials in the catalogue. The problem becomes even more complicated in a Meta Document. It will have neither a heading nor a title. Therefore, even these will have to be improvised by the cataloguers, by themselves or in consultation with the very limited users of them.

3 Future Work

Sufficient experience has not been gained in India with the kinds of documents enumerated in Sec VA1, other than manuscripts. Even in regard to manuscripts, certain traditions have been evolved largely by scholars using the manuscripts without much conformity to the current principles of cataloguing. However, time has come to work out the modifications necessary in the Catalogue Code in the case of manuscripts as well as the other kinds of documents under consideration. We appeal to the members of the profession who have begun to catalogue these kinds of documents, to communicate their experiences in our professional media such as the *Library science with a start to documentation*. If they do so, the time will soon come to collate all such experiences and arrive at an agreed standard in regard to the way in which the cataloguing rules should be modified to meet the needs of the respective kinds of documents. It is our hope that future editions of this book will be able to add progressively chapters in this part dealing with the respective kinds of documents.

PART W

END MATTER

CHAPTER WA

GLOSSARY OF TERMS

Abnormal	सुरक्षणीय
Absorption	विलय
Abstract	संक्षेप
Abstracting	संक्षेपण
Abstracting periodical	संक्षेप - उपेत - सूची - सामयिक
Abstractor	संक्षेपक
Accession	परिग्रहण
Accession-librarian	परिगृहीता
Accession number	परिगृहण - समङ्क
Adaptation	प्रकारान्तर
Added entry	अतिरिक्त - संलेख
Additional	अतिरिक्त
Administration	शासन
All-through-alphabetisation	वर्ण - केवल - व्यवस्थापन
Alphabetical	अनुवर्ण
Alphabetical catalogue	अनुवर्ण - सूची
Alphabetical index	अन्तवर्ण · निर्देशी
Alphabetical sequence	वर्ण - क्रम
Alphabetisation	वर्ण - व्यवस्थापन
Alternative	अवान्तर
Alternative name	अवान्तर - नाम
Alternative name entry	अवान्तर - नाम - संलेख
Alternative title	अवान्तराख्या
Amalgamation	एकी - भाव
Angle bracket	कोण - कोष्ठक
Annotation	विशिष्ट - विवरण
Arrangement	व्यवस्थापन
Array	पङ्क्ति
Artificial composite book	विसंगत - पुस्तक
Assistant	सहायक
Associated book	नैमित्तिक - पुस्तक
Associated book note	नमित्तिक - पुस्तक - अधिसूचन
Author	ग्रन्थकार

Author analytical	ग्रन्थकार - विश्लेषक
Author catalogue	ग्रन्थकार - सूची
Author, Corporate	समष्टि - ग्रन्थकार
Author entry	ग्रन्थकार - संलेख
Author index entry	ग्रन्थकार - निर्देशि - संलेख
Author, Personal	व्यष्टि - ग्रन्थकार
Auxiliary	सहाय
Auxiliary title	उपाख्या
Back of the card	पत्रक - पृष्ठ
Bay guide	खात - दर्शक
Bibliographer	ग्रन्थ - सूचीकार
Bibliography	ग्रन्थ - सूची
Bibliography, Analytical	ग्रन्थक - सूची
Bibliography of books and periodicals	कृति - सूची
Bibliography of periodical publications	सामयिक - सूची
Bibliography of periodicals	समुच्चित - सूची
Bibliography of serials	आवर्तित - सूची
Bibliographying	ग्रन्थ - सूचीकरण
Binder	संपुटक
Binder's catalogue	संपुटकीय - सूची
Binding	संपुटन
Binding collection	संपुटन - कक्षा
Biography	जीवन - चरित
Bipartite	द्विभागिक
Block	पद - गोष्टि
Block letters	विशिष्ट - लिपि
Book	पुस्तक
Book, Composite	संगत - पुस्तक
Book index entry	पुस्तक - निर्देशि - संलेख
Book label	पुस्तक - दर्शक
Book number	पुस्तक - समङ्क
Book, Simple	पृथक् - पुस्तक
Bookseller's catalogue	विक्रेत्रीय - सूची
Bracket	कोष्ठक
Bracket, Angle	कोण - कोष्ठक
Bracket, Circular	वृत्त - कोष्ठक
Bracket, Square	ऋजु - कोष्ठक

Call number	क्रामक - समङ्क
Call number entry	क्रामक - समङ्क - संलेख
Canon	उपसूत्र
Card	पत्रक
Card catalogue	पत्रक - आकार - सूची
Cardinal number	संख्या
Catalogue	सूची
Cataloguer	सूची - कार
Cataloguing	सूची - करण
Chain	निश्रेणि
Change-of-title note	आख्या - अन्तर - अधिसूचग
Characteristic	लिङ्ग
Choice	वरण
Circular bracket	वृत्त - कोष्ठक
City	नगर
Class	वर्ग
Class index entry	वर्ग - निर्देशि - संलेख
Class number	वर्ग - समङ्क
Classic	चिरगहन - ग्रन्थ
Classification	वर्गीकरण
Classificationist	वर्गीकरण - आचार्य
Classified bibliography	अनुवर्ग - ग्रन्थ - सूची
Classified catalogue	अनुवर्ग - सूची
Classified index	अनुवर्ग - निर्देशी
Classified sequence	अनुवर्ग - क्रम
Classifier	वर्गकार
Closed collection	सुरक्षणीय - कक्षा
Closed notation	पूरिताङ्कन
Code	कल्प
Collaborator	सहकारक
Collaborator entry	सहकारक - संलेख
Collation	पत्रादि - विवरण
Collection	कक्षा
Colon	लघु - विराम
Colon Classification	कोलन - वर्गीकरण
Colon notation	कोलन् - अङ्कन
Colon number	कोलन् - समङ्क
Colophon	पुष्पिका

Combination of complexities	जटिलता - मिश्रण
Comma	अल्प - विराम
Commentator	व्याख्याकार
Commentator entry	व्याख्याकार - संलेख
Committee	समिति
Compilation	संग्रहण
Compiler	संग्राहक
Compiler entry	संग्राहक - संलेख
Complex types	जटिल - प्राकार
Composite book	संगत - पुस्तक
Compound name	समासित - नाम
Conference	सम्मेलन
Connecting	योजक
Connecting symbol	योजक - अङ्क
Consecutive	अनुस्यूत
Consistent	अनुरूप
Consolidated	एकीकृत
Continued card	सन्तत - पत्रक
Contribution	प्रदानेय
Contributor	प्रदातार
Contributor index entry	प्रदातार - निर्देशि - संलेख
Co-ordinate	समाकृत
Corporate author	समष्टि - ग्रन्थकार
Corporate body	समष्टि
Corporate name	समष्टि - नाम
Court of Law	न्यायालय
Criticism	समीक्षा
Crooked bracket	वक्र - कोष्ठक
Cross reference	विषयान्तर
Cross reference entry	अन्तर्विषयि - संलेख
Cross reference index entry	नामान्तर - निर्देशि - संलेख
Crown	राष्ट्र - पति
Cumulative index	समूहक - निर्देशी
Current	प्रचलत
Dash (the symbol)	ऋजुरेखिका
Decimal Classification	दशमल् - वर्गीकरण
Decimal notation	दशमल् - अङ्कन
Decimal number	दशमल् - समङ्क

Department	विभाग
Dependent body	उपसमष्टि
Descriptive	वर्णक
Descriptive element	वर्णक - व्यक्ति
Dictionary	अनुवर्ण
Dictionary catalogue	सर्वानुवर्ण - सूची
Digit	अङ्क
Directing	देशक
Directing element	देशक - व्यक्ति
Director	निर्देशक
Directory	निर्देशिका
District	मण्डल
Division	परिभाग
Earlier title	पूर्वाख्या
Editing	संपादन
Edition	आवृत्ति
Editor	संपादक
Editor entry	संपादक - संलेख
Editor index entry	संपादक - निर्देशि - संलेख
Editor-of-series entry	माला - संपादक - संलेख
Encyclopaedia (generalia)	विश्वकोश
Encyclopaedia (of a particular subject)	ज्ञानकोश
Entry	संलेख
Entry element	संलेख - प्रथम - व्यक्ति
Entry word	संलेख - प्रथम - पद
Epitome	संक्षेप
Epitomisation	संक्षेपण
Epitomiser	संक्षेपक
Executive	मन्त्रि - मण्डल
Extract	उद्गृहीत
Extract note	उद्गृहीत - अधिसूचन
Extraction note	उद्ग्रहण - अधिसूचन
Facet	मुख
Facet formula	मुख - परिसूत्र
False Link	लक्ष्याभास
Fascicule	अवदान
Favoured country	इष्ट - देश
Favoured language	इष्ट - भाषा

Favoured script	इष्ट - लिपि
Festschrift	अभिनन्दन - ग्रन्थ
First series	प्रथम - माला
First vertical	प्रथमोर्द्धवा
Five laws of library science	ग्रन्थालय - शास्त्र - पञ्च - सूत्री
Focus	लक्ष्य
Forename	नामाद्य - पद
Formula	परिसूत्र
Full stop	पूर्ण विराम
Fundamental	मौलिक
Gang-way guide	अन्तर्मार्ग - दर्शक
Generalia class	समूह - वर्ग
Generic title	सामूहिकाख्या
Geographical area	क्षेत्र
Gestalt theory	रचना - तन्त्र
Group	समूह
Guide	दर्शक
Guide card	दर्शक - पत्रक
Half title	उपाख्या
Heading	शीर्षक
Head-quarters	केन्द्र
Helpful sequence	अनुकूल - क्रम
Hereditary	आनुवंशिक
Homonym	एकनामनि
Honorific word	मानपद
Horizontal line	समरेखा
Illustrator entry	चित्रकार - संलेख
Imprint	मुद्रणाङ्क
Inclusive notation	समावेशाङ्कन
Independent	स्वतन्त्र
Index	निर्देशि
Index entry	निर्देशि - संलेख
Indexer	निर्देशि - कार
Indexing	निर्देशि - करण
Indexing periodical	निर्देशि - सामयिक
Individualisation	व्यक्ति - साधन
Individualised	व्यक्ति - सिद्ध
Individualising	व्यक्ति - साधक

Individualising element	व्यक्ति - साधक - विषय
Initial	अग्राक्षर
Initionym	अग्राक्षरनाम
Institution	संस्था
Integer	पूर्ण - समङ्क
Inter-dependent	अन्योन्य - तन्त्र
Interrupted publication	व्याहृत - प्रकाशन
Inventory	अस्तित्व - पत्र
Inverted commas	उद्धार - कोष्टक
Irregular	निरवधि
Issue (of periodicals)	अवदान
Joint author	सह - ग्रन्थकार
Joint author entry	सह - ग्रन्थकार - संलेख
Joint author index entry	सह - ग्रन्थकार - निर्देशि - संलेख
Joint corporate author	सह - समष्टि - ग्रन्थकार
Joint editor	सह - संपादक
Joint personal author	सह - व्यष्टि - ग्रन्थकार
Judiciary	न्यायविभाग
Jurisdiction	अधिकार - क्षेत्र
Label entry	सजाति - नाम - संलेख
Last	अन्त्य
Later title	पराख्या
Law (as hypothesis)	सूत्र
Leading line	अग्ररेखा
Leading section	अग्रानुच्छेद
Learned society	विद्वत् - परिषद्
Librarian	ग्रन्थालयि
Library	ग्रन्थालय
Library catalogue	ग्रन्थालय - सूची
Library hand	ग्रन्थालय - लिपि
Link	लक्ष्य
Local variation	स्थान - विभेद - जनित
Main class	प्रधान - वर्ग
Main entry	प्रधान - संलेख
Major series	प्रधान - माला
Memorial	स्मारक
Memorial volume	स्मारक - ग्रन्थ
Micro document	ग्रन्थक

Minor series	उपमाला
Monograph	एक - आत्मक - ग्रन्थ
Multifocal	अनेक - लक्ष्यक
Multiple heading	अनेक - शीर्षक
Multiple series note	अनेक - माला - अधिसूचन
Multi-volumed	अनेक - संपुटक
Multi-volumed simple book	अनेक - संपुटक - पृथक् - पुस्तक
Museum	पुरातन - प्रदर्शन
New series	नव - माला
Notation	अङ्कन
Note	अधिसूचन
Number	समङ्क
Number, Cardinal	संख्या
Number (of a periodical)	अवदान
Number, Ordinal	क्रामक - समङ्क
Off-print	उन्मुद्रण
Open access	आसङ्ग
Open notation	अपूरिताङ्कन
Ordinal number	क्रामक - समङ्क
Ordinary composite book	सुसंगत - पुस्तक
Ordinary letter	सामान्य - लिपि
Organ (medium)	विचार - वाहक
Organisation	संघटन
Original work	मूल - कृति
Over-sized	महाकार
Pamphlet	पुस्तिका
Pamphlet collection	पुस्तिका - कक्षा
Parody	व्यनुकार
Part	भाग
Particular	विशिष्ट
Penultimate	उपान्त्य
Periodical	समुच्चित सामयिक
Periodical publication	सामयिक
Personal author	व्यष्टि - ग्रन्थकार
Personal name	व्यष्टि - नाम
Personnel	कर्तृ - गण
Phase	आश्लेष
Phased	आश्लिष्ट

Phase relation	आश्लेष - सम्बन्ध
Phrase	वाक्यांशक
Principle	न्याय
Printer	मुद्रक
Printer's catalogue	मुद्रकीय - सूची
Procedure	प्रक्रिया
Process	सरणि
Pseudonym	कल्पित - नाम
Pseudonym—real name entry	कल्पित - तथ्य - नाम - संलेख
Pseudo-series	कल्पित - माला
Publisher	प्रकाशक
Publisher's catalogue	प्रकाशकीय - सूची
Punctuation mark	विराम - चिह्न
Reader	सेव्य
Real name	तथ्य - नाम
Receptacle	आधार
Recto	पत्र - मुख
Reference librarian	अनुलयी
Reference service	अनुलय सेवा
Regulation	नियम
Rendering	उपकल्पन
Reprint	उन्मुद्रण
Reprinted	पुनर्मुद्रित
Reserved collection	निहित - कक्षा
Respective	प्रातिस्विक
Reviser	संशोधक
Routine	परिपाटी
Rule	धारा
Scheme	पद्धति
Second favoured language	द्वितीय - इष्ट - भाषा
Second series	द्वितीय - माला
Second vertical	द्वितीयोर्द्धवा
Secondary element	संलेख - प्रथमेतर - व्यक्ति
Secondary name	उपनाम
Section	अनुच्छेद
Semicolon	लघुतर - विराम
Separate	उन्मुद्रण
Sequence	कक्षा

Serial	आवर्तित - सामयिक
Serial number	माला - समङ्क
Series	माला
Series entry	माला - संलेख
Series index entry	माला - निर्देशि - संलेख
Series note	माला - अधिसूचन
Set	संघात
Schedule	तालिका
Shelf	फलक
Shelf arrangement	पुस्तक - व्यवस्थापन
Self-guide	फलक - दर्शक
Shelf-register	पुस्तक - क्रम - पञ्जिका
Shelf-register-card	पुस्तक - क्रम - पत्रक
Shelf work	व्यवस्थापन - कार्य
Short title	लघु - आख्या
Significant link	सार्थक - लक्ष्य
Simple book	पृथक् - पुस्तक
Single-volumed	एक - संपुटक
Sought link	वाञ्छित - लक्ष्य
Special cross reference entry	विशेष - विषयान्तर - संलेख
Specific	विशिष्ट
Specific subject	विशिष्ट - विषय
Specification	निर्धारण
Splitting	विच्छेद
Square bracket	ऋजु - कोष्ठक
Staff	कर्तृ - गण
Standard card	मानित - पत्रक
State	प्रदेश
Sub-class	उपवर्ग
Subdivision of a department	उपविभाग
Subheading	उपशीषक
Subject analytical	विषयान्तर - संलेख
Subject catalogue	विषय - सूची
Subject heading	विषय - शीर्षक
Subject matter	प्रतिपाद्य - विषय
Subject sub-heading	विषय - उपशीर्षक
Subordinate	परंपरित
Successive	क्रमागत

Supplement	अनुगत
Surname	वंश - नाम
Symbol	सङ्केत - चिह्न
Tab	पत्रक - दर्शक
Tag	ग्रन्थ - दर्शक
Taluk	उपमण्डल
Temporary collection	अस्थायि - कक्षा
Term	पद - व्यक्ति
Theory	सिद्धान्त
Thesis	प्रमिति
Thought, embodied	ग्रन्थ
Tier-guide	भूमि - दशक
Title	आख्या
Title (decoration)	विरुद
Title entry	आख्या - संलेख
Title index entry	आख्या - निर्देशि - संलेख
Title-page	आख्या - पत्र
Title-page, Back of the	आख्या - पत्र - पृष्ठ
Translator	भाषान्तरकार
Translator entry	भाषान्तरकार - संलेख
Transliteration	लिप्यन्तरीकरण
Tray	पात्रक
Tray label	पात्रक - दर्शक
Under-sized	अल्पाकार
Unifocal	एक - लक्ष्यक
Unipartite	एक - भागिक
Unique	अद्वय
Unit	मात्रा
Unit card system	ऐकिक - पत्रक - पद्धति
Unsought link	अवाञ्छित - लक्ष्य
Variant-form-of-word entry	रूप - अन्तर - संलेख
Verso	पत्र - पृष्ठ
Village	ग्राम
Volume	संपुट
Volume-number	संपुट - समङ्क
Volume-numbering	संपुट - अङ्कन
Volume periodicity note	संपुट - समयान्तर - अधिसूचन
Who's who	नाम वृत्त
Work	ग्रन्थ

CHAPTER WB

BIBLIOGRAPHICAL REFERENCES

Note: The Number of Section, which comes immediately after the serial number, is the Number of the Section in this book in which the reference to the book listed occurs.

A1	Sec	PF2	Am ER Educ. 32; 1927; 148.
A2	Sec	PD1	Amer J sc and arts. 92; 1866; 138.
A3	Sec	AA1	American Library Association, Cataloguing and Classification (Division of——). A. L. A. Cataloguing rules for author and title entries. Ed 2. 1949.
A4	Sec	BC2	——.——.Rule 92.
B1	Sec	PZY5	Biblio Newsletter (Unesco). 7, 1; 1958; 4.
B2	Sec	QA3	Brummel (L). Union catalogues; their problems and organisation. 1956. (Unesco bibliographical handbooks. 5).
C1	Sec	AC2	Cutter (C A). Rules for a dictionary catalogue. 1904.
C2	Sec	BF1	——.——.
C3	Sec	DA1	——.——. P12
C4	Sec	MB1	——.——. P34
C5	Sec	JF52	—.—. Rules 226 and 227.
E1	Sec	QB4	Egger (E). Burghoeffer system for union catalogue. (An lib sc. 5; 1957; 58-61).
F1	Sec	QA2	Filon (S P L). Union catalogues in Great Britain. (An lib sc. 5; 1958; 14-21).
G1	Sec	PZY5	Garde (P K). Directory of reference books published in Asia. 1956. (Unesco bibliographical handbooks. 6).
G2	Sec	KJ1	Goil (N K). Cataloguing reports of ad-hoc commissions (An lib sc. 7; 1960; 16-23).
G3	Sec	CG2	Gopinath. (M A). Reclassification of a library collection. (An lib sc. 9; 1962; 108-14).
I1	Sec	SB5	Indian Nat bibliog; experimental fascicules. (Decimal sequence). 1957.
			——.——. (Colon sequence).
J1	Sec	CB0	Jhalakikar (Bhimacharya). Nyayakosha. Ed 2. 1893.
K1	Sec	J62	Krishnamurti (C S). Rendering of names of organs of governments. (An lib sc. 7; 1960; 97-100).
O1	Sec	AC2	Osborn (Andrew D), *Tr.* Prussian instructions, rules for the alphabetical catalogues of the prussian libraries. 1938.
O2	Sec	BC2	——. Part 3.

O3	Sec	CF92	——. Rule 23.
P1	Sec	PE12	Phys Therap. 14; 1926; 56-7.
Q1	Sec	MF0	Quinn (J Henry) and Acomb (H W). Manual of cataloguing and indexing. P 104.
RA1	Sec	EH1	Ranganathan (S R). Alphabetical arrangement; a survey of basic principles. (ISI bul 2; 1950; 66-73).
RC1	Sec	KZD404	——. Chain procedure and dictionary catalogue. (An lib sc. 1; 1954; 220).
RC2	Sec	AD1	——. Classified catalogue code. Ed 1. 1934. (Madras Library Association, publication series. 4).
RC3	Sec	AD2	——.——. Ed 2. 1945. (Madras Library Association, publication series. 11).
RC4	Sec	AD2	——.——.——. Rule 0624.
RC5	Sec	BD4	——.——. Ed 3. 1951. (Madras Library Association, publication series. 17). Rule 1252.
RC6	Sec	BG0	——.——.——. Chap 7 and 8.
RC7	Sec	AD3	——.——.——. Sec 88.
RC8	Sec	AD3	——.——.——. Sec 91.
RC9	Sec	AD3	——.——.——. P 374-89.
RC10	Sec	AA3	——. Colon classification. Ed 1. 1933. (Madras Library Association, publication series. 3).
RC11	Sec	BC4	——.——.
RC12	Sec	QD4	——. Part 2. Chap 1.
RD1	Sec	TA1	——. Depth classification and reference service and reference material. 1953. (Indian Library Association, English series. 6). Sec 2.
RD2	Sec	FF98	Ranganathan (S R). Document, conventional and non-conventional. (An lib sc. 3; 1956; 22-32).
RF1	Sec	CA1	——. Five laws of library science. Ed 1. 1931. (Madras Library Association, publication series. 2).
RF2	Sec	PE12	——.——.——. Sec 1723.
RF3	Sec	BH2	——.——.——. Chap 2.
RF4	Sec	FN72	——.——.——. Sec 4781; 531-4; 64; 643-6.
RF5	Sec	MH7 MK2321	——.——.——. Sec 532.
RF6	Sec	DA1	——.——.——. Sec 53; 534; 64; 643.
RF7	Sec	MJ7	——.——. Ed 2. 1957. (Madras Library Association, publication series. 23).
RF8	Sec	MB7	——.——.——. Sec 687.
RF9	Sec	ED1	——.——.——. Sec 72.
RF10	Sec	CA6	——.——.——. Chap 8.
RF11	Sec	AB2	——.——.——. Sec 814.
RH1	Sec	AC2	——. Heading and canons, a comparative study of five catalogue codes. 1955.
RH2	Sec	BA0	——.——. Sec 33.
RH3	Sec	BJ0	——.——. Sec 338.

RH4 Sec QA6 ——.——. Chap 8.

RH5 Sec DE2 QA6 ——.——. Sec 93.

RH6 Sec SC2 ——.——. Sec. 932.

RH7 Sec DE3 ——.——. Sec 95

RI1 Sec DE4 FM5 SB5 ——. Indian national bibliography. (An lib sc. 4; 1957; 65-72).

RI2 Sec CE93 ——. International catalogue code. (An lib sc. 6; 1959; 13-20).

RI3 Sec GA2 ——. International Conference on Cataloguing Principles (1961). (An lib sc. 8; 1961; 19-25).

RI4 Sec GA3 ——. International Conference on Cataloguing Principles, Paris, 9-18 October 1961 and its findings. (An lib sc. 9; 1962; 15-38).

RL1 Sec MG1 RANGANATHAN (S R). Library administration. Ed 2. 1959. (Madras Library Association, publication series. 5). (Ranganathan series in library science. 3). Sec 2424:6:56

RL2 Sec MC2 ——.——.——. Sec 2531:2

RL3 Sec CG3 ——.——.——. Sec 2815

RL4 Sec CF2 ——. Library catalogue. Fundamentals and procedure. 1950. (Madras Library Association, publication series. 15). Sec 8242.

RL6 Sec CG3 ——. Library manual. Ed 2. 1960. Sec 564

RP1 Sec DE5 ——. Prenatal classification and cataloguing on its way. (An lib sc. 6; 1959: 113-25).

RP2 Sec BC8 ——. Prolegomena to library classification. Ed 2. 1957.

RP3 Sec BD0 ——.——. Sec 1434.

RP4 Sec QD31 ——.——.——. Sec 1438.

RP5 Sec KE0 ——.——.——. Sec 152.

RP6 Sec KD21 ——.——.——. Sec 171.

RP7 Sec KD21 ——.——.——. Sec 174.

RP8 Sec KF0 ——.——.——. Sec 1881.

RP9 Sec KF0 ——.——.——. Sec 1882.

RP10 Sec KZD401 ——.——.——. Sec 811.

RS1 Sec EE1 ——. School and college libraries. 1942. (Madras Library Association, publication series. 11). Sec 551 *et seq*

RS2 Sec BB5 ——. Social bibliography. 1952. (University of Delhi publications, library science series. 4). Sec 44.

RT1 Sec AB5 ——. Theory of library catalogue. 1938. (Madras Library Association, publication series. 7).

RT2 Sec MB3 ——.——. Chap 01 and 07.

RT3 Sec LC1 ——.——. Chap 12.

RT4 Sec MJ7 NA647 ——.——. Chap 31.

RT5 Sec FN72 MJ7 RANGANATHAN (S R). Theory of library catalogue. 1938. (Madras Library Association, publication series. 7). Chap 32 and 33.

RT6 Sec ED13 ——.——. Chap 62.

RT7 Sec MB71 ——.——. Chap 63 and 64.

RT8 Sec EH73 ——.——. Chap 64

RT9 Sec BA0 ——.——. P 60-75.

RT10 Sec BE7 ——.——. P 114-8.

RT11 Sec FL74 ——.——. P 294.

RT12 Sec AD2 ——.——. P 354-66.

RZM Sec CF3 —— and MUTHUKUMARASAMI (R). Commemoration bibliography. 1961.

RZN Sec AD3 —— and NAGAR (M L). Anuvargasuchi-kalpa. 1952.

RZR Sec PG32 —— and RAMAKRISHNAN (M N). Constructive destruction of a periodical. (An lib sc. 7; 1960; 117-24).

RZS Sec CB1 —— and SIVARAMAN (K M). Classification of allusion books. (Mod lib. 7; 1937; 127-33).

RZSU Sec FM4 —— and SUNDARAM (C). Reference service and bibliography. 1940. (Madras Library Association, publication series. 9). Part 4.

RZU Sec RC2 RANGANATHAN (SR), etc. Union Catalogue of learned periodical publications in South Asia. 1953. V1 Physical and biological series.

S1 Sec AD1 SAYERS (W C BERWICK). Manual of classification.

S2 Sec RF2 SCHOOL AND SOCIETY. 28; 1928; 529

S3 Sec TB3 SC INFORM notes. 4; 1962-63; 8.

S4 Sec AC2 SHAHANAN (THOMAS J) etc, *Tr*. Rules for the catalogue of printed books. 1948.

U1 Sec CF8 UNITED NATIONS, PUBLIC INFORMATION (Department of——) United Nations library service, 1948. P 7 and 11.

W1 Sec KL5 DE1 WELLS (A J). British national bibliography. (An lib sc. 4; 1957; Sec 681).

W2 Sec SC2 ——.——. P 83

W3 Sec QA5 ——.——. P 86

W4 Sec FM5 SB4 ——.——. P 73-89.

CHAPTER WC

INDEX

Note 1: The index number against each item is the number of the Chapter or the Section of its occurrence in the text.

Note 2: The following abbreviations are used:

def = defined
desc = described
irt = in relation to
qirt = quoted in relation to
rirt = referred in relation to

B

D

H

I

O

P

Q

R

S

U

V